MAHMOUD DARWISH
Exile's Poet

MAHMOUD DARWISH
Exile's Poet

Critical Essays

EDITED BY HALA KHAMIS NASSAR AND NAJAT RAHMAN

Foreword by Salma Khadra Jayyusi

OLIVE
BRANCH
PRESS

An imprint of Interlink Publishing Group, Inc.
www.interlinkbooks.com

First published in 2008 by

OLIVE BRANCH PRESS
An imprint of Interlink Publishing Group, Inc.
46 Crosby Street, Northampton, Massachusetts 01060
www.interlinkbooks.com

Library of Congress Cataloging-in-Publication Data
Mahmoud Darwish, exile's poet : critical essays / edited by Hala Khamis Nassar and Najat Rahman.— 1st American ed.
p. cm.
ISBN-13: 978-1-56656-664-3 (pbk.)
ISBN-10: 1-56656-664-9 (pbk.)
1. Darwīsh, Maḥmūd—Criticism and interpretation. I. Nassar, Hala Khamis
II. Rahman, Najat.
PJ7820.A7Z737 2007
892.7'16—dc22

2006031035

Bassam Frangieh's essay is based upon his article, "Modern Arabic Poetry: Vision and Reality," originally published in *Tradition, Modernity, and Postmodernity in Arabic Literature*, edited by Kamal Abdel-Malek and Wael Hallaq (Leiden: Brill, 2000).

Printed and bound in the United States of America

Contents

FOREWORD

Mahmoud Darwish's Mission and Place in Arab Literary History

Salma Khadra Jayyusi

THE PRESENT WORK PROVIDES AN ILLUMINATING, UPDATED CRITICAL account of a major poet who has been writing over many decades, and whose poetry has undergone the robust changes imposed on the genius of a creative mind by the social, political, and artistic aspects of this most critical of periods. It has been written by a group of critics and scholars with an evidently intimate knowledge of their subjects, and edited by dedicated scholars whose vision of what should be said at this juncture of modern Arabic poetry, about its foremost poet, is lucid and informed.

Multi-author works are difficult to organize effectively, in that the essays have to be selected with a specific view to supplying a balanced and multifaceted coverage of the subject in question; contributors must be chosen with care in the light of their respective specializations and interests, and of the way these latter combine to produce a rounded overall discussion. Essays should either complement one another generally, or else act upon one another in such a way as to cast light on points that have been obscured, or even completely overlooked, in earlier writings. In this way reader and scholar alike are served.

In the essays in this book, the humanizing capacity of Darwish's poetry comes fully into play, each contribution focusing on a specific aspect of his creativity. In this preface, however, I shall deal with Darwish's oeuvre as a whole, primarily from the viewpoint of the literary historian. If the value, the palpable flavor of a poet needs to be addressed from various sides, his place in the literary history of his language needs to be assessed and illuminated. The essays here demonstrate how this poet has never ceased to change and has never ceased to resist change. His poetry has developed constantly, embracing an authentic modernity where others have so frequently preached erroneous ones. As I aim to show, his sure poetic instinct kept him from going astray; in contrast to so many aspirants to modernity, he has been able, instinctively, to take account both of a poem's technical aspects (language, image, and form) and of the stance, attitude, and tone of a true modernist poet. Instinctively, too, he evaded a curse of the past few decades: the mad race toward innovation at any price, the passion for novelty that has so gripped numbers of young aspiring poets, to the total detriment of that controlling instinct that is the guardian angel of talent, and its guide.

Much benefit may be gained, too, from the interview with the poet, cogently conducted by Najat Rahman. It opens up to the reader numerous facets of the poet's critical mind, embracing not just art, but also history and life in general; more specifically, Palestinian life, his own life, which has never allowed itself to be severed from that of his country and its plight. It has become impossible now to think of Darwish without thinking immediately of Palestine, and of the terrible tragedy that has beleaguered its suffering people, the poet among them. The same consistently applies to writings on him, where no separation is possible between the poet and his country. This the present book beautifully demonstrates.

Mahmoud Darwish is the poet of Palestinian identity par excellence. I am speaking here both of the personal identity of the poet and of the collective identity of all Palestinians. The personal identity is rooted in the collective one, the latter being reinforced by the common plight and the common struggle people share. Their personal address, whether in poetry, fiction, or any of the other arts—created instinctively, but serving to relate the Palestinian dilemma to the world—depicts sharply the kinship among the vast community within and beyond Arab Palestine, and the incentives for struggle. The communal spirit draws them together, and often dictates both the tone of Palestinian literature and its essential appeal.

The Palestinian might suffer and die alone, but his personal tragedy is linked to the tragedy of the whole people. This collective identity forms an integral part of the national narrative, and plays a major part in the ongoing resistance in its countless aspects; it represents a unifying factor, one that speaks of a similarity of experience, of a common memory that warms the heart.

This personal/communal expression is the essence of Darwish's poetic address; it preoccupies him, heart, soul, and mind. He is the master of this stance and its faithful guardian, the most vibrant speaker of its spirit and meaning. Such is the essence of the authentic address this poet has conveyed to his people and to which they have clung; and he has likewise conveyed it to other Arabs, who have responded to him everywhere, and to the wider world—to the extent that it is now part of the way countless lovers of poetry view the tragedy of Arab Palestine. Such a comprehensive, warm, and uncontroversial reception is redeeming, revealing as it does the world's undying capacity, from Japan to the very heart of the United States, to support and uphold a human issue that the enemies of the Palestinian people, and the makers of their appalling tragedy, have surpassed themselves in portraying negatively, in a guise as stridently detrimental as it is false. In this lies Darwish's resounding poetic and human victory.

He is, then, profoundly concerned with his country; it is as though his people's tragedy has been a kind of talisman, binding him to a commitment from which he will not, cannot, part. Yet Darwish should not be viewed solely as a political poet. Political poetry has brought recognition and fame to many versifiers whose claim to genuine poetry is tenuous; who are, indeed, already obsolete in the eyes of serious criticism and literary history. Darwish is of a radically different order. What I find stunning and utterly distinctive in his art is that, for all his concentration on a single broad theme, which is at base political, he is neither a propagandist nor a political zealot catering to national frenzy (both of these last embodying attitudes liable to impair the value of poetic utterance). And it is interesting to note how many people, not addressing the matter in formal critical terms, perhaps incapable of doing so, have intuitively identified, in Darwish's work, the stuff of great poetry. The fact is that his commitment is not solely to a major political issue, but also—in fact primarily—to revelation of the daily human tragedy springing from it. This applies equally to the poetry dealing with his private experiences, which has as its source the deep well of Palestinian tragic experience. His primary incentive, then, is to consider the human condition; and it is this, not politics, that makes him a world poet.

Moreover, for all the unflinching focus on this issue, his poetic expression is forever renewed, pulsing with life, creating images that never jar—no matter how the style and form of expression may vary, they remain in rapturous harmony with themselves and with their basic message. The reader or listener can never predict what this poet will come up with in any new work he creates. Nothing seems able to assail his uniqueness and differentness; he speaks in the name of all, yet remains distinctive in his flavor and characteristic sheen. The only Arab parallel to this luminous, masterful concentration on a single major subject is the Libyan novelist Ibrahim al-Koni, that ardent lover of the Western desert whose fiction delineates the lives of its poor and eternally struggling people—providing, like Darwish, an unwavering focus whereby specific, strenuous experience, in place and time, is transcended so as to shed light on the universal experience of man on earth.

The Darwishian preoccupation may, though, have a parallel in a very different area of Palestinian art: namely, in the paintings of the major Palestinian artist Isma'il Shammout, whose very sad death I learned of while writing this. Shammout depicted the Palestinian tragedy over half a century; he was, indeed, the Darwish of the graphic arts, just as Darwish is the poet of all painters. The two stand out as proud emblems of the Palestinian tragedy in modern Arab history, as artists who have worked tirelessly to etch the many faces of the modern Palestinian experience on the minds and hearts of readers and viewers.

When the creative mind focuses on a vast subject, which becomes the essence of its creativity and its primary incentive, yet is never exhausted, never finds its address turning to cold repetition and lusterless predictability, then a rare genius indeed is proclaimed to the world.

Shammout, unlike Darwish, introduced the pastoral motif into his work, portraying Palestinian rural life as it was lived in the artist's own memory, before the onslaught of the catastrophe in the late 1940s. Darwish, by contrast, plunged immediately into the heart of the tragedy that had engulfed his world.

The truth is that Arabic poetry viewed in terms of pastoral is passé. The last such experiment I know of is that of the Lebanese Ilyas Abu Shabaka (1903–1947); and even then his work seemed more akin to simple Lebanese folk songs than to any living, robust tradition within modern Arabic poetry. Since 1948 and the onslaught of Zionism upon Palestine and the Arab world, poetic diction has been incompatible with the expression of simple, happy experience, has forged for itself a totally new tradition. Darwish is too great a poet not to be instinctively aware of the poetic possibilities of his time. The story of Arab painting is different. Its development has been a short one, burgeoning only in modern times. It is in fact the infant of modernity and openness on the world. The painter could begin anywhere he wished, could wield his tools in whichever way he chose. There was no entrenched tradition to hold him back.

There is a nostalgic element in Shammout's pastoral standpoint, which gives an immediate layered significance, a multiplicity of meaning, even to a simple portrayal of happy villagers celebrating the harvest. Such portrayals bring home the two poles of Palestinian experience: even as calm, joy, and peace are depicted, we are aware of the evil lurking behind, ready to pounce on the innocence of life. Writing could never express this in the same way. It would be bound to give at least a verbal hint of what was looming on the horizon.

If Darwish is instinctively aware of the poetic possibilities of his time, he is also intuitively conscious of the possibilities of all good poetry. He is, indeed, the finest Arab lyrical poet writing today. Lyricism, as Lukacs said, represents the highest level of poetry, and the most perfected. Where, with other poets, the lyrical flow dissipates, and the rhythm, which above all sustains the movement of poetic creativity, grows faint, Darwish still contrives a glittering power of creation, free of all mediocrity. The rhythms that constitute his overarching wealth remain within his grip, undefeated by the aggression and tireless cruelty of life around him. I find it fruitful to consider him alongside two poets who filled the Umayyad period (661–750) with poetry: Jarir and al-Farazdaq. Al-Farazdaq, an old critic said, sculpts in stone, while Jarir ladles out from a sea. The genius of Darwish is certainly of the Jaririan kind. It seems like a fountain pouring, forever, into a fathomless ocean.

It was just as Darwish was rising to fame that writings on modernity and the modernization of poetry began to appear, becoming, in due course, both ubiquitous and the abiding concern of numerous young poets experimenting in the genre. Some of these theoretical writings were of authentic value, but many others contained false rhetoric about modernity, linking it mainly to matters of poetic technique, especially diction and metaphor, and later to form itself. The call became a veritable obsession with a growing generation of poets, most of whom had little or no knowledge of foreign languages and depended for theory on the writings of other Arab poets and critics—and some of these latter, while dominating the scene, had themselves only a partial understanding of the history and essence of European modernity, and were attempting to set their own literature at the center of their theorization.

This call to modernity emphasized technique: language became open to every kind of innovation. Yet language in Arabic poetry has its own defenses, and will resist any radical encroachment on its robust history. The image was the element most profoundly affected; it became fractured, its two sides alienated, often to a degree that made the achievement of any meaning impossible. It became a tool for experimentation in strangeness, with internal logic often quite lacking; yet there was no fear of immediate rejection from a naïve audience eager to embrace what it supposed was modernist and fashionable. The main purpose seemed to be the acquisition of novelty at any price. A silent competition began, among the rising generation of poets throughout the Arab world, as to who could produce the greater novelty, the stranger image, the more autré metaphor.

And there were no limits; the possibilities were endless. A once good poet could be seen sinking toward the abyss. As for the critics of poetry, these either kept silent, or were simply at a loss to understand what was happening, failing to grasp the absurdity of the experiments that were strangling the new Arabic poem and cutting through its normal development; all in the name of a false modernity.

In due course the awesomely rich metrics of Arabic poetry were abandoned by many members of the new generation. The mystification and fascination with a novel interplay of words and metaphors, along with the ceaseless glorification of prose poetry in some quarters, seriously impeded any steady, flourishing development toward a true modernist expression in poetry—

particularly since, in theory and practice alike, almost no attention was given to the importance of vision and attitude, and to the role played by meaning and message in a modernist creation. There were two especially negative consequences of this: first, a mishandling of diction and a complete distortion of the image, together with a total misunderstanding of the latter's role within the poem; and second, an abandonment of the inexhaustible wealth of Arabic metrics in favor of prose poetry, itself generally mishandled and imprecise on the rhythmical and structural level alike. Poetry entered an age of blind confusion. It is as though contemporary poetry now works without any organic historical sense, outside tradition; as though it rejects all notion of creation within the continuum of an illustrious poetic history—so concerned with its own novelty that it seems to belong nowhere. Yet true innovation is at no time severed from the past. On the contrary, it is an addition to it and a modification of it; an enrichment of the whole corpus of literary contribution.

Further discussion of these crucially serious issues remains, unfortunately, outside the scope of this essay. Even so, this brief mention of them is relevant to an assessment of Darwish's highly successful experiment, a venture so fully modern and so fully coherent. He never succumbed to the prevailing frenzy, to the unspoken race to produce metaphorical novelties with no cogent relation to meaning and no true poetic punch. Yet he has achieved a rich modernity in his poetry, combining modernism's wholesome technical aspect with the stance and attitude of a truly modernist poet. And he has achieved this without ever stepping outside the continuum of one of the world's oldest and most vigorous poetic repertoires.

The greatest thing about his stance is that, unlike some poets, he never set himself up as teacher, admonisher, and prophet; as someone who pronounced from on high, as though untouched by the tragedy around him. Darwish stood alongside his audience, a man sharing their tragedy, partaking of the suffering they endured, one of the countless victims of his tragic world. This is a modernist stance par excellence. His poetry has a more modernist ring than that of others, while acquiring a deeper, more intimate tone. It has assimilated the spirit of the time and resonated with the poetic moment. By sheer poetic intuition, Darwish realized that modernism is more than an esthetic venture, more than an exercise in fracturing the inherited conventions of form, diction, and metaphor; that it entails, first and foremost, a standpoint that sees the world through modern eyes, taking full account of the yawning gulf now separating the poet-prophet of a rhetorical age from the poet of the present who shares the agony and the dreams of the world in which he lives.

Only a few of our modern poets share this stance. Most, even those who have raised the banner of modernity and underpinned their ideas with theory, have remained effective prisoners of their long-term poetic heredity: a heredity resonant with rhetoric and fixed standpoints, making of the poet an imam, a priest, and a soothsayer. In my view our modern poetry is no longer capable of accommo-dating such a stance, for esthetic fatigue has set in against all forms of rhetorical didacticism within poetry. The poet of the present moment must be kneaded into its suffering.

Never has the world been so big-mouthed about high ideals and spoken so resoundingly of human justice and right, yet so given itself over to a distorted vision of humanity, as it has today. Darwish had every reason to voice anger, even fury, against those who have made life so tragic and so dangerous. The urge to demolish, to tear away all those factors responsible for making existence intolerable, is a fully understandable one. Yet Darwish's poetic decorum has set a wedge between the violent expression of fury and the authentic exhortation of good poetry. And, finally, he pronounces no judgment of doom and final ruin, but rather upholds the human potential to resist and prevail. Great poets will always find their positive resonances. They will always proclaim the capacity for love, the possibility of denouncing evil while underlining human triumph over the wickedness of the world, over its blatant immorality and vicious intent. When poets find nothing to uphold, nothing to assert, they lose perspective. A great poet, indeed any great artist, will unfailingly embrace a vision of a world that bears within it the capacity, the moral force, the courage, and the will to face up to tragedy and resist its fracturing assault on the soul. No great poetry is ever a poetry of total defeat and disintegration.

Introduction

Hala Khamis Nassar and Najat Rahman

As for me—
Now that I am filled with all the reasons for departure
I am not mine
I am not mine
I am not mine
—Mahmoud Darwish, *Jidārīya* [Mural]

Farewell, farewell to poetry of pain.
—Mahmoud Darwish, in a tribute poem to Edward Said,
Like Almond Flowers and Further

EXILE CLAIMS NO PARTICULAR POET, FOR EVERY POET IS AN EXILE TO some extent, whether in relation to language, to tradition, to place, or whether it is the poet who withdraws from the demands of the everyday to write, finding both refuge and freedom to wander in that endeavor.[1] And yet, our title, *Mahmoud Darwish, Exile's Poet*, seeks to emphasize how intimately exile is connected to the poetics of Mahmoud Darwish. His is an exile that is displacement, dispossession, and siege.

Darwish has personally experienced an array of displacements: as a child of six in 1948, the initial flight with his family from his home village al-Birwa in the upper Galilee to Lebanon; the subsequent internal displacement when his family "infiltrated" home months later to find his village no longer existing under the newly declared state of Israel; the many imprisonments and house arrests that followed throughout his youth; the self-imposed exile in 1970 to Egypt and later to Beirut; expulsion from Beirut in the aftermath of the Israeli invasion of 1982; the returning to Ramallah in 1996 to live for the first time in the occupied Palestinian territories; the siege in Ramallah with the onset of the second intifada. Not surprisingly, given this personal history, the poetry of Darwish is preoccupied with displacement—a literal displacement, coterminous with the Nakba's rupture of history and the other losses that followed, and also a displacement of the self from itself. For Darwish, the testing of poetic limits is inextricably linked with his questioning of identity, whether in interrogating the role of poetry following the siege of Beirut in 1982 and the subsequent expulsion of Palestinians or in reflecting on the self that faces such a series of displacements. Exile, in one form or another, has always been at the heart of his literary creation.

A prolific poet, he has produced nearly 30 works and has been translated into over 25 languages. While Darwish's oeuvre is seminal in modern Arabic poetry and is often considered in that context, he is also without question one of the *world*'s most important living poets. Darwish has been recognized internationally and is the recipient of many prestigious international literary awards, including the Lotus Prize (1969), the Lenin Prize (1983), France's Knight of Arts and Belles Lettres (1997), and the Lannan Foundation Prize for Cultural Freedom (2001). Despite having been seminal in transforming the poetic landscape of Arabic poetry in the twentieth century, Darwish's poetry is only gradually becoming better known in North America.

No substantial critical study currently exists in English (or any language other than Arabic and French) that addresses the relevance and complexity of his later poetry in the articulation of exile and rewriting of the homeland.[2] Indeed, for a long time, anyone interested in modern Arabic poetry would have had difficulty finding substantial critical studies in English on the general subject, let alone focusing only on Darwish. Some exceptions to this are Terri DeYoung's study of al-Sayyab's poetry, *Placing the Poet: Badr Shakir al-Sayyab and Postcolonial Iraq* (1998), and before that her and Issa Boullata's *Tradition and Modernity in Arabic Literature* (1997), Salma Khadra Jayyusi's *Trends and Movements in Modern Arabic Poetry* (1977), and Mounah Khouri's *Poetry and the Making of Modern Egypt* (1971).

Critical writing in Arabic on Darwish, who has long been designated "poet of the homeland" and "poet of resistance," tends to focus on his earlier writing and on themes that reinforce nationalist readings of his work. Studies that have addressed his work since the early 1980s are few, even though the poems of this period constitute a significant portion of his oeuvre. Even as his later poetry consciously marks a move away from his earlier constructions of identity, of home, and of poetry, many of his critics have not taken sufficient notice of this shift, perhaps due to the force of the poet's identification as a "national poet."

Mahmoud Darwish's later work expresses an unfolding desire to forge new poetic forms and to establish poetry as a space of both survival and possibility. In this search for form, as evidenced from his experimentations with the lyric, epic, long poem, prose poem, and others, he has sought to safeguard a collective voice even as he ventured more personal reflections on death, love, poetry. Poetry can be a form of testimony when it offers itself as an alternative history (see Rahman 1996). As Darwish put it in an interview with Helit Yeshurun published in *La Palestine comme métaphore*, "a people without poetry are a conquered people" (154). It is precisely the fragility of poetry that allows a space of possibility for those historically silenced. Or, as Darwish put it in another interview published in the same collection, this one with Abbas Beydoun, "Poetry can be of little efficacy, but its force comes from recognizing human fragility" (47). At the same time, in such works as *State of Siege* (2002), Darwish writes of a collective that demands of the besieged poet continued attention to national themes and expects that he speak in their voice.

Darwish also recognizes the limits of poetry: how it is inhabited with a bygone temporality and a space of loss. Speaking with Beydoun, he states: "And poetry… remains incomplete if it does not resonate of echoes of the far past" (31). Darwish often deploys absence as structure—absence is generally a crucial thematic in his poetry—as in *Why Have You Left the Horse Alone?* At the same time, he is wary of the danger of further displacing an (absent) subject by writing about its absence—by absenting it again in writing. Palestine, argues Darwish, as it has been written about by Palestinian poets and writers, has been rendered strangely invisible—absented and displaced—by a fixed discourse of patriotism and nostalgia. In another interview, this with Liana Badr, Zakariyya Muhammad, and Munther Jaber, he says, "I am disconcerted by the absence of place, of its veritable attributes, in a poetry that pretends to celebrate it. I don't find in Palestinian poetry the flora and fauna, the landscape, in other words the real Palestine" (103). This absenting of Palestine in writing may not be for the lack of descriptive power, as Darwish also suggests, but may be inherent in the condition of all writing—an activity that seeks to make present again that which can no longer be recuperated through the work of representation. Nonetheless, it is significant that, for Darwish, Palestine needs to become mythical for the Palestinian writer, who must, as he said to Yeshurun, "import his language to concrete reality in order to transport it in the reality of words" (164). Absence is echoed more significantly in a language that is primarily rhythmic; that is, in a language in which time is spatially conceived between figures of home and poem. It is a language invoked from the limits of an Arabic mystic literary heritage where, once, poetic writing *was* home.

Darwish, who recognizes himself as the inheritor of the many civilizations that have passed through his land, has often defined his literary project as one of writing home. And poetry henceforth is a staging of a plurality of all the voices of home. And yet in his later works, the word "homeland" hardly occurs—in sharp contrast to his early period, in which it appears in profusion. Whereas other Palestinian poets who preceded Darwish, such as Abu Salma and Abdel Rahim Mahmoud, referred to the homeland conventionally as lost, raped, and wounded, Darwish's later works reveal a rich topoi of homeland. He transforms the homeland into a poem, for instance: "My homeland is my new *qaṣīda*" (in "Journey of the Mutannabi to Egypt," in *Dīwān* vol. 2, 108). As poetry might be named as an estrangement, so is home: "The homeland is this estrangement" (*Yawmīyāt al-ḥuzn al-'ādī* [Journal of an ordinary sadness] 156). And just as poetry is figured as a journey, so is home: "my homeland, my suitcase" (*Madīḥ al-ẓill al-'ālī* [In praise of the rising shadow] in *Dīwān* 58) This homeland is only possible as an echo, already mediated through loss. His late poetry is a marking of desire and the unattainability of the desired. If poetry is understood as home, it is also a desert of wandering. Since his "return" in 1996, Darwish has further complicated this conception of exile and of home, so that exile is no longer simply a self separated from a place. Exile is increasingly internal: the self severed from itself and from its language. For instance, he writes in *State of Siege*, "Here, there is no I" (179) and "My words besiege me/ Words I have not spoken/ They write me and they leave me searching/ For the remains of my sleep" (193).

The idea of a collection of critical essays on Mahmoud Darwish's poetry materialized in late November 2003 at a meeting of the Middle East Studies Association in Anchorage, Alaska, a location that seemed to many participants at the limits of any experience of home. The following year's MESA conference brought together for the first time scholars working individually on Mahmoud Darwish in the more hospitable environment of San Francisco. This collection, which grew from that panel, brings together twelve critical essays that address the complexity, diversity, and depth of Darwish's poetry. The contributors write from Palestine, Syria, Jordan, Israel, Germany, France, Canada, and the United States, and as teachers, readers, students, writers, and scholars of Arabic literature we have worked to situate Darwish's texts for English-speaking students and readers. While each essay focuses on a particular aspect of the poetry of Mahmoud Darwish, the essays together suggest points of intersection in their attention to the political, historical, and cultural contexts and concerns of Darwish's creativity.

Darwish has had a profound influence on generations of readers and poets throughout the Arab world: his poetry readings are hugely popular, attracting audiences of thousands, and he is credited with reviving Arabic lyrical poetry, taking it beyond, as the critic Hassan Khader puts it, "immediate political concerns into more metaphysical subjects" (Shehadeh 2000). His status as one of the foremost poets of the Arab world urges us not only to place the poet within the movement of Arabic poetry, but also to look at the historical, political, and literary contexts that started this movement. Therefore, *Exile's Poet* begins with a historical overview. "Modern Arabic Poetry: Vision and Reality" by Bassam Frangieh details the Arab poets who appeared on the cultural scene from the mid-1950s and traces their active roles in the social, political, and national realities of their societies. Frangieh's essay also argues that Arab poets are looked upon as persons of vision and prophecy, and for this they have been feared by many Arab authoritarian regimes. Thus in the "last few decades," Frangieh writes, "most prominent

Arab poets have been imprisoned, tortured, and forced into exile, or have lived outside the borders of their homelands." In addition, Frangieh demonstrates the influence on Arab poets of the political defeats and tragic events that swept the Arab world in the last half of the twentieth century. By the 1950s a sense of loss, despair, and disillusionment demanded "a new language," not only to cope with the gloomy reality, but also as a vehicle demanding social and political change. In such a context, Darwish excelled in his commitment to the Palestinian cause, which earned him the designation as Palestine's poet of resistance.

Situating her discussion within the parameters of "home" and "exile," Najat Rahman in "Threatened Longing and Perpetual Search: The Writing of Home in the Poetry of Mahmoud Darwish," demonstrates how the notions of "home" and "exile" are no longer in opposition or merely geographical, but are also metaphorical within the poetic space they occupy. Through the *qaṣīda* and the *nashīd*, Darwish is "engaged in a historical struggle and in a poetic project, one that inaugurates poetic writing as home." In addition, the poet's lyrics sing of the tension of desire and loss of the homeland. Thus to Darwish, home is poetic creation in a condition of perpetual exile.

Darwish never ceased deconstructing and questioning his previous poetic creations, but since the 1980s he has turned inward to explore the self in poetic exile. The poetic self and its transfiguration in Darwish's poetry are further elaborated in Faysal Darraj's critical essay "Transfigurations in the Image of Palestine in the Poetry of Mahmoud Darwish." Darraj charts the poet's relentless effort to put Palestine on the poetic map. He argues that the poet also reveals the poetic "self," which is sometimes depicted as angry, romantic, prophetic, or as a refugee, an occupied land—whereas the *qaṣīda* is complete, pure, and intact. Nevertheless, the poetic "self," which is the homeland, ends up outside the self and in everlasting exile. The transformation of the self/Palestine reaches its peak when, in *State of Siege*, the poet ends up simply as one among many under siege. Furthermore, Darraj argues that this poetic "self" goes through yet another stage of transformation, a kind of poem that embraces all humans, in which love and beauty become rites of passage, if not the principles of existence. Although over time the young, angry Darwish departed from his "first" *qaṣīda*, he continued to create other ones without abandoning his cause.

Tracing another important transformation in Darwish's poetry, Sulaiman Jubran, in "The Image of the Father in the Poetry of Mahmoud Darwish," focuses on the use of imagery of fathers and Darwish's relationship to his own father figure. While the mother image remains a constant source of love and care in Darwish's poetry, early images of a father who tills the earth, cares for the harvest, and provides for the family give way to a pervasively critical attitude toward his own father's generation of Palestinians.

Subhi Hadidi's "Mahmoud Darwish's Love Poem: History, Exile, and the Epic Call," focuses on *Sarīr al-gharība* [*The Stranger's Bed*] (1999) and shows how the simple act of writing love poems cannot be taken for granted in this poet's work. Long considered the "lover of Palestine," the poet who is expected to speak for the collective resists such an expectation, according to Hadidi. The love poem that is integral to an aesthetic project becomes a defense for it as well. Hadidi argues that this poem of Darwish's does not resemble other love poems: not only does it differ from his other lyrics, but also from the love poems in the Arabic tradition. His love poems "contemplate history" and "evoke the pains of exile," presenting estrangement of love in "the inseparability of love and exile." Estrangement, however, poetically develops as a fruitful possibility of expression. Furthermore, his poems, though they showcase the sonnet, do not strictly adhere to its conventional form. Darwish's innovations of meter and prose collaborate to create "better poems."

Darwish's technical innovations have influenced the form, style, and substance of modern Arabic poetry. He is considered the first to have written in a "nontraditional way" such that "the poem was not built on one single rhyme" (Shehadeh 2002, 57). It is known that Darwish prepares meticulously before writing. In an interview, Darwish says "I feel that no poem starts from nothing. Humanity has produced such a huge poetic output [...] you are always building on the work of others. There is no blank page from which to start" (Shehadeh 58). But Darwish also builds on both the Hebrew Bible and the New Testament, on Greek and Roman myths and legends in order to de-narrate and deconstruct the authoritarian and homogenous master-narrative. In this context Reuven Snir's essay "'Other Barbarians Will Come': Intertexuality, Meta-Poetry, and Meta-Myth in Mahmoud Darwish's Poetry," concentrates on *Ward aqall* [Fewer Roses], a collection written by Darwish in 1986 while residing in Paris. Here again we notice the poetic persona is a chronicler of Palestinian collective agonies and aspirations. Through the interplay of reality, meta-poetry, meta-myth (whether Biblical, Roman, or Greek), and intertextuality, the poet aspires to be simply a poet. Snir's meticulous structural and thematic analysis of selected lines of poetry shows how they are all "linked by the persona, who represents all the members of a collective and as their poetic proxy suffers on their behalf."

As Darwish continued to transform his poetry, he endeavored to move away from his identification as the "poet of the Palestinian resistance," yet without ceasing to articulate collective and political issues in his work, as Angelika Neuwirth argues in "Hebrew Bible and Arabic Poetry: Mahmoud Darwish's Palestine from Paradise Lost to a Homeland Made of Words." Neuwirth follows Darwish from the time he wrote his first long poem *'Āshiq min Filasṭīn* [A lover from Palestine] (1966), a poem that reflects an experience recorded in his early memoir *Yawmīyāt al-ḥuzn al-'ādī* [Diary of ordinary sadness] to *Ḥālat ḥiṣār* [*State of Siege*] (2002). Neuwirth argues that on the road to exile, the young poet came full circle in his poetical narration of re-reading the Hebrew Bible. In the beginning of his career, Darwish "had given the Palestinians a Genesis-story, de-narrating their exile." But in later works celebrating the figure of the *fidā'ī* and the *shahīd*, Darwish "created a Palestinian Exodus drama, dramatizing their 'return' from exile."

Referring to one alluring but thorny aspect of exilic life, Edward Said writes in *Reflections on Exile*: "Exile is never the state of being satisfied, placid, or secure. Exile, in the words of Wallace Stevens, is 'a mind of winter' in which the pathos of the summer and autumn as much as the potential of spring are nearby but unobtainable" (186). "Exile and the City: The Arab City in the Writing of Mahmoud Darwish," by Hala Khamis Nassar, examines the poet's attitude toward the cities he has lived in during his exile. For Darwish, the city is both a realm where he can feel anonymous and a space where he can be in touch with his readers. The city can also be a refuge; living on the margins, he no longer feels the need to integrate into a specific culture and can derive a sense of home from his poetic discourse. In concentrating on Darwish's latest collections, Nassar, however, argues that Darwish's life of exile in large cities mirrors his ambivalent attitude toward the metropolis that is closely connected with the political events and turmoil of the Palestinian experience.

In an essay on the recurrent theme of exile in Darwish's poetry, Sinan Antoon concentrates on one of the poet's latest collections *Lā ta'tadhir 'ammā fa'alta* [*Do Not Apologize for What You've Done*] (2004). In Antoon's essay, "Returning to the Wind," we join Darwish on a journey, following his desire to "return" to the "homeland" and nonetheless ending up in a state of unending exile. Anchoring himself in Arabic poetic tradition, Darwish uses the poetic persona to create a myth that is not limited to speaking about the "self" and the "home," but speaks on behalf of others as well. He creates a poetic myth only to demythologize it at the end in order to celebrate exile instead of return.

In "Language Places," Jeffrey Sacks describes the poet's choice of language as "a force that cuts, displaces, disfigures, and divides. It is a force which attests to the fact that, as Darwish wrote [...] in 1973, 'language doesn't settle down.'" Darwish wrote *State of Siege* in Ramallah when the Israeli army besieged it in 2002, leaving the city full of rubble. The poet is under siege; his language besieges him; he is besieged by his text—only to shatter into a future language that liberates him from his own previous texts.

In "Alternative History, Expanding Identity: Myths Reconsidered in Mahmoud Darwish's Poetry," Ipek Azime Celik considers Darwish's resistance to and liberation from narratives of history and the myths that sustain hegemony. Celik revisits Darwish's use of myth, concentrating particularly on his work in the 1990s, and considers how in deconstructing master mythical narratives Darwish is not only rewriting myths and contesting their historical validity, but carving out a new, complex, multilayered Palestinian identity that can withstand destruction and annihilation.

Stuart Reigeluth, in "The Art of Repetition: The Poetic Prose of Mahmoud Darwish and Mourid Barghouti," presents another comparative perspective on Darwish's literary prose, looking at Darwish's *Memory for Forgetfulness* (1986) and Mourid Barghouti's *I Saw Ramallah* (1997). Reigeluth argues that both Palestinian poets, on respective journeys to cities from their past, "are acutely aware that repetition within existence is not possible. They will not return from exile with a full sense of belonging." As modern embodiments of the nineteenth-century flâneur, Darwish and Barghouti create essential Palestinian manifestos of memory.

The critics whose essays appear in this collection write from a wide range of geographical, critical, and cultural locations. As contributors, we all have our say on Darwish's work; however, we leave the last word to him, so the final piece in this collection is an interview with Darwish. In this interview, Najat Rahman reflects on her first encounter with the poet in 1996. Then the dialogue focuses on his latest works and the roles of the poet, the critic, and the reader. The interview is by no means a closure to the multiple visions of Mahmoud Darwish's poetry that are united by a passion for his work, but an invitation to continued critical engagement.

1
Modern Arabic Poetry: Vision and Reality

Bassam K. Frangieh

Write down I am an Arab
You stole the groves of my forefathers,
And the land I used to till.
You left me nothing but these rocks.
And from them, I must wrest a loaf of bread,
For my eight children.
Write down on the top of the first page:
I neither hate others nor steal their property,
But, when I am hungry,
I will eat the flesh of my usurper!
—from "Identity Card," 1964

THESE ARE THE VERSES OF MAHMOUD DARWISH, THE NATIONAL POET OF Palestine and one of the greatest Arab poets of our time. Darwish has been a symbol of defiance in the Palestinian struggle against the Israeli occupation and his verses have been recited throughout the Arab world as an effective means in the political mobilization of the Palestinian people in the last 40 years particularly in the 1960s and 1970s. Mahmoud Darwish has indeed played a leading role in his political commitment to Arab national causes and in enriching the modern Arab poetics as a whole. Darwish has been a poet of national authority and a mighty force in provoking the people through the power of his words.

For the poet to be defender of his people, or even to die for them, is not new to Arab society. The Palestinian poet Abd al-Rahim Mahmoud (1913–1948) was the first poet-martyr in modern time: one who carried his "soul in the palm of his hand," as he expressed it in his verse, and who threw himself, indeed, into "the caravan of death." His premature death at age 35, fighting a battle in an attempt

Translations in this chapter are by Bassam Frangieh unless otherwise noted.

to keep Palestine free from foreign occupation, brought dignity to the hearts of his people. He translated his verses into death and eliminated the gap between words and action. Abd al-Rahim Mahmoud was a courageous poet and a man of purpose who changed his vision into reality and the reality of his life into a myth—and he shall remain a symbol of heroism.

The Arab poet has at no time in history been entirely free from political and social commitment. Since pre-Islamic times, Arab poets have played a critical role in their society. The Arab poet was the voice of his tribe, its defender and representative—above all, its provocative force. The ideal Arab hero has always been embodied in the warrior poet who fought against injustice and oppression. In modern times, the role of the Arab poet has not changed a great deal. The poets Hafiz Ibrahim (d. 1932), Jamil Sidqi al-Zahawi (d. 1936), Ma'ruf al-Rusafi (d. 1945), Ibrahim Tuqan (d. 1941), and Muhammad Mahdi al-Jawahiri (d. 1997), to name only a few, fought for social and political justice, reaffirming the continuing involvement of Arab poets in their societies. Mahmoud Darwish, serving as a representative and spokesperson for Palestinians, is one fine example of the importance of the Arab poet in contemporary Arab society.

Also, perhaps nowhere else are poets more actively involved in the social, political, and national realities of their societies than in the Arab world. Arab poets are considered persons of vision and prophecy, and because of this they have been a source of fear for many Arab leaders. In the latter part of the 20th century, as challenges and crises intensified, the poet became even more involved and his role became increasingly critical. Today, the Arab poet has become a "fighter against his time," to use Nietzsche's words. In the last few decades, most prominent Arab poets have been imprisoned, tortured, and forced into exile, or have lived outside the borders of their homelands.

As a consequence of their brave words, Qassim Haddad (b. 1948), Muhammad Afifi Matar (b. 1935), and Abdellatif La'ābi (b. 1942) were tortured and imprisoned. Kamal Nasir (d. 1973) was murdered, Abd al-Wahab al-Bayyati (d. 1999) lived in continuous exile, and Muzaffar al-Nuwwab (b. 1934) lives underground, while Adonis (b. 1930) resided in Lebanon then France, and Nizar

Qabbani lived in several places before he died in 1998 in England.

The Arab world in the period following World War II suffered a series of tragic events and confronted increasingly harsh realities in the political, social, national, and cultural spheres. Arabs were faced with complicated international conspiracies and foreign interventions, harsh economic conditions, and internal and external threats. By far the most devastating blow to the Arabs came in 1948 with the creation of the state of Israel and the transformation of the Palestinians into a stateless people. The newly independent Arab states became corrupted, and most were ruled by military dictators or monarchies supported by foreign powers. Palestine became a helpless nation of refugees, its citizens bankrupt not only of their land, but also of their dignity.

The Arab defeat in 1948 brought a loss of faith, despair, disbelief, and demoralization, which deeply affected the collective Arab psyche. This same catastrophe, however, became, as Salma Jayyusi writes in the *Anthology of Modern Palestinian Literature*, "a turning point for modern Arabic literature on a pan-Arab scale," with poets reacting in unison to a new reality in which literature could participate in the battle for change (16). Arab poets confronted these tragic events with a new attitude of defiance. In light of these dramatic occurrences, the School of Romanticism, which had dominated the Arab world's literary circles between the two world wars, became totally inappropriate.

Albert Hourani has said that in order for poetry to reflect the dramatic and rapid developments occurring in the Arab world after World War II, a revolutionary change had to take place in the conception of Arabic poetry, and in the role and the function of the Arab poet. Indeed, there was a change in the "intent and content of the poem." Individual poets may have differed in their emphasis on various aspects of reality, but all were concerned with the theme of the Arab nation and its weaknesses, and expressed the "discontent of the Arabs with themselves and the world." What is more, they felt that poetry should play an active role in rebuilding and revitalizing Arab society and bringing about revolutionary change. "A new Arab nation and a new Arab man," Hourani wrote in *A History of the Arab Peoples*, "needed to be brought into being." The poet should be a "creator of a new world" (396–397).

Poetry needed a new language for this new world, and a new language was created. New symbols and images were drawn from ancient Arab culture, classical mythology, and modern European poetry. All were given a local resonance. The rigid constraints of classical poetic forms, traditional rhyme schemes, and the conventional metric patterns that had prevailed for more than fifteen centuries were rejected in favor of free verse poetry with no restrictions.

This new "free verse" movement, which began in the late 1940s and blossomed into fruition in the 1950s, was a poetic revolution in both content and form and a reaction to, and reflection of, the new social and political realties. It serves as an excellent demonstration of the close connection between literature and society in the Arab world.

Soon, there was no major poet who did not use his or her voice as a weapon for political and social change, and *iltizām* [commitment] became for many years "a key term in the Arab critic's vocabulary" (Badawi, *Short History* 58). The word was a translation of Sartre's *engagement*, a term coined by the French philosopher in 1948, and popularized by the influential Lebanese periodical *Al-Adab*, founded by Suhail ldris and devoted to emphasizing the need for literature to have a message. This pan-Arab publication, established in 1953, played an important role in shaping the course of modern Arabic literature. Another leading and influential literary periodical was *Shi'r*, which played the most important role in the development of modern Arabic poetry. The poets of *Shi'r*, which was founded in Beirut in 1957 by Yusuf al-Khal and Adonis, were extremist and revolutionary in their rejection of stagnation and traditional values, and in their use of the language. The content and form of their poetry had metaphysical and mystical dimensions and was influenced by contemporary Western poetry, especially the French symbolist and surrealist trends.

Meanwhile, on the political front, several new movements emerged seeking to recover the dignity of the Arabs, and to achieve independence, freedom, and unity within the Arab world. Pan-Arabism, with its rallying cry for Arab unity and demands for a strong moral relationship between the people and their rulers, resonated in the hearts of Arab poets and the Arab masses at large.

The Ba'ath party's platform of pan-Arabism and socialism attracted the support of large communities outside of the Muslim Sunni majority, including the Druze, Christians, and Alawis. Founded in Syria, it spread to Lebanon, Jordan, Iraq, and other surrounding areas. Among those challenging the Ba'athists for political and social power were the Marxists, Communists, and the Syrian Nationalist Party. The latter, founded in Lebanon by Antoun Sa'ada, was supported by many intellectuals and attracted a handful of prominent poets. Another response to the hardships facing the Arabs took the form of the Islamic movement, which also emerged as a major political force at this time, particularly in Egypt and Syria (Hourani 401–425).

But not until 1952 did the vision for the rebirth and renewal of Arab society really take hold. At a time when the entire Arab world was groping for a way out of its misery, Jamal 'Abd al-Nasir, the new president of Egypt emerged as the promise of salvation. The father of Arab nationalism and an advocate of secularization and modernization, he called on Arab nations to transcend narrow factionalism and party alliances, and unite as one. Nasir soon became the unquestioned leader of the Arab world, capturing the hearts and souls of the Arab peoples, who saw him as a savior who would return the Arabs to their long lost glory. Nasir's confidence and popularity increased with his victory during the Suez crisis in 1956, the construction of the Aswan High Dam, and the unity with Syria in 1958. He enacted broad measures of social reform and promised strong leadership in defense of the Palestinian cause. Regardless of their ideological orientation, most leading Arab poets dedicated poems to Nasir, hailing him as a hero and the leader of a new Arab world.

Nevertheless, the sudden and unexpected Arab defeat in 1967 shattered the hopes and dreams for Arab unity and the restoration of Arab glory. The promises of absolute victory made by Nasir and other leaders and political parties were suddenly broken and shattered, and everything that had been proclaimed to be true was found to be no more than false illusions, empty words, lies, deceptions. What followed in the Arab world was a psychological state of profound depression, and, in the words of Jabra I. Jabra, a "complete spiritual impotence." Arab poets expressed feelings of intense anger, resentment, and alienation in their writing, and their verses echoed the bitterness of the Arab reality with voices of discontent and total disillusionment.

The Lebanese poet Khalil Hawi, a fervent champion of Arab nationalism whose poetry is dominated by the idea of the resurrection of Arab civilization, fell into despair after the disintegration of the union between Syria and Egypt in 1961. In his prophetic and tragic poem "Lazarus" (1962), he predicted the disaster of the June 1967 War. The poem is based on the myth of Lazarus, who was resurrected by Christ three days after his death. In Hawi's poem, however, Lazarus, who symbolizes Arab civilization, does not want to be resurrected. Hawi's Lazarus is in love with his death and, instead of accepting his resurrection, he asks the gravedigger to deepen his grave:

> Deepen the hole, gravedigger,
> Deepen it to an unfathomable depth
> That extends beyond the orbit of the sun
> Into a night of ashes,
> Ruins of a star
> Buried in the beyond.

Hawi's Lazarus feels that all of his values have died and his life has become more painful than death. Why be resurrected to live such a life? He views his resurrection by Jesus as an act of accursed mercy:

> Why would the God of love
> Resurrect a corpse
> Petrified by the lust for death?
>
> This mercy is accursed—
> More painful than spring fever.

Lazarus remains a lifeless soul and a dead face. His wife, who symbolizes the lust of Arab civilization for life, had long been awaiting her husband's resurrection. But her burning desire to be united with him is crushed by the tragedy of his return. She sees her husband, a cold body and a dead spirit, and is shocked and devastated. She says:

He was a black shadow
Looming over the mirror of my breast
And in my eyes the shame of a woman
Undressed to a stranger.
Oh! Why did he return from his grave
A dead man?

In his introduction to the poem, Hawi addresses Lazarus: "[Your wife] longed for an existential renewal that would satiate the body and the soul, but you failed her, you, her rancorous dead husband!" Indeed, as a consequence of Lazarus' dark resurrection, his wife loses faith in her husband and in the God who resurrected him. She challenges Jesus:

Of what use are my tears and prayers
To a phantom God,
To a ghost hiding in blue clouds,
In soft light,
Where my sighs, laden with hunger
Go unheard.

The poem opens at Lazarus' grave and ends in his wife's grave, for Lazarus drags her with him to the world of the dead, into a dark and barren existence. She is too weak to resist, so she loses her lust for life and follows him into the ditch. In this nihilistic vision, Hawi is suggesting that the Arab nation, like Lazarus, is too broken to embrace efforts at its resurrection, and like his wife, too weak to resist being dragged into the grave. Hawi's tragic vision was realized and his prophetic poem did indeed anticipate and embody the collapse of the Arabs (see Abu Deeb).

The poetry of the Iraqi Abd al-Wahab al-Bayyati is also concerned with the resurrection and revival of Arab civilization. But while Hawi had a very pessimistic vision of the future, al-Bayyati generally ends his poems on a note of hope for the future and confidence in ultimate victory and positive change. Nonetheless, in his collection *Death in Life* [*Al-Mawt fī al-ḥayā*], written after the 1967 defeat, he depicts the Arabs in a state of "refrigerated deathlessness," to use Northrop Frye's phrase, and expresses a great despair born from the reality that the Arabs are suffering from the death of their civilization. His poem "Elegy to Aisha," written in 1968, is similar in tone to Hawi's Lazarus. The poet, ashamed and suffocating, stands before Aisha, a symbol of Arab civilization, and sees that "her hands are cut off on a cushion," symbolic of powerlessness and disability. In the darkness of Aisha's braids, rats scuttle about; worms "devour her eyes"—all is corrupt and decaying. Aisha goes to her grave not quite dead; she is unable to live and unable to die. The poem reflects the inability of rebirth and revival, and symbolizes that the resurrection was false and that all the waiting was in vain. In the words of Muhyi al-Din Subhi, Aisha symbolizes a "false pregnancy" (55).

> On your mattress, Ishtar, I laid you down to die
> I walked sober and drunk through the house of the dead.
> Through the ruins of Babylon,
> Along the river shore,
> Alone
> I spoke to clouds,
> Wallowed in dust,
> Shouted out in despair.

In "Lament for the June Sun," a moving poem of self-condemnation written immediately after the 1967 defeat, al-Bayyati highlighted the deficiencies of Arab society and the death-in-life of the Arab nation. He bitterly criticized the Arabs and attacked the corruption of Arab rulers who deceived their people with propaganda, cover-ups, and misleading news broadcasts about the reality of their situation. In beautiful images and simple language, al-Bayyati laments the condition of the Arabs:

> We were ground in the coffeehouses of the East by
> War of words, wooden swords
> Lies and empty heroes.
> We did not kill a camel or a grouse
> We did not try the game of death
>
> Trivia preoccupied us
> We killed each other and now we are crumbs.
> In the coffeehouses of the East we swat at flies
> We are the generation of meaningless death

the recipients of alms.
The sun of June left our genitals naked
Why did they leave us for the dogs, corpses without
prayers
Carrying the crucified nation in one hand and dust in
the other?

Still, al-Bayyati ends his poem on an optimistic note, saying that the leaders, not the people, were defeated:

We were not defeated
The giant peacocks alone were defeated
Quicker than the flicker of a flame.

In a more sophisticated and complicated poem, "The Nightmare of Day and Night," from his collection *Writing on Clay* [*Al-kitāba 'alā al-ṭīn*] (1970), al-Bayyati composed in a quieter tone, but used rich, powerful, surrealistic images and symbols to convey the state of psychological siege of the post-1967 years in the Arab world. He revealed the transformation of a disillusioned dream into a nightmare in which one is unable even to find a place to bury one's own corpse. This poem demonstrates a profound awareness of the complexities of Arab life in this confused age of defeat and absurdity as well as the sharp contradictions between reality and dream:

While the earth dreams of the birth of a prophet
Who will fill the horizons with justice,
And dreams of the birth of the seasons,
I carry a corpse in the street
At nightfall
I will bury it in a brothel or a park
Or a coffeehouse or a tavern of light,
Hiding my face from God and from you,
Ashamed and drunk, I cry.

The Syrian poet Adonis, one of the most committed to cultural and poetic change in the Arab world, is known as a "tireless advocate" of modernity. His book *Al-Thābit wa al-mutaḥawwil* [The static and dynamic] (1974), was a landmark in the intellectual provocation for radical and immediate change. "In the verses of

Adonis," M. M. Badawi writes, "the modernism in modern Arabic poetry has been achieved" (*Short History* 75). In a poem written after the 1967 defeat and published in the poet's 1969 collection *This Is My Name* [*Hadhā huwa ismī*], Adonis touches upon the same theme as al-Bayyati's "Lament for the June Sun." He views the Arab nation as broken and defeated, and as a dead corpse wrapped in shrouds. Nothing remains save madness:

> I have said,
> This broken jar is a defeated nation!
> I see the shadow of a crow
> Upon the face of my country.
> I name this book a shroud,
> I name this city a corpse.
> Madness!
> Only madness remains!

While al-Bayyati suffered continuous exile for his political belief, the Bahraini poet Qassim Haddad was tortured and imprisoned for five years for his belief in the need for a radical revolution in Arab society in order to achieve freedom and justice. An important figure in the process of modernity, he called for democracy and protested tyranny and oppression. In his poem "Sin Number Three," Haddad voices disgust at oppressive Arab regimes, along with a challenge:

> O King:
> We are the flocks, of which you boast to other nations
> But we are fed up with this false glory. (28)

The Syrian poet Nizar Qabbani, the most renowned contemporary love poet in the Arab world, also became a powerful voice in the battle of social and political change. After the 1967 defeat, he wrote, "woman has been my beloved and she still is, but I am now taking a second wife; her name is Homeland":

> Oh, my homeland
> You have changed me in a single moment
> From a poet writing of love and longing
> To a poet writing with a knife. (32)

His poem "Marginal Notes on the Book of Defeat," which he wrote immediately after the 1967 defeat, was harshly critical of both the Arab peoples and the Arab leaders:

> This is the secret of our tragedy:
> Our cries are more powerful than our voices
> Our swords are taller than our men
> O Sultan, O my lord,
> I was beaten with shoes,
> Your soldiers forced me to eat out of my shoes.
> Twice you have lost the war
> Because you cut out the tongues of half your people.
> What use are a people who cannot speak?

The Iraqi poet Muzaffar al-Nawwab faced dire personal consequences for his political verses; he was forced to live underground most of his life because of his biting satire focusing on the corruption of Arab leaders and their establishments. Although his poetry was officially banned in all parts of the Arab world, it has been photocopied and memorized. He spent his life in exile, hiding from one place to another to avoid imprisonment and torture. Al-Nawwab attacked virtually all Arab leaders and many, if not all, major political events in the Middle East. In his collection *Watarīyāt Laylīyya* he calls all of the Arab leaders "traitors" and "defeated," and in a poem addressed to them entitled "Sons of Bitches without Exception," he depicted Palestine as a young virgin being raped by the Israelis, while Arab leaders gathered behind the door to hear her sounds of pain at her deflowering. According to al-Nawwab, even ants and dogs would have fought or done something about such an insult; instead, these leaders shouted at her from behind the door not to scream—to avoid a scandal. Al-Nawwab became the voice of the silent majority who saw that their leaders and their governments had conspired against them.

The Iraqi poet Badr Shakir al-Sayyab (d. 1964) was also forced into exile and hunted by the authorities of his country. In "Hymn of the Rain" (1954), which is, in the words of Naji Alloush, "the most committed political poem written by al-Sayyab" (1–4), the poet, who was living in exile in Kuwait at that time and swept by homesickness, describes the injustice of the political and social situation in Iraq. The poet watches Iraq from across the border—the rain falling and the crops growing, only to be eaten by ravens and locusts, symbols of corrupt Iraqi government officials and an oppressive social system. The rain, a life-giving force and symbol of fertility, serves only to perpetuate the hunger and misery of the Iraqi people, who never get to reap the harvest of their slave labor:

> Despite the rain,
> Not a year has passed without famine in Iraq!
> Do you know what sadness the rain evokes?
> And how the roof-gutters of the poor
> Sob when it pours?

Nevertheless, in the final verse of the poem, he gives hope for political salvation:

> Iraq will grow green with the rain,
> And the rain pours.

As for Palestinian poets, they focused their anger and bitterness on the Israelis, the Arab states, and the West, particularly the United States for supporting both Israel and the Arab dictators. They have long described their countrymen as victims of history, but also as courageous heroes fighting to redeem their people. The underlying tenets of Palestinian poetry have been resistance and defiance, determination in their struggle, and continuing faith in their ultimate victory. But attempts to rigidly classify Palestinian poetry have been invalidated by the writing of such poets as Fadwa Tuqan. Although Ahmad Dahbour classifies her as a romantic poet, she has been deeply committed to her national cause. Salma Jayyusi, in her introduction to *A Mountainous Journey: An Autobiography of Fadwa Tuqan*, calls this poetess one of the "most powerful voices raised in defense of her people and their rights." In fact, Jayyusi writes, so powerful was her political poetry that it caused the prominent Israeli personality Moshe Dayan to say that just one of Fadwa Tuqan's poems "is enough to create ten fighters for the Palestinian resistance" (see also Jayyusi, *Anthology* 8, 20).

The Palestinian poet Tawfiq Zayyad (d. 1994) used simple language and expressions of daily life, often mixed with colloquial dialect, to transform his verses into weapons of defiance in support of the Palestinian liberation movement. His defiant verses were put to music and became national emblems of the Palestinian struggle. So powerful is their language and so enchanting their musicality, that they have been an enduring source of inspiration and spiritual strength for Palestinians; they were even chanted by children during the intifada. As such, Zayyad's songs have become an integral part of Palestinian resistance ideology:

> Here we shall stay
> Like a wall upon your chest
> And never leave.

The defeat of the Arabs in June 1967 strengthened the will and determination of the Palestinians against Israeli occupation. Palestinian poets such as Samih al-Qassim (b. 1939) emerged out of the Arab defeat as the strongest poets in the Arab world in their unwavering determination to continue the struggle. Not only did their earlier poetry play a formative role in mobilizing the Palestinian people to revolt, but their works also helped restore and strengthen the spirit of the Arab people by calling for renewed resistance and dedication to the cause of Arab nationalism.

Mahmoud Darwish (b. 1942) left Israel in 1971 and joined the Palestinian diaspora in the Arab world. He was received as a hero and maintained his status as the foremost Palestinian poet. He has continued to draw attention to the great problems facing the Palestinians in their struggle for a homeland, and to the internal and external conspiracies to abort this struggle. After the Israeli invasion of Beirut in 1982, when the PLO headquarters was forced to move to Tunis and the Palestinian revolution seemed to have come to a standstill, Darwish remained determined to continue the Palestinian struggle:

> A dark night will come,
> When there will be fewer roses.
> But even then,
> I shall continue my song
> With the same force.

The theme of exile and continual Palestinian displacement is most elegantly conveyed in the following of Darwish's verses:

> I gave my picture to my beloved:
> "If I die, hang it up on the wall."
> She asked: "Is there a wall for it?"
> I answered: "We will build a wall."
> "Where, in what house?"
> "We will build a house."
> "Where, on which spot of exile?"

In an effort to rescue Arab society from its prolonged spiritual death, Arab poets have resorted to myths and archetypal images of the "savior" and the "redeemer" in their struggle to keep alive the dream of Arab renewal. They employed a variety of myths from the ancient Near East including Ishtar, Tammuz (Adonis), Baal, and variations on them. In addition, they invented their own symbols and assumed the personas of archetypal figures from history, the Bible, the Qur'an, and Greek mythology. Some poets put on the mask of Noah in an attempt to express to readers the possibility of building a better world after the flood, which symbolizes the destruction of Arab civilization. Others become Ulysses or Sindbad and express the restlessness of the Arab man on an endless quest toward a far-off destination. Some poets invoked Prometheus, Sisyphus, Mihyar, Job, and Hallaj, as well as other myths that make up what Carl Jung calls archetypes of the collective unconscious.

The fact that the poet Ahmad Ali Sa'id deliberately chose to write under the pen-name "Adonis" since early in his poetic career is reflective of his deep belief in the myth of resurrection after death. Adonis has used several different variations of the "myth of the eternal return," including the myth of the phoenix, a legendary Arabian bird, who, when facing imminent death, consumes itself in fire and rises renewed from the ashes to start another long life. In his poem "Resurrection and Ashes," Adonis begins with a dream:

> I dream that I have an ember in my hands
> Which came to me on a wing of a bird
> From a far-off horizon.

The ember, which was brought to the poet on the wings of the phoenix, united the poet with the myth and infused new life into the poet's lungs:

> I am carried away by its incense
> To a country which I both know and do not know.
> Where it is said:
> There is a bird in love with its death
> Who, for the sake of a new beginning
> Will burn itself alive.

Thus, the poet becomes like the phoenix; holding fire in his lips and breathing fire out of his lungs, he burns the corruption and stagnation of his society, purifies its spirit, and gives it a new beginning. Then the poet detaches himself from the bird, and addresses it:

> O Phoenix,
> At this moment of your resurrection,
> From ashes, sparks and flames
> Spring crept into the roots!

He links the phoenix with the myth of Tammuz, whose blood fertilized the entire country. Here, the poet's words are his blood and his sacrifice, which will fertilize his nation and bring new life to the Arabs. In the end of the poem Adonis prostrates himself in ritual supplication to the phoenix, praying that it should carry through with the death process in order that its dream be realized:

> Here I bend my knee
> In humility.
> O Phoenix! Let me dream for one last time!
> Let me embrace the flames and vanish in them!

Other poets employed Jesus and his crucifixion as a myth of resurrection. They gave the story of Christ a national dimension: it became a symbol of sacrifice and martyrdom necessary for the forthcoming resurrection of a nation. Salma Jayyusi writes in *Trends and Movements in Modern Arabic Literature* that for al-Sayyab, who was able to Arabize almost all the myths he used, "Christ and the Cross became, in his hands, a part of a human heritage no less Arab than anything else" (vol. 3, 722–724). In his poem "Christ After Crucifixion," the poet speaks in the voice of Jesus, thus drawing the parallel between Jesus and the Arab man: both are victims of tyranny, injustice, and corruption, and both are tortured, beaten, and murdered. But the nail that pierced the body of the speaker in the poem does not kill him:

> The wounds from the cross which they nailed me to,
> The whole afternoon, did not kill me.

Both poet and Jesus serve as god, redeemer, and lifegiver to the people:

> I died that the bread might be eaten in my name,
> That every season they will sow me in the earth!
> So I will become the seed of future generations.

Thus, in the poem, Jesus becomes symbolic of the revolutionary Arab fighter, who martyrs himself for his cause. Only with such a death will the birth pangs of the Arab nation begin:

> After they nailed me
> I cast my glance towards the city,
> And saw a flowering forest.
> Everywhere there was a cross
> And next to it, a sorrowful mother.
> Blessed be the Lord
> These are the birth pains of the city!

Khalil Hawi also saw himself as a Christ figure carrying the suffering of his nation as a burden on his shoulders. With a boundless love for his people, he stretched out his body as a bridge, just as Jesus stretched out his body on the cross to save humanity. The ribs of the poet's body become a bridge on which revolutionaries will march toward a brighter future:

> They cross the bridge at dawn, light-footed
> My ribs laid out before them as a solid bridge.
> From the caves and the swamps of the old East,
> They cross into the new East.
> My ribs are their solid bridge.

The very same poets who viciously criticized their society are the ones who actually loved it the most fervently. They rejected the slow death of the Arab nation and took on the role of savior, redeemer, and prophet of change. They made use of myths of death and rebirth as an expression of hope for the resurgence of the Arab spirit after a long period of stagnation. Unfortunately, the vision of these Arab poets, who thought of themselves as prophets and saviors, was not achieved. Some poets began to be disillusioned and to lose faith in their ability to inspire change in their society. Their struggles, their battles fought with words, began to seem futile. As a consequence, more and more poets fell to despair.

In his poem "Jaykūr wa al-Madīna," al-Sayyab's vision for change ended in despair. Issa Boullata writes that, while al-Sayyab "remains the revolutionary he has always been, he begins to express the sentiment that the struggle is in vain" (96). The city in this poem is associated with evil oppression, political and social corruption, and spiritual death, while the poet's village, Jaykūr, represents peace, purity, and goodness. Al-Sayyab depicts the roads of the city as "ropes of mud" wrapping around his heart, and "cables of fire" devouring the fields, leaving in them only ashes of hate. A wall with a locked gate is built around the village, keeping it beyond reach, and the poet is powerless to return. As Jaykūr becomes drowned in stillness, the poet surrenders.

Al-Bayyati's city is also a symbol of the unfortunate situation in which the Arabs are living today. The Arab city, like Arab reality, is full of confusion and contradictions, corrupt leaders and thieves, gallows and prisons and incinerators. Al-Bayyati likens the Arab man of this age of defeat to "a postage stamp" glued on everything. The orphaned children of society wander about, searching in garbage dumps for a bone or for a "moon dying upon the corpses of houses." The Arab man is for sale, displayed in the storefronts of the city, while:

> The policemen, the sodomites, and the pimps
> Spit in his eyes
> As he lies shackled.

The city has become a major theme in modern Arabic poetry. The city, Ihsan Abbas writes, is used in poetry as a mirror to "reflect the poet's ideological position." Without exception, the Arab artist's position toward the city is one of hatred and rejection. In al-Bayyati's poetry, for example, the city symbolizes the ebb and flow of Iraqi political life. The city is a center for corruption, injustice, and political conspiracies; it is employed as a symbol of evil, oppression, and alienation. It is also a symbol of cruelty, inhumanity, and lost innocence. As a result, poets are rejecting the ills of contemporary Arab society when they reject the modern city (*Directions* 175).

The Egyptian poet Ahmad 'Abd al-Mu'ti Hijazi (b. 1935) wrote in his poem "City without Heart," that the city is like death, both spiritual and physical. It is a source of fear and uncertainty, where humanity is cheated and betrayed by fellow humans. People are alienated from each other, they live and die alone and feel nothing. In this poem, a boy, coming from the village to look for a job in Cairo, is run over by a car:

> Not an eye wept because,
> In the big city people are no more than numbers:
> One boy came, one boy died.
> They dumped his body in a white car
> A green fly hovered above the spot
> Stained by his blood.

Even New York City has not escaped attack by Arab poets. In his poem "A Grave for New York," Adonis depicts the city of New York as a woman "lifting in one hand a rag called liberty, and with the other suffocating a child called the earth." He sees New York as an "archetypal city" of imperial power that dominates the entire world while its black community lives in desperate misery. Adonis also attacks Arab cities for being the willing customers, or victims, of New York cultural exports. Likewise, al-Bayyati, in his poem "A Funeral Mass for the City of New York," describes New York as "a ferocious beast" and as a place where everything is for sale. "Pay a dollar and Kill a man"—all is in the "name of the law." According to al-Bayyati, leaders from all continents come to New York to sell themselves.

The future of the Arabs in the eyes of Khalil Hawi remains dark and the struggle is futile. Hawi could see no fight in the future, only darkness and corruption. His Lazarus dragged to death not only his wife, but the whole Arab nation. For Hawi, Arab society can no longer be revived, and the Arab man can no longer be saved:

> The light in his eyes is dead.
> Nothing can save him:
> Neither a heroic deed nor a humble prayer.

Al-Sayyab's vision in "The City of Sindbad," is equally as nightmarish and tragic as Hawi's, and serves as an example of another poet's loss of faith in the future. This poem describes a deformed resurrection—this time, when God finally answers prayers for rain, He sends blood in the form of rain. Such rain brings not the fulfillment of years of waiting and expectations, but futility and death:

> Flowers are not blooming,
> Black fields have no water
> Sickles reap nothing.

Al-Sayyab, like his contemporaries, looked around himself and saw that heroism was defeated, streets crowded with the dead, fields barren, and leaders brutal and corrupt. Not only was Christ nailed to the cross and crucified, but also the poet and the prophet Muhammad:

> Blood boiled up in the feet of the prophet,
> In his hands and in his eyes.
> In his eyelids, the God was burned.

Al-Sayyab tells us in this poem that Christ was not resurrected but that the hungry people only imagined that he rolled back the stone from the tomb, cured the leper, and made the blind see. He also tells us that Christ never brought Lazarus back to life, but that he left him to sleep while his flesh dried in strips and was sold in the city of sinners, blood, and bullets, while:

Women are aborting in the slaughterhouses!
The flames are dancing on the threshing floors!
Christ will perish before Lazarus.

The poet sees only bones in the country, daggers, and dogs—no water or green fields. Even the moon has disappeared. Only Judas is active, serving as a symbol of treachery, deception, and the secret police, who wear the colors of blood and who "set the dogs on houses" and the cradles of little children.

The Lebanese poet Yusuf al-Khal (d. 1987) shares this tragic vision in his poem "The Deserted Well," in which he describes a well that people pass by, but neither drink from nor even toss a stone in. They feel apathetic after they discover that their toil was in vain; their tears of waiting for salvation change into tears of humiliation and defeat. Al-Khal comes close to calling on people to give up the struggle:

Someone shouted at them: retreat, retreat!
In the shelter at the rear there is a place
Safe from bullets and death.
Some said it was madness
Perhaps it was.

Al-Bayyati once said that a poet is compelled in the core of his being to be "burned with others when he sees them burning and not to stand on the other side of the bank absorbed in prayer," a statement that demonstrates his commitment to the use of poetry for social and political change. And yet he, too, had doubts about the ability of poetry to affect reality, and often his verses are darkened by this skepticism. His verses are those of a wounded man who continues to raise questions about salvation. After years of continuous struggle, al-Bayyati asks in "Eye of the Sun" (1971):

Who will stop the bleeding in the memory
Of the man destined to be hanged?
Who will wear the robe
Of the saint and the martyr?
Who will burn like me
In the fire of yearning?

Al-Bayyati doubts whether anyone will wear the robe of a martyr. In his poem "Reading from the Book of al-Tawwasin by al-Hallaj" (1975), he puts on the robe of such a martyr, an archetype of heroism and great courage, who was crucified mainly for his social and political beliefs. Through him al-Bayyati laments the Arab reality. The poet becomes another Hallaj, who sees only a wall of stone separating thousands of poor, desperate people from freedom and justice. The poet comes closer to this wall, which also separates words from actions, and true from false, only to discover that it is surrounded by another wall, then another wall, which keeps rising and rising. He sees that the polar star has disappeared and that there is no way out:

> I shout, terrified, at the base of the wall
> Why is man crammed with death in this exile.
> Why, O lord, this silence of man?

When he hears nothing, he asks the Lord for an answer:

> Why, my Lord, did you not raise your clement hand
> In the face of evil coming through all doors?

As God does not answer him, al-Bayyati ends his poem on a note of doubt tempered with hope. All the poor gather, around the fire:

> In this night
> Haunted by the fever of something
> Which might or might not
> Come from behind the walls.

In moments of despair, al-Bayyati believes that the Arab man has been sentenced to death by leaders who use him as a puppet in the game of death that has been repeated throughout history. He betrays such a trap in "A Conversation of a Stone" (1989):

> One stone said to another:
> I am not happy by this naked fence
> My place is in the palace of the sultan.
> The other said:
> It is no use!
> Tomorrow this palace will be destroyed, as will this fence

By an order of the sultan's men
Who will repeat this game anew.

Khalil Hawi in "The Cave" (1965) is far more pessimistic. In this contemporary era, he sees in the Arab world only dead fish and rotten fruits, corpses and ghosts and boats tipping into the sea. He senses a spell of darkness falling over the Arab world, a complete stagnation and a slow death. A process in which minutes seem like centuries, in which time is frozen still:

The hands of the clock do not turn:
My God, how the minutes stretch their legs
And freeze, changing into ages.

This frozen desert of time is matched by the dead clay that Hawi describes in "The Sailor and the Dervish." Nothing amounts to more than "clay for clay":

How often I died with dead clay!
Leave me alone with the sea, the wind, and death
Which spreads blue shrouds for the drowned.

For Hawi, the Arab tragedy has escalated to such an extent that death became the only solution. As expressed in "Lazarus," Hawi perceived the resurrection of Arab society as deformed and disfigured since, as Rita 'Awad writes, "he saw the present reality as a continuation of the age of decline." Although "this very vision was painful to the poet and he wished it to be different," he felt that the only protest left for him was to take his own life (13–22).

Hawi, a man of great passion and sensitivity, never overcame his disillusionment. He shot himself in the head the day after the Israeli army invaded Lebanon on June 6, 1982, the day that also marked the fifteenth anniversary of the June 1967 war. Thus he united his reality with his vision, decrying and proclaiming, in the words of Mahmoud Shurayh, "the defeat of an entire nation" (33).

This leads us to the following questions: Can poetry change the world? More specifically, can Arabic poetry, with its revolutionary vision, change the reality of Arab society? Can it help to bring justice, unity, and freedom? Or can any literary, ideological, or political movement succeed in bringing change? And what is the future of Arab society?

The world in the past few decades has been in a state of constant flux. With the collapse of the Berlin wall, the fall of the Soviet political structure, and the end of cold war, many oppressive regimes were overthrown and new nations were born. In many instances, visionaries have replaced dictators, geographical borders have been redrawn, and the promise of change has been realized. Significant steps toward freedom and democracy have been achieved in all corners of the globe except in the Arab world. Unfortunately, the Arab peoples on the whole still enjoy little or no democracy or freedom. They continue to live in fear of dictators and oppressive governments with full hold on the reins of power. Arab poets, along with other literary activists, and other intellectual and political movements have long been calling for change, but these efforts seem to have failed in bringing results. The Arab world has not only remained stagnant but, in some instances, governments seem to be getting even more oppressive.

In a lecture at Yale University, Philip Khoury noted that "not even the idea of Arab nationalism has helped," while Hisham Sharabi stated that what is needed is a radical upheaval of the entire social and political system in order to free Arab society from corruption and patriarchy (86). Halim Barakat maintained that the only hope for the future of Arab society is the institutionalization of democracy, freedom, secularism, and social justice (157), while Constantine Zurayk argued that the only way out of stagnation is to change Arab powerlessness into power (35). Yet none of these intellectuals has been able to articulate exactly how these changes could be achieved.

Badr Shakir al-Sayyab writes that poetry, by its nature, is a reflection of reality. If the reality is dark, so must be the poetry. Yet he also believes that as long as life continues, there remains hope for salvation and for the reawakening of the spirit. The responsibility of poetry is to keep alive this hope and nurture it to fruition (Boullata 176). In fact, at one point, al-Sayyab believed that the salvation of Arab society would come about through his own personal death. He spoke as though he were another Christ and another redeemer. In his poem "The River and Death," he wrote:

In the depths of my blood,
I long to carry the burden of the people
And to resurrect life.
My death is a victory.

Kamal Abu Deeb rejected the last line of this poem, remarking that the death of al-Sayyab was not victorious, but pathetic! It was no more significant than a normal death. The deaths of Ghassan Kanafani and Hussayn Muruwwa, Abu Deeb says, were more tragic; yet even their deaths did not change the world. We live in a frightening age, he writes; at some moment in history there was "an Arab dream and a vision of a glowing future," but the dream has "shattered as well as the world." The Arab man is paralyzed by fear and therefore his "ineffectiveness in making change has reached an extremely tragic point." What is left is "absurdity and madness," which is "the new vision and the new reality." The world has truly collapsed and modern Arabic poetry is a reflection of such a collapse: "It is a poetry of conflicts, oppositions, and negations, and fragmentations of self and of text." Abu Deeb adds that with the "crumbling of the socio-political nationalist revivalist projects, a process of fragmentation began and is still going on," a process reflected in the development of "structure-less poetry" (34).

Issa Boullata contends, on the other hand, that poetry is not meant to provide philosophical or tangible solutions to the problems of society, but only to raise questions about the mysteries of life, death, human existence, and human anguish, and to shed light on difficult existential matters. Thus, by depicting man as lonely, confused, and powerless in challenging his fate, or by portraying the tragedies of the modern age, Arabic poetry assists humans in confronting these questions head-on and in dealing with their anxiety and pain (46).

Perhaps Qasim Haddad best expressed the tragic reality of these psychological and spiritual disturbances. He has rejected this entire age and expressed the bitterness of Arab intellectuals toward their governments, a bitterness mixed with restlessness and disgust. He speaks in his poetry about the misery, anguish, and absurdity of the present, and reflects the deep anxiety of the Arabs and their loss of direction. He portrays the fear and the deep inner void of the oppressed Arab man in a shattered age and "formless" society, where "the dead ask the dead for directions," death is slow and "dragged by mules," and women are raped by "mad horses" and impregnated with their tyrannical genes in order to give the kingdom "clones of their tyranny." On the horizon, there is only the "guardian dust which writes its false commands." For Haddad, nothing makes sense and all is "tragic." There are no longer bold sailors to save him from drowning in the sea. As he mentioned in his poetry, only his "hallucinations" have delayed his suicide (36).

In *Al-Jawāshīn* (1989), co-written with Amin Salih, in a poetic text entitled "We Tell the Meaningless Tale," the authors wrote about the upside-down and insane world around them, with a voice comprehending such absurdness, but with strength and rejection:

> "You are ignorant. You do not understand."
> "O.K. I do not understand. I do not understand what you understand. But at least I did something. I spat on one of their faces."
> "And what did it bring you? He slapped you on the face and left you on the floor."
> "Fine. But when I looked in his eyes, I saw fear. He was afraid of me. Nobody noticed. I am the only one who saw it. And that is enough for me to feel a little proud."

In *Space*, Haddad confesses that he does not know the answer to the questions that plague him, he only sees towers of chaos:

> I do not know why
> I sit this way:
> My head the hat of the universe and my hands in a frenzy.
> I see only whiteness—towers of chaos.

In *Delirium*, he describes the diffusion of the dream into a cloud of chaos and fear. Everything takes on a misty, ethereal, transitory, and nebulous quality. The dream is arrested, as is the Arab man who clings to it:

> I am neither asleep nor awake,
> Yet the enchanted dream dazzles me.

The same dream interrupts my every waking and my
every sleep.
A group of angels leads me. They say:
Do not open your eyes and do not close them.
Do not sleep and do not wake.

There are no answers, Haddad writes in *Interrogation*, because:

We are terrified rabbits,
Falling into whiteness.

Al-Bayyati contributes to this dismal vision the images of a present and future inhabited by fears and ghosts, prisons and police, exile and banishment. In "Love Poem at the Seven Gates of the World," he writes:

I now discover the oppressors of the new world.
The actors have changed their masks.
The world has fallen into the clutches of the prompter,
Who crouches in the shadow.
They killed us before we loved each other
And then they dyed the theater with our blood.

The Syrian poet Muhammad al-Maghout (b. 1930) speaks about the Arab man as a victim oppressed by a frightening reality. While most contemporary poets voice protest, al-Maghout voices resignation. Not only does al-Maghout express the sentiment of defeat, but also the despair born from a total defeat in a defeated land:

You have defeated me!
But in all this beaten land
I can find no proper hill
On which to hang my banner of surrender!

The terror voiced in the poetry of al-Maghout and Qasim Haddad hearkens back to the visionary words of Tawfiq Sayigh (d. 1971), written more than three decades ago. When the poet was still alive, his words were dismissed by critics as being irrelevant to the spirit of the times. Now, however, long after his death, his words have become extremely relevant:

My summer is emptiness

My winter is horror
And my life is a train passing between them
whistling!

For Sayigh, poetry is what sustained him in an absurd and frightening world. In the words of Mounah Khouri, it allowed him to "endure the tragedy of more than one paradise lost." Thus, when his words dried up, he did not find the strength to keep living, and he "found in death his trustworthy savior" (87).

In the last fifty years, seeing that the dream of Arab renewal has not been materializing, and seeing that their pain and struggles were in vain, many Arab poets became disillusioned and fell into despair. Many poets, seeing that their words fell on deaf ears or evaporated in the darkening air, fell silent. Some began to write in circles, or became introverted and wrote only for themselves. Nevertheless, many poets continue to struggle. And they continue, because they must continue, to fight the battle for national, cultural, social, and political change. They know well that they are not fighting alone, but representing an entire people. More than once in his poetry, Adonis writes, "I am not alone." Al-Bayyati writes for the "oppressed Arab poor from shore to shore"; Qabbani is the "voice of the voiceless"; Unsi al-Haj states, "I must continue to dream." Indeed, Arab poets have vowed to continue the struggle, and they have continued to pay the price for their courage. In spite of, and because of, these injustices, Arab poets continue to be involved and continue to fight "against their age."

When Abd al-Wahab al-Bayyati accepted an invitation in 1996 to participate in a literary conference in Saudi Arabia, the Iraqi government considered his participation to be a public statement of his personal political opposition to Baghdad. As a result, the greatest Iraqi poet in modern times was blacklisted and his passport invalidated. He responded with the words:

Who owns the homeland, my lady?
The commissioned killer,
The jailer,
The man of rain,
Or the poets?

Further, in 1996, al-Bayyati published "The Dragon," which symbolizes the dictators in the Arab world. Although it could apply to any dictator who corrupts his country, steals the bread of his people, and drives them to their deaths, it was clearly addressed to the former Iraqi President Saddam Hussein:

A dictator,
Masking his brutality,
Claiming he cannot kill a bird,
Kills men and crushes them.

He named all the rivers
In his name.
All the streets and prisons
In this oppressed nation.

Eventually, this dictator will be deposed, only for another beast to emerge as his reincarnation. The new dictator will be crowned leader of this "betrayed nation," and one will find:

His photo on display everywhere
In the cafes, cabarets, brothels
And markets.

Nizar Qabbani, in a poem written in 1991 in *Marginal Notes on the Book of Defeat 1967–1991*, criticizes the Iraqi invasion of Kuwait:

All is illusion!
We have achieved no victory
Only one defeat after another.
Every twenty years, another military leader
Who aborts our dream and destroys our unity.
We die meaningless deaths,
Like flies in Africa.
We are voiceless, our lips are parched and sealed.
Madness dictates our decisions.

Several years later, in his poem, "I Am with Terrorism" (1997), Qabbani strongly criticized the peace treaty with Israel following particularly violent clashes due to renewed and enlarged Jewish settlements on land to be negotiated with the Palestinian Authority. Drawing a distinction between surrender and peace, he proclaimed that he himself had been accused of being a terrorist many times when defending the rights, civilization, culture, and dignity of the Arabs and their existence. He was accused of being a terrorist because he spoke out against the Arab leaders who had suddenly changed their role from "devoted nationalists" to "middlemen and agents." In cases such as this, according to Qabbani, one is compelled to come down on the side of "terrorism."

Due to similar concerns, Mahmoud Darwish resigned from his position in the PLO after a disagreement with Yasir Arafat about the content of the peace treaty with Israel, which became the Oslo Accord, signed September 13, 1993. He later protested the agreement in his long poem "The Native American Speech,"

> Take my motherland by sword
> But I will not sign my name on a peace treaty
> between
> The victim and the murderer.

And in his book *Why Have You Left the Horse Alone?* [*Limādhā tarakta al-ḥiṣāna waḥīdan?*] (1995), Darwish reconfirmed his complete rejection of that accord with Israel. He expressed a deep sorrow for the victims who died as martyrs, because their deaths turned out to be for nothing. His words echo with the same tone—quieter, perhaps, but they have remained clear and firm. He repeats many times that "everything shall start all over again," stressing that the battle has not ended, but will begin again. Darwish returned to the land, but continued to articulate his personal fears that "tomorrow" would not fulfill the long-awaited Palestinian dream, and that "this war will never end."

Darwish and other leading Arab poets have long hoped that their writing and positions on national, social, and political issues of the Arab world would result in significant and positive change. If poetry failed to change reality, and if the ideological movements and political parties failed as well to bring change, then how could change come about? And what is the role and function of poets and intellectuals in society?

Nietzsche wrote, "The ideal condition cannot be achieved by dreaming, we must fight and struggle to achieve it" (81). Clearly, the fights and struggles of isolated poets and individuals have not succeeded in making change. Even if the hundred best Arab poets loaded themselves with dynamite and exploded in the streets of Arab capitals, it would make little difference. For real change to come about, only massive popular revolution can succeed in overturning the political regimes of the Arab world. Only then can significant and radical change take place.

Goethe once said that if the age in which the poet lives is bad, then "the poet will encounter nothing to inspire him in the life that surrounds him." But modern Arab poets dispute the truth of this quote as they have continued to struggle. These poets will never lose faith and shall continue their roles as visionaries and involved leaders. As the Arab scholar Hisham Sharabi said, "to fight the pessimism of the intellect, one must hold fast to the optimism of the Will" (155). This, above all, is the function and the role of the modern Arab poet: to provoke the people through the power of words—to inspire them and to give them hope.

This is exactly what Mahmoud Darwish has done. Darwish, along with other leading poets like Samih al-Qasim and others, continues to write about the national, social, and political issues of the Arab world in order to give the people the vision that might change positively their social and political conditions. Darwish's poetic verses have indeed continued to inspire the people and to create hope in them. He has kept his position as a political leader in society and as a poetic genius in literature. Darwish is very aware today that the political and social reality of the Arab world has become much more complicated, but he nevertheless has kept his political involvement as strong as it was during the last 40 years, with unyielding determination for the continued struggle for a better Arab reality.

2

Threatened Longing and Perpetual Search: The Writing of Home in the Poetry of Mahmoud Darwish

Najat Rahman

"Home, for we have no home"
—Al-Mutannabi, quoted in Adonis, Al-Kitāb: ams al-makān al-ān

"Poetry is the original admission of dwelling."
—Martin Heidegger, "...Poetically Man Dwells..."

THE POETRY OF MAHMOUD DARWISH HAS LONG BEEN PREOCCUPIED with a reflection on home. His later writing, approximately the stage of the "epic song" from *Ḥiṣār li-madā'iḥ al-baḥr* [Siege for the praises of the sea] (1984) until *Limādhā tarakta al-ḥiṣāna waḥīdan?* [*Why Have You Left the Horse Alone?*] (1995), precisely the period after the Israeli siege of Beirut in 1982, responds to nationalist demarcations of collective identity that have failed and that have brought on the critical situations of the present, and this is reflected in his conceptions of "home" and "exile." Even as his poetry consciously marks his move away from his earlier nationalist formulations, many of his critics have not taken much notice of this shift in his later writing due to the force of the poet's identification as a "national poet." Home is no longer constituted by land or people but by the possibility of a poetic gathering of voices. The reasons for such a shift in Darwish's work are both literary and historical: exile from the physical home, exile from the physical refuge, and exile in the poetic condition. Darwish had to address the complexity of the experience of the siege of Beirut in 1982 that resulted in another displacement of the Palestinians: not from their original home but from their place of refuge.

Translations in this chapter are by Najat Rahman unless otherwise noted.

Poetry for Darwish becomes a space of survival after Beirut 1982. His poetry seeks an inheritance that will not dispossess and that will open toward a future. It is through playing with the tension of lyric as desire and loss that Darwish charts the possibilities for home. The creation of homeland becomes the work of the poet: "the countries between my hands are the work of my hands" ("Rubā'iyat," *Arā mā urīd*, in *Dīwān* vol. 2, 382). In so far as he approaches home as absence, he sees poetry as the only guard against absence: "It is absence of countries that I form in words" ("Usamīk Narjīs hawla Qalbi," *Hiya ughniya*, in *Dīwān* vol. 2, 299). Poetic language, despite its limitations—mainly that it absents again that which it seeks to represent—becomes a way of guarding against disappearance. Poetry is akin to history for him, in its desire to write the beginning of things; and, ultimately, he presents poetry as an alternative to dominant history. An examination of the complex connections between poetry (specifically lyric opening onto epic), myth, and history in Darwish's later work will reveal how his notions of "home" respond to textual delineations of heritage that have become historical. Through a rigorous reflection on the song, the *nashīd*, and the *qaṣīda*, Darwish announces lyric in his work as threatened longing, perpetual search, and the possibility of poetic belonging. His distinctive lyrical poetry remains faithful to a long tradition of Arabic poetry, while also being innovative and receptive to international poetic influences.

This shift in the expression of home in his work takes into account the connection between home and writing as established by a plural and dynamic literary heritage. In his attempt to reconstitute the trope of home differently from its inherited configurations, he recalls moments of interruption in his heritage that grant new possibilities for thinking about home. Darwish, for example, turns to pre-Islamic and Andalusian moments of Arabic heritage, as I will elaborate further, to constitute poetry itself as home in this interruption, as lyric is identified with perpetual search rather than with loss.

Darwish identifies a long literary heritage that not only speaks of dispossession and effacement, but also suggests that those very predicaments are historically enacted through nationalist and religious readings of inherited stories. He directs himself to a paternal heritage that emerges from the myths of monotheism, one that forged collective identity through these stories. A common monotheistic heritage delivers Abraham as a figure of paternity and of heritage. The patriarchal narrative that forges collective identity by way of submission to the authority of the father and to the exclusion of others is revisited and reopened, since the Abraham myth binds monotheistic narratives of submission and nationalist delineations of identity. He considers these myths before they are foreclosed by history, thereby revealing history's encroachment upon myth. His work exploits these ruptures of heritage in order to reclaim that heritage, revealing that it was always open to contestation.

Darwish's notion of home confronts textual delineations of heritage that have become historical. As a result, a dialogue with the father ensues. In *Why Have You Left the Horse Alone?*, the titular question posed to the father, Darwish invokes the father who exiles, the father who sacrifices the future for the past. In Darwish's poetry, the fathers are often the ones who absent themselves and who allow for the absence of home. Through dialogue with the father, the son who only recognized the departure of the father sees how home is inhabited by a paternal heritage and a paternal failing and cannot be dissociated from the question and the words between father and son: home is ultimately a process of articulation, constructed through dialogue with a paternal heritage. Darwish writes in *Why Have You Left the Horse Alone?*: "I look upon a procession of ancient prophets/ as they climb barefoot towards Orshalim/ And I ask: Is there a new prophet/ for this new age?" ("I See My Apparition Coming from Afar," *Limādhā*13) The ancient prophets, who in their departure also marked the history of this early place, loom over its present. It is an age in crisis that demands new prophets and, by extension, new stories.

The monotheistic writing that constitutes heritage also marks a desire for home, a desire rendered sacred through its ties to land and lineage as evident in the Abraham myth. For Darwish that heritage has also been paternal due to the absenting of a maternal source, figured previously as land. The tradition of the transient and ephemeral father, however, provides possibility for words and for home, but only in displacement: "As you used to carry me, my father/ I will carry this longing to my beginning and its beginning/

and I will walk this path to my end and to its end!" ("To My End and to Its End," *Limādhā* 42)

Darwish, who dedicates himself to the song, defines his literary project as one of writing home. He writes in "Anā min hunāk": "I learned all the words and how to take them apart so I can form one word, homeland" (*Ward aqall*, in *Dīwān* vol. 2, 327). He also valorizes the *qaṣīda*, a poetic form from pre-Islamic Arabia that recounts events from the life of the poet and his tribe with motifs of journey and desire:

> The *qaṣīda*... has the power [...]
> to return, with a gardenia's cry, a homeland! [...]
> The *qaṣīda* between my hands has the power
> to command the affairs of myths,
> through the work of my hands, but I
> since I found the *qaṣīda* have displaced myself
> and asked her:
> Who am I?
> Who am I? ("Poetic Planning," *Limādhā* 102)

His incorporation of home from the pre-Islamic and Andalusian moments chooses less prevalent motifs, and insists on desire rather than loss and on the perpetual journey rather than the nostalgic return, as Barbara Harlow has argued (Harlow, "Palestine" 43). Darwish's poetry unfolds a desire to forge new collective forms and to establish poetry as a space of survival, "for a people without poetry are a conquered people," he states (Yeshurun 154). It is also in the recital of his poems, which the musicality of his poetry allows, that a collective voice takes shape. As Elias Khoury writes, "Homeland, which becomes in the *qaṣīda* an address for the long travel, is *an act* and not oranges or things" (*Al-Dhākira* 272). In this search for a form capable of safeguarding a collective voice, lyric is valorized and refashioned, as it is no longer simply a genre that marks individual loss but one that allows for the expression of the desire for home and for a collective voice.

For Darwish considers poetry to be primarily lyric, or *inshād:*

> Poetry is that which we do not know, that in which the interweaving of prose and poetry intersect on the threshold of presence. And poetry may be simply the

> search for the poetry [*shi'rīya*] of reality. But what is this *shi'rīya*?... My experience is a continuation and not a rupture... My poetic reading of reality is developing, from transporting it to the text to enmeshing the text in its *nashīd*, without reality being the text and without the text being reality. (Darwish, "Bayt" 162–163)

Darwish already in this brief pronouncement announces poetry as an inheritance and a horizon, locating it at the threshold as *movement*, a continuous questioning that inhabits the poem-song, *nashīd*. Poetry then not only interrogates the "real," it is also a questioning of poetry. He also defines poetry as "a quest for what has not yet been said" (Yeshurun 154). In this context, it is important to note that the Arabic word *nashīd* etymologically signifies as a noun "poem-song" and as a verb "the search for a lost object" (see for example Wehr, *Dictionary*, and al-Bustani, *Muḥīṭ*). Thus his attempt at *inshād*, his inheritance, is a double effort to sing and to search for what is absent. Darwish writes: "And here is the *nashīd* pushing us for another search" ("Mu'in Bsseisso" 5).

Furthermore, Darwish insists on the sensory and musical aspects of poetry, which is consistent with the pre-Islamic conception of poetry as metered and rhymed. And it is this musicality of poetry that may distinguish Darwish's later poems. Darwish chooses the song, breaking away from his earlier poetry, in which the acclamatory style tended to predominate. The song is necessary, for while it embodies loss, absence, and the unknown, it is for Darwish "at the threshold of presence," "without reality being the text and without the text being reality." In the song, where absence and loss seem intrinsic, as I will discuss further, poetry seems to have a fragile force for those silenced. It is this possibility in poetry—that those who have experienced loss might be able to draw force from it—that is its lure.

Darwish further considers that it may be possible for poetry to testify in the form of history, since both poetry and history are concerned with inscribing a certain "beginning." His proclaimed project then is a rewriting of the originary myths that allude to contemporary defeats upon which the narrative of the word of the victor is predicated. For the homeland has already been written and enacted by a narrative that dispossesses. This desire to write the beginning of things not only links history and poetry for Darwish but is also fundamental to the poetic drive. He writes: "There is no poetry without *genesis*..." (Beydoun, "Qui impose" 45; my emphasis) He also writes: "I am searching for a locus for the *nashīd* in an open historical space" (Hadidi and Baker 81). The testing of poetic boundaries is therefore inextricably linked with his questioning of identity.

In this median locus between history and myth, there can be no contradiction for Darwish between lyric and epic. For Darwish, epic is lyric enfolding history. In his poetry, he brings together epic as the genre of homeland, following the tradition of the *Iliad* and the *Odyssey* as well as the *Aeneid*, and lyric as the genre of loss in the tradition of Sappho and Horace. Darwish valorizes lyrical epic texts because they speak to collective predicaments of struggle and loss, and, in his words "are preoccupied with universal themes including the tragic perception of history and the expression of a collective conscience in the face of loss and mourning" (Hadidi and Baker 87). The epic, which gathers both the past and the present and directs them toward the future, arguably makes Darwish remain within a national register without being limited to its formulation of identity. The clear privileging of the epic over the mythic has to do with epic's open struggle and form, whereas myth is and has been historically closed: "the only difference is that the notion of destiny does not exist as long as the conflict is open. This is precisely what makes our texts epic and not mythic" (80). To write the beginning again, against what has been written, is to render the dominant narrative, which has been foreclosed and historicized, open to contestation.

Darwish's task of writing a "beginning," a mythic narrative prior to history's encroachment, which he defines as the desire of poetry, and which is simultaneously his longing for the homeland, is inextricably linked with his lyrical endeavor. To pose the question of this ancient mode is necessarily to get entangled in desire. As Darwish puts it, "he who does not desire does not sing" ("Thalāthat" 222). Desire in his poetry is akin to that of the Sufi, where the intermingling of loss and desire figures loss "not as nostalgia or regret but as a horizon [*bu'd*]."[1] And if we follow the legacy of the orphic, desire and loss are intrinsic to the song. Maurice Blanchot writes in "Orpheus's Gaze":

> ... Only in the song does Orpheus have power over Eurydice. But in the song too, Eurydice is already lost, and Orpheus himself is the dispersed Orpheus; the song immediately makes him "infinitely dead." He loses Eurydice because he desires her beyond the measured limits of the song, and he loses himself, but this desire, and Eurydice lost, and Orpheus dispersed are necessary to the song, just as the ordeal of eternal inertia is necessary to the work. (Blanchot 173)

Blanchot locates the particularity of the song in being a site of power and loss. The song that grants Orpheus power over Eurydice is also that which "infinitely" kills him. Desire is necessary for the song, for its excess—desire extending beyond the "*measured* limits of the song"—is what creates loss (my emphasis). The song, predicated on the double loss of Eurydice and of Orpheus, cannot contain desire, which is always excessive, or retrieve the loss. Orpheus's quest for Eurydice in the world of shades, which is an attempt to presence her, fails because of that critical, instantaneous, transgressive gaze, which refuses re-presentation for the sake of the song. For Blanchot, failure is not a lack of success, as he puts it; it is "in its beginning all over again" (243).

The musicality of poetry, although fleeting, makes it endure, granting it a certain permanence. Not only does Orpheus die, but he is also fragmented to pieces while his floating head continues to sing.[2] For Blanchot this "Orpheus dispersed" is also necessary for the survival of the song. Lyric in this formulation is the disembodied voice on a continuous journey. The poet responds to loss in his failed attempt to sing. Thus poetry's identity is its attempt, albeit failed, to redress this loss. It is precisely this failure, and the desire born of it, that leads to the continuation of the song. The song then is the movement of desire and this space of the search and of the loss.[3]

Darwish's poetry not only follows the orphic in marking desire but also in announcing this desire as a threatened longing. He writes: "We restrain the longing in us, for it is not for us to reveal it, if for no other reason than this, that it is a threatened longing." What threatens desire? In both cases it is desire itself, the desire to make present what is desired and what has been absented, a desire that absents the desired a second time. In turning back toward

Eurydice, Orpheus fails in the excessive desire of his gaze to make her present, and this is what allows for the song. Similarly, Darwish's entire poetic corpus faces the absence of the homeland and its impossible attainability. The poem is then necessary for the poet who "builds on sand what the wind carries/ from battles and desires" ("Crypts, Andalusia, Desert," *Ḥiṣār li-madā'iḥ al-baḥr*, in *Dīwān* vol. 2, 90). It is a locus of desire where the loss is double, that of the homeland as well as that which supplants the homeland. In his recent works, it is the exile of Palestinians in 1982 from Beirut that he invokes, as if to seal the original displacement from home.[4] For Darwish to focus on the displacement from Beirut rather than the original one from Palestine is to introduce exile as perpetual: "I have no harbor/ to say I have a home" (*Madīḥ al-ẓill al-'ālī*, in *Dīwān* vol. 2, 55).

The poet also has power over the poem in his ability to interrupt the repetition to which the song is inclined, as we see in the caesura Darwish forces in his poem "Crypts, Andalusia, Desert":

> and sing of the fields in which sun and heart run and
> never tire... and desert
>
> and desert! From one thousand years to the light I came.
> (*Dīwān* vol. 2, 91)

This interruption is necessary for foiling desire in its very intense appearance. Darwish states in an interview that "... poetry is better when it folds upon itself" (Yeshurun 132).

Moreover, the threatened desire ensues from the poet's predicament: the poet is always in exile because the poem is exile. According to Blanchot, exile is in a sense the "space of literature," the space of withdrawal that offers solitude for the writer wandering in an inescapable desert and which spares him the demands of the everyday but denies him the power derived from active engagement in the affairs of daily life. It is nothing short of risking the world that he knows and the certainty in which he thinks he lives. It demands "ruinous desire." So while it is necessary for Blanchot's Orpheus to look back and face the essence of the night, losing Eurydice in order to safeguard the song, Darwish confronts not the temporal otherness of the night but the spatial otherness of the crypt as a locus of nowhere that will guard home in the poem. Hence the figuring of the desired (and poetry as locus of desire), as we will see, as a crypt, inaccessible, hidden, yet providing a refuge and protecting this longing.[5]

In "Crypts, Andalusia, Desert," Andalusia, a heterogeneous, cultural encounter of strangers, is invoked not as "the lost paradise," but rather as the future promise and a point of intersection (Rahman 1996). Darwish writes:

> In every poet there is a loss or an absence. In every poet there is an Andalus. Otherwise how do we interpret the sadness of poetry and its thrust into two contradictory directions: the past and the future. And poetry is the search for an Andalus that is possible to recall, able to be presenced. From here grows the mysterious happiness, not in reality, but from creation, when the words are able to capture the impossible. (*Libération* 11)

Andalusia is this fragile possibility of presencing absence. It is poetry's possibility, since poetry for Darwish is "this search for an Andalus," which is the essence of the *nashīd*. In "Aḥada 'ashara kawkaban," Darwish points to the essential literary construction of Andalusia when he asks: "Was Andalusia/ here or there? On earth... or in the poem?" (*Dīwān* vol. 2, 476).

In "Crypts, Andalusia, Desert," Andalusia is furthermore figured as the impossibility of return. The poetic voice announces: "I cannot go to Cordova" (92). For Darwish, Cordova is simultaneously the past, the displaced home, the disconnected identity, and the loss. But it is also the desire for a future. This rupture with the past is the foreclosure of any possibility for "return." Return is no longer a response to the journey but becomes a going toward the future. It is eternally deferred and belated (Rahman 1996). "And why do you want to journey to Cordova?/ —Because I don't know the path. Desert and desert" (90). It is the singularity of the journey that has tied the Palestinian poets to Andalusia, a journey that demands impossible suffering. "Nor do they ride to Andalusia/ singularly" (91). It is also revealed as an absurd journey.

They opened the lonely door of confinement so I
came out.
I found a path so I walked.
Where do I go? To the issue I said: I'll teach my
freedom how to walk, she leaned on me,
I straightened up, and straightened her up...
and I carried her
over my back like they carry countries on camels and
lorries, and I walked. (92)

To look to the open-endedness of the future, Darwish invokes the older poetic theme of the pre-Islamic desert journey. He marks the journey as a passage that may not lead anywhere and that has already begun. "I'd travel again on the roads that may or may not lead to Cordova" (325). Though the desire for the past remains, it has no place in the journey. The wandering of the ancient poets is tied to no space. It neither originates nor attempts to arrive at a specific destination. But the journey is now a lonely wandering.

The valorization of the pre-Islamic poetic motif of the journey over the Andalusian notion of the return changes the construction of the idea of home by rejecting a presumed accessibility to the past. It also valorizes the movement of desire over loss (Harlow, "Palestine" 43). The homeland in this construction is no longer a project or a fulfillment of a destiny as it has been articulated in nationalist narratives and in Darwish's earlier poetry. Rather, it is an echo mediating desire and loss.

Having ruptured with the "past," Darwish encrypts it as if to keep its death alive but as impossible to access or return to: "It's effortless and difficult this egress of the doves from the wall of language, so how do we pass to the small orange grove?" (89) Although the return to the homeland is conjured in the conventional image of the land of oranges, it is very difficult to read the past without re/construction; it is unreadable, like the "egress of the doves from this wall of language." The title of Darwish's poem already encloses Andalusia spatially between crypts and a desert. In its singularity it juxtaposes the crypts but slips into them rhythmically. It is as if the crypts recall Andalusia, which in turn recalls the desert, an empty space that is marked but marks nothing. His poem announces itself as a crypt, a crypt that in the poem implies a topos of death. Throughout the poem, Darwish speaks of enclosed spaces of death such as the crypt, the cell, the enclosed wall, and the vault. Home then is that which conceals itself and which resists access. This poem, written in the wake of Beirut 1982, does not name Beirut, the supplanted homeland, but transplants itself in time and space to Andalusia. By not naming it, the poem encrypts it. Once it is encrypted it cannot be left; it becomes a journey that the poet bears with him.

What remains is the poem, which is encrypted just like home, or as home. "It's effortless and difficult this ingress of the doves to the wall of language, so how do we bide before the lyric in the crypt?" (89) Darwish locates the lyric in the crypt, and the reader is situated before it. The encryption of the poem preserves it so that any reading of the poem is bound to misidentify it. The crypt is then the only threshold of presence and absence that offers safe refuge for a poet who has had to lose even his exile. He writes: "... I lifted down my freedom/ like a sack of coal/ and escaped to the crypt;/ does the crypt resemble my mother your mother? Desert and desert" (92). What space can the poet claim after the loss of a supplanted homeland except the space of the poem? Poetry is the closest thing to granting a sense of belonging for the poetic voice that poses it as a question. Furthermore, this sense of belonging is evident in the emphasis on the mother. He defines the loss, toward the end of "Crypts, Andalusia, Desert," as the loss of the string in the crypts. The string is allegorical for the melody or the lyric that one associates with it, a lyric that cryptically bespeaks a desire for home. Loss here is protected, guarding the lyric. For the poem ends right after declaring the loss by an affirmation of the song where there is rhythmic harmony between the Arabic words "crypts" and "song." [*aqbiya*, *ughniya*]: "and don't cry, my friend, for a string lost in the crypts./ It's a song/ It's a song!" (94)

The song becomes the only belonging possible, not only poetically but politically as well, assuming the collective voice of a displaced and threatened community. In another poem, "Qaṣīdat Bayrūt," Darwish writes: "Our crypt is dug so we sleep like ants in the small crypt/ as if we were secretly singing/ Beirut is our shelter/ Beirut is our star" (from *Ḥiṣār li-madā'iḥ al-baḥr,* in *Dīwān* vol. 2, 95–96). The poetic voice points to a suspension of identity and to a threatened desire to belong. The collective singing done in secrecy is qualified by an "as if," which makes the claim for a collective identity, grounded in the song that is predicated on the loss of Beirut, further removed and based only on the confines of this singing which has to be done in secrecy. The song is made manifest as concealment. The "assertion" of identity is also enunciated as a secret. So while there is a claim to a common identity, the basis for that claim is not revealed, as if to further protect it.

The poem that begins with the continuation of lyric [*nashīd*] ends by affirming the individual song [*ughniya*]: "It's a song!" Darwish's affirmation of the song as the only belonging possible, as the threatened memory that insists on desiring in the face of loss, has to begin again and to continue for new songs to emerge.

Darwish performs a secret identification between death and song at the end of his poem where disappearance—not survival—becomes song. But disappearance is not an experience that begins and that comes to an end, according to Blanchot. And in this poem, the poetic voice proclaims the loss of the string in the crypt, and hence the search begins again in the song. This movement of disappearance becomes paradoxically the survival of the song.

> And wait for me little by little so I can hear the sound
>   of my blood
> cross the street that explodes
> (I almost survived)
> —You will not win!
> —I will walk.
> —To where, my friend?
> —To where the doves have flown clapping the wheat
>   to uphold this space by a chaff that waits.
> So you continue your lyric in my name
> and don't cry, my friend, for a string lost in the crypts.
> It's a song
> It's a song! (*Dīwān* vol. 2, 94)

The continued search for the absent is a continuation of the *nashīd*. The rupture with the past is coterminous with this continuation. So while Darwish mourns his separation from the earlier poets, he is simultaneously aware of the continuity of the heritage of poetry through the *nashīd* or lyric, "so you continue your lyric in my name." The poem is naming the *nashīd* as something that has already begun and continues even after the individual poetic voice is silent. The first word of the poem, "So," performs this, as if the poetic voice is engaging in a dialogue that has already commenced. This beginning of the poem also announces the withdrawal of the poetic "I," so that the lyric is not claimed by the "I" but belongs to the interlocutor who has already started it. The impersonality of the poetic voice is reinforced when the poetic "I" claims an "ancient heart" (93).

Moreover, it is suggested that other poets continue the *nashīd*, that it may take the collective effort of several poets. *Nashīd* emerges as a collective song. In modern terms, it is often associated with nationalist songs that are recited in groups. But Darwish names it a song for a people without an effective home. In an interview he states: "The long *nashīd*... founds a land which cannot contain one pace, and which opens a horizon that cannot contain one idea...." ("Fī waṣfi" 4). The *nashīd* in his work is instead associated with the communal [*qawmīya*] song and not the national [*waṭanīya*] *nashīd*. In addition, the *nashīd* endures and expresses journey and displacement. In *Why Have You Left the Horse Alone?*, he writes: "I look upon the name 'Abi Tayib al-Mutannabi'/ traveling from Tiberia to Egypt/ over the horse of *nashīd*" (12). "Crypts, Andalusia, Desert" is about *nashīd* and is a *nashīd* itself.

Darwish's poetics distinguishes between *nashīd* (lyric), *ughniya* (song), and *qaṣīda* (the pre-Islamic ode). Both the song and the *nashīd* are open-ended. While the *nashīd* is a continuation of the lyric and the voice of the *qaṣīda*, the song [*ughniya*] is the individual voice. The *qaṣīda* is a dialogue, containing a plurality of voices (Rahman 1996).

Lyric is the only remnant continuous with an Arabic heritage of poetry via the songs of Andalusia and the *qaṣīda*. Adonis points to the oral origins of pre-Islamic poetry, when poetry was *nashīd*, transmitted through memory. He writes: "Pre-Islamic poetry was born a *nashīd*, I mean that it developed through listening and not through reading, a song not writing..." (Adonis, *Al-Shi'rīya* 7–8) But memory and the act of *nashīd* had the status of the written word in both disseminating and conserving poetry. The song is different from the *nashīd* since it usually follows from the poem, composing music to the metered words. For Adonis, *inshād*, the act of saying the *nashīd*, is one form of song. And poetry was often recited/sung by the poet himself. "This implies that the Arabs of pre-Islam considered the *inshād* of poetry to be another talent, in addition to the talent of saying it" (7). Predicated on listening, the art of this oral poetry was not just in what it said but how it said it.

In what it said, pre-Islamic poetry was one of testimony, according to Adonis, since it did not seek to change things or to follow them but simply to describe them. What it depicted is a collective existence, and it sought a dialogue with that reality (Adonis, *Hā anta*) Adonis writes: "The pre-Islamic poet used to say… what the listener already knew: he said his customs and habits, his battles… he did not express himself as much as the group, or he did not express himself except through articulating the group. He was the singing witness" (*Al-Shi'rīya* 6). Darwish, too, is a "singing witness" of the critical present. He is also engaged in a historical struggle and in a poetic project, one that inaugurates poetic writing as home.

As opposed to his earlier work, home in the later work of Darwish announces itself as a trope and is figured specifically as a metaphor, as in the biblical words translated as "Man goeth to his long home" (Eccles. 21:5). Home performs itself as a temporal and spatial metaphor and can be deployed infinitely. It betrays itself as absence and at the same time as the possibility of form, due to metaphor's materialization of an invisible union between apparent dissimilarities (see Benjamin, *Illuminations* 13–14). The prevalent associations of home with belonging and dwelling are extended in the above biblical formulation to death and to an unbounded temporality in which the passage through time and space neither begins nor ends. Darwish writes: "And travel led me to travel/ and I don't see a country there" (*Dīwān* vol. 2, 107).

Poetic language becomes a way of guarding off disappearance, even as Darwish acknowledges the limitations of his poetic project:

> Past is what I see
> for one a kingdom of dust and his crown. So let my
> language

> triumph over time the enemy, over my descendants,
> over me, over my father, and over disappearance that
>   does not disappear.
> This is my language and my miracle…
> […]
> and the sacred of the Arab in the desert,
> who worships what flows
> from rhymes like stars on his cloak,
> and he worships what he says.
>
> Prose is necessary then,
> divine prose is necessary for the Prophet to triumph…
> ("A Rhyme for Mu'allaqāt," *Limādhā* 118)

In seeking to be part of a continuing, collective work of reconstruction, Darwish is engaged in an endeavor that would allow new figurations of home to emerge from the inherited myths. Darwish's poetry seeks alternate forms of history that would overcome readings and enactments of dominant histories. In his search for form, he poses poetry as such a possible alternative. Poetry can face dispossession; it can carry this threatened longing for home and the promise that lies within it. Darwish's poetry, which insists on interruptions, has the capacity to continue its tropic figurations of home endlessly. The notion of poetry that emerges in his work is that of a perpetual search.

Walter Benjamin reminds us, as Hannah Arendt points out, "that although the living is subject to the ruin of the time, the process of decay is at the same time a process of crystallization" (Arendt, introduction to *Illuminations* 51). It is this possibility of transformed and fragmented poetic survival that guides Darwish's poetic endeavor. In examining Benjamin's relation to the past, Arendt writes that

> insofar as the past has been transmitted as tradition, it possesses authority; insofar as authority presents itself historically, it becomes tradition. Walter Benjamin knew that the break in tradition and the loss of authority that occurred in his lifetime were irreparable, and he concluded that he had to discover new ways of dealing with the past. In this he became a master when he discovered that the transmissibility of the past had been

> replaced by its citability and that in place of its authority there had arisen a strange power to settle down, piecemeal, in the present and to deprive it of "piece of mind," the mindless peace of complacency. (38)

The loss of authority in the transmission of one's collective past is precisely what Darwish confronts, responding to the fracturing of the past by attempting to reconstitute it from the perspective of the defeated and silenced. Benjamin's strategy was to destroy in order to preserve; his is a writing that wrenches fragments out of their context and puts them in new ones in order to create new figurations of history and to avoid easy identification. Benjamin uses quotes, as Arendt indicates, with "the double task of interrupting the flow of the presentation with 'transcendent force'... and at the same time of concentrating within themselves that which is presented" (introduction to *Illuminations* 39). If Benjamin's work is one of identifying moments of rupture, those that tradition does not deliver from their heritage, Darwish follows him in his emphasis on the discontinuous. For tradition is able to impose its order and authority onto the past by denying discontinuities (44). Those discontinuous moments are very important, then, because it is only through them that "the past [speaks] directly" (40). Reading, being attentive to the rhetorical complexities and plays of the text, becomes a crucial preliminary aspect. Such a reading ideally does not recreate another continuist narrative along the axis of oppressive nationalist tradition, but reveals how tradition is revived and simultaneously challenged at each moment. Hence the necessity, in a critical present, of confronting effacement and the tyranny of tradition.

3
Transfigurations in the Image of Palestine in the Poetry of Mahmoud Darwish

Faysal Darraj
Translated by Hala Khamis Nassar and Areeg A. Ibrahim

MAHMOUD DARWISH HAS CREATED A BROAD POETIC SPACE, PRESENTING aesthetic variations that never cease to renew and representing a world that knows no boundaries. Between 1964 and 2005, the Palestinian cause witnessed numerous phases, and so the poet too has lived through many changing experiences of homeland, exile, and poetry. He commenced his career with a poem about the Palestinian land, and ends his latest collection with a universal poem that places the "un-reclaimed" land in a new poetic form. In the course of this evolution, he has not abandoned his earlier subject, but rather is attentively listening to the "wisdom of poetry," which permits liberation from time and place.

What Palestine means in Darwish's most recent collection of poems, *Ka-zahr al-lawz aw ab'ad* [Like almond flowers or further] (2005), is not, therefore, what it meant in his first collection, *Awrāq al-zaytūn* [Olive leaves] (1964). This essay attempts to read these transformations in the meaning of Palestine over the decades of Darwish's career as if they constituted a greater "poem"—one that is itself continually changing, constantly bringing the homeland and the longings of the exiled into new poetic relationships with each other.

Homeland within the "Romantic Self"

In *Ḥalat ḥiṣar* [*State of Siege*] (2002) Darwish says, "when I am liberated, I will know that homeland panegyric is similar to homeland satire" (50). The homeland cannot become a subject of poetry unless it is occupied; once it is liberated, the poet will move on to worthier themes. The liberated homeland is unworthy of either eulogy or satire. It tiptoes into poetry, side by side with the immortal

Translations of poetry in this chapter are by Hala Khamis Nassar unless otherwise noted.

poetic themes of love, death, and the torment of time. Perhaps when eulogy is imposed upon it, the homeland becomes unworthy of praise, and this is the core of Darwish's creativity, which derives the meaning of homeland from topics unconstrained by time and place.

At the beginning of the 1960s, when he was in his early twenties, Darwish earned the title of "the poet of the Palestinian resistance." At first, the "resistance" referred to the Palestinians who stayed on their land after the establishment of the State of Israel, and later to the Palestinian Liberation Organization, which came into being in 1965.

The poet did not seek out this title. He wrote what he lived, sharing the pains and hopes of his people, leaving to Arab critics the liberty of bestowing titles. Even though other Palestinian poets shared Darwish's suffering, his talent distinguished him early on, as expressed in four consecutive collections: *Awrāq al-zaytūn* [Olive leaves] (1964), *'Āshiq min Filasṭīn* [A lover from Palestine] (1966), *Ākhir al-layl* [At the end of the night] (1967), and *Al-'Aṣāfīr tamūtu fī al-Jalīl* [Birds die in Galilee] (1969). After the publication of these collections, Darwish's name came to signify both his occupied land and Palestinian poetry itself.

The expression "the poet of the Palestinian resistance" has two implications: first, of an occupied land that awaits liberation, and secondly, a national ideology that celebrates the "poetry of commitment" to the liberation of Palestine. In reality, Darwish wrote what he wanted, but since his beginnings, he has been surrounded by the aura of the romantic poet who is leading his people to the land of truth. The truth, which is personified in the poet, promises the people certain victory. This romanticization that unifies the land, the poet, and truth itself drove the poet into unremitting anger, as he worked expansively for the triumph of both land and poetry. In the first poem of his first collection, *Awrāq al-zaytūn*, Darwish says, "O my reader!/ Do not ask me to whisper!",[1] thus inaugurating a different kind of poetry, one delivered in an angry voice. In the second poem, he speaks of a rhyme that is like "swords of fire," carving and burning. In the third poem, he calls for poetry that "creates prophets," thus equating poet and prophet, and in turn, equating the poet/prophet with a reformer who will regain lost righteousness. In his poem "Lorca," also from the first collection, Darwish describes the ideal poet: "that's how the poet is, an earthquake... and a hurricane/ [...] That is how the poet is, music, and a hymn of prayer" (in *Dīwān* vol. 1, 68–70). Within the poet lie contradictions present in no one else: a reconciliation of prayers with hurricanes, and water with fire. These contradictions, which occur only in a prophet, compel the poet to prevail on behalf of the occupied land, because the poet belongs to both the truth and the land.

Darwish commences his first dīwān [collection of poems] by declaring himself a shattered poet who does not deal in popular poetry. He says, "the wrath of my hands.../ The wrath of my mouth.../ And the blood of my veins is a sap of wrath!"[2] From the poet's internal anger comes a poem that is equivalent to his anger: "The poet must have a new pledge and new anthems."[3] Therefore, the poet advises the reader to abandon "whispered poetry" and revert to the "poetry of the prophets." Whatever the meaning young Darwish assigned to the poet and the idea of poetry, he was laying a new poetic foundation for new times that embraced a prophetic poetry and a Palestine free of imperfection and corruption. This inauguration of a new poetic foundation needs to recapture the idea of the pure, ancient origin, which assigns the founding poet as an origin to others, an origin from which the land emerges—just like truth and poetry—as a pure space, without iniquity or imperfection.

In this romantic/prophetic representation, Palestine becomes nothing but an extension of the poet or one of his manifestations, and the land, lost and regained, will be a qualitative space embodied in the poet. The land is temporarily lost; however, it is also regained because it has never departed from the being of the poet/prophet.

In "Sirḥān yasrabu al-qahwa fī al-kafātīrīya" ["Sirhan Drinks His Coffee in the Cafeteria"] in (*Uḥibbuki*, *Dīwān* vol. 1, 445–457), the poet celebrated the "refugee," of whom he says:

> You could not find the [one] difference
> Between its curved [corn] fields
> And my palm.
> [But it is my homeland]
> You could not find the difference
> Between the night that sleeps in memory
> And the night upon the Carmel.

> But it is my homeland
> (*Sand* 22; trans. modified)

There are no differences between the land and the refugee because the land is his origin. There are no differences between the poet and the land because he is its origin. Everything is within the poet since he has appointed himself an origin and a truthful protector of what he creates: humans, flowers, birds, and fruit. Perhaps "Qaṣīdat al-arḍ" ["Poem of the Land"], which represents a specific development in Darwish's poetry, is an expression of his romantic phase. In it we read,

> —I am the land
> And the land is you
> [...]
> —The Galilee air wants to speak on my behalf
> The Galilee gazelle want to break my prison today.[4]
> —[...] The smell of the land
> in early morning
> awakens me, my iron chain
> Awakens the land in the early
> evening.[5]
> [...]
> —I am the awakened land
> [...]
> Plough my body

This prophetic/romantic representation leads to beautiful and homogeneous themes, also revealing a beautiful origin from which they have become emancipated. More specifically, it leads to a lonely, harmonious world, reflected in both the poet and the poem: "I am [...]/ the family apricot blossom[6]/ [...] I am the hope and the vast meadow [...] /[...] I am the land awakening/[...] I am the eternal lover[7]/ I am the witness of the massacre/ [...] Only the land: has it/ Arisen? My child the earth!"[8] The self emerges as vast, capacious, and prophetic, embracing Palestine's nature, people, and history. Since this self represents Palestine in all its different manifestations, it stands for all things, keeping them in a pure, unified, and intact form.

Therefore, the poet says, "plants of Galilee can bloom among my fingers."[9] He embodies the plants as well as the air, the deer, and the clear sky. His sentence, "the land has told us," does not change anything as long as the self/origin is the ancient forefather to all subsequent things. Everything is within the romantic self and its poem, and there is no space between the romantic poet and his poem. We read, "The birds/ pointed their beaks/ at the song and at my heart" (Jayyusi, *Anthology* 146). Or, "For all the pathways in the mountains are extensions of this song./ All the songs in you are extensions of an olive tree that swaddled me" (147). Or, "The land and the grass told me." This is a harmonious, organic, complete, and concordant world where all things have an ancient, pure origin and where the poem/the poet embodies everything.

Since the origin is constant regardless of time, and since the future of the origin is an image of the past, the romantic poem promises a return of the land to its owners, a return guaranteed by the poet/prophet whose vision never fails him. We read, "As if temples asked now about the prophets of Palestine/ And about her continuous beginning" (Jayyusi, *Anthology* 147). The poet/origin combines the beginning with the end, calling for an absolute, constant beginning, without definite time and place, whereby all times and places are in harmony:

> As if I returned
> to what has been
> As if I walked
> in front of myself
> I restore my harmony.
> (148)

In such harmony, where times are presented as constant, the future emerges pure, content, and in continuity with past images, which is an absolute present: "We will throw them out of the Galilee air./ [...] It will rain today/ [...] The land will explode."

The future tense, which is supposed to represent the future, does not do so here, since all times are equal in the memory of the prophet/poet who represents all prophets:

> O country of prophets: Come to your fruition!
> O country of planters: Come to your fruition!
> O country of martyrs: Come to your fruition!
> O country of refugees: Come to your fruition!
> (Jayyusi, *Anthology* 149)

The usage of the words "planters," "martyrs," and "refugees" is unnecessary since the poet has already personified them all. On the surface level, these words, which refer to the poet's outside world, distinguish between the romanticism of young Darwish and a different kind of romanticism that is self-enclosed.

Darwish's romanticism connects the voice of the poet/prophet with the history of his country, thus expanding the poem and varying its themes. This history, of which the poet is proud, is disturbed by an external foreign occupation that, he predicts, will eventually come to an end. Therefore, young Darwish's poetry comes across as both serene and angry: serene in narrating the story of the homeland's ancient origin that will defeat temporary obstacles, and angry because the enemy has disturbed this timeless Palestinian harmony.

The poet's pride in his country promises the recapture of historic Palestine, and reveals a love that knows no boundaries. The romantic self, which asserts itself as a mirror for existence, disseminates love in a variety of manifestations. In such a way, prophethood becomes a synonym for love, the voice of the self grows to be the voice of collective love, and divine anger becomes an antonym to hatred. Such all-embracing love inspires the beauty of the poetic language, a trend that Darwish has expressed to an unprecedented degree as one of the pioneers of modern Arabic poetry. Hence, the aesthetics of language become a concrete expression of prophethood. In addition, love, without which poetry cannot exist, separates Darwish's poetry from hatred. That is, "the lover of the homeland," i.e., young Darwish, asks simply for the right to exist. It is not surprising, therefore, that love is at the crux of Darwish's poetry and that this is reflected in many of the titles of Darwish's collections: 'Āshiq min Filasṭīn [A lover from Palestine] (1966); *Ḥabībatī tanhaḍu min nawmihā* [My lover awakes from sleep] (1970); *Uḥibbuki aw lā uḥibbuki* [I love you or I do not love you] (1972); *Tilka ṣūratuhā wa hādhā intiḥār al-'āshiq* [That is her picture and that is the suicide of the lover] (1975). In addition, his collections include many poems with titles referring to love: "Ajmal ḥubb" [Most beautiful love], "Qaṣā'id 'an ḥubb qadīm" [Poems of an old love], "Ughnīyāt ḥubb 'alā al-ṣalīb" [A love song on the crucifix], "Lā tanāmī… ḥabībatī" [Do not sleep… O my love], "Uḥibbuki akthar" [I love you more], "Qirā'a fī wajh ḥabībatī" [Reading in the face of my beloved], "Ughnīyāt ḥubb ilā Afrīqīya" [Love songs for Africa], "Ka' annī uḥibbuki" [As if I love you], "Mawt 'ākhar… wa uḥibbuki…" [Another death… and I love you].

In its incessant presence, love becomes an expression of a world that embraces the reader, the poem, and the homeland, and reveals an urge to reform that world. The romantic self declares that the founding time knows no hatred, which is evident in the vocabulary that tints Darwish's qaṣīda in general—"the green, the pigeons, the blue, and the marble…"—for the green stands for life, the pigeons for peace, the blue for dream, and the marble for smoothness. These words compose a complete vision of the world, and make the future ever-present in Darwish's poetry.

The poet bestows the status of beloved upon all creatures: the mother, land, sister, friend, martyr, riverbank, an eyelash, and the family's apricot tree. This trait is both present and absent in the love poems or amatory odes [*ghazal*]. It is present in beauty, longing, and the need for self-actualization. It is absent due to an existential experience that surpasses the arguments between the lover and beloved. In addition, within the homeland the love poem represents alienation. Outside of it, there is exile, continuous wandering and immigration, renewed separation, and yearning for a time when the word "martyr" will not be as common. In this situation, the ghazal becomes a journey into different worlds, and a way to question the meaning of existence and the moral values of different times.

To bring the notion of history into our discussion: Darwish begins his poetic oeuvre with the face of the beloved, and ends it with the face of human beings. Therefore there is more than one history: that of the land, love of the land, and love in its manifestations. This love, which is inclusive of history, human beings, language, and Palestine, renders Darwish's ghazal different from the traditional ghazal of both ancient and modern Arabic poetry. In this manner, Darwish's romantic self becomes open to the reader, to history, and to poetry.

Based on the definition of love that is associated with the prophetic/romantic self in Darwish's poetry, this self represents two main aspects: on the one hand, the urge to reform an existence that is tainted by corruption (i.e., the occupation of Palestine); on the other hand, the certainty that this corruption/occupation is temporary and about to end. A quick look at Darwish's poems shows similarities in the endings. For example, "Poem of the Land" ends with the following: "I am the land awakening/ You shall not pass/ You shall not pass/ I am the land but you/ Who walk over the land/ In her awakening/ You shall not pass./ You shall not pass" (Jayyusi, *Anthology* 151).

This optimistic self has a tragic sense due to the discrepancy between the daily sufferings it endures and the human idealism in which it believes. Thus, what violates the land violates the poet/prophet. The poet/prophet—who is used to dealing with familiar innocence, which is a metaphor for the land, ancient and pure—is momentarily violated by the Israeli occupation. Thus, Darwish's poetry does not endorse an ideological stance that we might label "resistance"; rather it stems from something deeper and more lasting: a defense of the land's violated innocence. This prevailing tragic sense is a response to the violation and destruction of innocent existence. In "Al-Qatīl raqam thamāniyata 'ashara" [Victim number 18], from his collection *...Ākhir al-layl* [End of the night] (*Dīwān* vol. 1, 214–216), we read:

> The olive grove was once green
> It was... and the sky
> [...]
> What changed it this evening?
> [...]
> It was, my lover
> Fifty casualties
> made it... at sunset
> a red pond... fifty casualties
> (trans. Nassar and Ibrahim)

In a rhythm reminiscent of some of Lorca's poems, the ancient innocence of the homeland has been tragically violated and is innocent no longer. The color red overtakes the green, and the expected beauty is not there. The romantic poem depicts the distance between what should exist and what does exist, always idealizing the return to the familiar origin of the ancient and innocent homeland.

Young Darwish's poetry unvaryingly represents beauty as disturbed by external elements or by injustices, which deprive it of its earlier innocence. We read in "Poem of the Land," "And in the month of March come the silken shadows (and without shadows the invaders)" (Jayyusi, *Anthology* 148). It seems as if the shadows of the invaders are in conflict with the shadows of the good, or as if the invaders' presence is a temporary spring that opposes the ancient Palestinian spring. Even though innocence is at the crux of Darwish's romantic poetry, the occupiers have replaced it with an alien innocence.

> —Silken are the thorns of my days, until tomorrow,
> silken are the thorns of my days
> [...]
> —Of shackles, I dream to explain my cries to the
> passers-by,
> Of shackles I dream, to see my freedom, and count
> the ages of the years.
> [...]
> —A river of love songs flows in a piece of shrapnel.
> [...]
> —There are seasons and countries in my corpse.
> (*Dīwān* vol. 1, 620; trans. Nassar and Ibrahim)

The above lines describe a set of contradictions: thorns and silk, shackles and freedom, shrapnel and love, corpses and seasons, red and green, and shadows of the invaders and silken shadows. These contradictions portray the Palestinian estrangement, instigated by the Israeli occupation that obliterated and claimed their history.

The romantic poem resolves the contradiction between what is and what should be, counting on the inherent goodness of the self to triumph. Resolution will emerge from this self because it is an origin: all-encompassing and collective. Therefore, the Palestinians do not die in battles, but are resurrected. That is, they do not perish, since they are themselves the image of the immortal land. In "Poem of the Land," Darwish says,

> I name my ribs
> trees
> Gently I pull a branch
> from the fig tree of my breast
> I throw it like a stone
> to blow up the conqueror's tank
> (Jayyusi, *Anthology* 146)

There are no differences between the poet and the branch or between the branch and the stone. For the land has its defenders. And the poem only celebrates imminent and forthcoming joy. In this structure, death takes the form of anthems or spring rituals dedicated to fertility, child labor, and childbirth. Perhaps the poem "A'rās" [Weddings] (in Dīwān vol. 1, 583–584), known to be about the martyr, is Darwish's celebration of the collective resurrection, in which the martyr and wedding rituals are indistinguishable:

> A lover comes from war to the wedding day
> [...]
> Above the ululations, come the airplanes
> Airplanes
> Airplanes
> Kidnapping the lover from the butterfly's embrace
> [...]
> The girls sing:
> You married all girls,
> O Muhammad!
> You spent the first night
> on Jaffa's red tiled roofs,
> O Muhammad
> [...]
> You married the vineyards
> and the jasmine bushes,
> O Muhammad

When elegizing a Palestinian martyr, Darwish does not begin with "the Palestinian," but with the lover, thus extending the human dimension of the poem. Hence, Darwish substitutes love for death, singing for bereavement, and the definite for the indefinite.

The romantic poem thus emphasizes two things: first, the poet's belief in the power of words as signifiers of truth (that is, the truthful right to defend the occupied land); and second, the poet's faith that love can defeat the occupiers. The romantic poem created the legend of Darwish (who, ironically, will not remain that romantic figure throughout his career). Moreover, it crafted the legend of a Palestine woven out of the olive tree, the martyr, the refugee camp, alienation, and exodus.

Homeland Outside the Self

In Darwish's collection *Limādhā tarakta al-ḥiṣāna waḥīdan?* [*Why Did You Leave the Horse Alone?*] (1995), the son asks the father, "Where are you taking me, Father?" The father answers, "Where the wind blows, son" (*Unfortunately*, 65). In earlier poems, the answer would bring confidence and optimism into the son's soul. We read in *Ākhir al-layl* [End of the night] (1967),

> They took away a door… to give you wind
> opened a wound to give you a morning
> razed a house so that you could build a homeland
> (*Dīwān* vol. 1, 203–204)

During the phase of the romantic self, the poet substituted prophetic time for historical time, so that the story of the land was, in the poetry, the story of the rightful liberation of the land. After thirty years of poetic experience, however, Darwish's work came to depict truth, tragedy, and history. Tragedy has remained, in the form of continued occupation, replacing the certainty of liberation with its probability instead. What has changed is the role of the envisioning poet, who now chooses to follow others in order to depict the naked truth, without propaganda and without any golden future built on the idea of the past.

State of Siege (2002), in which the poet contemplates his own and his people's siege, is a testimony to this transformation. There is neither a place for collective resurrection nor for the poet to contemplate green trees. *State of Siege* ponders the meaning of siege and the well-being of the besieged, thus transferring the siege from the land of Palestine onto the cosmic horizon and shedding light on the besieged of every time and place. The poet begins his dīwān with the following:

> Here on the slopes before sunset and at the gun-mouth
> of time,
> Near orchards deprived of their shadows,
> We do what prisoners do,
> What the unemployed do:
> We nurture hope
> (9; trans. Elbendary 2002)

Recall how in the poem "Victim Number 18" (in *Ākhir*, *Dīwān* vol. 1, 214–216), the romantic self placed the one in all and all in one, and at the same time substituted itself for the one and all:

> My heart was once a blue sparrow… O nest of my
> love
> I had your handkerchiefs, all white, were O my love
> what stained them tonight?

No such imagery can be found in the *State of Siege* collection. For in *State of Siege* the poet is content with simply presenting a tragic scene, the elements of which are the siege, the uprooted trees, and the ironic possibility of hope. All themes are shattered and shaky, with the constant threat of reemergence or relapse. In spite of the change of images in *State of Siege*, the scene is liberated from the impact of time, as if the poet has eliminated time from the scene and left it constant. Repetition, in this case, occurs only in the description of the many faces of the siege, mixed either with direct or embedded irony. Therefore, the poet is sometimes concise:

> Here, after Job's poetry we waited for none…
> (11; Elbendary 2002)

Or the poet repeats himself:

Here, on the heights of smoke, on the stairs of home,
There is no time for time.
We do what those who ascend to God do:
We forget pain.
(15; Elbendary 2002)

There is a parallel between the lines "we nurture hope" and "we forget pain." The space between them is a dead time in which the whole poem is colored with images that convey the feeling of waiting. The poem starts and ends in a static manner, illustrating the many faces of siege. The collection is structured on the basis of controversial images and contemplation, where every image invokes another and every thought opens up onto another without ever reaching a resolution. It seems as if the poet has placed himself both inside and outside: he is inside because he personifies everything, and he is outside in order to observe the path toward resolution and the possible end of the siege. In both cases, the poet is aware of the relationships within the poem, fully aware of the beginning and the end. In this collection, the poet is situated in the position of the individual who is equal to others, thus giving him the opportunity to be one of them—unlike in the earlier image of the visionary prophet, in which all relationships were homogeneous. Even if the absence of prophetic vision leads to a sense that hope is unattainable, it nevertheless allows the poet to observe ordinary life.

Contrary to the treatment of time in Darwish's earlier work, which recalls history and erases it at the same time, time in *State of Siege* appears to be ordinary, measurable, embodied in real-life situations. It can be said that the martyr is seen, but not his resurrection; the bride is seen, but not compared to a butterfly. In reality, in his romantic phase, the poet dealt with a specific aspect of the Palestinian tragedy, with its clear causes and ramifications. However, during the time of siege, he contends with describing daily life under brutal siege. Moreover, he describes a restricted period of time, not that which precedes or follows it.

Darwish ends his collection by talking about peace. However, peace would not seem to be the culmination of the long-lasting siege that is about to end; rather it appears to be a static and continuous aspect of the numerous scenes of siege, just like the state of hope that is nurtured by the unemployed. Therefore, the poet only defines peace as it is dictated by the siege, soliloquizing as he looks into a scene that promises nothing:

> Peace be upon him who shares my cup
> In the darkness of a night spilling over the two seats:
> Peace be upon my ghost
> (90; Elbendary 2002)

This alienation, comparable to the feeling of being orphaned, transforms peace into a mere description, another tree without shade. There is no dialogue; the poet must search for the meaning of peace as permitted by language:

> Peace is two strange pigeons sharing a last coo
> on the edge of the abyss
> (91; Elbendary 2002)

Or:

> Peace is the breakage of swords in front of natural beauty,
> when iron is ruptured by the dew
> (93; trans. Nassar)

From the point of view of literary criticism, the poet does not occupy the center of his new collection: he sees only his own day, places his voice among others, and even lets others speak on his behalf. The romantic self is no longer the only source of articulation. In this collection we have a unique poetic self that is neutral and contemplative, speaking on behalf of the soldier, the martyr, the bereaved mother, the grieving father, the enamored young woman, and the doomed critic, thus allowing daily scenes to speak for themselves, where previously the poet used to speak on their behalf. We read:

> —A woman told the cloud: Cover my loved one
> My clothes are wet with his blood[10]
> [...]
> —[To the night:] No matter how you advocate equality
> [you are for all]... for the dreamers and those who guard

their dreams; we have an incomplete moon, and blood
that does not change the color of your shirt,
oh night...[11]
—[To a poet:] Whenever you feel absence becoming
more absent
You slip into isolation akin to that of the gods
So be the wandering "subject" of your object
And the "object" of your subject. Be present in
absence[12]

These multiple images reflect silence and human suffering, whether Palestinian or not, expressed from within the new poetic self: Darwish announces a disseminated voice, in which certainty is absent but everything possible. The various attitudes of the besieged to their situation collectively constitute the meaning of siege and reveal the vision of the poem. In fact, there are three ways in which Darwish defines his specific position in the poem. The most prevalent is dark irony, which is detached from the ancient rituals of birth and death, thus eliminating what comes before and after the siege, and contending with the daily as it is compressed into one day without the larger elements of a narrative. His poetry recalls dark irony, especially when he connects the "nurturing of hope" and the "unemployed" (9). The more the poem advances, the clearer the irony becomes, until it veers into absurdity:

We are not going to argue
about the martyrs' share of the land,
here they are equal[13]
They lay down the meadows for us
in order to get acquainted![14]

Or:

And if there must be joy,
Let it be
Light on the heart and on the waist
"A [practiced] believer is not bitten
[By joy]... twice!"
(27; Elbendary 2002)

Or:

> Quiet, quiet, for the soldiers now want
> To listen to the songs
> The martyrs listened to, and which remained,
> Like the aroma of coffee in their blood, fresh.
> (86; Elbendary 2002)

There is no place here from which the collective self may speak on behalf of the land. Neither is there a place for a fig branch to be transformed into a grenade by the poet. Even though the dark irony is literally combative, it describes a state of mind that is rested and free from rationality, and at the same time describes the irrationality of the daily scene suspended on the horizon. Therefore, and this is the second approach, the poem is similar to the scene with which it deals: serene and composed of many stanzas with different themes, thus transforming scattered daily life into poetic images.

In the past, the romantic poem used to derive its ending from the beginning, declaring without hesitation the triumph of Palestinian goodness. It was an organic poem, in which the voice of the poet embraced everything. In *State of Siege*, the site of the siege is filled with the shrapnel of time and possibility. The poet does not care about a guaranteed victory. Instead, he is only concerned with the aesthetics of poetry, which contemplates everything but promises nothing. Liberating the poem from the idea of assurance is what makes it free and hence transforms it from its organic status—where meaning is given all at once—to an open situation in which meaning is gradually divulged. This transformation allows the poet to counter the time of Palestinian siege with poetic time, liberated from time and space:

> A little boundless, absolute blue
> Is enough
> To ease the burden of this time
> And clean the mud of this place
> (53; Elbendary 2002)

The poem becomes serene and the images orbit each other. Because there is no conflict in its themes, and because the poet does not see any more than anyone else under siege, there is neither development nor growth in the poem. The poet describes; he neither analyzes nor predicts. He has transformed the Palestinian cause from a tragic situation, proclaimed by the romantic self, into a daily reality, captured by open poetic contemplation. Even though the phrase "state of siege" implies a contradiction between siege and peace, the poem's detailed descriptions limit such implications. This is because the poet is preoccupied with the sorrows of the people at a specific time.

The third way is a transformation of Darwish's poetic voice, as if his poetry has become a reaction to the uncertainty of life under siege. This new poetic form expresses bloodiness, destruction, dispersion, and wastefulness. The poet derives poetry from everywhere: from the rubble of destroyed themes, from the absurdity of hate, from the accumulation of daily ordeals, from the flickers of bombs that rob the night of its color, and from the silence of the inner isolation that torments the soul. This is a poetry that defies the siege, using the rubble and the freedom of poetry to resist the siege. It is a proclamation of Darwish's exceptional poetic creativity, which starts from the "here and now" and extends to all times. This exceptional talent gives Darwish's poetry multifaceted traits yet keeps his poetic creativity as the ultimate source.

On several occasions, Darwish has written poems with specific themes, including "Aḥmad al-Za'tar" and *Madīḥ al-ẓill al-'ālī* [In praise of the rising shadow]. His great poetic talent is reflected in his ability to document and contextualize in time and place without actually contextualizing the poem itself. *State of Siege*, which observes the Palestinian situation in a new context, is a continuation of Darwish's creativity in its simultaneous acceptance and defeat of contextualization. In his poetry, which is committed to a just cause, "liberation" has a double significance: a people's fight for liberation, or a poetic structure that liberates the poem. Darwish structured *State of Siege* from the now and then, extending time and place into binaries that do not offer closure: siege and death, peace and life, time of day and time of soul, the peacefulness of writing and the gravity of the military artillery of the occupiers, the azure of the sky and the blood of the dead, the despotism of the colonizer and the fragility of the doves, the beauty of the infinite and the sadness of confined spaces. All these dualities lead to the unexpected:

> Siege is: waiting,
> Waiting on a leaning ladder in the middle of the storm.
> (32; Elbendary 2002)

This waiting, which "nurtures hope," emerges as the poem is liberated from these dualities. The besieged poet paints a long and tragic human scene, which opens onto the unexpected insight:

> Peace is the apology of the strong to the one
> who is weaker in weapons but powerful in range
> (93; trans. Nassar)

State of Siege is itself part of this "powerful range" of response, as well as an attempt to accentuate it. In his early work, Darwish documented the image of the Palestinian "who is weaker in weapon" rebelling against occupation. At another stage, his poetry represented Palestinian transformations during times of exile. At a later phase, his poetry contemplates the tragedy of hoping for peace with those who do not seek it. In all of these situations, the poet is defending a liberated Palestinian identity and creating a cosmic poetry free from the siege of identity.

The Cosmic Poem of the Self

In his most recent dīwān, *Ka-zahr al-lawz aw ab'ad* [Like almond flowers or further] (2005), Darwish seems to have attained that freedom, using free verse that debates the many faces of the human. There is no mention of Palestine, except in a poem elegizing the late Edward Said. In its avoidance of comparative forms, the dīwān seems to suggest that the poet has withdrawn from the urgent and the limited, and has chosen instead a place to observe the human cosmos in its multifaceted poetics, illuminated by love.

It seems as though the poet is responding to unrestrained Israeli brutality by presenting its absolute opposite. Darwish believes that poetry is one aspect of the "powerful range" of responses in *State of Siege*. The poetic "range" is a contemplation of the simple beauty hidden within both miniature and massive objects, which is concealed by daily hatred and traditional language.

> To describe the almond flower, neither a botanical
> encyclopedia nor a dictionary will help me...
> Words will mislead me to the tangles of rhetoric/
> Rhetoric will wound the meaning and praise the wound,
> like a male pronoun dictating the female's feelings/
> How could the almond flower bloom in my language,
> when I am the echo?
> (47; trans. Nassar)

The poet reaches for the spirit of the familiar objects, and retreats from the "tangles of rhetoric" as though rhetoric were a form of violence or violence one of the aspects of rhetoric. Therefore, he begins his collection with a classical Arabic proverb reconciling poetic composition with prose, thus negating the division between the two styles of writing. The proverb expands the horizon of the poem and opens it up to the reader in a familiar way—as if the reader were co-writing with the poet. However, there is still a celebration of multiplicity, which is a principle of tolerance and reconciliation. Once poetry and prose finally reconcile on the level of poetics and world depiction, this reconciliation becomes an invitation to end isolation and an optimistic openness toward existence in all its various colors and possibilities. Darwish says,

> If I could talk to someone on the road,
> I would have said: my privacy does not define me,
> It is unnamed (107)

The "unnamed," i.e., the unknown, or what appears on the surface level, is what drives the poem to an eager encounter with a "strange woman on the road," with "love, the ghost of death, and God..." Admitting the unknown is a path to knowledge, a space in which to compose the poem, and a defiance of the prejudiced self that celebrates itself as it eliminates the other:

> I do not know myself well
> for fear of losing it.
> I am what I am
> And I am my other in a duality
> that harmonizes between words and signals. (184)

The poetic self cannot exist without an other. There is no existence but of a temporary self because it awaits the other to complement it and, at the same time, leaves the other unfulfilled. Accepting the other is an invitation to solidarity, familiarity, and forgiveness. The poetic self represents humans, classical poetry, the four seasons, and the bystander, as if the poet casts his warmth upon all existence, or as if he is looking forward to a happy day that will overshadow bygone times. Becoming intimate with existence is what makes the poet begin his collection with a poem entitled "Fakr bī-gairik" [Think of the others], which is an invitation to loving both the small and the enormous.

> When you sleep and count the planets, think of the others
> [Some do not have a place to sleep]
> When you liberate yourself with slogans, think of the others
> [Some have lost their right to speak] (16)

The principle of forgiveness for which the dīwān calls leads to the principle of multiplicity, opening the forgiving self up to the infinite: humans, birds, roses, colors, silent and spoken places, or "an orange scared of a hungry mouth" (37). There is no existence but in multiplicity, and this multiplicity is also found in a forgiveness that implicates no one in particular:

> [If the canary did not sing
>   for you my friend... then know
>   that you overslept
> If the canary did not sing] (114–115)

Darwish does not structure his poems upon a moral principle, but rather upon the principle of poetics that recalls love, because his poetry embraces both love and beauty. It is not strange in this case that in the whole collection Darwish uses only four pronouns (you, he, I, and she), leaving space for multiple voices. This choice liberates the poem from the romantic self that monopolizes discourse, and makes every personal pronoun speak through every other pronoun. There is no lonely "self" that continues discoursing because it does not quite know itself. Just as the voice of the self cannot exist without another voice, poetic composition does not become clear unless it appeals to prose, recalling explanation, comment, irony, and the opposition between the elegance of seriousness and a sarcasm that is no less elegant.

> A stranger's funeral might be mine
> But a divine order is delaying it
> For many reasons,
> One of which:
> A great error in the ode! (68–69)

Darwish penetrates the meaning of life, appealing to its contradictions, which include: the sensory and the spiritual, the visual and the hidden, the real and possible, the concrete and the allegorical, the present and the absent. In the end, all these binaries lead to the binary of life and death, which yearns for love and builds upon the encounter between the male and female. If love is built upon the harmony of the "self/I," which is an extension of the "you," the continuity of life is based upon the relationship between the "he" and "she," without which life is impossible.

Darwish made out of his new collection, *Ka-zahr al-lawz aw ab'ad*, a unique pattern of "intimate poetry" that cancels the distance between different things and closes the space between the point of view and the theme, not for the sake of possession, but in order to declare love. Nothing is inside or outside the poet, for he embodies everything. Thus, he aspires to worlds without identity and finds solace in the identity of love. The poet has created new, vast, and beautiful worlds, through a spontaneity that is mixed with poetic wisdom, which liberates the ordinary from its commonality by uncovering its image and making it visible. He also upholds the principle of illumination, which recreates the object and returns its dignity, after the poet has bestowed upon it an acknowledgement long denied by daily life. It is as though the poet, who derives themes from within poetry and outside it, is returning to the world its essential existence, or as though he is bringing us back to an innocent, transparent, and pure world, masterfully created by poetry:

> Orange in color, the sun immerses into the sea/
> And the orange is a lantern of water on a cold tree
> Orange in color, the sun delivers the child of divine
> sunset/

> And the orange, one of its bridesmaids, contemplates
> its unknown (26)

The world, wrapped in love, is born from poetry just as light is born in a child's eye: a world that is tender and pure, with no place for conflict and belligerence, a magnificent world that is closer to a dream.

The poet in his youth, filled with rage, derived the whole world from "a Palestinian poem" or a poem for Palestine. In a later stage, he created a different poem, searching for a universal truth, from which he derived the meaning of the Palestinian tragedy. Darwish has remained true to his cause but without adhering to his first style of poetry. For poetic creativity carried him to vast and different horizons, contemplating the sorrows and joys of humanity and pleading for peace and reconciliation.

Darwish began with Palestine and ended up contemplating the human universe as it reveals itself in a cosmic poetry, admitting all creatures and admitting to the universality of poetry. If, in his earlier collections, Darwish reached the level of national and just cause, then in his later collections his work has been elevated to the level of poetry as it should be.

4
The Image of the Father in the Poetry of Mahmoud Darwish

Sulaiman Jubran

I

Mahmoud Darwish (1941–), one of the best Arab poets of the second half of the twentieth century, and certainly the most renowned, owes his unique status in modern Arabic poetry to a rare poetic talent, forty years of constant output, and unceasing efforts to innovate and improve himself. During these long decades Darwish has pursued various occupations, mainly journalism, but he has always considered poetry to be his most important vocation, to which he has devoted most of his time and effort, in fact, most of his life.

Certainly, the fact that he has become known as "the poet of Palestine" has contributed to his fame. But his standing did not tempt him to stagnate and maintain the constant artistic level that his readers expected and enjoyed:

> I find it problematic when some of my readers and fans of my poetry demand that I tread in one place, that I stay with the one text in which they saw themselves. When I would go beyond that text I took the risk of losing my readership. But I chose the way that was best for my poetry and that best fit my artistic criteria. In this I made the right choice, which also reflected the respect in which I hold my readers. (Beydoun, interview 110)

II

In his decades-long career as a poet, Darwish has published more than twenty collections of poetry. His first collection, 'Aṣāfīr bilā ajniḥa [Birds without wings], was published in 1960. Darwish believes its contents to "express unformed experiments" and therefore does not count it among his works (Dakrub, interview 55). His latest collection, *Lā ta'tadhir 'ammā fa'alta* [*Don't Apologize for What You've Done*], came out in 2004.

All translations in this chapter are by Sulaiman Jubran.

Darwish's poetic works can be divided roughly into three main phases.

At first his poetry was more or less "realistic," an attempt to describe the harsh realities of Palestinian existence in the State of Israel using simple tools, a declarative tone of voice, and highly rhetorical prosodic structures. It should be pointed out that at that stage Darwish was a member of the Communist Party and was no doubt influenced by Marxist doctrine, which considered poetry, and literature in general, as a revolutionary tool whose purpose was to win over the masses and bring about change. This is an attitude he expressed, perhaps with a whiff of exaggeration, in one of the poems in his collection *Awrāq al-zaytūn* [Olive leaves] (1964), as follows: "Our poetry shall be without color/ without taste... and without sound/ if it will not carry the lamp from house to house!/ And if the simple [people] will not understand its meanings it should rather be scattered to the wind/ and we... should stick to silence" (*Dīwān* vol. 1, 55; see also Dakrub, interview 57). At this stage his writings consisted of "fighting poetry" in every sense of the word. This was a poetry that protested sharply against the oppressive regime in Israel and expressed the bitter tragedy of the Palestinian people as a whole, but at the same time was also full of the kind of optimism and hope one expected from "socialist realism." Still, his "fighting poetry" also possesses a winning lyrical tone, particularly when the individual and society, the beloved and the homeland, are combined into a single entity, as happens for example in one of his best-known poems, *'Āshiq min Filasṭīn* [A lover from Palestine] (*Dīwān* vol. 1, 79–85).

In 1971 Darwish left for Egypt and for what was in fact a new life and a novel stage in his artistic development. His decision to leave Israel permanently made a considerable impact both in Israel and in the Arab world, but what is relevant for our purposes here is that this step meant the end of his role as "poet of the resistance" [*shā'ir al-muqāwama*], as the poet of political and social protest against Israeli rule, and that he now stood at an important crossroads in his artistic career: should he stick to his old poetics and recycle the themes and texts that he had written so far, or should he choose a new, more sophisticated and more complex method of expression, despite the danger that such a path might hurt his standing among his readers and fans? In his words:

> I was twenty-eight years old. My feathers were still soft as I walked toward the unknown. I did not notice that my figure, whether I wanted it or not, was to be crucified in Galilee, that I had no right to get down from the cross, put on my shoes and walk away, since that would destroy the figure. For this reason I feel that readers were more generous than I was, and granted me more than I granted them. When readers forgot my sins they forgave me and assigned me tasks in return for their forgiveness. But how? Should I be an echo repeating what I was before? Should I preserve the old figure, or perhaps should I search for a new language and a new poem? That is indeed what I have done, without breaking my ties to the country of my longing. (al-Qasim et al., *Al-Mukhtalif* 30)

Darwish's poetry now went into a new phase, with an attendant new poetic form. He gradually moved away from Marxist views on literature, abandoned the direct rhetoric with which he had expressed his people's collective voice, and began writing profoundly artistic poetry that relied heavily on symbols and motifs from the Old Testament and the heritage of Islam, of Christianity, and of the ancient civilizations of the region. While he continued dealing with the Palestinian question in his poetry, his new perspective was more universal and his language was brimming with a multiplicity of voices, intertextuality, and abstract, at times even surrealistic, images.

In an interview he revealed how much he reads in preparation for writing a poem: "When I wrote 'Eleven Stars,' which is not a long poem, I read nearly fifty books about Muslim Spain. And when I wrote 'The Indian' I read twenty books on the history and literature of the [American] Indians. I also read Indian literary texts and speeches" (Beydoun, interview 70). Interestingly enough, despite the rich historical and mythological knowledge he claims to bring to bear on his writing, Darwish manages to produce easily flowing verse that possesses an outwardly "simple" mode of expression in which a tremendously broad cultural background is reflected by means of a sophisticated intertextuality, a dominant artistic element in his poetry:

> The matter of intertextuality, or allusions, which I use very consciously, is a major element in my work. For I assume that there cannot exist writing which begins now. There is no first writing or writing that begins with a clean slate. And poetry, by all means, has a history. Therefore it is appropriate, at a time of cultural mingling, multiple references and a tremendous development of poetic compositions, whether in classical Arabic or in the modern world, to use intertextuality [...] If you do not write about what has already been written you remove poetry from its historical essence, for poetry possesses first and foremost a cultural identity. On the other hand, the matter of talent, and of how a culture should express itself, these are technical questions. (al-Qasim et al., *Al-Mukhtalif* 17)

In 1982 Israel invaded Lebanon, and the PLO, including Darwish himself, were forced to leave. In the wake of these events he wrote a fascinating poem entitled *Madīḥ al-ẓill al-'ālī* [In praise of the rising shadow] (*Dīwān* vol. 2, 7–77), an extraordinary composition whose very anomalousness testifies to the nature of most of his other work during this period. The poem is very long, about seventy pages, and is written in the rhetorically oriented *kāmil* meter. Its expressions are biting and direct, as are his poetical images, and the voice of the ego is very dominant, overshadowing all of the work's other artistic components. This poem, so unusual for the period in question, reminds one of the early Darwish who wrote the famous poem "Biṭāqat hawīya" ["Identity Card"] (*Dīwān* vol. 1, 73–76). The poet himself admitted that this poem was anomalous. He argued that this manner of writing was justified by the tension, the anger, and the frustration he felt following the above-mentioned events, and was in no way to be construed as a "concession" to the reader:

> I did not present a concession, since I did not write a text meant to appease the reader. For I was angry, and my point of view was always in agreement with that of the reader. My anger at the world made me scorn poetry, the language of the poem as well as its aesthetics. That is why I called it a documentary poem [*qaṣīda tasjīlīya*]. The extent of my anger determined that there

> are times in which there is no place for aesthetics. This, of course, does not constitute a concession, but rather expresses in a way the desire to explode. (al-Qasim et al., *Al-Mukhtalif* 23)

The year 1995 saw the publication of another collection of his poetry, entitled *Limādhā tarakta al-ḥiṣāna waḥīdan?* [*Why Did You Leave the Horse Alone?*], which marked a new, rather surprising turn in Darwish's poetic art. The change consisted in the introduction of "self-observation," in giving his own ego pride of place, and in a profound existential philosophical perspective. Darwish in this collection goes back into the past to delve into childhood memories, whose scenes he now presents in a complex mythical context. Perhaps the best description of this new direction in his poetry is the following by Subhi al-Hadidi:

> This collection opens a truly novel phase in the work of Darwish, that of autobiographical writing, wherein he provides a very generous (perhaps unprecedented in his poetry) opportunity for the emergence of the "I," "I" the poet, in a mosaic of associations with himself, with history, with his place and time, until it equals, or perhaps at times even overtakes, the human and national representation of the collective. (al-Qasim et al., *Al-Mukhtalif* 50)

The atmosphere in the collection's poems is calm and restrained, with a prosodic rhythm that "disguises" itself as narrative prose interspersed with dialogue and replete with historical and religious allusions. Darwish maintained this formula more or less through his next four collections, and even *Ḥālat ḥiṣār* [*State of Siege*], which describes the siege of Ramallah by the IDF, is written from a personal perspective and in a calm, often also ironic, personal style.

III

Before we turn to the main topic of this paper, the father image in Darwish's poetry, we should point out that other members of his family appear in his poetry as well. Even when he still lived in Israel, he lived in the city of Haifa, far from his family in the village, and was frequently in prison or under house arrest. It was therefore only natural that he should miss his family and express his longings in his poetry: "Mahmud has a special 'weakness' for his home and everything in it: his mother, his father, his sister and brothers, and all the usual things that are to be found in any home, the door, the threshold, the fence, the fireplace, the laundry rope, and so on" (Ziyad, "Darwish" 7). Indeed, in the 1960s, when he was in prison, he dedicated to his sister a beautiful and stirring poem with the title of "'Uhdīhā ghazālān" [I shall present her with a gazelle] (*Dīwān* vol. 1, 100–102). Occasionally he also mentioned his grandfather, and to his mother he dedicated another poem he wrote in prison, "Ilā ummī" [To my mother] (98–99). A Lebanese singer who set this poem to music and sang it won extraordinary fame as a result. Darwish's mother is represented there as a stable figure in his poetry: a warm oriental mother, doting and full of love. The poem opens with the words:

> I miss my mother's bread
> my mother's coffee
> the touch of my mother's hand…
> childhood grew up within me day after day
> and I am in love with my life because
> if I shall die
> I shall be ashamed of my mother's tears!

This image of his mother did not change over the years, and in his collection *Why Did You Leave the Horse Alone?*, Darwish describes her in the following lyrical lines:

> My mother counts my twenty fingers from afar
> combs me with her golden braid
> searches my underwear for strange women
> and mends my torn sock
> I did not grow under her care
> as we wanted, she and I
> We parted by the marble slope. (*Limādhā* 18)

His mother has thus remained more or less the same beautiful and loving feminine figure that she always was.

IV

Whereas Darwish's mother represents, as we saw above, the "home" as a whole, the source of warmth, love, and care for the son, the figure of his father does not appear in the same colors, nor is it stable and unchanging over time. Darwish himself attempted to define the difference between the two figures as they are reflected in his poetry in metaphorical terms: "Fathers there were many throughout history, but the mother is one. The mother possesses a stable identity whereas fathers change. The land in which I was born is, as is well known, a meeting place of invaders, prophets, missions, civilizations and cultures. But all of these passed away sooner or later. So that the father was not one, eternal and constant. That is why culturally we relate to the land, to the mother" (Beydoun, interview 21). In more prosaic terms the Palestinian mother represents love and protection to her son, while the father is the "chief": he deals with relations to the outside world and is responsible for protecting the home and ensuring its future. As a result the father-son relationship, including that between Darwish and his father, is complex, which is also why he presents the image of the father differently in different periods. In the same interview in *Masharif*, Darwish described his father as a simple man, busy working his land, and somewhat distant from both his children and his home:

> It was my grandfather who was the real father, because of my father's agricultural work and the need to run after the seasons. He would go out in the morning and return in the evening, leaving me and my brothers in my grandfather's care. He was our real father. He spoiled us, took us out on walks, and we accompanied him to the cities. My father, like the other peasants, was immersed in his work on the land as if he formed a part of it. (Beydoun, interview 72)

Such an image of a father laboring hard to earn a livelihood of course fit in with Darwish's philosophy during the first phase of his career, before he left Israel. Already in his famous poem "Identity Card," which in time became a kind of political manifesto in the eyes of many Palestinians in Israel, he points to his "proletarian background," and at the same time expresses his pride at the heritage of his grandfather, not his father:

> My father is... from the family of the plow
> He is not one of the noble lords
> And my grandfather was a peasant
> with no status... and no lineage
> who taught me the pride of the sun before book
> reading.

In another poem, called "Talātha Ṣwar" [Three pictures] (*Dīwān* vol. 1, 27–28), the poet dedicates the third "picture" to a description of his father. Here again the father is described as a hard-working laborer who finds it difficult to provide for his many children:

> My father was
> as usual, laden with worries, running after the loaf of
> bread wherever it was to be found [...]
> And everyone in our household presents him with
> their demands
> while my father, as usual
> reconstructs the lofty traits, twists his moustache!
> and produces children...
> soil...
> and stars!

This poem clearly also contains gentle criticism of his father, who remains indifferent to the family's situation, continues to produce children and to twirl his moustache.

During this same period Darwish dedicated an entire poem to his father, entitled "Abī" [My father] (144–146). Here again the father is represented as working the land and quarrying rock, adhering to his religious faith despite all his worries and troubles, like the prophet Job who serves as an example. At the end the father commands his son to stay in the homeland and not to go abroad:

> He turned his eyes away from the moon
> bent down to hug the soil
> and addressed his prayers...
> to a rainless sky,
> and forbade me to leave
> [...]

My father once said:
Whoever has no homeland
has no grave in the soil
... And forbade me to leave!

In this poem, too, the phrase "turned his eyes away from the moon," which is repeated further down when the father gives advice to his son, implies that the father is bereft of hope and ambition, and that he has patiently reconciled himself to his hard lot, as Job did.

To summarize so far, we may say that during this early period the father is represented as a peasant, struggling with soil and rock in order to provide for his family, patiently reconciled to his lot, who in the end clings to the land of his birth and refuses to consider emigrating or abandoning his homeland. On the other hand, we see some gentle criticism of the father's indifference, the many children he produces unthinkingly, and his lack of ambition. There is thus some inaccuracy involved in the claim that in this period Darwish presents the figure of his father as free of any faults or blemishes, a claim made by the Egyptian critic Raja' al-Naqqash (*Udabā'* 247).

V

In the second phase, following his emigration from Israel, Darwish became emancipated from his Marxist environment and became a Palestinian national poet par excellence. From that time on he was able to write anything he wanted without having to fear the Israeli authorities and censorship, or the criticism of his "comrades" in the Party or the newspaper. This change caused him to reexamine his father, and his father's generation, from a national, not class, perspective. He "settled accounts" with his father, on the personal as well as the national level, mentioning his and his generation's resistence to British rule, but at the same time also leveling sharp criticism against him on both counts.

We shall not deal here with poems in which his father appears not as a figure on his own but rather as an addressee before whom the poet, in an individual as well as a collective voice, recounts the tragedy of the Palestinians throughout history, as he does in the poem "Ḥajar kan'āni fī al-baḥr al-mayyit" [On a Canaanite Stone in the Dead Sea] (*Dīwān* vol. 2, 515–524), or in another poem entitled "'Anā Yūsuf, yā abī" [I am Joseph, Father] (359), which is an allegory of sorts on the condition of the Palestinian people among its "brother" Arab states. After all, in these poems it is the son who is the topic, whereas the father is a marginal figure about which nothing is actually said and whose sole purpose is to provide an audience for the poet's words.

We encounter a first reference to his father in a lengthy poem entitled "Qaṣīdat al-arḍ" [Song of the earth] (*Dīwān* vol. 1, 618–631), in which the month of March functions as a central theme unifying the description of girl students who were murdered during that month in the intifada, of the awakening of nature, and also of the poet's birth: "And in the month of March, thirty years and five wars ago/ I was born on a heap of glowing tomb grass/ My father was in the hands of the English. And my mother cultivates her braid/ and my stretching out on the grass." The poem thus describes succinctly, in the context of the poet's birth, how his father was under British arrest at the time, a biographical detail that will appear again below.

After his father's death Darwish wrote a long poem about him entitled "Rabbi al-ayā'il yā abī... rabbihā" [Raise the deers, Father...; or The lord of the stags... Father] (*Dīwān* vol. 2, 387–399). The poem is spoken by the poet himself in the first person, and the figure of his father appears throughout, sometimes in the second person and sometimes in the third. It can hardly be called an elegy; rather, it constitutes a harsh accounting with his father, couched in a sharp and picturesque language.

It should be pointed out at the outset that a number of factual items from the poet's life appear in the poem: the carob tree, for Darwish a characteristic feature of his village al-Birwa (Darwish and al-Qasim, *Al-Rasā'il* 45); his father being crucified by the British on a prickly-pear cactus, a fact mentioned twice in this poem and then again in the collection *Why Did You Leave the Horse Alone?*; his father's devotion to cultivating the soil, quoted above; and, finally, the description of his father as shy [*khajūl*], twice in the poem and then once again in the interview with Darwish in the journal *Masharif* (Beydoun, interview 72).

Darwish's first criticism of his father is personal: he accuses him of not having drawn his son near to him, nor encouraging him to take the path of struggle and sacrifice, nor even cultivating him as he did his fields (*Dīwān* vol. 2, 391, 398):

> ...You would habitually drive me away from what I
> was trying to be and not to be... for you knew
> that I desired the virtues of flowers before those of
> salt. More than once you brought me near,
> my father, to the far-away star of absurdity. Why did
> you never once in your life say to me:
> Son! So that I would run to you when I returned from
> school?
> Why did you not try to cultivate me as you cultivate
> sesame, corn and wheat in your field?
> [...]
> You are the one who hid from me his heart, my father,
> and so my life
> has brought me among creatures who are not my
> creatures...
> and now your distant fatherhood is pulling me back
> from my hands and my exile.

He also accuses his father of observing his stolen land, to which he only returns in his imagination in order to pick a flower, but not fighting to get it back (393–394): "Watching his lost Paradise behind his hands, he casts his shadow/ above the soil—his soil, and draws it... in order to pick a chamomile/ [...] What kind of father is my father? He casts the arrows of his shadow at his stolen land.../ in order to steal from it a chamomile?"

Another complaint that the poet has against his father is the latter's excessive preoccupation with the farm, which prevented him from teaching his son "the book of the soil" and the history of his people, who have lived in this land from time immemorial (390–391):

> Do not give me love, I whispered to him, I want to
> give my land
> a gazelle. Explain your distant beginning so that I can
> see you as I should see you
> A father who teaches me the book of the soil from A
> to Z... and plants me there

> [...]
> He does not tell me about the history
> of his days: here we were before time and here we
> shall remain, so that the fields will become green
> Raise the gazelles...
> Raise them in the large yard of the house, oh father!
> But he turns his gaze away from me, attends to a vine
> branch, serves barley and water to the horse
> [...]
> smokes his tobacco, counts the grape chandeliers
> and says to me: Calm down! And then I fall asleep on
> his knee, weak from fatigue.

Here we see quite plainly that the very same traits, of commitment to working the soil and providing for the family, which the poet lauded in his first, Marxist phase, have now become drawbacks, because they are not accompanied by a concomitant struggle to retake possession of "the stolen land" and an effort to inculcate national values. Darwish in this poem "settles accounts" with his father, very harshly, and in fact he appears to have been conscious himself of having overstepped the limits of propriety, especially in view of the fact that the poem was written on the occasion of his father's death. That is probably why twice in the poem he asks for his father's forgiveness for having abandoned him after he had reached adulthood, and also for having "turned my back toward his horses" (393, 398).

VI

In the third phase Darwish published his collection *Why Did You Leave the Horse Alone?*, which constitutes, as mentioned already, a kind of "poetic autobiography." Here the quantity of autobiographical elements becomes considerable, although it is difficult at times to determine whether they are indeed taken from the poet's own biography or rather from the mass displacement of the Palestinians in 1948. The following autobiographical details are certainly factual: his birth, the village church that survived to mark the village after the latter's destruction, the carob tree next to the main road, the exodus to Lebanon through Galilee, Napoleon Hill near Acre, and more. These are elements that any reader can identify as actual autobiographical facts, although we should point out that such realistic elements usually appear within a single context, and sometimes even within a single sentence, together with historical and mythological elements, including a plethora of allusions to the Old Testament as well as both Islamic and Christian tradition, turning this collection into a rich Palestinian epic. Darwish himself described this "admixture" felicitously:

> In my latest collection of poems, *Why Did You Leave the Horse Alone?*, I come back to all my lyrical poems. But these poems, when taken together cumulatively, possess a mythical tone. In other words, the book as a whole, when read from beginning to end at one sitting, consists of a mythical epic poem in which everyday details are embedded. We are faced with a problem, since we live in a historical situation that presents us as if we did not possess a past. Therefore, one of the strategic motives for writing myths is as an attempt to grasp at a past which is otherwise in danger of being entirely torn away from any historical process. (Beydoun, interview 84)

In this autobiographical context, the poet's father occupies considerable space. The father is accorded a considerable measure of justice, as if out of a wish to compensate for the harsh picture the poet painted before. He thus gives the "accused" an opportunity to present arguments in his own defense, in his own words. The collection contains many pieces of dialogue between father and son, from various periods in their lives, written according to narrative norms, enabling the father to present his own "version" of the events that were to lead to defeat and displacement in 1948.

It is the father who leads the son into exile to Lebanon, and it is he, too, who decides to go back to the homeland, although he avoids answering his son's question, why they left their home in the first place (*Limādhā* 33–34):

> He handled his key in the way he feels
> his limbs, and calmed down. He said [to the child]
>   when they skipped over a prickly fence:

> Remember, my son! Here the English crucified
> your father on the thorns of the prickly pear for two nights
> and he did not confess at all. You will grow up
> my son, and tell those who inherited their rifles
> the story of the blood over the iron…
> —Why did you leave the horse alone?
> —So that he'd be a companion of the house, my son,
> for houses die when their inhabitants abandon them!

The father also provides his own version of their defeat in the war: their enemy enjoyed military superiority; they fought as well as they could but in the end were forced to leave the land (37):

> —Are you speaking to me, father?
> —They signed an armistice in Rhodes,
> my son!
> —And what is it to us, what is it to us, father?
> —The matter is at an end.
> —How many times does our matter end, father?
> —The matter is at an end. They did their duty:
> they fought against the enemy's aircraft with
> broken rifles
> We did our duty and moved away from the
> Chinese cherry tree in order not to move the
> military commander's cap.

The collection is full of childhood recollections, descriptions of his home and village, and dialogues between father and son. This is not the place to describe them all in detail. Still, three additional comments are in order here:

1. In this collection Darwish's father is described as the one who initiated and carried out the family's exile to Lebanon (40), even carrying his son on his shoulders when they begin their journey back. But in reality it was the grandfather who was responsible for the move to Lebanon: "He [the poet's grandfather] was the one who took us out [to Lebanon]. He thought like all the Palestinians, that their emigration was temporary, no more than vacating the area for armies and war for a short time, after which he would return to his village and to his land" (Beydoun, interview 73).

2. As just mentioned, the poet's father is portrayed as having carried his son on his shoulders when they began their journey back from Lebanon. However, later the situation changes: his father sweats and becomes tired, and then it is the son who carries his father; he is the one who knows the way back, to the village and to their home, and it is he who will continue marching, all the way to the end of the path, and of his life (*Limādhā* 41–42). Here is another symbolic expression of the hope that the younger generation, the generation of the future, will at the end of the day succeed in bringing back home the Palestinians who had been displaced.

3. In this paper we have dealt only with thematic aspects of Darwish's poetry. There can, however, be no doubt that the artistic aspects of his poetry, prosody, structure, language, and his rich and complex intertextuality are all deserving of our interest no less than its thematic aspects, which cannot in fact exist without them.

To conclude, we may justly say that Darwish's image of his father, in contrast to the stable image of his mother, went through three distinct phases, or three periods, which are in fact identical to the stages of his own personal and artistic development.

5
Mahmoud Darwish's Love Poem: History, Exile, and the Epic Call

Subhi Hadidi
Translated by Najat Rahman and Rim Bejaoui

I

Does Mahmoud Darwish have a right to produce a book of poetry solely dedicated to love? He is considered the "poet of resistance," "the conscience of Palestine," "the lover of the land," as Arabic literary criticism has so often represented him and confined him. Does he have a right to a love poem, free and light except for the weight of the heart, where no gun comes between Rita and his eyes,[1] and where he is not the lover of one unique beloved who is the land? And can Darwish utter the simple words "I love you," without continuing:

> Your face
> upon the water is
> the evening shadow
> confronting my shadow,
> and the windows of my people
> prevent me from being
> alongside this evening.
> When do flowers wither in memory?
> When do strangers rejoice?
> So that I can render the moment
> Floating on the water—
> a myth or a sky…
> (From "Taqāsīm 'alā al-mā'" [Divisions over water],
> in *Uḥibbuki aw lā uḥibbuki*)

A natural first response should, of course, be yes! It goes without saying that Darwish should be able to love as others do, and should be allowed to write a love poem for a woman; a beloved may be of flesh and blood and not only a metaphor for Palestine, or the land,

Translations of poetry and other extracts in this chapter are by Najat Rahman unless otherwise noted.

or the cause. Yet this simple affirmation of his obvious right proves not so simple when we look more closely.

The issue is in fact much more complicated than this first exercise in surprise around a poet's rights would make it seem. It is a question of the poet's obligation vis-à-vis the "rights" of the reader who demands to be given topics of interest to him. Perhaps the reader is obligated to defend the unique position granted to the poet, as the voice of Palestine (the lost paradise of the Arabs), the lover from Palestine (the beloved of the Arabs), the steadfast one from Palestine (who stands in opposition to the defeated Arab), and the transcendent symbol (whether in Jaffa, Cairo, Beirut, Paris, or Ramallah). He is the lyre of Palestine that heals as it wounds, that animates the soul when the body is without breath. The voice of Darwish seems clear even when obscure, optimistic even when pessimistic, and alluding to the collective even when openly proclaiming itself as that of the individual.

Darwish is the poet of whom we ask lessons for the future. People recognize the lucidity of his vision, and he is duly claimed by the crowds. He is the awaited lover who replaces the defeated leader. Yet this adulation forbids him his right to be a poet first, and we forget that his vocation is to be a poet. He wants to be a poet and no more, one who is sometimes tempted to resign from the functions that have been proscribed for him (of "poet of resistance," "the Palestinian conscience," and the "lover of Palestine"). He bristles to resign for personal reasons or without needing to offer personal justifications. Indeed, Darwish is a poet who makes us learn a great deal. His vision scrutinizes; his voice expresses. He warns us—unites our voices when darkness veils our sight—against those who have chosen to condemn themselves to silence. He defends the dignity of poetry when poetry itself gives up, when its relation to others is destroyed. We, his audience, forbid him from walking away from his moral duties (in the literary, political, and aesthetic domains) and even from resigning from his functions.

Is it necessary to mention how few poets have seen themselves attributed such power by their readers? In the history of Arabic poetry, only the great poets were able to influence the people so extensively, and this was during the glorious periods of Arabic poetry. It was a time when Arabs considered poets as prophets, when Arabs identified themselves with the unique voices of their poets, trusting their prophecies in order to contemplate their own past and prepare for the future. It was a time when Arabs made poets their guides and followed them down the meandering roads of the unknown that only poets knew how to travel. Whether in victory or in defeat, it is to poets that crowds turned. All cultures, like Arabic culture, attributed a special role to their poets at a particular moment of their history. It became incumbent upon poets everywhere to speak for their communities, to find answers to existential questions, to give poetry a power that was national and cultural, spiritual and material, aesthetic and informative.

Circumstances, both personal and impersonal, have led Darwish to occupy a position of significance similar to that of the great poets of the Arab past. Indeed, the interaction between these sets of circumstances has contributed to Darwish's poetic project, when external reality puts pressure on his poetry; it leads him to make the national question a priority, and this at the expense of his own aesthetics. However, in both cases, Darwish manages to continuously affect changes at the level of language and theme, and to explore new sources of inspiration. His artistic stubbornness can only arouse our admiration and even our solidarity when we know the pressures placed on him, mentioned at the beginning of this essay. The poems he has published during the last two decades express a more harmonious relationship between poetics and moral and cultural authority.

When Darwish left Israel in 1970 and began to gain greater literary authority, he became aware of the task that was assigned to him and conscious of the problematic position of the poet who is made into a spokesman for the collective. Darwish, not wanting to lose aesthetic control of his poetry, decided to determine for himself his relationship with his public. He did not hesitate to distance himself from the public when it asked for political responses. He insisted that his voice must remain different from that of the public. In order to retain control of his poetry, Darwish was forced to innovate, to constantly rethink the material of his poetry, as well as its subject. In this context, he was obliged to establish a certain balance between his poetic quest and public expectations. It was not without clashes that this distinction was made. By refusing to surrender to ideology and to populism, Darwish wanted to express something different from the simplistic "we" of the collective.

Even if his famous poem "Identity Card"[2] continues to excite the public and continues to be widely applauded by Arab audiences because it rekindles national pride, Darwish often refuses to recite it. He prefers to read new and less immediately graspable poems instead. In certain situations, Darwish succeeds in not answering the expectations of the public, as justifiable as these may be. By challenging his public in a daring way, he is only confirming the image which the public has of him, an image of the poet/prophet of new visions, who must always surprise and uplift. Going from one register to another is never an easy task for readers of Darwish, even for the most mature among them. Because every reader has at least a favorite poem, every attempt at innovation coming from the poet seems suspect at first. This ambivalence does not take long to dissipate, however, because Darwish is a particularly gifted poet who has an extraordinary capacity for renewal. He is fully conscious that he has come to embody one of the pillars of contemporary Arabic poetry. It is thanks to his artistic stubbornness that he has been able to protect the integrity of his poetic project, to renew it constantly. The reader, as well, has always been receptive to this poet's offerings and has welcomed, without distrust, the new form that Darwish's poetry has taken since the 1970s.

Indeed, the writing of long epic poems constitutes one of the most important phases in the poetry of Darwish, insofar as the epic reflects iconographic preoccupations. Each of his poems takes on iconic status as it prepares for the next. His poems become the icons he himself breaks as he writes new ones. The poem "Sirhān yashrabu al-qahwa fī al-kafātīrīya" ["Sarhan Drinks His Coffee in the Cafeteria"] (*Uḥibbuki aw lā uḥibbuki*, 1972), with its character of Sirhan, identified with Sirhan Bishara Sirhan, the Palestinian assassin of Robert F. Kennedy, remained iconic until "Ahmad al-Za'atar" (*A'rās*, 1977), a poem that came to vie in the mind of Darwish's readers with "Sirhan..." This poem in turn took on an iconic status in relation to the poem *Madīḥ al-ẓill al-'ālī* [In praise of the rising shadow] (1983), and the latter in relation to *Qaṣīdat Bayrūt* [The poem of Beirut] (1983), and so on and so forth. *Aḥada 'ashara kawkaban* [Eleven stars, or planets] (1992) marked a decisive stage in the poetry of Darwish, for it confirmed the double vocation of Darwish as poet/prophet, for this work predicted the critical phase of contemporary Palestinian history, the Oslo agreements.

Other poems, in which the national content does not hinder the project of elaborating an aesthetic, are more numerous than the iconographic poems: "Mazāmīr" [Psalms] and "Taqāsīm 'alā al-mā'" (both in *Uḥibbuki aw lā uḥibbuki*, 1972) most of the poems of the collections of *Muḥāwala raqam sab'a* [Attempt number seven] (1973), the one-poem book (*Tilka ṣūratuhā wa hādhā intiḥār al-'āshiq)* [That is her image and this is the lover's suicide] (1975), "Kāna mā sawfa yakūnu" [What was to be came to be] (in *A'rās*, 1977), "Qaṣīdat al-arḍ" [The poem of the land] (1977), and "Sana ukhrā, faqaṭ" [Another year] (1983). After this phase, Darwish set about organizing an aesthetic project, writing whole collections with the aim of achieving it. Iconography was no longer what distinguished one poem from another. Collections now distinguished themselves from one another by composition and by theme. This is certainly the case of *Hiya ughniya, Hiya ughniya* [It is a song, it is a song] (1986), *Ward aqall* [Fewer roses] (1986), *Arā mā urīd* [I see what I want] (1990), *Aḥada 'ashara kawkaban* [Eleven stars] (1992) and *Limādhā tarakta al-ḥiṣāna waḥīdan?* [*Why Did You Leave the Horse Alone*?] (1995). This last collection introduced a new and fundamental element in Darwish's poetics, in which autobiographical writing dominates, allowing for an open manifestation of the self apparent for the first time. It presents the poet's subjectivity, the complexity of his relationship with his various self-constructs, with history, time, and space, the whole of humanity, as well as the national entity and the community.

It was right for Darwish to begin to express himself without constraint.

It was time for him to set free his subjectivity.

II

At first glance, it does not necessarily occur to us to think of the poems gathered in the collection *Sarīr al-gharība* [*The Stranger's Bed*] as love poems. They are not poems of pleasure, or *ghazal* in the classical sense, nor do they speak of sensual and fascinated courtship, or lament past courtship. This does not mean that Darwish is anxious to express the opposite of these distinctive elements of Arabic poetics. It is, however, relevant to note that Darwish's love poems differ from others' in terms of their aesthetics, which is of crucial importance at the artistic level; sociological concerns also distinguish his love poems, because even when he is not addressing nationalist subjects, the public continues to demand that he express himself in the name of the collective "we."

Apart from some poems grouped together in the collection *'Āshiq min Filasṭīn* (1966), in which Palestine is the idealized beloved, "with Palestinian eyes/ and ṭattoos/ a Palestinian name/ worries and dreams/ a Palestinian scarf and feet/ Palestinian body/ Palestinian silence and words/ a Palestinian voice/ a Palestinian birth and death" (*Dīwān* vol. 1, 84), the love poems of Darwish radically distinguish themselves from Arabic love poetry. Instead of being introspective, as is the case in the Arabic poetic tradition, Darwish's love poems contemplate history. Instead of describing the calm of a lovers' meeting, his poems evoke the pains of exile. Already in 1964, Darwish withdrew his book *'Aṣāfīr bilā ajniḥa* [Birds without wings], published in Acre in 1960, to inform the reader in his second book, *Awrāq al-zaytūn*: "I wagered with my sadness/ I shook the hand of hunger and destitution/ my hand grew angry/ my mouth angry/ and the blood of my veins streams of anger!/ My reader!/ Do not ask me to whisper/ Do not ask me to enrapture" (7–8). On the other hand, the first love poem he wrote, entitled "Al-maw'id al-awwal" [The first encounter], reflects the influence of the Syrian poet Nizar Qabbani, but it describes a meeting between two lovers that does not take place. Earlier, and specifically in the poem called "Ajmal ḥubb" [Most beautiful love]—which begins with these verses: "As within the fissures of stones/ herbs grow/ we found ourselves strangers one day..."—Darwish treats one of his favorite subjects, which is the relationship between lovers who are strangers to one another. This theme will come to dominate the majority of his love poems.

Darwish's first love poems elaborated his aesthetic project. At that time, his poetry was an integral part of what was called "poetry of resistance," and which grouped together other Palestinian poets, such as Samih al-Qasim, Tawfiq Zayyad, and Salem Gibran. But he had already distinguished himself from them by his abundant creativity (in Palestine he published five collections of poems between 1960 and 1971), by his wider horizons, his remarkable use of myths and symbols from Middle Eastern and ancient Greek sources, the epic dimension he gave to everyday life, the role of women as symbolic of the land, the capacity to mix romantic lyricism with revolutionary mood, the simplicity of his rhythms, the warmth of his language, and his preference for sensual over intellectual poetry.

During this early period, his poems represented the individual aspect to the act of resistance. This continued after his departure from Palestine, but his poetry transformed into a defense of an aesthetic project. Darwish is intent on proving that he is a poet with a project, that he is actively involved in experimentation, so we cannot confine him to the sole role of "poet of resistance." Darwish entered into a conflict with his readers, who wanted him to be above all, if not exclusively, the bard of the struggle. Darwish tirelessly retorted that even a poet of resistance had to start by being a poet. In 1972, *Uḥibbuki aw lā uḥibbuki* [I love you or I do not love you] came out. It was his first collection published outside of Palestine. He showed innovation and a clear shift in poetic style. This tendency continued further with the publication of *Muḥāwala raqam sab'a* [Attempt number seven], and became clearer in *Tilka ṣūratuhā wa hādhā intiḥār al-'āshiq* [That is her image and this is the lover's suicide] in 1975, and "Hīlīn, yā lahw min maṭar" [Helen, what a rain] (which appeared in the collection *Limādhā tarakta al-ḥiṣāna waḥīdan?*). A decisive step was taken in this last collection, with autobiographical writing. This collection was followed by *Sarīr al-gharība*, which is completely dedicated to love poems.

Why did Darwish start such a new project at this specific moment? Why this poetic project in particular? What constitutes the singularity of the love poems that appear in this collection, and how do they distinguish themselves from classical and modern Arabic love poems?

The reader who tries to find answers to these questions will inevitably raise other questions about the relationship between Darwish and his public. I, for one, noted that Darwish was no longer writing love poetry to release himself from the wounds of the heart. In *Sarīr al-gharība* there are no references to lovers' quarrel, to a change in mood by these lovers, and even less to lovers' complaints. His love poems do not comply with the leading classical Arab critic Kadama Bin Ja'far's conception of love poetry—as poetry rich in reference to perdition in youth, longing, fragility, and decadence—which constitutes a valid vision for the great majority of the love poems of the classical and modern Arabic tradition. Yet Darwish's love poems should not be located outside this tradition either, for they convey a vision of love similar to that of the Andalusian Ibn Hazm's. In his definition of love, Ibn Hazm wrote:

> And we learned that the secret of intermingling in creatures is communication, and the secret of separation among them is difference. Form always calls for similar form; we tend to lean towards resemblance, and affinity is tangibly at work and has visible influence. Within us can be found discord in opposites, agreement in aversion, and struggle in resemblance, so how do we account for the self and its world, which is light and pure, whose essence is temperate ascension, and whose root is inclined toward acceptance, agreement, longing, yearning, desiring, deviation, fleeing, avoidance, running away.

Darwish, in turn, writes in *Sarīr al-gharība*: "Let's go as we are:/ a free woman/ and a loyal friend/ let's go together on two different paths/ let's go as we are united/ and separate" (5). The lover says to his beloved, "we were missing a present" (5). And he continues: "And soon there will be a new present for us./ If you look back you will see only/ the exile of your looking back" (5).[3] Romantic encounters anticipate estrangement, and are the witnesses of the war between Athens and its rivals, as well as the reconciliation between Rome and Carthage. They return tirelessly to the past, to Babel, from where the lover comes and asks: "Am I another you/ and you another I?" (9)

> … Because soon
> the birds will relocate from one epoch to another:
> Was this path only dust
> in the shape of meaning, and did it march us
> as if we were a passing journey between two myths
> so the path is inevitable, and we are inevitable
> as a stranger sees himself in the mirror of another
>   stranger? (5–7)

III

From the first verses of the poem, the theme of love combines with that of exile; it is a question of the fundamental duality of the lover and beloved, who are strangers, as seen from the Ibn Hazm definition, "discord in opposites and agreement in separation, and struggle in resemblance." In the same poem, historical circumstances give an epic dimension to the theme of love as well as to the lovers' quest for identity. The following passages from *Sarīr al-gharība* illustrate the originality of Darwish's lyric poems and reveal the particular attention given to the symbiotic relation between epic and love:

> No cultural solutions for existential concerns (7)
>
> No collective solutions for personal scruples (9)
>
> Soon the sea will suck you in
> so walk leisurely to your death (13)
>
> Will you come with me, or walk alone
> in your name as an exile that adorns exile
> with its glitters? (15)
>
> and here I have my life as my bread's worth
> and my questions about a destiny a passing present
> tortures, and I have a beautiful chaotic tomorrow (19)
>
> [...] Night diffusing a mystery
> that illuminates my language, whenever it is clearer
> I become more fearful of a tomorrow in the fist. (23)
>
> There's no name for us, woman, when the stranger
> stumbles upon himself in the stranger (27)
>
> [...] Who will say to me
> now: Let go of yesterday and dream with all
> of your subconscious? (29)
> and I sat with my freedom silently staring into our night:
> Who am I? Who am I after your night
> night of the last winter? (29)

In the evening, by the freckled light between
your breasts, yesterday and tomorrow approach me
(31)

We were two strangers in two faraway lands a while ago,
so what will I be tomorrow when I become
two? What have you done with my freedom? Whenever
my fear of you mounts I rush into you,
my beloved stranger, since my ardent desire
is my only credit. (53)

[...] And say we are
two stranger birds in Egypt
and in Syria. Say we are two stranger birds
in our feathers. (61)

So go as memories go to their endless
wells, you won't find a Sumerian woman carrying an urn
of echo waiting for you. (65)

[...] go
to any east or west that exiles you more,
and keeps me one step further from my bed
and from one of my sad skies. The end
is beginning's sister... (65)

And what will we do?
What
will we do?
without
exile? (91)

For Darwish, the theme of love cannot be separated from that of exile. His love poems are the theater of a double struggle between freedom and necessity. The love encounter becomes the place of what is possible, of destruction, of doubt, and an attempt to recover what was lost. A love poem that engages such philosophic concerns certainly cannot be considered a common lyric poem, especially in that the existential questions that haunt the Palestinian soul do not cease to arise here. *Sarīr al-gharība* is therefore a love poem and an epic at the same time. Furthermore, this collection marks the beginning of a new phase in Darwish's poetry, in the elaboration of a lyric-epic. This project, which Darwish began and has been developing since the early 1970s, constitutes today the essence of his poetry, insofar as his repertoire of sung epic keeps growing richer in surprising ways, thanks to his formal as well as aesthetic innovations.

Another theme in *Sarīr al-gharība* is the estrangement of love. The inseparability of love and exile allows us to question our conception of love. The poems of this collection explore various and unexpected aspects of the theme of love, as perceived through the prisms of history, of reality, and of everyday life. "There's a love walking on two silken feet/ happy with its estrangement in the streets" (13). And Darwish proclaims: "a love small and poor made wet by a passing rain/ that it overflows onto passersby," "a poor love staring at the river/ in surrender to summoning," "a poor love, one-sided/ and quite serene" (13), "a poor love, and two-sided/ it diminishes the number of those in despair," "a love passing through us,/ without us noticing/ and neither it knows nor do we know" (15), "a poor love, it contemplates/ at length the passersby, and chooses/ the youngest moon among them" (17). In his writing of epic love, Darwish defines love as follows:

> [...] No one can
> return to another. Eternity performs
> its manual chores out of our lives then thrives...
> So let love be an unknown, and
> the unknown a kind of love. How strange
> to believe this and still love! (19)

In Darwish's love poem "Anā wa Jamīl Buthayna" ["Jameel Bouthaina and I"], the lover asks Jameel Bouthaina, a classical poet of ghazal and a famous lover: "Would you explain love to me, Jameel,/ to remember it one idea at a time?" (95) And Jameel answers: "People who know love best are the most perplexed,/ you must burn, not to know yourself, but/ to illuminate Bouthaina's night..." (95) Introduced to love by Jameel, the lover learns that lovers are created in the image of their beloveds' desires, and that the writing of a love poem is in itself a declaration of love. "Which time do you want, which time/ that I may become its poet, just like that: whenever/ a woman goes to her secret in the evening/ she finds a poet walking in her thoughts./ Whenever a poet dives into himself/ he finds a woman undressing before his poem…" (15) Thus it is with Majnoon Laila, another famous classical poet of ghazal, that the lover identifies himself. "I am Qyss Laila, I am/ and I am… no one!" (99) Subsequently, the truth of another tradition is evoked, that of Indian erotic poetry, in which the lover looks for a remedy and is taught patience: "with the patience of the horse prepared for mountain descent/ wait for her,/ with the manners of the refined and marvelous prince/ wait for her,/ with seven pillows stuffed with light clouds/ wait for her […]" (101) The meeting with Jameel takes the form of a dialogue, while the meeting with Majnoon Laila raises existential questions. Thanks to the Indian erotic tradition, the lover learns the secrets of anticipation, of waiting. This poem is a dialogue first of all, an intersection of existential notions, and an attempt to transmit knowledge.

The third distinctive feature of *Sarīr al-gharība* concerns dialogues. Indeed, this collection succeeds in establishing a certain balance, from varied points of view, between the replies of women and those of men. Seven poems express exclusively a female voice, without any intervention from the male lover, valorizing a vision of love as conceived by the female lover. The plurality of voices is one of the notable qualities of the collection, since Darwish does not limit himself to the historic and epic dimension (which is also existential and philosophical) for the form of the lovers' encounter and separation: the lover and his beloved seem overtaken by history, which will lead to their estrangement of one from the other. However, neither historicity nor this feeling of estrangement prevents them from expressing themselves. On the contrary, the insularity of the lovers appears characteristic, neither original nor peculiar. Estrangement is developed as a fruitful possibility of expression that distinguishes it from the familiar. In the poem "Lā aqall wa-lā akthar" ["No More and No Less"], the female character expresses herself in this way:

> I am a woman, no more and no less
> […]
> I am who I am, as
> you are who you are: you live in me
> and I live in you, to and for you

I love the necessary clarity of our mutual puzzle
I am yours when I overflow the night
but I am not a land
or a journey
I am a woman, no more and no less (49)

One of the particularities of the seven poems dominated by female voices is that they present another dimension to the plurality of these poems and return us to a world of women: the woman who devotes herself to weaving a cloth for herself, who dreams of picking rare flowers beyond the mountains of Moab, who imagines her lover comparing her to a majestic palm tree, who sometimes asks him to caress her back and untie her hair, who quotes a verse of Yannis Ristos, "in the streams of marble milky words run and call out to the poets to write me," and who whispers that she should never have loved. The man speaks in turn, compares his love to that of Qyss, tells his beloved the same words that Adam once secretly uttered, tells her that he longs to return to exile's night and to the figs of home, that he will go to any East or West to add to his exile, and refuses to die out of love. Nevertheless, the melodic notes, lullabies, or festive songs succeed in uniting the lovers' voices. The details of everyday life occupy a dominant place in Darwish's poetry: they are used as titles of poems, repeated insistently or allusively, or constitute the main themes of certain poems.

History serves as the primary inspiration for such love dialogues as these last ones, which have as their subject the place of man in history. In these poems, history allows the epic to interfere in the love dialogues. Nevertheless, the numerous references to history, that is, to its mythological, universal, and geographical constituents, are far from being the only components of the love dialogue. The evocation of history is conducted at several levels: it is never the same evocation; the encounter with history varies from one poem to another. In *Sarīr al-gharība*, Palestine is omnipresent though only alluded to. Sodom and Gomorrah, Moab and Jericho, the Song of Songs, the Virgin Mary, Jesus and the Gospels, Sumer, Babylon, Egypt, Syria, Andalusia, and Samarkand are all elements used as metaphors for Palestine, and serve to reference her.

IV

Addressing the French public during the cultural events of the "Palestinian Spring" organized in Paris in 1997, Darwish described the Palestinian condition of post-Oslo as follows:

> ... Peace was supposed to resolve the tensions of Palestinian identity, Palestinian culture, to withdraw us from our mythical existence, to remind us of our real condition, and to teach us that reality is richer than any text. We effectively began to ask questions about how to move away from a mythic text of victims and executioners to a commonplace history, to a common people worried about their everyday life and about their human weakness, where each one of us would pay more attention to his voice and would complain about disease, about laziness, and about boredom. We do not want to be heroes and we do not want to be victims. In other words, what we began to do is to try to lead a normal life. But, it seems to me that to live a normal life in conditions which are not that normal is to seek another heroism.

And Darwish further responds to a question on the link between poetry and exile:

> ... Regarding poetic language, poetry is in a general way a journey between cultures, languages, and different temporalities. Poetry cannot be nationalist in the strict meaning of the word; but, because of the fact that there is a link between poetry and community and because the poet belongs in some way to this community and is the product of a particular historic configuration, has a role in shaping the cultural identity of his people. I don't know if I could one day extricate myself from exile's cultural influences. I also don't know if the Palestinians who were born and grew up outside their homeland, in exile, would be able one day to recover their individual memory somewhere else far from exile. I also don't know if we would be able, once return is possible, to continue to oppose exile to homeland. It is still too early to raise these questions and to answer them; Palestinians have to be entitled to a homeland that they will curse or hate in their own way. As for me, I cannot praise exile as long as it is

> impossible for me to curse the homeland. But, the dreamed Palestine comes to my mind more readily when I write poems than the real Palestine... It is a problem that is at the same time personal and national and that prevents the Israelis from continuing to exile me. This is why I have to write better poems!

The bitterness and sarcasm of this last expression, "I have to write better poems," already announces how the new poetic project that Darwish was to begin after the conclusion of the Oslo agreements was going to get Palestinians interested in their own individual worries. After these events, Darwish began to write poems in which the autobiographical element was dominant. This is notable in the case of the collection *Limādhā tarakta al-ḥiṣāna waḥīdan?* [*Why Did You Leave the Horse Alone*?] and especially in *Sarīr al-gharība*, which is largely preoccupied with love. In these two collections, Darwish's poems benefit from all of his knowledge of literary and aesthetic principles as well as his profound knowledge of the art of composition, although they are less political in appearance. This poetic achievement, which embraces both autobiography and the tradition of love poetry, distinguishes him all the more from his contemporaries and confirms once again the uniqueness of his aesthetic. He puts to work his talents and tests his powers: in relation to the other, in relation to both the dreamed and the real Palestine, in relation to history and reality, as well as in relation to the "other heroism," both individual and communal.

The main observations we put forth in the first part of this essay are the following:

1) Most of Darwish's love poems have always differed from one another because of the particular aesthetic appropriate to each of them. The first distinctive quality of Darwish's poems is his artistic innovation; the second is of a sociological nature, due to the pressures to express himself in the name of an entire people, pressures that the poems resist.

2) Darwish's love poems, apart from some that appeared in the collection *'Āshiq min Filasṭīn* (1966), differ from the love poems of the Arabic tradition. History plays a bigger role in the poems than the description of feelings. Exile, absence, and dispossession have replaced stability, ease, and pleasure in the relationship with the other.

3) Darwish's love poem serves as a form of double resistance. On the one hand, it carries the burden of representing the solitary human aspect of resistance against occupation, dispossession, and the eclipsing of Palestinian identity; on the other hand, it is also a resistance against the reader. By making aesthetics a project and a means of resistance, Darwish leads the reader in unanticipated directions and is able to surprise him at any time. This is what he dedicated himself to doing when he left Palestine. The love poem thus complies better with the new aesthetics of Darwish in its patriotic and iconographic elements, as in such poems as "Sarhan Drinks his Coffee at the Cafeteria," "Ahmad al-Za'tar," *Madīḥ al-ẓill al-'ālī* [In praise of the rising shadow], and *Qaṣīdat Bayrūt* [Beirut poem].

In the second part of this study, I will analyze the artistic dimensions of the resistance aesthetic of Darwish's poetry: how he defends and develops an aesthetic project. Of particular interest will be the following aspects of Darwish's love poem:

—The structure of *Sarīr al-gharība*: the way the poems are arranged.

—The use of the sonnet form in six poems: the reasons and implications of this unusual choice.

—The use of the same metric unit [*taf'īla*] throughout the collection, which bridges the gap between the choice of meter and the choice of prose in poetic writing. He proposes for the first time a median unit close to "prosaic meter" or "metered prose," which makes the composition of the poems unique.[4]

—The dynamic manipulation of rhymes.

The poems published in *Sarīr al-gharība*, like those that appeared in the collection preceding it (*Limādhā tarakta al-ḥiṣāna waḥīdan*?) were written to be published together. The poems of this last collection were written between 1996 and 1997, and none of them were published separately. Darwish establishes a dialogue between the poems of *Sarīr al-gharība*; he decided to publish this collection only when he was convinced that the interaction between these lyric poems would contribute to his whole poetic project. He places specific love poems in the same collection and adopts a singular organizational method. Critics of Darwish's poetry cannot ignore this detail, because the arrangement of the poems in the collection is executed according to a particular logic. He put all his knowledge and experience into writing the love poems. He has managed to bewilder those who maintain that he is exclusively the "lover of Palestine." The love poems allow greater individual freedom and offer a spontaneous expression of profound emotions. Darwish's love poetry thus possesses a psychological infrastructure. This organizational method is certainly relevant to Darwish, his poetry, and his readers. Indeed, the structure negotiates the limits of the reader's interpretations of the poems as well as the emancipation of the poet's and reader's subjectivities.

Also, the aim of this particular organization of the poems is to make the reader aware that feelings—those of the reader and those of the poet—should be more temperate. Poems published in *Sarīr al-gharība* establish a moderate balance between emotions and reason. Darwish does not cease to remind the reader (and himself) that the lover has other anxieties, and that the preoccupations of love and individual fears can be put in perspective at any time. These verses show that Darwish aims to engage in a dialogue with the reader and to confront him with his reading: "The likes of us don't die/ not even once, from being in love with the nimble modern song/ and they don't stand alone on the sidewalk/ because trains are more numerous than words/ and we always reconsider" (81). He goes further by insisting that yesterday will follow the lovers, that the lovers' lyric will be interrupted at the poem before the last and will announce what is more extreme than dying of love.

> On the bridge, near your life, I lived
> as a guitar player lived near his star.
> Sing for me, she said, a hundred of your love songs
> and you will enter my life! So he sang ninety-
> nine songs about love, then killed himself (87)

Sarīr al-gharība can be structured into sections, not unlike *Limādhā tarakta al-ḥiṣāna waḥīdan?*, which uses a more direct division.[5] In *Limādhā tarakta al-ḥiṣāna waḥīdan?*, every phase of age is represented: childhood, adolescence, exile, refuge, youth, love, poetry, prison, past/present. *Sarīr al-gharība*, can be divided into nine parts:

1) The "Prologue": a dialogue between two strangers who are lovers about the conflict between men and women; they argue about the present, about exile and the irrecoverable past, about the impossibility of naming things, about the way to freedom, to the body, to meaning, about war and peace between Athens and its rivals as well as between Rome and Carthage, and between lovers, who say to each other that they are inseparable. This prologue has the task of contemplating, announcing, warning, and attributing to the expression of love epic dimensions that will be reechoed in the collection because of the pressure exercised by history and because of time, since the lovers will realize that the future quickly changes into the past and that the fact that they are together is not enough: "We missed the present."

2) Sections two, three, four, five, six, and seven contain three poems preceded by sonnets, which Darwish calls "Sonata."[6] These sonnets separate the parts or link them together. They perform significant artistic functions (which I will analyze further in the essay). These six parts constitute the main body of the collection. In twenty-four poems, Darwish handles with different thematic registers the relationship between the stranger/lover and the stranger/beloved, the fields of love, and references to historic, cultural, geographic, mythic, and poetic events that infuse the expression of love. (Note for example the references to Rome, Carthage, Sumer, Babel, Iraq, etc.) However, if the six sonnets are regularly structured (each is fourteen verses, with variations on the usual sonnet form), eighteen other poems are particularly long (between 27 and 100 verses) but differ in their forms (the poem "Tadbīr manzilī" ["Housework"] is made up of four parts; the poem "Rubbamā li'anna al-shitā' ta'akhkhara" ["Maybe, Because Winter is Late"] consists of twenty quintets). The poems are shared between the female and male voices, between the contemplative and the communicative, between the individual and collective voices, and between different temporalities (past, present, future).

3) The eighth section of the collection is made of three poems: "Anā wa Jamīl Buthayna" ["Jameel Bouthaina and I"], "Qina' li-Majnūn Laylā" ["A Mask… for Majnoon Laila"], and "Dars min Kāmā-Sūṭrā" ["A Lesson from the Kama Sutra"]. Unlike in the previous seven sections, the epic dimension of the lover's speech is

withdrawn in this section. The lovers' meeting takes place, as the title indicates, in an atmosphere not divested from tension in "Wukū' al gharīb 'alā nafsihi fī al-gharīb" ["The Stranger Stumbles upon Himself in the Stranger"]. The stumbling on the self becomes historical, but history exercises a certain pressure on the love relationship. It is the ephemeral, the distant, and exile caused by historical events that govern the relation of the lover to the woman, rather than togetherness, intimacy, and stability. Furthermore, the eighth chapter introduces new speakers, namely Jameel Bouthaina, who evokes the idea of love and its concordance with the image of Bouthaina, the woman he loves; Majnoon Laila is another speaker, but he considers that love and writing about love are both acts that condemn the lover to wandering and to uncertainty. The lover later makes reference to the Indian erotic tradition in order to learn how to coincide time, space, and self before meeting with the beloved. This section also contains erotic scenes that lack Darwish's usual restraint, and the poet's delicate sensibility is apparent in his rendering of these scenes.

> I married her. And we shook the heavens and they
>   streamed
> milk on our bread. Whenever I came to her my body
> blossomed flower by flower, and my tomorrow spilled
> its wine drop by drop into her jugs (95)

4) "Ṭawq al-ḥamāma al-Dimashqī" ["The Damascene Collar of the Dove"], the last poem in the ninth section and which closes the collection, consists of 22 stanzas. It is the site of fusion between the lover's speech and the love song, the love of a place and of a woman in that place.

The poem is a poetic, linguistic, and musical affirmation of what Darwish means by "better poems"; these poems employ a language and musicality he had not previously explored. Darwish accomplishes what the poet Nizar Qabbani would have wanted to produce: a pictorial representation in words, and even more, as the words succeed in bursting into choral singing, possessing rhythmical dancing, reconfiguring language. Poetry is simultaneously narrower and more expansive than language: narrower since it only possesses the name "Berada"; more expansive since it quickly surpasses the known name and ascends to new horizons.

> In Damascus:
> a gazelle sleeps
> besides a woman
> in a bed of dew
> then the woman takes off her dress
> and covers Berada with it (109)

V

The American critic Paul Oppenheimer goes so far as to argue that the invention of the sonnet marks the birth of contemporary thought and of modern literature (see *Modern Mind* 171). He argues that the sonnet was from the start a specific form of lyric poetry, created to be read but not to be sung. Consequently, the sonnet would have been the poetic form most capable of reflecting individual consciousness as well as the self in all its complexity. Oppenheimer describes the historic and intellectual circumstances that made possible the emergence of this new poetic form in early thirteenth-century Italy, when the decline of the Roman Empire had already given free reign to two crucial developments: first, the replacement of the god-hero model with the ordinary man, as well as the ideal of heroic, predestined conduct with that of individual, emotional comportment; and second, the transition from tragic hymns to the lyric love poems.

It turns out that the structure of the sonnet reflects these major changes. The sonnet, characterized by a carefree tone, requires a shortened form. Sonnets are composed of fourteen verses, eight of which bring forth a stream of emotions and six of which, by contrast, ease the rhythmic movement of the first eight verses. Plato had already built a system that presumed a similar relation between the soul and the universe. So, the advocates of the sonnet wanted to model this poetic form on the Platonic system so that it could establish a relation between emotional states. These advocates wanted to be attentive to the "silent melody" of the human soul, as the English Romantic poet John Keats (1795–1821) would have said.

According to much literary research, Giacomo da Lentini first invented the sonnet. Now, it is particularly surprising that he was not inspired by the musical form of the troubadour and the provincial songs that were widespread then. Giocomo da Lentini was inspired by other songs, particularly the songs of Sicilian farmers. It is noteworthy that certain studies of the history of the sonnet attribute the origin of these Sicilian songs to Arabic traditions. They were brought by Arabs who came from Andalusia. Dante Alighieri (1231–1265) and Francesco Petrarch (1304–1374) contributed to the development of the Italian sonnet, which quickly spread to the rest of Europe. The French, German, and Spanish poets appropriated the sonnet as well. In England, the sonnet knew a revival with Edmund Spenser (1552–1599), William Shakespeare (1564–1616), and John Milton (1608–1674). A certain restraint appears when it comes to the sonnet as it was practiced by Milton, who avoided lyric expansion. Sonnets were performed in German by Goethe, Schlegel, von Platen, Rilke, and Schroder. Gaultier, Nerval, Baudelaire, Verlaine, Mallarmé, Rimbaud, and Valéry wrote the most beautiful sonnets of the French language. In Spanish, Lope de Vega, Antonio Ferrara, and Garcia Lorca adopted, as did so many other poets of different cultures, the form of the sonnet.

Why does Darwish privilege the sonnet in his collection *Sarīr al-gharība*? And why in this collection in particular? I think Darwish chose the sonnet for several reasons: ones having to do with the philosophy of the birth of the sonnet form, as I previously discussed (replacing the gods as heroes with ordinary individuals); the particularly (and intentionally) subdued rhythmical options distinguishing the poems of *Sarīr al-gharība* in general; the love theme, which has always dominated sonnets; and, of course, the challenge the form offers a poet who declared his intention to write "better poems": for all these are reasons, Darwish chose the sonnet.

Why at this precise moment? It is likely that this particular phase in Darwish's poetry demands a certain degree of "thematic specialization" such as love poems or autobiography, which requires consequently certain forms such as the sonnet. Darwish might have judged that it was high time for him to show his poetic skill through a new form for him, the sonnet. It might be that he wished to regain a precious poetic form that Europeans borrowed from his Andalusian ancestors, especially as the sonnet remains highly attractive.

However, one of the distinguishing features of Darwish's poetry is that it is nonconformist. This noncompliance is with both the conventions of Arabic poetic tradition, as mentioned, and those of the sonnet. Darwish makes changes to the division of stanzas and to versification. If Darwish initially keeps the number of verses of the sonnet, he nevertheless violates certain rules of the form. Rhyme is not repeated, or it is situated in the middle of the verse and not at the end, or the sonnet consists of three quatrains and a stanza of two verses. To change the usual order of the sonnet is not to disdain it. The first sonnet consists of two quatrains and two tercets, and the rhymes are distributed as follows: *-aab bccb b-- --b*. [*fal-yakun/ lanā/ hunā/ wa al-yamāmu// al-kalāmu/al-qaṣīda/ al-ba'īda/ al-rukhāmu// al-zuḥamu/ athwābahunna/ al-qāfiya// shi'ru/ qālahu/ al-kalāmu*]. The four rhymes are rhyming couplets, the second verse rhymes with the first one and the last rhymes with the fourth. The rhymes are irregular or absent in five verses. Furthermore, the rhymes are not at the end of verses. The third sonnet is composed of two quatrains and of two tercets, and its rhymes are distributed according to the conventions of the sonnet: *aaab cccb ddb eeb* [*ma'ā/ maqta'ā/ tusri'ā/ mut'aba// qalīlā/ Jamīlā/ al-wuṣūlā/ 'ataba// al-khāfiya/ al-qāfiya/ al-tajriba// bābilī/ dākhilī/ al-ṭayyiba*]. This form is not among the commonly used rhyme schemes, and it is difficult to execute because of the caesura or break of rhyme *a* and because of the distance between the recurrences of rhyme *b*. This demands that the poet secure the musical connections throughout the segments that are not connected through a homogenous rhyme scheme, and choose lexical and sound units that allow the reader to temporarily leave the musical atmosphere without breaking away from the outflow of rhythm. The phonetic accentuation can constitute a break within the cadence without slowing down the rhythm.

In the following passage from Darwish's third sonnet, the poet incites the reader to continue to read the poem, and contemplate it without leaving the art of poetry:

> Both of your silks are hot. But the flute should be
>   patient [a little, *qalīlā*]
> and polish a sonnet, when you two descend on me as a
>   lovely [*Jamīlā*] mystery,

like a meaning on the verge of nakedness, incapable
of arrival [*al-wūṣūlā*]
and of long waiting in front of speech, it chooses me
as a threshold [*'ataba*]

Of poetry, I love the spontaneity of prose and the
hidden [*al-khāfiya*] image
without a moon for rhetoric: when you walk barefoot
rhyme [*al-qāfiya*] abandons
copulating speech, and meter breaks in the climax of
experience [*al-tajriba*] (33)

Darwish's use of the sonnet is not, however, a mere exercise in composition, to prove the poet's mastery, or even how diversified Darwish's form has become. In the sonnet, Darwish shows a certain restraint in emotion, achieves a certain balance between the private and the public, between the subjective and the objective, the form and the content, the heart and the mind. One day, the literary critic will have to be interested in the reasons that make the sonnet the poetic form most convenient to the expression of the most opposed feelings. The sonnet succeeds in gathering the heart and the mind, the spiritual and the sensible, the melodic and the epic, as well as artistic and intellectual concerns. One of the many distinguishing features of the sonnet is its flexibility; it is a form that all languages know how to innovate.

Darwish often repeats this sentence, "What I particularly like about poetry is the spontaneity of its prose." This brings us to examining the link between poetry and prose. It is first of all necessary to explore what Darwish means by the "spontaneity of prose," given his admiration for Arabic rhythmic meters, which he exploits in their wealth and possibilities. Prose is obviously not for Darwish what it is for Monsieur Jourdain, a character invented by Molière, who did not know how to express himself except in a kind of poetry called "prose" (*The Bourgeois Gentleman*, act 1, scene 4). Darwish's prose is not at all imitative and does not lend itself to the Arabic prose poem; otherwise, Darwish would have contented himself with modeling his prose on the best prosaic texts of the Arabic tradition.

The spontaneous prose of Darwish is rhythmic, free and easy poetic language, with density of style and content as its main attributes. This language succeeds in expressing everyday life in everyday language, in its most elegant form. It is a transformation of language in a way not possible by other linguistic uses. The spontaneity of poetic language is deliberate, but we note all the same a certain insouciance in the restraint. Finally, Darwish's poetic language conceals the eternal mystery by which the poet recognizes himself in his prose while feeling a stranger at the same time. Poetic language, if it emanates from the depths of the soul of the poet, does not look like the standard Arabic used in journalistic media; the poet recognizes that it is his language and not his language at the same time. In the poem "Layluki min laylakin" ["Your night is of lilac"], Darwish appropriates the sense of the word *layl* [night] and redefines it in his own way, also playing on the words *layl* [night] and *laylak* [lilac, but also "your night"].

> The night sits wherever you are
> [...]
> And your night is your shadow—
> a fairytale piece of land to make our dreams
> [...]
> I am not a traveler or a dweller
> in your lilac night
> [...]
> Whenever night grew in you I guessed
> the heart's rank between two grades
> [...]
> And all of you
> is your night... radiant night like planet ink
> [...]
> Night in the covenant of night
> [...]
> Night diffusing a mystery
> that illuminates my language
> [...]
> Night
> staring at itself safe and assured in its
> endlessness, nothing celebrates it except its mirror
> [...]
> Night that flourished in its *jāhilī* poetry
> on the whims of Imru' el-Qyss and others,

> and widened for the dreamers the milk path to a
> hungry
> moon in the remoteness of speech [...] (23)

The spontaneity also results from the fact that Darwish disperses[7] rhythmical forms. He chose meters of *mutaqārib*, where there is a higher and lower unit, in all the collected poems, the short ones and the long ones, the *rubā'iyāt* and the *al-khumāsiyāt*[8] as well as the sonnets, from the first verse of the opening poem to the last one in "Ṭawq al-ḥamāma al-Dimashqī" ["The Damascus Collar of the Dove"]. And there is a poetic attempt here to close the gap between an Arabic poetry that still relies on meters (in which variations in meter have narrowed slowly so that it is now restricted to single meters with single feet since they are easier to handle, especially for poets with limited experience with meters) and an Arabic poetry that relies solely on prose, as in prose poems, in an attempt to withdraw poetry from the language of prevailing discourses (in which imitation proliferates and artistic variety is narrowing). The *mutaqārib* meters, which are flexible and low in resonance, can mediate between meter and prose, where meter is not determined by measure alone and where prose is not determined by prose alone, in a shared space between "a prose metered" and "metered prose."

The search for this spontaneity in "metered prose" may have been the reason for Darwish's many new poetic works, anchoring spontaneity without undoing the vital role of rhyme in shaping the meaning and musicality of poetry. He develops further his search for new forms of internal rhyming, so that he goes against the anticipated place of the rhyme. In *Sarīr al-gharība*, he proposes the following forms:

1) Distanced rhyme: as in the poem "Ughniyat zafāf" ["Wedding Song"], where there are eight poetic lines between one rhyme and another.

2) Sectional rhyme: as in the poem "Tadbīr manzilī" ["House-work"], where a rhyme connects four different and independent sections, and connects the first and last segments of a section:

> How often [*kam anā*]?
> [...]
> and sleep, my love, a blissful sleep [*hanā*] (55)

How often [*kam anā*]?
[…]
or the image
of a woman from Athens running her emotional
errands as I do here [*hunā*] (55)

How often [*kam anā*]?
[…] Whoever the victim between us should dream
now, more than the other [*baynanā*] (57)

How often [*kam anā*]?
[…]
how often! Who am I [*anā*]! (57)

3) Alternating rhyme: as in the poem "Rubbamā, li-anna al-shitā' ta'akhkhara" ["Maybe, Because Winter is Late"], so there is a rhyme scheme that connects stanzas one with three, six, eight, ten, twelve, fourteen, sixteen, twenty, but not stanzas two, five, seven, nine, eleven, thirteen, fifteen, eighteen; for instance:

Verses from section 10:

I have in me what's in you of night's craving.
A man screams in his sleep: "I am my woman!"
And a woman screams: "I am my man."
Which one of us are you? You? We become narrow
narrow, and the descent widens… [*al-munḥadar*] (83)

Verses from section 11:

I embrace you, until I return to my void
an eternal visitor. No life and no
death in what I sense
as a bird passing beyond nature
when I embrace you… [*aḍummuki*] (83)

Verses from section 12:

What will we do with love? you said
while we were packing our suitcases
do we take it with us, or hang it in the closet?
I said: Let it go wherever it wants

it has already outgrown our collar and spread
[*intashir*] (83)

4) Hidden rhyme: the rhyme is echoed throughout a section without being contained necessarily within the words themselves, not unlike consonance and internal rhyme, as in the case of such letters as "kāf," "hā'," and "Qāf" that designate the sounds of "ka," "ha," "Qa," in the following example:

For you [*laki*] the twins: for you [*laki*] poetry and
prose unite, as you
fly from one epoch to another, safe and sound
[*kāmila*]
on a howdah made of your murdered victims'
[*qatlāki*] planets [*kawākib*]—your kind guards
[*ḥurrasiki al-ṭṭayibīn*]
[*wahum*] who carry your seven heavens [*samāwātiki*]
one caravan at a time [*qāfilatan qāfila*].
And between the palm trees and your hands' [*yadayki*]
two rivers [*nahrayki*], your
horse-keepers [*khuyūliki*] approach [*yaqtaribūn*] the
water: The first goddess [*al-ilāhāt*] is the one
most [*aktharuhunna*] filled
with us. And an infatuated [*'āshiqu*] creator [*khāliqu*]
contemplates his work [*af'ālahu*], becomes mad
with her [*bi-hā*] and longs for her [*ilay-hā*]: Shall I
make again what I did before?
And the scribes [*kuttābu*] of your lightning [*barqiki*]
between in the sky's ink, and their offspring [*wa-
aḥfāduhum*]
Strew the swallows over the Sumerian [*sūmarīya*]
women's parade [*mawkib*]...
Be she [*kānati*] ascending [*ṣa'idatan*], or descending
[*nāzila*] (41)

5) Open rhyme: an absence of visible "voweling" for the ending of the words, and the sudden break in the poetic line at a possible rhyme is an occasion for the reader to expose or not the rhyme, as in the *damma* or *taskīn* of the word *al-mushāt* [*mushātu* or *mushāt*, respectively], or as in *kasr* or *taskīn* of the word *al-ḥayāt* [*ḥayāti* or *ḥayāt*, respectively], in contrast to the word *dhikrayātī*[8]:

And we listen to what pedestrians [*mushātu*] say
on the bridge:
"I have other things to do"
"I have a place on the ship"
"I have a share in life" [*ḥayāti* or *ḥayāt*]
"And as for me,
I must catch the subway
I am late for memories [*dhikrayātī*]
[...]" (19)

6) The use of a single repeated word as a substitute for rhyme, as in the case of the word *intaẓirha* [wait for her] in the poem "Dars min Kāmā Sūṭrā" ["A Lesson from Kama Sutra"]:

With the drinking glass studded with lapis
wait for her [*intaẓirha*],
by the pool around the evening and the rose perfume
wait for her [*intaẓirha*],
with the patience of the horse prepared for mountain
descent
wait for her [*intaẓirha*]
[...]
with seven pillows stuffed with light clouds
wait for her [*intaẓirha*] (101)

Other research tracks could also have been envisioned. It would have been relevant to compare the poetic language used by Darwish in *Sarīr al-gharība* with that of his previous collections, to analyze the poetic images and their relation to spontaneous prose, to study the contrast between songs of lower tones and intense emotions, and finally to situate this collection in the context of Darwish's larger aesthetic project.

This collection of poems constitutes a new phase in the poetics of Darwish. It redefines the relationship of the poet to Arabic poetry generally. By revealing an incredible capacity for innovation, by challenging the usual poetic ways of expression as well as preconceived categories of national literature, Darwish already joins the space of universal literature, explores while making us discover... and resists! And he is victorious. And so we triumph with him!

6
"Other Barbarians Will Come": Intertextuality, Meta-Poetry, and Meta-Myth in Mahmoud Darwish's Poetry

Reuven Snir

Now what's going to happen to us
without barbarians?
—C.P. Cavafy, "Waiting for the Barbarians"

I wanted to live outside the History
that Empire imposes on its subjects.
—J.M. Coetzee, *Waiting for the Barbarians*

UNTIL THE SECOND HALF OF THE TWENTIETH CENTURY, POETRY WAS the principal channel of literary creativity and served as the chronicle and public register of the Arabs [*al-shi'r dīwān al-'Arab*],[1] recording their very appearance on the stage of history. No other genres could challenge the supremacy of poetry in the field of belles lettres across more than 1,500 years of literary history. The high status poetry enjoyed in Arab society as a whole is reflected in a passage by the eleventh-century scholar Ibn Rashiq al-Qayrawani:

> When a poet appeared in a family of the Arabs, the adjacent tribes would gather together and wish that family the joy of their good luck. Feasts would be got ready, the women of the tribe would join together in bands, playing upon lutes, as they were wont to do at bridals, and the men and boys would congratulate one another; for a poet was a defence of the honour of them all, a weapon to ward off insult from their good name, and a means of perpetuating their glorious deeds and of establishing their fame forever. And they used not to wish one another joy but for three things: the birth of a boy, the coming to light of a poet, and the foaling of a noble mare.[2]

Translations in this chapter are by Reuven Snir unless otherwise noted.

Only in the second half of the twentieth century was poetry pushed to the margins,[3] and prose, especially the novel, became the leading genre.[4] In the early 1970s, the Egyptian magazine *Al-Ṭalīʻa* issued a feature called *Al-Riwāya mir'āt al-shaʻb* [The novel is the mirror of the people] (1971: 10–57), and more than twenty years later, upon his nomination as head of the prose committee of the Supreme Council for Culture in Egypt, ʻAli al-Raʻi (1920–1999) asserted: "This is the time of the novel.... the novel is the new chronicle of the Arabs [*al-riwāya dīwān al-ʻArab al-jadīd*]."[5] Al-Raʻi's imputation to the novel of an historical role may be considered an intertextual, ironic allusion to Ibn al-Rashiq's above quote. "Glory to the Arabic novel!" declared al-Raʻi, "The best of its writers have made it a mouthpiece of the nation, the new annals of the Arabs, and a reservoir of the hopes and agonies of our great but torn nation" (1991: 19). A book published in 2001 by the Egyptian Taha Wadi (b. 1937) bears the title *Al-Qissa dīwān al-ʻArab* [Fiction is the new annals of the Arabs], and the author explains that the narrative genres have become the new Arab chronicle because "they truly reflect their general and personal reality, the social and subjective one" (Wadi 9).

This change in the status of literary genres is not exclusive to Arabic literature. It is a worldwide phenomenon, and has much to do with the hermetic nature of modern poetry, which has become self-regarding and employs obscure imagery and very subjective language. Several reasons have been given for this phenomenon, such as it being the poet's way of passing a negative judgment on the complexities of modern life—on the relatively inaccessible sciences, on the multiple belief systems among which people are asked to discriminate, on the separation of arts from everyday life. Also Arab poets, especially since the mid-1950s, have played down poetry-as-communication or as message and concentrated on exploiting poetry as medium. They tend to write less about public matters and more about themselves and for themselves—or for small coteries equally sensitive.[6] Obscurity is a well-known trait in ancient Arabic literature, especially poetry (Arazi 473–505), but the nature of that obscurity is different—the difficulties in understanding the traditional Arabic ode, the *qaṣīda*, with its conventional form and strict theme sequence, was largely owing to linguistic, rhetorical, and stylistic reasons and to the affectation and mannerisms that began to influence Arabic literature beginning in the Abbasid period (Dayf 275–406). During the second half of the twentieth century, however, canonical Arabic poetry underwent a radical change with the emergence of new sensitivity—the public, clear, and unambiguous style was replaced by a more personal, obscure, and ambiguous one. Additionally, the role of the reader in the concretization of meaning has become crucial and the idea of a matter-of-fact interpretation dictated by the author has gradually disappeared. The awareness that it is the reader who makes sense of a text at both a cognitive and emotional level is now very common. In fact, the same person reading the same text in another time and place may understand it differently from the first time he read it. Furthermore, the process of reading itself becomes significant, or as Stanley Fish put it, "a reader's response to the fifth word in a line or sentence is to a large extent the product of his responses to words one, two, three, and four" ("Literature" 73). It is not only the rational process of constructing meaning that happens gradually but also that of aesthetic experience. "In art," as Viktor Shklovskij put it, "the process of perception is an aesthetic end in itself and must be prolonged. Art is a device for experiencing the process of becoming; that that has already become is of no importance for art" (*Theorie* 14).

The marginalization of poetry, within the already marginalized role of literature in the age of mass media and the internet, has consigned it to being an intimate activity of the lonely reader, far removed from the declarative traditional tone of neoclassical poetry. Yet, although the relationship between poet and reader has undergone an essential change, poetry still functions as a register of the experiences of human beings, recording their miseries, feelings, hopes, and trials, if in new modes. Moreover, poetry as a means of expressing the struggles of a collective is still being written. One example is the poetry used by the Palestinians to chronicle their Nakba (the catastrophe of 1948) and its unending agonies. The present article deals with a chronicle of the Palestinian people in the mid-1980s, against the backdrop of the Israeli invasion of Lebanon in 1982, and prior to the outbreak of the first intifada in the West Bank and Gaza Strip in December 1987; in fact, that chronicle as undertaken by a single poet, Mahmoud Darwish (b. 1941),[7] mainly in one collection, *Ward aqall* [*Fewer Roses*] (1986), and more specifically in one poem, "Sa-ya'tī barābira ākharūn" ["Other Barbarians Will Come"]. The Nakba is always there as a kind of background without which this poetry cannot exist, but the work's main concern is a dialogue with other texts and the interplay not only between reality, poetry, and myth but between poetry, meta-poetry, and meta-myth.

The present essay is an attempt to study the thematic and structural pattern of the collection *Ward aqall* on various levels. Special attention is given to the rhetorical, metrical, graphical, rhythmic, poetic, meta-poetic, and mythical dimensions of the poems. Also, I will argue that each poem of the collection is a microcosm of the entire collection—a detailed analysis of one poem will thus be presented. Throughout the essay I will show that in the mid-1980s Darwish started to present in his poetry "pretexts" in order to explain his uncontrolled desire to write poetry. Also, although being aware of the inadequacies of language and that it can never fully be a substitute for reality, and recognizing the limits of poetry in effecting change in the social and political spheres, especially its limited power in the face of suffering, he must and does return to language; it is all he has recourse to. In other words, he was eager to show that as a poet he cannot be but a poet.

The Persona: "I Am the Last Arab's Sigh"

In one of the first poems in *Ward aqall*, "Idhā kāna lī an u'īda al-bidāya" [If I were to start all over again],[8] the persona asks himself what he would do if he were given the chance to start his life all over again:

> If I could start all over again I'd choose what I have
> chosen: roses on the fence.
> I'd travel again on the roads that may or may not lead
> to Cordova.
> I'd hang my shadow on two rocks for fugitive birds to
> build a nest on my shadow's bough.
> I'd break off my shadow to follow the scent of
> almonds as it wafts on a cloud of dust
> And feel tired at the foot of the mountains; come and
> listen to me. Have some of my bread,

> Drink from my wine and do not leave me on the road
> of years on my own like a tired willow tree.
> I love the countries untrod by migration's song, and
> held captive to neither blood nor woman
> I love women who in their desires conceal the suicide
> of horses at the threshold.

Andalusian Cordova here is the place the persona was exiled from, the mythological homeland he is longing to return to. But reaching this homeland may always remain an illusion:

> I will return, if I can, to my own rose and to my own step,
> But I will never go back to Cordova...[9]

The persona in Darwish's poetry is not only a man expelled from his homeland but a poet who records the feelings and aspirations of his tribe—a single person from a *jamā'a*, a collective that imposed on him the task of representation. The personal and public voices are always co-mingled and the persona-poet's distress is the synecdoche for that of an entire people.

Darwish is only one among numerous Arab poets who, ever since the nineteenth century, have been invoking the image of al-Andalus—Muslim Spain—in their poetry.[10] As such they are part of a much wider phenomenon: a conscious effort on the part of contemporary Arab poets and writers to highlight al-Andalus experience and the benefits Western civilization has gained through its interaction with Arab civilization.[11] Furthermore, when poets recall the cultural achievements of the Arabs in al-Andalus—from the time Arabs and Berber troops crossed the Straits of Gibraltar into Iberia in 711 and overthrew the Visigoths, commencing nearly 800 years of Muslim rule on the peninsula—they do so to remind their audience that their bitter state in modern times is only a transitory period, a temporary clouding of the skies between a glorious past and a splendid future. Though the Andalusian period was one of political fragmentation and local dynasties (known as *mulūk al-ṭawā'if*, "party kings"), it was also a period of great cultural efflorescence which lasted continuously in one form or another up until the fall of Granada in 1492 to the Christians. Inspired by nostalgia, the picture that most frequently appears in modern Arabic literary writings is that of al-Andalus as the lost paradise [*al-firdaws al-mafqūda*] or God's paradise on earth [*jannat Allāh 'alā al-arḍ*].

For Mahmoud Darwish, the main Andalusian sites (Cordova, Granada, Toledo, and Seville) are icons whose meanings go far beyond the historical, external, or sensuous dimensions of these places. Cordova, as the famous center of Andalusian learning and culture, is not just the historical city but also a trope for the "Palestinian" experience, signifying the lost paradise. As one Palestinian scholar says: "If circumstances prevented the poet from reaching Jerusalem and he was forced to go to Cordova, the idea is that his creative journey stopped as well and remains a dream with a chance of ever being fulfilled" (al-Ju'aydi, "Ḥuḍūr al-Andalus" 17). In Darwish's poetry, Andalusian sites have the same emotional resonance as "tears, dance and the long embrace of a woman. Al-Andalus is a universal aesthetic and artistic property, but Jerusalem is an aesthetic, spiritual and juristic property" (36). In Psalm 16 from his *Mazāmīr* [Psalms] (in *Dīwān* vol. 1, 396–397), Darwish flirts with time "as a prince caresses a horse."

And I play with the days
As children play with colored beads.

Today I celebrate
The passing of a day from the previous one
And tomorrow I shall celebrate
The passing of two days from yesterday.
I drink the toast of yesterday
In remembrance of the day to come
And thus do I carry on my life!

When I fell from my indomitable horse
And broke an arm
My finger, wounded a thousand years ago,
Caused me pain!

When I commemorated the passing of forty days in
    the city of Acre,
I burst out weeping for Granada
And when the rope of the gallows tightened around
    my neck

I felt a deep hatred for my enemies
Because they stole my tie.
(translation follows that of Johnson-Davies in
Darwish, *Music* 50)

One of the prominent themes in Darwish's poetry after the Israeli invasion of Lebanon in 1982 is the use of al-Andalus as a mirror for Palestine.[12] His series of poems entitled "Aḥada 'ashara kawkaban 'alā ākhiri al-mashhadi al-Andalusī" [Eleven stars at the end of the Andalusian scene], from the collection *Aḥada 'ashara kawkaban* [Eleven stars], is one long repetition of the equation al-Andalus = Palestine = Paradise Lost. Apart from the clear allusion to the advent of the miseries of the "present" following the end of the "Andalusian scene," the title also "justifies" this end by evoking the biblical and Qur'anic story of Joseph and his brothers (see below). Significantly, Darwish published the collection in 1992, that is, 500 years after the end of Arab rule in al-Andalus, when on January 2, 1492, the combined armies of Castile and Aragon captured the city of Granada, followed by a royal edict that decreed the expulsion of all non-Catholics from the peninsula. The fourth star poem is called "Anā waḥid min mulūk al-nihāya" [I am one of the kings of the end]:

... And I am one of the Kings of the end... jumping from
My horse in the last Winter, I am the last Arab man's
sigh [...]
There is no present remaining for me,
So I could pass near my past. Castile is raising her
Crown over Allah's minaret. I hear the rattling of keys in
The door of our golden history, good-bye our history,
will it be me
Who will close the last gate of heaven? I am the last
Arab man's sigh. (*Ahada* 15–16)

Against the glory of the past, which elicits the image of al-Andalus in the present, the only remaining hope—in this long poor "present" that has been enduring for more than 500 years—is survival. Al-Andalus is mere mirage:

> Where should we go after the last border? Where do
> the birds fly after the last sky?
> Where do the plants sleep after the last breeze?
> (*Ward aqall* 17; for a translation of the entire poem,
> see *Unfortunately* 9)

For the time being:

> Thirty seas have we passed, and sixty shores
> And our days of wandering continue. (*Hiya* 43)

Each abode is a temporary shelter in a "series of moveable shelters" (*Dhākira* 73; *Memory* 90). "My bundle is my village" (*Ward* 17), declares one woman in the Athens airport. The men are despairing:

> We said to our wives: yield us offspring for hundreds
> of years so we can complete this journey.
> Toward an hour of a land, and a meter of the
> impossible.
> (*Ward* 21; for an alternative translation, see
> *Unfortunately* 11)

The airport becomes a cross road of repressed desires and frequent frustrations:

> Where will I fight? asked the fighter. A pregnant
> woman
> Shrieked to him: where will I bear your child? [...]
> Where did you come from? asked the customs'
> officials. We responded:
> From the sea. And where are you heading? they asked.
> To the sea, we said. [...]
> A young lad married a maiden, but they could not find
> any place for a hasty marriage.
> Where will I pierce her maidenhood? he asked. But
> we laughed and said:
> O lad, there is no place for such a question.
> (*Ward* 23; for an alternative translation, see
> *Unfortunately* 12)

A Palestinian man has been shunted about from emigration to exile, from sea to desert, from detention camp to slaughter:

> Thus, he confronts other questions besides those of freedom and independence, the questions of normal human existence on the face of the earth: Where to go? Where to give birth? Where to sleep? Where to work? Where to learn? Where to love? Where to write poems? And where to be buried? (*Al-Karmel* 16 1985: 249–252)

Meanwhile:

> We go toward a land not of our flesh. The chestnut
> trees are not of our bones
> And its stones are not a goat in the mountain hymn
> [...]
> We go toward a land where a personal sun does not
> shine above us.
> (*Ward* 19; for a translation of the entire poem, see
> *Unfortunately* 10)

What an irony, after being expelled from Beirut and Tripoli, thousands of miles away, to find refuge in a place named for the Garden of Eden:

> We went to Aden [...]
> We went to the poverty-stricken paradise of the poor
> people, so as to open a window in the stone.
> The tribes besieged us, O my friend, and cast us into
> tribulations,
> Nevertheless we didn't exchange the bread of the trees
> for the enemy's loaf.
> (*Ward* 47; for a translation of the entire poem, see
> *Unfortunately* 24)

Rather than surrender they prefer death on the battlefield—"We will write for the thousandth time on the last air: we shall die, but they will not overtake us" (*Ward* 35; for a translation of the entire poem, see *Unfortunately* 18)—but without losing sympathy for the victims among their enemies:

> We saw the faces of those who will be killed in the
> last defense of the spirit by the last of us.
> We wept for their children's holiday. And we saw the
> faces of those who will throw our children
> From the window of this terminal emptiness.
> (*Ward* 17; for a translation of the entire poem, see
> *Unfortunately* 9)

There is not only despair but self-flagellation: "there is no more hope to be placed in the Arabs. A nation which does not deserve to live. A nation in the image of its rulers" (*Dhākira* 81; *Memory* 100). When the fighters were about to leave Beirut in 1982, the question remained— whither?

> —Is it true we are leaving?
> —We are leaving.
> —Where to?
> —To any Arab place which will take us.
> —Won't they be willing to accept us when we leave?
> —Some of them won't even take our corpses. The United States is asking some of them to agree to receive us.
> —The United States?
> —Yes, the United States.
> —Do you mean that [the Arabs] want us to commit suicide and stay in Beirut?
> —They can't stand our steadfastness. They aren't telling us to commit suicide, like the Libyan Colonel [Qadhafi]; they just don't want us to stay in Beirut, or any other place on earth. They want us to leave, to leave Arabism and leave life.
> —To leave it for what destination?
> —Nothingness! (*Dhākira* 105–106; *Memory* 132–133)

A substantive change has taken place over the years in the attitude of the Arabs:

> There were times when a blow to Palestine filled the Arab street with gloom, turmoil and rage. The Arab street would overthrow the ruler for any injury

> whatsoever to this collective heart. Now, the rulers are bribing the street in order to make it renege on this consensus. The official Arab weaponry has been turned publicly against Palestinian activity and ideology and is making them fully responsible for the wretchedness and subjugation of the Arab nation. Were it not for Palestine—the mirage, the unattainable, the imaginary [...] our freedom would be fuller and our prosperity even greater. (*Dhākira* 84; *Memory* 105)

Moreover:

> Palestine has been transformed from a homeland into an empty slogan, a commentary on events, adorning the rhetoric of revolutions, dismantling political parties and preventing the sowing of wheat, the exchange of labor for quick profits, and the development of the industry of revolution. (*Dhākira* 40; *Memory* 49)

The various conferences that convene to discuss the Palestinian tragedy are a source of bitter irony. At one of them, the persona takes the floor to ask:

> Good ladies and gentlemen: is the earth of man for every man
> As you claim? Where thus is my little hut, and where am I?

The best that the Arabs could supply is

> Three minutes of freedom and recognition. The conference affirmed
> Our right to return, like all chickens and horses, to a dream made of stone.
> One by one, I shake their hands, and bow my head, and continue this journey
> To another land, to say something about the difference between the mirage and the rain.
> (*Ward* 25; for a translation of the entire poem, see *Unfortunately* 13)

"The Empire of Arabic Words," as described by the Syrian poet Nizar Qabbani (1923–1998), becomes greater and greater "and our defeats grow bigger… and our hopes dwindle" (Qabbani 6–7). Even the Palestinian revolution itself has clearly gone off course:

> Perhaps it is appropriate to judge the revolution for its absence of a tradition for judging its leadership's crimes, which cry out to heaven. Instead, the judging was limited to following the moral crimes of the future martyrs while pursuing the transitory pleasures of a hashish cigarette or seductive women, before their bodies become a podium for speeches. (*Dhākira* 27; *Memory* 31)

But, as the poet describes in an earlier collection, there will be harder days ahead:

> There will be blacker night. There will be fewer and
> fewer roses
> The trail will split even more than we have seen, the
> plains will be sundered,
> The foot of the mountain will heave out upon us, a
> wound will collapse upon us, families will be
> scattered.
> The slaughtered among us will slaughter the
> slaughtered, to forget the slaughtered's eyes,
> and to erase memory.
> We will know more than we knew, we will reach an
> abyss beyond the abysses when we rise above
> A thought which the tribes worshipped then roasted it
> on the flesh of its originators, when they had
> grown fewer.
> We will see among us emperors etching their names in
> wheat in order to refer to
> Ourselves. Haven't we changed? Men who slaughter
> with the faith of their daggers, and more and
> more sand,
> Women with the faith of what is between their thighs,
> and less and less shadow…
>
> Still, I will follow the path of song, even though I
> have fewer and fewer roses.
> (*Ward* 45; for a translation of the entire poem, see
> *Unfortunately* 23)

In "Al-Kamanjāt" [Violins], the memory of the lost paradise also becomes the lost territory of love:

Violins are weeping, seeing the gypsies coming to al-
Andalus
Violins are weeping over the Arabs leaving al-Andalus

Violins are weeping over lost time which will never
return
Violins are weeping over a lost homeland that could
return

Violins are burning the forests of that very far darkness
Violins are causing knives to bleed and are smelling
the blood in my veins

Violins are weeping, seeing the gypsies coming to al-
Andalus
Violins are weeping over the Arabs leaving al-Andalus

Violins are horses on the string of a mirage, and
weeping water
Violins are a field of wild lilacs to-ing and fro-ing

Violins are a wild animal tortured by a woman's
fingernail
Violins are an army building a cemetery of marble and
music

Violins are a chaos of hearts maddened by the wind
blowing at the dancer's foot
Violins are groups of birds escaping the missed flag

Violins are the complaint of the creased silk during
the beloved's night
Violins are the voice of distant wine on a former
desire

Violins are walking after me, here and there, to take
revenge on me
Violins are looking to kill me, wherever they can find me

> Violins are weeping over the Arabs leaving al-Andalus
> Violins are weeping, seeing the gypsies coming to al-
> Andalus[13]

In another poem Darwish asks his friend to "tear the arteries of my ancient heart with the poem of the gypsies who are going to al-Andalus/ and sing to my departure from the sands and the ancient poets" (*Ḥiṣār* 23).

The Palestinian miseries as illustrated in the image of the Andalusian paradise lost are the major stimuli behind the collection *Ward aqall*, whose poems were written during and in the wake of the 1982 Israeli invasion of Lebanon.

The Collection: Variations on One Theme

Ward aqall, which includes 50 poems, is a very coherent and cohesive—like the verses in a 50-verse *qaṣīda*, each poem echoes the same ideas. At the same time, each poem is a microcosm of the entire collection. The Palestinian poet Salman Masalha (b. 1953) understood this peculiarity of the collection immediately upon its publication and composed a poem that consists of the titles of the poems ("'Anāwīn lil-nafs" [The soul has addresses]). In order to emphasize the collection's cohesion and organic unity, several techniques and strategies were employed by Darwish on various levels. We will concentrate in the following sections on the most outstanding of them, from both aspects of form and content, that is, the peculiarity of choosing the titles of the poems, the homogenous meter, the flexible and simple rhymes as well as the poetic, meta-poetic, and mythical dimensions.

Titles

Grammatically, the titles are complete independent clauses [*jumal mufīda*]: either nominative, with a subject and predicate [*jumla ismīya: mubtada' + khabar*], or verbal, with a verb and subject [*jumla fi'līya: fi'l + fā'il*]. The title of one poem, "Maṭār Athīnā" ["Athens Airport"] (23), is not a complete grammatical clause, but even this title may be read as the predicate of an omitted subject: "[Hādhā] Maṭār Athīnā" [This is Athens Airport]. Moreover, it may be understood as a subject whose verb has been omitted, since the function of an airport is to serve as a spatial and temporal transitive point; the first complete independent sentence of the poem reflects this aspect of the airport: *maṭār Athīnā yūwazzi'unā lil-maṭārāti* [Athens airport disperses us to other airports]. Each title consists of between two and six words—all of which are taken from the first part of the first line. Only the titles of six poems are not precisely the first words of the poems, but the changes herein are minor. An examination of the few diversions reveals what was important to the poet from the standpoint of the poem and the structure of the title.

First, he condensed some titles to keep them short; for example, in "Yaḥiqqu lanā an nuḥibba al-kharīf" [We have the right to love Autumn] (25) the first words are: "Wa-naḥnu yaḥiqqu lanā an nuḥibba nihāyati hādhā al-kharīf" [And we indeed have the right to love the end of this Autumn]; three words were omitted because the title would have been too long. In another poem, "Ilāhī limādhā takhallayta 'annī?" [My God, my God, why hast Thou forsaken me] (81), the first words of the poem are: "Ilāhī ilāhī limādhā takhallayta 'annī?"; one word was omitted. In "Astaṭī'u al-kalāma 'ani al-ḥubb" [I can talk about love] (99), the first words are: "Wa-hā anadhā astaṭī'u al-kalāma 'ani al-ḥubbi" [And here I am able to talk about love]; one word was omitted. In "Nu'rrikhkhu ayyāmanā bi-farāshi" [We write the history of our days with butterflies] (103), the first words are "Nu'rrikhkhu ayyāmanā bi-farāshi al-ḥuqūli" [We write the history of our days with the butterflies of the fields]; also one word was omitted.

Second, the internal music of the poem was important to the poet. For example, in the poem titled "Ṣahīlun 'alā al-ssafḥi" [Neighing at the foot of the mountain] (37) the first words of the poem are "Ṣahīlu al-khuyūli 'alā al-ssafḥi" [The neighing of the horses at the foot of the mountain]. He adds the word *al-khuyūli* [the horses] although it is not essential for conveying the meaning, since *ṣahīl* [neighing] in Arabic is used only for horses. The title is much more poetic and condensed; however, without this word the first line would have been devoid of its peculiar musical dimension: it may be divided into two parts—as if they were *ṣadr* [first hemistich] and *'ajuz* [second hemistich] of a classical verse [*bayt*] in a *qaṣīda*. In addition, the same line is repeated in line four; and in line nine there is a variation of the line but with the same musicality. This line thus serves as a sort of *lazima*—a refrain, a kind of "filler" or key sentence that outlines the "melodic structure" [Racy 82, 224]—of the poem and combines its various elements into a single entity, as may be seen in the following transliterated version:

(1) Ṣah**ī**l**u**lkh**uyū**l**i** 'alāl-ssafḥ**i**, **i**mmālh**ubū**ṭ**u** wa-**i**mmālṣ**u**'**ū**d**u**.
(4) Ṣah**ī**l**u**lkh**uyū**l**i** 'alāl-ssafḥ**i**, **i**mmālh**ubū**ṭ**u** wa-**i**mmālṣ**u**'**ū**d**u**.
(9) Ṣah**ī**l**u**lkh**uyū**l**i** 'alāl-ssafḥ**i**, **i**mmālṣ**u**'**ū**d**u** wa-**i**mmālṣ**u**'**ū**d**u**.

The alternation of the short and long vowels of i/i and u/u may be seen as a kind of simulation of the movement of the horses at the foot of the mountain.

Meter

According to the conventional metrical system that was unchallenged in Arabic poetry from the pre-Islamic times till the mid-twentieth century, every verse [*bayt*] in a *qaṣīda* [the classical ode] consists of a certain number of feet [*taf'īla*, plural *tafā'īl*], divided into two hemistichs. Every foot [*taf'īla*] consists of short (U) and long (-) vowels. Each one of the sixteen meters consists of different sequences of feet. A common rhyme is used at the end of each verse throughout the entire poem even if it consists of hundreds of verses. In the late 1940s, there emerged a new metrical system of "free verse" called in Arabic *shi'r ḥurr* [free poetry] or *shi'r al-taf'īla* [poetry of *taf'īla*]. The essential concept of this system entails a reliance on free repetition of the *taf'īla*, the basic unit of the conventional Arab prosody—i.e., the use of an irregular number of a single foot instead of a fixed number of feet as was dictated by the classical meters. Additionally, in *shi'r ḥurr* there is no need for a common rhyme throughout the poem. The poet varies the number of feet in a single line and the rhymes at the end of the lines according to his need. In Darwish's collection all the poems use the new system of "free verse," but what is highly peculiar in this collection is that a single foot, that of the *mutaqārib* meter (U - -), is used in all of the poems. This is a rare phenomenon in Arabic poetry; ever since ancient times poets, even if they wrote on the same theme, generally used various meters for different poems, as in the case of the *qaṣīda*; modern poets have used various feet for different poems. Here Darwish uses the same single foot for all the poems, as if to direct the attention of the reader to the unified character of the collection. Of course, it is this unity of the meter that enabled Salman Masalha to compose a poem from the titles of all the poems, serving as a kind of summary of the entire collection.

Graphic Appearance

The poems share approximately the same graphic design; the length and number of lines are very similar. Forty-three poems have ten lines, four poems have eleven lines, two poems have thirteen lines, and one poem has nine lines. Most of the poems pretend to be prose paragraphs, far away from the traditional structure of the *qaṣīda* or even the familiar structure of the *shi'r ḥurr* with its short lines.

Rhymes

Darwish employs various rhyme schemes in *Ward aqall*, but in all cases the rhyming is functional and by no means dictates the meaning, as we frequently find in traditional poetry when poets are tempted to use a "successful" rhyme even if it does not help express the desired meaning. Darwish's rhymes are very simple and usually feel effortless. None of the rhymes may be attributed to the kind of *ḥashw* [stuffing; i.e., the use of a word only because it fits the rhyme or meter] so frequently found in classical and neoclassical poems. The poems in the collection may be divided into the following groups based on their rhyme schemes:

Mono-rhyme poems: Eight poems pretend to be a one-rhyme classical *qaṣīda*; three of them have one united rhyme (19 [*nu*], 25 [*ar*], 103 [*mina*]). In two poems, one united rhyme is used (35 [*ru*], 45 [*lu*]) but the last line of each poem is separated from the other lines. In two cases the poems are strophic, but with one rhyme (99 [*di*], 101 [*la*]). In one poem the united rhyme (*dah* with one case of *ha*) is broken by the last line—which does not share the same rhyme—in order to emphasize the voice of the poem (the last word is *waṭan* [homeland]) (13).

Duo-rhyme poems: Thirteen poems use rhyme schemes with only two different rhymes:

ABBABBBBBA (5)
AABBAABBAA (21 [*ar* / *il*], 31 [*mu* / *ihim*])
ABABABABAB (27 [*ah* / *ma*], 29 [*ad* / *am*], 57 [*at* / *ah*])
ABBABBAAA (37 [*du* / *ar*])
AABAABAABB (43 [*a'* / *ah*])
ABA/BAB/ABA/B (47 [*ar* / *an*])
ABABABABA/B (91 [*ah* / *aq*)
AABABBAABA (49 [*ii* / *lak*])
AABBAAB/BBA (51 [*aa* / *qa*])
ABAABBABBA (61 [*a'a*])
ABBABBBBBA (69 [*ah* / *an*])
AB/BA/AB/BA/BA (83 [*ab* / *lah*])
ABBBAABAAB (97 [*si* / *ad*])
Trio-rhyme poems: Eight poems use rhyme schemes with three different rhymes:
ABABABABCA (7)
AABCAACAAA (15)
ABACBABAAAA (55)
AABA/AACAAA (73)
ABACADAABA (75)
ABBABBBCA (81 [A=Maryam])
AAA/BBA/CCA/A (85)
ABBBBBCBBB (93)
Quadro-rhyme poems: Seven poems use rhyme schemes with four rhymes:
ABCBCBBBDB (9)
ABBBBBCDBB (17)
AAA/BBB/CCD/D (39)
A/BCDDDDDD/D (65)
ABCABADAAA (71)
ABBBBCDEBB (79)
ABCCCC/CCDD (89)
Casual rhymes: Two poems use only casual rhyming:
ABCBDEBFBFBF (53)
ABCBCDCEF/A (59)
Unique scheme: One poem has three stanzas, each of them beginning with the same sentence (*'alā hadhihi al-arḍ mā yastaḥiqqu al-ḥayāt*) and the end of each stanza rhymes with this

sentence (*āt*). Each stanza is a kind of long line divided into three or four lines according to the format of the page (11).
No rhymes: Six poems are without any rhyming; the page layout generally determines the number of lines. These poems are structured like prose poems, but unlike them they have the same metrical foot (23, 33, 41 [the first line is broken], 63, 77, 87). In one poem the lines are broken (95).

Poetic, Meta-Poetic, and Mythical Dimensions

All the poems are linked by the persona, who represents all the members of a collective and as their poetic proxy suffers on their behalf. It means that not only the reality is represented but also the manner of representation is also questioned, including issues related to the value of poetry and its relationship to universal questions. Two poems in the collection provide the persona with the mythical foundations through two biblical myths, the first being "Yu'āniqu qātilahu" [He embraces his murderer], which appears as poem number fifteen in the collection:

> He embraces his murderer in order to win his
> compassion: Will you be much angry if I survive?
> My brother, oh my brother! What did I do that you
> want to kill me? Two birds are overhead—shoot
> Upward! Shoot your hell far away from me. Come to
> my mother's hut so she may cook for you
> Broad beans. What do you say? What is that you say?
> You grow tired of my embrace and my smell.
> Are you tired of
> The fear within me? So throw your revolver in the
> river! What do you say? There is an enemy on
> The riverbank aiming his machine gun at our
> embrace? So shoot toward the enemy
> So that we may avoid the enemy's bullets, and you
> may avoid falling into sin. What do you say?
> You will kill me so the enemy can go to his own
> home/our home and you can return to the
> game of the cave. What
> Have you done with the coffee of my mother and
> your mother? What crime did I commit that you
> want to kill me, oh my brother? I will

> never unloose the knot of the embrace,
> I will never leave you!
> (*Ward* 33; for a freer translation that omits several
> sentences, see *Unfortunately* 17)

Embracing his brother, Cain, who is about to slay him, Abel is not ready to relent, striving desperately to elicit his brothers' mercy.[14] The intertextual allusion to the ancient myth is reinforced by the sentence "Two birds are overhead"—an allusion to the Qur'anic story about Cain and Abel, when God sent a crow to scratch in the earth and show Cain how he might hide his brother's shame (al-Ma'ida 30–34). In the poem a rhetorical question is repeated in two modes: *mā ṣana'tu li-taghtālanī*? [What did I do that you want to kill me?] (line two) and *mādhā janaytu li-taghtālanī*? [What crime did I commit that you want to kill me?] (line nine)—the murder foretold has no rationale at all. At the same time the speaker is eager to hear his brother reply, and so repeats the question *mādhā taqūlu*? [What do you say?] four times in this short poem, but his brother utters no reply and the poem concludes with an exclamation mark; the speaker has been slain by his brother and his last cry—"I will never leave you!"—is in fact also a curse, the Curse of Cain.

In a certain way, Gabriel Garcia Marquez's *Chronicle of a Death Foretold* is here recalled, the story of a murder everyone knows about before it happens—with the exception of the murdered man, Santiago Nasar. But unlike in Marquez's novel, in Darwish's poem the victim does know of his impending murder and demands an explanation for it—in fact, he is more concerned with plumbing the murderer's motives than preventing the murder itself. As in Marquez's novel even though everyone knows the murder is going to happen no one intervenes to stop it. Why not? The more that the reader learns, the less he understands, and as the story races toward its inexplicable conclusion, an entire society is placed on trial. Elsewhere, Darwish mentions a "knight who stabs his brother/ with a dagger in the name of the homeland" (*Ḥiṣār* 136).

In another poem, number 37 in the collection, "Anā Yūsufun yā abī" [Oh, Father, I Am Joseph], the persona, Joseph, complains to his father that his brothers want to kill him:

Oh, Father, I am Joseph. Oh, Father, my brothers
neither love me nor want me in their midst, oh
Father, they assault me and cast stones and words at
me. They want me to die so
They can eulogize me. They closed the door of your
house and left me outside. They expelled me
from the field. Oh, Father, they
Poisoned my grapes. They destroyed my toys, oh,
Father. When the gentle wind played with my
Hair they were jealous, they flamed up with rage
against me and against you. What did I do to
them, oh, Father?
The butterflies landed on my shoulder, the wheat
spikes bent down toward me and the birds
hovered over
My hands. What have I done, oh, Father? And why
me? You named me Joseph and they
Threw me into the well and accused the wolf, and the
wolf is more merciful than my brothers, oh,
Father!
Did I wrong anyone when I said: "I saw eleven stars,
and the sun and the moon; I saw them
bowing down before me."[15]

The persona addresses his father, stating "I *am* Joseph," as though the father does not know his own son, and he complains about the brothers who assault him—the dialectical tension is thus between the son, the father, and the brothers. The father shares responsibility for the persona's fate for having sired him and named him Joseph and by doing so caused his misery, as if the very act of naming could define the fate of human being (on the evil inflicted by the father, see also below). The last words of the poem employ the fourth verse from Sūrat Yūsuf, in which Joseph address his father Jacob (both of them revered in Islam as prophets):

When Joseph said to his father, "Father, I saw eleven
stars, and the sun and the moon; I saw them
bowing down before me."

The singer Marcel Khalifa (b. 1940), who earned a cult following in the Arab world and the diaspora through his nationalistic songs during the Lebanese civil war, set the poem to music and sang it.[16] Besides the repetition of sentences, only minor changes were introduced to the lyrics: a few words were substituted (*'indamā* instead of *ḥīna*; *aqfalū* instead of *awṣadū*; *katifī* instead of *katifāyya*; *ṣana'tu* instead of *fa'ltu*; *wahum* instead of *wahumu*), a sentence was omitted ("wa-hum ḥaṭṭamū lu'abī, yā abī" [They destroyed my toys, oh, Father]), and the song's beginning does not follow exactly the order of narration in the poem. However, the changes made in the song do not have any influence on the meaning of the original but only reinforce the dramatic tension and conflict between the persona and his brothers.

In September 1996 the chief prosecutor of Beirut charged Khalifa with blasphemy for allegedly "insulting Islam" by singing the Qur'anic verse,[17] but following the protests of many Lebanese Muslim and Christian poets, writers, and journalists, the Lebanese Prime Minister Rafiq al-Hariri ordered that the lawsuit against Khalifa be dismissed.[18]

Darwish's poem depicts a relationship between the persona and the collective similar to that presented in "He Embraces His Murderer" as well as showing a like degree of astonishment as to why the persona's life is in danger; the same kind of questions are presented here: "fa-mādhā fa'ltu anā yā abī?" [What did I do to them, oh Father?] and "hal janaytu 'alā aḥadin?" [Did I wrong anyone?] (line 9). The latter is nearly the same wording as the second hemistich of a famous verse by the ascetic poet Abu al-'Ala' al-Ma'arri (973–1057), which he wished to have inscribed on his grave: "hādhā janāhū abī 'alayya wamā janaytu 'alā aḥad" [This wrong was done by my father to me, but never by me to another] (al-Ma'arri 184; cf. Husayn, *Al-Majmū'a* 189–190, 306–307). Because al-Ma'arri's ascetic proclivity made him angry at his father for having sired him, he abstained from sexual congress so as not to spawn any offspring of his own. Darwish stresses the evil inflicted on Abel and Joseph by their own fathers—both of whom, Adam and Jacob, are considered in Islam as prophets—through an allusion to al-Ma'arri's verse.

The two aforementioned myths, together with the above series of poems entitled "Aḥada 'ashara kawkaban 'alā ākhiri al-mashhadi al-Andalusī" [Eleven stars at the end of the Andalusian scene] which evokes the story of Joseph by recalling the Andalusian lost paradise, are in fact presenting the same theme: the cause of the Palestinians' suffering is not only due to external threats—for example, for the persona, some of his own "friends" even "desire my death in order to say: he was one of us, he was ours" (*Ward* 41; for another translation, see *Unfortunately* 21). Echoing the desperate cry from "Oh, Father, I Am Joseph"—"They want me to die so/ They can eulogize me"—the mission is to protect the martyrs from such eulogy-lovers:

> When the martyrs go to sleep, I wake to guard them
> from the eulogy-lovers;
> I say to them: I hope you awaken in a homeland of
> clouds and trees, of mirage and water.
> I wish them well-being from the impossible.
> (*Ward* 43; for another translation, see *Unfortunately* 22)

Here the poet-persona in fact confronts the "eulogy-lovers" on the meta-poetic level, one of the main discursive levels in *Ward aqall*. He addresses his complaint to God, just as Jesus did on the cross (Matt. 27:46):

> My God, my God, why hast thou forsaken me? [...]
> Why did you promise the soldiers my only vineyard,
> why? [...]
> You created two peoples from a single stalk,
> You betrothed me to an idea, and I obeyed; I
> completely obeyed your future wisdom.
> Have you divorced me? Or have you hastened to save
> another, my enemy, from the guillotine?
> (*Ward* 81)

Against this main theme of the collection, it is obvious why the intertextual allusions and the meta-poetic and meta-mythical dimensions of the collection come to the fore: the persona is a poet confronting other poets of his community, who desire his death in order to have some "inspiration" or to make a living by writing eulogies. Poetry is for them no more than a means to gain material profit. The following section traces the aforementioned allusions and dimensions in one poem from the collection.

The Poem: "Will Homer be Born After Us?"

Other Barbarians Will Come

Other barbarians will come. The emperor's wife will be abducted. Drums will beat 1
Drums will be beaten so that the horses will trample corpses from the Aegean Sea to the Dardanelles 2
But what have we got to do with it? What have our wives got to do with this horse race? 3

The emperor's wife will be abducted. Drums will beat. And other barbarians will come 4
Barbarians that will fill the vacuum of the cities, somewhat higher than the sea, stronger than the sword in times of madness 5
But what have we got to do with it? What have our children got to do with the offspring of this impudence? 6

And drums will beat. And other barbarians will come. The emperor's wife will be abducted from his house 7
And from his house the military expedition will be born to bring back the bride into his Highness's bed 8
But what have we got to do with it? What do fifty thousand victims have to do with this quickie marriage? 9

Will Homer be born after us, and the myths open their gates to all? 10
(*Ward* 39; for an alternative translation, see *Unfortunately* 22)

Rhetorical Structure

The poem, which uses the same *mutaqārib* meter as the other poems in the collection,[19] consists of ten lines with the following rhyme scheme: aaa/bbb/ccd/d—each line ending with a silent vowel [*taskīn*]. The lines are arranged in three stanzas and the last line is isolated as if to form a kind of fourth stanza.

Each of the three main stanzas has the same structure. The first line of each stanza consists of the same three verbal sentences but in a different order. The three sentences are as follows: "Other Barbarians will come" (a); "The Emperor's wife will be abducted" (b); "Drums will beat" (c).

The second line of each stanza consists of a direct link to the last component of the first line in each stanza (c, a, b respectively), and then of an action that develops from that link (d).

The third line of each stanza consists of two questions, the first of them identical in all stanzas (e); the second has the same structure and the same broad meaning (f).

The last line (g), which is isolated from the main body of the poem, does not have a direct connection to the three stanzas; it is connected by a rhyme with the last line of the third stanza. We can present the rhetorical structure of the poem as follows (the letters illustrate the aforementioned components in each line and the numeral is a variation of the component):

(a)(b)(c)
(c1)(d1)
(e)(f1)

(b)(c)(a)
(a1)(d2)
(e)(f2)

(c)(a)(b)
(b1)(d3)
(e)(f3)

(g)

From first glance it seems that changing the three components in the first line of each stanza undermines the usual sequence of cause and effect: is it because the emperor's wife will be abducted by the barbarians that war will be declared? Or will war be declared before they come and will they be a kind of excuse for the war, which will be declared only so as to provide entertainment for the emperor?

Verbs

The use of verbs in the poem betrays a dynamic motion by means of two modes: *taswīf* (henceforth S) and *muḍāri'* (henceforth M). The *taswīf* is used in Arabic, with the prefix *sawf* or only *sa*, to express an action which will occur in the remote future; the *muḍāri'* is used in order to express events in the present or near future. For example, the first stanza begins with three verbs in the *taswīf* mode: *sa-ya'ti*, *sa-tukhṭafu*, and *sawfa taduqqu*. In the second line there are two verbs in *muḍāri'* mode. The third line is without any verb at all. As one reads, the number of verbs denoting the remote future gradually decreases while the number denoting the present and the near future increases, as if to reflect the movement of the barbarians toward the persona and the collective he represents. The first word of the title, which is also the first word of the first line—*sa-ya'ti* (S)—alludes to the style of religious texts about the coming of prophets and the Day of Judgment (cf. Post 6–7, s.v.; 'Abd al-Baqi 6, s.v.; Wensinck and Mensing 9–10, s.v.). Together with the second word, it might be understood as future-oriented or as an eschatological myth (Sivan 9). In order to show the balance between future and present, what follows is a scheme of the verbs in the poem and their temporal denotation:

sa-ya'ti (S)/ *sa-tukhṭafu* (S)/ *sawfa taduqqu* (S) 1
tudaqqu (M)/ *li-ta'lū* (M) 2
no verbs 3

sa-tukhṭafu (S)/ *sawfa taduqqu* (S)/ *wa-ya'ti* (M) 4
yaml'ūna (M) 5
no verbs 6

sawfa taduqqu (S)/ *wa-ya'ti* (M)/ *wa-tukhṭafu* (M) 7
tūladu (M)/ *tu'ida* (M) 8
no verbs 9

'a-yūladu (M)/ *taftaḥu* (M) 10

In the first stanza three of the five verbs are in *taswīf*; in the second only two of four; in the third only one of five; and none of the two verbs in the last line denotes the remote future. The event in the poem starts off by being in the remote future, but as one reads this future becomes the present. The third line in each stanza in the original is without any verbs at all, as if to show that events that will happen in the remote future have already marked the present. It should be noted that in Arabic there are two kinds of clauses, verbal and nominal. The nominal clause may be either with a verb (but not in the beginning of the sentence!) or without. Here, the third line of each stanza consists of two nominal clauses without verbs at all. However, although the use of the verbs in the poem reflects the movement of the barbarians toward the persona, by the absence of verbs at the end of each of the three stanzas the reader is led to the conclusion that the barbarians will not come. The poem has thus two motions: on the thematic, grammatical, and rhetorical levels the barbarians are advancing, but it is clear that what has already come is only the catastrophe for which the Emperor wants the people to believe that the barbarians are to blame.

Intertextuality

The title of the poem makes several allusions, the most famous of them being to the barbarians who brought about the destruction of the Roman Empire. The barbarians are perceived in the general public discourse as agents of destruction who are teeming at the gates of civilization. However, due to the marginal status of poetry in the public discourse, it is evident that the poem's mainspring is not a dialogue at the public level but on the meta-poetic one. In this sense Darwish is following in the footsteps of ʻAli Ahmad Saʻid (Adonis) (b. 1930) who stated that the readership of the revolutionary Arab poet consists not of consumers [*mustahlikūn*] but of producers [*muntijūn*] (Adonis, *Zaman* 95–96). Darwish's poem thus conducts a dialogue on the meta-poetic level with other texts, the most famous of these being "Waiting for the Barbarians" (1904) by the Greek poet Constantine P. Cavafy (1863–1933):

> What are we waiting for, assembled in the forum?
>
> The barbarians are due here today.

Why isn't anything going on in the Senate?
Why are the Senators sitting there without legislating?

> Because the barbarians are coming today.
> What's the point of senators making laws now?
> When the barbarians are here, they'll do the
> legislating.

Why did our emperor get up so early,
and why is he sitting enthroned at the city's main gate,
in state, wearing the crown?

> Because the barbarians are coming today
> and the emperor's waiting to receive their
> leader.
> He's even got a scroll to give him,
> loaded with titles, with imposing names.

Why have our two consuls and praetors come out
today
wearing their embroidered, their scarlet togas?
Why have they put on bracelets with so many
amethysts,
rings sparkling with magnificent emeralds?
Why are they carrying elegant canes
beautifully worked in silver and gold?

> Because the barbarians are coming today,
> and things like that dazzle the barbarians.

Why don't our distinguished orators turn up as usual
to make their speeches, say what they have to say?

> Because the barbarians are coming today;
> and they're bored by rhetoric and public
> speaking.

Why this sudden bewilderment, this confusion?
(How serious people's faces have become.)
Why are the streets and squares emptying so rapidly,
everyone going home lost in thought?

> Because night has fallen and the barbarians
> haven't come.
> And some of our men just in from the border say
> there are no barbarians any longer.
>
> Now what's going to happen to us without barbarians?
> They were, those people, some kind of solution.
> (*Collected Poems* 14–15)

Cavafy's barbarians have not come; moreover, some even say that "there are no barbarians any longer," a fact that creates a problem: how will life be without those who were "some kind of solution." The voice of Darwish's poem is very clear: the poem's other barbarians—that is, other than Cavafy's barbarians—will not come either, thus leaving the emperor without any scapegoat to rely on. The dialogue Darwish's poem conducts with Cavafy's poem is not only on the meta-poetic level but also on the meta-mythical level. This myth of the barbarians is used by those who have the power to create myths, the poets included, in order to deceive people and lead them astray. A clear distinction is thus drawn between what is conceived as "true" poetry and a type of poetry that bears an animus against such poetry by propagating false myths.

Another intertextual allusion is to the novel *Waiting for the Barbarians* (1983), by J.M. Coetzee (b. 1940), which also addresses issues of power and justice through the allegory of a war between oppressors and oppressed. The novel is set in an isolated outpost where the magistrate, the novel's narrator, has been a loyal servant of the empire, ignoring constant reports of a threat from the "barbarians" who inhabit the uncharted deserts beyond the village. But when military personnel arrive with captured "barbarians," we witness an episode that manifests the cruel and unjust attitudes of the empire. Determined to find enemies, Colonel Joll interrogates the prisoners, assuming that acts of the empire, while excessive in force, are necessary to the security of the people. Powerless to prevent the persecution, after the prisoners are released the magistrate finds himself involved in an affair with one of the victims, a girl orphaned by the torturers, begging in the streets, temporarily blinded and crippled as a result of the torture inflicted upon her. The magistrate befriends her and eventually invites her to sleep in his room; the relationship, however, is not based on sexuality but a deeper physic, emotional need. They both partake in a relaxing cleansing ritual in which the magistrate washes the girl's body—a symbolic way of washing his hands of the terrible deeds of the oppressors. After the girl's eyesight returns and she regains some use of her feet, the magistrate decides to return the girl to her people. His relationship with the girl—a quixotic act of rebellion—brands him an enemy of the state and he becomes the newest object of the empire's suspicion.

The narrator, however, is not satisfied with contemplating the events solely on the fictional plane; he is also interested in how these events will be viewed by history:

> What has made it impossible for us to live in time like fish in water, like birds in air, like children? It is the fault of Empire! Empire has created the time of history. Empire has located its existence not in the smooth recurrent spinning time of cycle of the seasons but in the jagged time of rise and fall, of beginning and end, of catastrophe. Empire dooms itself to live in history and plot against history. (Coetzee 133)

The process of perception which the reader passes through in reading the novel is, as Shklovskij put it, "an aesthetic end in itself"—especially in how Coetzee shows compassion for victims and villains alike. When the narrator is reflecting on the events he witnesses, the reader finds that he too is a witness of the suffering in his own society: "'When some men suffer unjustly,' I said to myself, 'it is the fate of those who witness their suffering to suffer the shame of it'" (139).

The narrator's conclusion at the end of the story is also relevant to the reader:

> I wanted to live outside the History. I wanted to live outside the History that Empire imposes on its subjects, even its lost subjects. I never wished it for the barbarians that they should have the history of Empire laid upon them. How can I believe that that is cause for shame? (154)

Coetzee's novel—published some years before Darwish's poem—follows in the footsteps of Cavafy's poem and uncovers the use of myth to deceive and oppress people. The person who tries to confront this process is considered an enemy of the empire, thus deserving to be numbered among the barbarians.

A third intertextual allusion, mainly limited to Arab readers, is to the destruction of Baghdad by Hulagu in 1258. This incident has been engraved on collective Arab memory as the fundamental reason for the destruction of the Arabs' great medieval civilization and the cause for the cultural stagnation of the Arab world until the nineteenth century. Because Hulagu became part of the myth of the anti-civilization barbarians, emphasis has been laid by Arab historians and educators on the killing of many of the men of letters in Baghdad and the destruction of cultural institutions and libraries by the Mongol army—even throwing books into the Tigris and using them as a bridge to cross the river. This narrative of the demonic, cruel, and uncivilized Mongols was originally formulated by European orientalists[20] and later adopted by the Arabs—it can be already found, for example, in a manifesto of Arab nationalists disseminated from Cairo by the Arab Revolutionary Committee at the beginning of World War I. The manifesto mentioned Genghis and Hulagu who "slaughtered your upright and pure ancestors, destroyed their flourishing civilization, trampled with hooves of their horses on the books of their libraries, or else stopped up the course of the Tigris with a great number of these books which they flung into it." The Turks, according to the manifesto, are descendants of Genghis and Hulagu—"they have destroyed what the ancestors left standing, and have thus prevented Arab civilization from recovering its scattered elements and returning to its former glory" (al-A'zami 113; translation according to Haim 86). Later it could be found in history books,[21] literary histories,[22] and both poetry and prose.[23]

Arab officials also used this narrative for their own ends, as did, for example, Egyptian President Jamal 'Abd al-Nasir (*Falsafat* 45–46, 61). Also, Arnold Hottinger, a Swiss writer on Middle Eastern affairs, quotes "a high Syrian government official" as saying "in deadly earnest" that if the Mongols had not burnt the libraries of Baghdad in the thirteenth century, "we Arabs would have had so much science, that we would long since have invented the atomic bomb. The plundering of Baghdad put us back centuries" (qtd. in

Lewis, *Islam* 179). This is of course an extreme example, but the thesis it embodies, as Bernard Lewis elucidates, was not confined to, and was not invented by, romantic nationalist historians. Deriving ultimately from the testimony of contemporary sufferers, it was developed by European orientalists, who saw in the Mongol invasions the final catastrophe that overwhelmed and ended the great Muslim civilization of the Middle Ages. This judgment of the Mongols "was generally accepted among European scholars, and was gratefully, if sometimes surreptitiously, borrowed by romantic and apologetic historians in Middle Eastern countries as an explanation both of the ending of their golden age, and of their recent backwardness" (*Islam* 179).

Yet it is clear that this thesis is quite unjustified, as the signs of the stagnation had appeared long before Hulagu arrived in Baghdad. The successive blows by which the Mongols hewed their way across western Asia, culminating in the sack of Baghdad and the toppling of the independent caliphate, scarcely did more, as H.A.R. Gibb writes, "than give finality to a situation that had long been developing."[24] Even some modern Arab intellectuals and historians feel that this description of the sacking of Baghdad was much exaggerated. Constantine Zurayk, for example, says that "the Arabs had been defeated internally before the Mongols defeated them and that, had those attacks been launched against them when they were in the period of growth and enlightenment, the Mongols would not have overcome them. On the contrary the attacks might have revitalized and re-energized them."[25]

The above allusions use both the linear (the barbarians and Roman Empire; Hulagu) and ironical (Cavafy; Coetzee) modes of intertextuality: the linear mode is derivative, drawing mostly on what is already in existence in the literature of the past; in the ironical mode, the use of the myth is designed to create a new meaning rather than to invoke the conventional one.[26] In Arabic literary texts we generally find the barbarians as agents of destruction and devastation, and only rarely do we find them in texts using the ironical mode of intertextuality.[27] Significantly enough, Darwish's poem "Other Barbarians Will Come" was included in the anthology *100 Poets Against the War*, first published online in January 2003, because the editors referred to the barbarians in the poem as agents of destruction. The anthology contains a selection from the poems submitted by peace protesters across the world and features some of the leading contemporary poets and peace activists. The aim was to protest the plans of the Americans (here the barbarians) to invade Iraq. Darwish's poem was given in a translation that does not preserve the structure of the original poem, but still the aforementioned intended message was clear:

> Other barbarians will come along.
> The emperor's wife will be abducted.
> Drums will roll.
> Drums will roll and horses will trample a sea of corpses
> all the way from the Aegean to the Dardanelles.
> And why should we care?
> What on earth have our wives got to do with horse races?
>
> The emperor's wife will be abducted.
> Drums will roll.
> And other barbarians will come along.
> The barbarians will take over abandoned cities,
> settling in just above sea-level,
> mightier than the sword in an age of anarchy.
> And why should we care?
> What have our children got to do with the progeny of
>   the rabble?
>
> Drums will roll.
> And other barbarians will come along.
> The emperor's wife will be abducted from the palace.
> From the palace a military campaign will be launched
> to restore the bride to the emperor's bed.
> And why should we care?
> What have fifty-thousand corpses got to do with this
>   hasty marriage?
>
> Will Homer be born again?
> Will myths ever feature the masses?
> (Swift 143; translation by Sarah Maguire with Sabry
> Hafez)

In an article published twelve years after the publication of Darwish's poem and entitled "Barbarians at the Gates," Edward Said (1935–2003) wrote about the military actions the United States had been conducting against Iraq "in the guise of sanctioned police action authorised by the United Nations." Said, whose *Orientalism* (1978) undoubtedly inspired Darwish's poetry in the 1980s, considered the American actions as part of a "history of reducing whole peoples, countries and even continents to ruin by nothing short of holocaust... This starts with the native American peoples, 90 percent of whom were massacred during the first two centuries of this country's life, all in the name of progress, doing God's work and eradicating barbarians." In one place Said alludes to the same power relations that structure Darwish's poem. Speaking about the Iraqi regime as a government of unprincipled tyranny that has led "the most modern, secular and advanced of Arab countries" into ruin, he says that "neither Saddam Hussein nor his military and political supporters in Iraq are bearing the major brunt of the suffering imposed by the US: it is innocent Iraqi people who are paying the price." Said's conclusion is that serial American aggression embodies "the clash of civilisations, or rather the clash of untrammeled barbarism with civilisation, with a vengeance."

In an article published in 2004, after Said's death, the Arab-American poet and critic Naomi Shihab Nye (b. 1952) adds a new dimension to Said's conception. She relates that Said supported a single-state solution for Palestine and Israel, writing that "the question is not how to devise means for persisting in trying to separate" Israelis and Palestinians, "but to see whether it is possible for them to live together as fairly and peacefully as possible." She draws attention to the fact that his favorite poem, "Waiting for the Barbarians" by Constantine Cavafy, includes the lines: "What are we waiting for, assembled in the forum? The barbarians are due here today. Why isn't anything happening in the senate? Why do the senators sit there without legislating?" Nye thus understands the act of "waiting for the barbarians" as useless—the two sides should be engaged in legislating the single-state solution instead of waiting, which only complicates the problem. Unlike the traditional interpretation of Cavafy's poem, in which the myth of barbarians as a destructive force is used only as a *pretext*, the barbarians are conceived by Said, according to Nye, only as a destructive force.

The linear mode of intertextuality also uses the myth of the barbarians as a kind of reversal of the well-known Western conception of the Arabs as barbarians. Before the occupation of Iraq by the Americans, Palestinian historian Elias Sanbar (b. 1947), editor-in-chief of *Revue d'études palestiniennes* and translator of some of Darwish's works into French, argued that the Americans and Israelis created the barbarians in the image of the Arab and thus "it is certain that the deterioration in Palestine will be permanent... until this fall when the declared war against Iraq is unleashed. Then Ariel Sharon will hitch his vehicle onto the American convoy, send his provincial legions to be posted at the steps of the Empire 'waiting for the Barbarians' who, refuting the eponymous poems by Cavafy and Darwish this time, will surely arrive by virtue of having been created."[28] Sanbar's argument is supported by the Zionist discourse, two examples of which suffice to show that in this sense Zionism has adhered to the same conception; and the span of time separating them proves that the same attitude remains at the heart of the Zionist toward the Arabs. In 1896, Theodor Herzl (1860–1904), the founder of modern Zionism, wrote about the desire to establish in Palestine a national home for the Jews: "We should there form a portion of the rampart of Europe against Asia, an outpost of civilisation as opposed to barbarism" (*The Jewish State* 30). More than 100 years later the historian Benny Morris described the Arabs and Muslims as "barbarians," arguing that "due to the nature of Islam and Arab people, it was a mistake to think that it would be possible to establish here a quiet state that would live in harmony with its neighbors."[29]

Helen of Troy vis-à-vis "the Emperor's Wife"

The Arabic text of Darwish's poem encourages one to read it in the ironical mode of intertextuality. The third line of each stanza ironically links with one of the components of the first line ("The Emperor's wife will be abducted"). In the first reading, this sentence might evoke the myth of Helen of Troy.[30] Yet the reader gradually becomes aware that, in contrast, Darwish's Helen is only a one-night-stand for the Emperor. This transformation is expressed in the choice of words.

In the first stanza, "the Emperor's wife" [*imra'at al-imbarāṭūr*] of the first line is contrasted with "our wives" [*zawjātinā*]. But then "What have our wives got to do with this horse race?" gives a hint of the Emperor's interests as against the interests of the people. For the Emperor it is only entertainment—for *us* it is our beloved wives.

In the second stanza, "the Emperor's wife" is contrasted with "our children" [*awlādinā*]. The impression that there is no balance between the Emperor's desires and the sacrifice of the people is reinforced. "What have our children got to do with the offspring of this impudence?"—For the Emperor it is only impudence—for *us* it is our dear children.

In the third stanza it is only casual sex [*zawāj sarī'*] with the "mattress bride" [*'arūs al-firāsh*] that brings about this catastrophe, of 50,000 men killed, "but what have we got to do with it? What have 50,000 men killed got to do with this quickie marriage?"[31] For the Emperor it is only casual sex—for *us* it is a massacre. The birth of the military campaign [*wa-min baytihi tūladu al-ḥamla al-'askarīya*] was a kind of frustration that the Emperor could not make love to his new "bride" (cf. Snir, *Rak'atān fī al-'Ishq* 192).

Through the process of reading, one discovers that the barbarians are not so terribly barbaric and at the same time that the possible abduction of the Emperor's wife is only a pretext, if that. The real suffering is endured by the people, who have no interest in the sexual life of the Emperor. As in Cavafy's poem and Coetzee's novel, the barbarians are only an excuse for committing greater crimes against civilization. As previously mentioned, the changing of the three components in the first line of each stanza in Darwish's poem undermines the usual sequence of cause and effect and the reader is led to the conclusion that the Emperor and the barbarians are in fact two sides of the same coin.

Before publication of the poem, Darwish published an article in *Al-Karmel* (which he himself edits) under the title "Fī intiẓār al-barābira" [Waiting for the barbarians].[32] Serving as epigraph to the article are Cavafy's lines: "Now what's going to happen to us without barbarians?/ They were, those people, some kind of solution." The article begins with the question: "when they will strike?" They, the barbarians, never did arrive in Cavafy's poem, but they "settled down in our reality and consciousness for a long time in order to enable the Arab establishment to solve its problems with us." We, the collective in the poem and in the article, are the victim, whose body has become a theater of war between two murderers, between two kinds of terror, internal and external—we are a space that has nothing to do but wait for the new strike. Here, the myths of the barbarians, Hulagu, Cain and Abel, and Joseph and his brothers, as well as the aforementioned intertextual allusions, are intermingled and find their manifestation in the myth of Ayyūb, the biblical Job. Both the article and the poem are unquestionably indebted to Said's *Orientalism*, especially in their attempt to illustrate the discourse of power, but they also should be read as trying to engage his main arguments. The article concludes as follows:

> But what could you do, when the big terror and the small terror disagree regarding you? How would you cry when the spears of the enemies are broken on your waist? And when your body is the battleground between your big murderer and your small murderer, where could you send the call? This question should not be put because you are betrayed, oppressed Job. You must close the gap between the cry and the body, you must listen alone to your silence, and from this small gap the airplanes of the barbarians will pass, and you might be accused, you will be accused if you cry from pain and from betrayal that you take part in the conspiracy against your small murderer. You should support him, you should embrace him, you should help him plunge his dagger into your liver so that he might defend himself against your big murderer—these are the obligations of brotherhood. Don't mention the name of him who assassinated you, and thus the severed parts of your corpse struck a number of foreign passersby, so that America will not hear the deep secret. Don't say anything. Help your brother to kill you, or say that you are killing yourself. Nobody killed you. Nobody killed anybody. Say that he had conducted a remedial operation on your liver and that you died from excess surrender. Say again that you are the murderer of yourself. You are the cost of everything. You are the cost of nothing. Say that you are the murderer of yourself in order to save one oil well, and a weapons deal, or to

> save a revolutionary sentence form inflation. You don't have any part in what is divided in you and in your corpse, because you are the victim of the victim. Nobody killed you. You are the murderer. Say it and don't regret, soon both murderers will embrace each other over you, and you are the cost which does not look for any result. You should stand now, with all your wounds, and apologize to the dagger that injured your body and injured the form of your spirit, because it could disgrace the murderer, could disgrace him somehow. Have the barbarians already arrived? Have the barbarians already arrived? They were some kind of solution.

Between the lines the reader may sense a certain disappointment that the barbarians did not come. The repeated question, "Have the barbarians already arrived?" [*hal waṣal al-barābira?*] may be read in Arabic as a kind of wish: "if only they came." They could have been some kind of solution not only for the complicated reality but also for the poet recording the chronicle of the collective. The conclusion of the article echoes the doubt imbued in the last line of the poem.

Conclusion: "The Poet Cannot Be But a Poet"

On May 1, 1964, a young Mahmoud Darwish, only 23 at the time, stepped onto the stage of one of Nazareth's larger movie houses and, to an unsuspecting but eager crowd, proceeded to read his latest poem, in which the imperative *sajjil anā 'Arabī!* [Write it down! I am an Arab!] is repeated in each of its six stanzas; the first of them is as follows:

> Write it down!
> I am an Arab
> And my identity card number is fifty thousand.
> I have eight children
> And the ninth is coming after the summer.
> Makes you angry, doesn't it?

The last stanza combines the persona's good will and anger:

> Write it down! At the top of the first page:
> I do not hate people

Nor do I encroach on anyone,
But if I become hungry
I shall eat the flesh of the one who violated me –
Beware, beware of my hunger
And of my anger![33]

The tension among the audience was palpable from the moment Darwish began reading, and when he finished the reaction was tumultuous. Within days the poem, "Biṭāqat hawīya" ["Identity Card"], had spread throughout the country and the Arab world—its straightforward language and forceful images imprinted themselves easily on the minds of the very same people of which it spoke. In August 1982, in a Beirut that was being bombarded from the air by Israeli fighter jets and besieged on the ground by Israeli army tanks, Darwish's mind went back to that May Day gathering in Nazareth eighteen years before:

> For the first time [since 1948] they [the Israeli authorities] had given us permission to leave Haifa, but we had to be back at night to report to the police station next to the park, that is, the city park—for each of us to say in his own way, "Write it down!—I exist! Write it down!" An old familiar rhythm that I recognize instantly. "Write it down"—I recognize the voice, then 25 years old. Oh, what a dead time! Oh, for a living time to emerge from this dead time. "Write it down: I am an Arab!" I said that to a government official whose son may very well be flying one of these jets overhead! I said it in Hebrew, to provoke him, but when I put it in a poem the Arab audience in Nazareth was electrified, as if a secret current had sprung the genie from the bottle. At first I didn't quite understand the secret of this discovery—as if, in a yard full of bombs, with the gunpowder of my identity, I had succeeded in defusing the thunderbolt. This cry of mine soon turned into my poetic identity—not satisfied with bowing to me, it pursues me even now! (*Dhākira* 140; translation in *Memory* 173–174, modified; cf. Darwish and al-Qasim, *Al-Rasā'il* 151).

The poem was written against the background of the extensive Israeli–Zionist efforts "to rob that [Palestinian] minority of its Arab personality, culture and identity" (Sulaiman 200), or in the forceful words of the Palestinian Anton Shammas (b. 1950), the Israeli policy aimed at "initially phasing out the Arab personality in Israel and then, as a follow-up, demanding that this personality accommodate itself to the state." What Israel wanted to raise were "people whose tongue had been amputated... with no cultural past, and no future. Just an improvised present, and a free-floating personality" (qtd. in Hareven 44–45).

In the 1980s, Darwish had no need to assert his Arab or Palestinian identity—it was a solid, unshakable identity that daily sufferings and miseries only served to consolidate and strengthen. Crowned as the unchallenged Palestinian national poet, he wanted to widen his poetic identity. This was the time when he felt totally convinced that the poetry of declarations and slogans had exhausted itself.[34] His major concern now was not solely to narrate reality—in order to engrave new verses in *dīwān al-'Arab*—or to join his voice to those poets who were satisfied by national or didactic poetry with simplistic and nationalist interpretations. Being aware of his own mythmaking capability, the persona was no longer only a witness at the time of the events but also an outsider looking upon them from a specified point of view in time and space. *Ward aqall* reflects this intention of the poet to be a witness of his time and place, and at the same time to wonder about poetry's place in reality and its relationship with myth and about the place *his* poetry will eventually occupy, if any, in the future. The process of reading and the role of the reader in his efforts to concretize the meaning became much more dominant in Darwish's poetry, and instead of the imperative *sajjil!* [Write it down!] the question "But what have we got to do with it?" became the *lāzima* [a refrain, a kind of "filler" or key sentence]. The poet has many more questions than answers; even if each question somehow conceals an answer, this answer depends on the readers' responses as well as on each reader's own answer and personal preferred meaning.

Yet the reader may remain merely a *consumer* and be satisfied by reading the poems as he read Darwish's previous poems, tracing the footsteps of the persona in his experience as a refugee. This is the story of the Nakba from the viewpoint of the victim and through the process of reading the reader identifies with the persona. But the poem is also addressed to the community of poets, the *producers*, whose texts may conduct a dialogue with Darwish's texts. The process of reading is thus also a process of poetic dialogue whose core is poetic and aesthetic, the purpose and value of the poetry written on the Nakba, and its continuous aftereffects. In this sense the reader assumes not only the role of a poet but also that of a critic who is interested in the internal connections in the poems and their relationship to the myth as well as the process of the creation of myths.

This interplay between reality, poetry and meta-poetry, myth and meta-myth, as well as the role of the reader in the concretization of meaning and the significance of the reading process, grant the poems of *Ward aqall* their particular significance. "Other Barbarians Will Come" illustrates this singularity of the collection—the question "Will Homer be born after us, and the myths open their gates to all?" is imbued with all the above components and dimensions—and the reader is expected to take part in a poetic and critical discourse that asks whether the poetry of Darwish could be considered the equivalent of Homer. Can Darwish sing the poetry of Palestine and the days of its lost paradise as Homer sang the story of Troy?

At the same time, despair and frustration are deeply ingrained in the poems of *Ward aqall* and other poems written in the 1980s. Suicide is sometimes seen as a possible solution to the persona's crises. For example, receiving a pistol as a present, he hastened to hide it "for fear of a rage that cannot be contained" (*Dhākira* 7; *Memory* 5). Yet, he "placed the pistol in his vision, and tried to sleep":

> If I find no dream to dream, I will fire my bullet
> And I will die like a blue-tailed fly in this darkness,
> Without appetite. (*Hiya* 73–74)

But because there is no dream to dream—"The Time Has Come for the Poet to Kill Himself":

> Not for a reason, but rather in order to kill himself
> [...]
> The time has come for the poet to leave me forever.
> (75–78)

The persona wishes not only to renounce his poetic abilities but also thinks of actual suicide. Wandering in Beirut, the poet looks at the balcony of the Lebanese poet Khalil Hawi (1925–1982) and muses:

> The twilight of twilight [...] Where will I go after this twilight? [...] Here is the balcony of the poet who saw all things fall, and chose the time of his end. Khalil Hawi grasped his hunting rifle and hunted himself, not in order to witness something, but in order not to see anything, and not to bear witness to anything. He was bored with this garbage, hated to observe the bottomless abyss [...] He was alone, without an idea, without a woman, without poetry, and without promise [...] I don't want to look at his balcony. I don't want to see what he did that I did not do. (*Dhākira* 123–124; *Memory* 153–154)

In his hours of distress the poet is aware of the fact that poetry has no value:

> The wounded and the thirsty, and those who seek water and bread do not want melodies from you, and the fighters pay no attention to your songs. Sing if you want, or be quiet. We are marginal in war. We have the ability to offer other services to people: a small can of water is equal to the 'Abqar valley.[35] What is demanded of us now is not creative aesthetics but human action. (*Dhākira* 52; *Memory* 62–63; cf. Leeuwen, "The Poet" 265–266)

But this poet who believes that poetry cannot be of any benefit is at the same time a very prolific writer. The same paradox is known from the mystical experience: it is ineffable[36] and the mystic himself inclines to be silent regarding his divine experience, because it is an intimate experience with the divine beloved. At the same time, paradoxically, mystics are very prolific. This conflict between the mind [*'aql*] and the heart [*qalb*] brings us to the meta-poetic dimension. It is sometimes argued that those mystics who speak about their experiences are "weak"—they could not help but surrender to the temptation of disclosing what happened to them. The greatest of the mystics resist the temptation of speaking and thus we will never know anything about them. But they will remain mystics even if they don't speak because, like lovers, their experience is not conditioned by language. Can we say the same about the psychological structure of poets? That is, that those poets who write and publish their poetry are weak for preferring to speak about their experiences rather than keeping them for themselves? Moreover, ever since Theodor Adorno argued that "to write poetry after Auschwitz is barbaric" (34), all kinds of artists, not just poets, have been debating whether poetry has any value vis-à-vis reality. Should we also see poetry through the eyes of Walter Benjamin?

> There is no document of civilisation which is not at the same time a document of barbarism. And just as such a document is not free of barbarism, barbarism taints also the manner in which it was transmitted from one owner to another. A historical materialist therefore dissociates himself from it as far as possible. He regards it as his task to brush history against the grain. ("Theses" 256)

In his most recent collection, *Ka-zahr al-lawz aw ab'ad* [Like almond flowers or further], Darwish dedicates a poem to Edward Said in which he states: *qad yakūnu al-taqaddum jisra al-rujū'/ ilā al-barbarīya* [progress might be the bridge of return/ to barbarism] (2005: 181).

Darwish, whose interest in Sufi texts had been mainly limited to cultural and literary allusions (see, for example, Neuwirth, "Restaging"), started in the mid-1980s to present in his poetry a persona whose poetic experience is sometimes intermingled with the mystical one, culminating in his long poem "Al-Hudhud" [The hoopoe].[37] Thus it is no wonder that in his exchange of open letters with Palestinian compatriot Samih al-Qasim (b. 1939) he used a mystical "pretext" in order to explain his desire to write poetry even if he was very much aware that poetry has in fact no "real" value. Speaking about the generic relationship of poetry to prose, Darwish asserts the dominance of fiction over poetry, "if television has left to it any remnant." But if the poet himself is also writing prose he should not mix the two activities, because poetry is "an explosive desire." Just as the mystic cannot help but speak of his experience because love overflows his heart, so the poet cannot resist this desire; he must "put himself in the wind and madness, because the poet cannot be but a poet" (Darwish and al-Qasim, *Al-Rasā'il* 72). Nevertheless, for Darwish it is not only overflowing emotions but also a rational choice—mind and heart are in harmony:

If I could start all over again I'd choose what I have
chosen: roses on the fence
I'd travel again on the roads that may or may not lead
to Cordova.

7
Hebrew Bible and Arabic Poetry: Mahmoud Darwish's Palestine—From Paradise Lost to a Homeland Made of Words

Angelika Neuwirth

I Introduction

> I come from there.
> I return the sky to its mother when for its mother the
> sky cries
> And I weep for a cloud that returns to know me.
> I have learned the words of blood-stained courts to
> break the rules.
> I have learned and dismantled all the words to
> construct a single one: homeland.
>
> —"I Come From There" in *Ward aqall*
> (in *Dīwān* vol. 2, 327),
> trans. 'Abd al-Rahim al-Shaykh

IS THE VOICE THAT CLAIMS A TRANSCENDENT STATUS, TO COME "FROM there," aspiring to the role of mediator between heaven and earth and boasting the achievement of having subverted language as such to form one particular name, merely the lyrical "I" of a particular poem, or is it the poet's own personal voice? The problem has, of course, a long history: The ancient *qaṣīda* poet who figured as a guardian of collective memory and traditional norms in pre-Islamic society used to speak in the I-voice, but though the experiences he related were highly stereotypical and the heroic deeds he claimed for himself were to serve as examples for tribal virtues, he nevertheless figured as the personal representative of his message, with whom the listeners would identify, when he recited his poetry. In times of crisis he bore personal responsibility for the political stance he had represented.[1] With little exaggeration one might claim

Translations in this chapter are by Angelika Neuwirth unless otherwise noted.

that early Arabic poetry was immanently political. Mahmoud Darwish, who early in his career had joined the universal scene of modern poetry through his broad reading in international modern literature, did not completely change paradigms concerning the public role of the poet, but remained committed to both functions of poetry: poetry as a personal celebration of life and as a weapon in the strife for political freedom. This was very much in accordance with his paragons, revolutionary poets such as Nazim Hikmet, Louis Aragon, Pablo Neruda, and García Lorca, who through their poetry acted as tribunes for their oppressed societies striving for political change.[2]

The verses quoted above, however, raise a particularly ambitious claim. The speaker of the poem presents himself as no less than a cosmic agent[3] reconciling heaven and earth, a kind of Prometheus who shatters the symbols of ruling power structures, and the re-embodiment of a biblical figure: the First Man, Adam, who on divine order gives every created being its name. Is this poem a purely poetic and thus licitly hyperbolic articulation of an artist triumphing over a situation of perverted values, or is it a "prophetical," covenantal—and thus autobiographical—statement of "the poet of Palestine"? This is a controversial question among the readers of Mahmoud Darwish. The following observations will shed some light on the problem inherent in modern political poetry that has in Darwish's case invited an immediate and long-lasting reinterpretation in the sense that readers, or more often listeners, claimed autobiographical validity for poetical statements presented in the first person "I." Indeed, it is no exaggeration to state that they thus created a kind of "meta-literary," prophetic autobiography for the poet from his poetical speech (see interviews in Darwish, *Palästina*).

It is noteworthy that Mahmoud Darwish has not written an autobiography in the strict sense of word, but has composed some dīwāns that deserve to be considered (and have been accepted) as a kind of autobiography in the shape of a sequence of poems: in 1995, *Limādhā tarakta al-ḥiṣāna waḥīdan?* [*Why Did You Leave the Horse Alone?*] and in 1998, *Sarīr al-gharība* [*The Stranger's Bed*]. In these works, a component that has always been latently and at times overtly[4] present in Darwish's earlier poetry clearly and explicitly comes to the fore: his reading of the Hebrew Bible. In the following we will try to trace some instances of his reading of the Bible in their peculiar entanglement with the Arabic canon, which is not only the Qur'an, but also the great poetic tradition. Darwish's poetical rereading of the Hebrew Bible, pursued on different levels, must be considered as a politically significant act. The Bible is at once the canon of the hegemonic majority in the young Jewish state in which Mahmoud Darwish grew up and—in its Zionist reading—a document used politically to legitimize the exile of the Palestinians. An Arab poet's critical rereading, as will be shown, can amount to a counter-text, a kind of replacement of the original text by a new understanding, thus enabling the reader to confront the canon of the "other" with a newly established or newly affirmed canon of his own. But it may equally serve the opposite purpose: to dissolve the antagonism between the other and the self, by relocating both in the same world of estrangement, in the *ghurba*—the particular *conditio humana* to which the title of the new dīwān *Sarīr al-gharība* alludes. It is hardly surprising that in such a context kindred spirits make their appearance, thus the great Jewish poet Paul Celan,[5] who in German tradition figures as the poet of exile par excellence, and his disturbing reading of the Hebrew Bible find a place in Darwish's new poetry.

The Poet: Individual Artist and Publicly Claimed Symbol

Mahmoud Darwish is, together with Adonis, the most significant Arab poet of our time. Born in 1942 in a Galilean village, which was destroyed in 1948, and educated in both Arabic and Hebrew, he as a young man joined the editorial staff of the communist literary journal *Al-Jadīd* in Haifa (Embalo et al., *Kulturelle* 3–60). He wrote poetry with overtly political overtones from early on. He emerged as the outstanding voice of his community, however, with his first long poem, *'Āshiq min Filasṭīn* [A lover from Palestine], written in 1966. The poem is concerned with an experience recorded in his early memoir *Yawmīyāt al-ḥuzn al-'ādī* [Diary of ordinary sadness] that in my reading epitomizes his personal call to poetry:

> Suddenly you remember that Palestine is your land. The lost name leads you to lost times, and on the coast of the Mediterranean lies the land like a sleeping woman,

> who awakes suddenly when you call her by her beautiful name. They have forbidden you to sing the old songs, to recite the poems of your youth and to read the histories of the rebels and poets who have sung of this old Palestine. The old name returns, finally it returns from the void, you open her map as if you opened the buttons of your first love's dress for the first time. (140)

Lost times, the land, her beautiful name, forbidden old songs and histories of the rebels, poets singing about Palestine—all these material and textual components converge to make up the homeland. What had been forcibly banned from the speaker's consciousness re-emerges in a kind of vision, whose erotic radiance restores to him reality in its full dimension. It seems to have been this vision that inspired him to write the poem *'Āshiq min Filasṭīn*, whose poetic claim to a "redemptive" role was to establish him as the poet of Palestine.

Mahmoud Darwish at that time was 24 years old. As a consequence of his growing fame as a politically critical poet he had been imprisoned several times, and it is reported that he wrote the piece while in prison. Soon after the poem's publication, his talent was discovered by Ghassan Kanafani, the famous Palestinian prose writer, who succeeded in smuggling the poems of a number of young Palestinian writers from Israel to Beirut, thus introducing them to the broader Arab public. Kanafani presented his literary protégés as authors of "resistance poetry," who were soon claimed as representatives of the movement of "committed literature" then en vogue (Klemm, *Literarisches*)—a label that Darwish was later vehemently to reject. Increasing confrontations with the Israeli authorities, imprisonments, and house arrests finally made life in Israel impossible for Darwish and induced him to leave the country in 1971. In his exile—he lived in Beirut from 1972 to 1982—he produced some of his most impressive poems, creating the figure of the *fidā'ī* [devoted fighter] or *shahīd* [martyr], as an alter ego of the poet himself. Forced to leave Beirut with the expulsion of the PLO and the Palestinian fighters by the Israeli army in 1982, Darwish chose Paris as his new exile, where he was to write his war memoir *Dhākira lil-nisyān* [*Memory for Forgetfulness*] and several collections of new, pronouncedly personal poetry.[6] But whatever he wrote, he was to remain in the consciousness of his wider public the voice of Palestine, the translator of those most intimate desires and aspirations of the Palestinians that could only be expressed poetically, through myths and symbols. Though Mahmoud Darwish from the 1990s onward had started to rewrite his past poetically, viewing it from the angle of the "estranged," the exile, it certainly came as a surprise that the poet who for thirty years has been claimed as the voice of Palestine, whose recitals attract thousands of listeners, whose dīwāns reach innumerable readers over the Arab world, in 2002—six years after his return to the Arab world—published a collection of poems in which he explicitly steps down from his rank of the mythopoeic poet of this people and questions an essential part of his own mythic creation.

II Re-creating the Promised Land: A Palestinian Genesis

What has been claimed for German Romantic poetry seems to apply in some important aspects to modern Arabic poetry as well:

> Since poetry is credited with a world-transforming and time-devaluating dimension, reflections about poetry often touch on eschatological horizons. The poet [in Novalis' work] bears the traits of the ancient poet Orpheus. Like Orpheus he appears as a powerful magician who devaluates the laws of space and time, who connects between remote realms of being and invites all creatures into a comprehensive dialogue....[7]
>
> The poet occupies a privileged rank, since he commands a sort of mystical access to the Golden Age. He is capable of experiencing the unity of the ideal, primordial world even through the most disparate phenomena of the present appearances.[8]

Although it is problematic to claim a particular Golden Age for (nonreligious) Arabic culture, the topos of an ideal past is certainly no less powerful in the Arab context than it is in the West. Postcolonial Arabic poetry has been recognized as markedly nostalgic. Poets endeavor to invert reality and recover the vision of a precolonial paradisiacal state of their living space beneath its real appearance, which has been disfigured by political circumstances (DeYoung, *Placing*). This applies to Palestinian poetry in particular, which for its understanding relies—as Richard van Leeuwen has stressed—on the premise that the land is the structuring principle that organizes individual and collective perceptions of life:

> There are various versions of history inscribed on the land, both by the occupier and by the Palestinians. The relations of power however, imply that the Israeli version is dominant and that the Palestinian 'textual' homeland is threatened by elimination. What remains for the Palestinians is not so much 'history,' as 'memory' consisting of recollections of childhood and of the exodus, emotions symbolizing the attachment to the land and the natural right of the Palestinians to the land. (Leeuwen 270)

But these recollections remain dispersed as long as no catalyst is available. It is the task of the poet to reconstruct the disrupted Palestinian identity

> ... by reintegrating it into the domains from which it was evicted: time, or the continuity of history, and place, the repossession of the homeland. This reintegration can only be achieved in one way, by recreating the two domains in texts, by enabling their essence to transcend a distorted reality and to return to their natural course of deployment. (268)

But poetry in Darwish's case goes a step further. Poetry is a response to a pre-existing writing that is inscribed on the land serving to assert the legitimacy of the dominance of the others: the Hebrew Bible. There are many witnesses to the exclusiveness of the biblical tradition, one of whom, the American writer William M. Thomson, author of a work called *The Land and the Book* (1858), was recently rediscovered and discussed by Hilton Obenzinger in his study *American Palestine* (1999). Obenzinger has summarized this and similar works:

> The country was considered strange, but it was a strangeness emanating from divine meanings waiting to be 'read' as they oscillated between sacred ground and biblical text, a strangeness considerably more intense than the mere excitation of the exotic expected to be found in the Orient, one redolent with meanings about the divine and the destiny of "God's New Israel." Palestine is "where the word made-flesh dwelt with men," as Thomson explains

> and as a consequence it "is and must ever be an integral part of the divine Revelation." (39)

The American Protestant perception thus anticipates the later Zionist view that the Bible is inscribed into the land:

> American Protestants traveled to Palestine to read this entire, all-perfect text, to engage in a complex interpretive practice of reading a female land inscribed with a male pen that by the coupling of soil and story would provide evidence of faith and providence in a unified, eroticized entity, created by the traveler who has come with great purpose to 'read' it. (7)

Meanwhile an extensive America–Holy Land Project at the Hebrew University has been established, initiated in the early 1970s by Moshe Davis, Yehoshua Ben-Arieh, Robert Handy, and other Israeli and American scholars, which tends to view the nineteenth-century history of the region as Israeli prehistory, expecting that the proper study of the Western "rediscovery" of Palestine and the various pre-Zionist, Christian notions of Jewish restoration will prove the historical inevitability of the founding of the Jewish state.

It is true that Mahmoud Darwish's coming out as a poet, which may be dated to the year 1966, predates the emergence of these debates as well as the response to them, including Edward Said's *Orientalism* (1978), with its critique of orientalism and imperialism in the formation of Western cultural and power relations. Yet Darwish's extended cooperation with cultural and political figures such as Emile Habiby[9] in the context of the communist periodical *Al-Jadīd* leaves no doubt that he was very aware early on of the inseparable entanglement of text and land in the minds of the dominant society in his country, the Israeli Jews, an awareness also affirmed by his *Yawmīyāt al-ḥuzn al-ʿādī* [Diary of ordinary sadness], which was published 1978 but written pre-exile. In Darwish's view, as he has spelled out at a later stage:

> [P]oetry is essentially to strive to rewrite or to create its own Book of Genesis, to search for beginnings and to interpret myths of creation. It is through these myths that the poet can return to his origins and ultimately touch upon daily life in the present. History and myth have become an unavoidable detour to comprehend the

> present and to mend the gaps created by the violent usurpation of the land and its textual representations. (in Leeuwen 270; see also Darwish, *Palästina* 38)

The master narrative of the eviction has to be de-narrated.

Darwish Acting as the First Man, the Writer of a Scripture

The Palestinian public, however exaggerated their desire to be represented by the poet may be, were not entirely arbitrary. The poem that mirrors the above quoted experience of the recuperation of the land can indeed be read as a covenantal document. It starts with the line "Your eyes are thorns piercing my heart"[*'Uyūnuki shawkatun fī al-qalbi*]—thus obviously drawing on experience that is not limited to the merely individual but reaches deep into literary tradition. The Beloved's gaze at the poet's persona is the violent gaze known from the mystical ghazal: the Beloved's eyes violate the poet-lover, only to make him more attached [*'Uyūnuki... tūji'unī fa-a'buduhā*]. The addressee of the ghazal, which in early Islam was the individual beloved and later became the great unattainable other, the divine Beloved, has in the postcolonial era been re-embodied as the similarly unattainable lost or occupied homeland. It is thus in the ghazal mood of addressing the high-ranking unattainable Beloved that the poet in *'Āshiq min Filasṭīn* approaches his homeland. But to be able to address "her," he has first to restore her to reality. In 1966, the name "Palestine" was still politically taboo, having been officially abolished with the foundation of the state of Israel. The word was likewise made taboo for the Palestinians of the West Bank after its annexation by the Kingdom of Jordan. There was nothing called Palestine existing.

It is no exaggeration to state that the poem *'Āshiq min Filasṭīn*[10] re-creates Palestine. To achieve that momentous act of creation, Darwish employs a pre-existing poetic model for the process of overcoming nostalgia, regaining a stable mental composure, and reinitiating social communication. The modern poem is shaped in the standard form of the classical *qaṣīda*, with a sequence of three sections, each conveying a different mood: a nostalgic *nasīb* lamenting the loss of a Beloved; followed by a description of a movement in space, a journey, *raḥīl*, portraying the poet regaining his self-consciousness; and culminating in a pathetic *fakhr*, a self-praise confirming the heroic virtues of tribal society. In Darwish's poem, the *nasīb* laments the absence of the homeland and the resulting muteness, a topos that in pre-Islamic *nasīb* sections usually refers to the natural milieu of the deserted campsite, but which in our poem, however, affects not only the space, but the homeland's loved ones. Her absence affects poetry itself as well, their shattered relation allowing only for the sad genre of elegy:

> Your words were a song
> But agony encircled the lips of spring.
> Like swallows, your words took wing.
> Led by love, they deserted the gate of our house
> And its autumnal threshold.
> Our broken mirrors shattered
> My sorrow into a thousand pieces;
> We gathered the splinters of sound,
> We could perfect only our homeland's elegy.
> (Sulaiman, *Palestine* 156–160; lines 10–18; trans. modified)

Darwish's *raḥīl* section, which leads to his vision of a triumphal union with the homeland, presents a prolonged visual pursuit of the Beloved, leading the poet through various sceneries of exile, suffering, and misery: to the harbor, locus of involuntary emigration; to abandoned hilltops grown with thorn bushes; to the storerooms of poor peasant houses; to cheap nightclubs; to refugee camps.

> I saw you yesterday at the harbor
> —a voyager without provisions. (line 25)
>
> I saw you on briar-covered mountains
> —a shepherdess without sheep. (line 40)
>
> I saw you in wells of water and in granaries
> —broken.
> I saw you in nightclubs—waiting on tables. (lines 47–48)

The landscape is a "world deserted by its creator," *'Ālam bi-lā khāliqin*, as Darwish terms it in a later poem. It has yet to be recreated. The long sequence of visions of the Beloved in the state of need and humiliation eventually comes to a turn, when the Beloved presents herself in a clearly erotic emanation—as we already know from the poet's recollection of his rediscovery of the homeland—as a sleeping beauty, displaying life in its most perfect aesthetic form:

> I saw you covered all over with salt and sands,
> Your beauty was of earth, of children and jasmine.
> (line 58)

With this final vision the speaker himself achieves a new state of mind: he regains his composure and swears an oath of absolute devotion to the homeland. He thus concludes—in the understanding of his listeners—a pact, an "autobiographical pact," so to say, with the Palestinian collective that is behind his poetical addressee. This oath, a meta-textual section, placed exactly in the center of the poem, through a complex metaphor presents the process of poetical creation of the other as the production of a textile, a garment for her made from parts of his body, thus constituting a kind of self-sacrifice:

> I swear to you
> I shall weave a veil from my eyelashes embroidered
> With verses for your eyes
> And a name that, when watered with my heart, will
>   melt to song
> That makes the tree spread its branches again.
> I shall write a sentence on the veil, more precious than
>   kisses and the blood of martyrs:
> Palestinian she is and will remain. (lines 60–66)

The speaker in the poem thus acquires a mythical dimension, that of the biblical Adam, the First Man, who was entitled to give names to the newly created beings. Like Adam, the speaker even cedes a part of his body to make the creation of his female companion possible. The new Eve, Adam's companion who is thus emerging and who receives her name through the poet's creation act, is none other than Palestine.[11] The poem that echoes the Qur'anic creational imperative *Kun fa-yakūn* [Be—and it is] is a Palestinian transcript of the creation story from the Book of Genesis (Qur'an 2:117, 3:47, 16:40,

19:35, 36:82, 40:68). The lyrical "I" of the poem is Adam, who, at the same time, since he writes down the covenant, figures as the writer of a new Scripture. This new poetic bestowal of identity on the Beloved, demanding the poet's utmost devotion, is deemed comparable, even superior, to a real, bloody sacrifice; it is *aghlā min al-shuhadā'* [more precious than martyrs' blood]. It has redemptive value, as the speaker is aware when he ranks himself typologically among the bearers of the highest rank in love, the martyrs of love.

In the central strophe of the *madīḥ*, the newly created figure is evoked as the bride in a wedding ceremony, whom the women praise by describing her body from her head to her feet (see Weir, Dalman):

> You, whose eyes and tattoo are Palestinian,
> Whose name is Palestinian,
> Whose dreams and sorrows are Palestinian,
> Whose veil, whose feet and body are Palestinian,
> Whose words and silence are Palestinian,
> Whose voice is Palestinian,
> Whose birth and death are Palestinian! (lines 96–102)

The strictly arithmetic crescendo and decrescendo of the adjectival clauses seems to reflect the geometric structure of the patterns used in the embroidery of the dresses produced and worn by the traditional Palestinian women.

Now that the Beloved has received a name, this name can be employed as a password in the strife of the poet for personal and collective dignity. The *fakhr* ends in a fearless self-assertion of the poet, who relies on his poetical medium in his exchange with the other:

> In your name I shout to the valleys:
> I know the horsemen of Byzance, I know them,
> Though the battlefield has changed.
> Beware of the lightning,
> My song engraves on granite. (lines 106–110)

Having achieved the re-creation of the Beloved, the speaker in the last verse steps into the role of an ancient Arab hero poet, the legendary 'Antara, borrowing 'Antara's motto for himself[12]:

> I am the fire of youth and the knight of knights! (line 122)

III Exodus: The Poet's Alter Ego: The Fighter

Four years after the publication of *'Āshiq min Filasṭīn*, Darwish left his homeland to join the Arab intellectual elite in Beirut. Here for a second time he had to distance himself from the way his poetry was read, this time from its being read as ideological propaganda, a reading purportedly sanctioned by him. It is true that he had, during his stay with the Palestinian exiles in Beirut, extolled the resistance fighter as a hero, a figure that since the beginning of armed struggle in the mid-1960s had kindled new hope of regaining possession of the land. The *fidā'ī* in Darwish's poetry came to be regarded as a redeemer, as a figure who through a highly symbolic act of self-sacrifice leads his people to freedom, without himself participating in it—like the biblical Moses who led the Israelites in their Exodus to the Promised Land—he himself dying before treading on its ground.

The struggle for the land that in the 1960s became manifest in the military operations of the *fidā'ī ūn* thus took textual shape with Darwish's placing the fighter in the mythical context of his poetry. The poetic achievement of the creation of a being called "Palestine," the nucleus of a Palestinian Genesis, was thus followed by another act of inventing sacred history: elevating the fighter to the rank of a redeemer figure. It is not surprising that Darwish's poetry celebrating the *fidā'ī* was again received as a "canonical expression" of the new collective experience: to be part of a decisive movement promising liberation, to live the miracle of an Exodus.

Reclaiming the land is not an exclusive matter of poetic words. The poetic tradition of Palestine is closely connected with the deeds of fighters and martyrs, who were celebrated in the 1930s as the heroes par excellence. "My land is my honor, either living in dignity or dying for the sake of it" [*arḍī 'irḍī*] was the motto of the patriotic young men during the period of the British mandate (Peteet, "Male Gender" 103–126). The power of the poet, however effective, had to be measured against the power of the fighter. This ideal was to be revived after the Nakba, the fall of Palestine in 1948. Since the mid-1960s, Palestinian reaction to the occupation expressed itself in acts of resistance. In this context, the poet's self-sacrifice could not claim to be more than a kind of metaphorical reproduction of the real self-sacrifice of the fighter. The poet is a martyr only virtually, or, viewed from another perspective, the poet is the spokesman of the *shahīd* (see Neuwirth, "From Sacrilege" 259–282), who in turn becomes the poet's alter ego. During the siege of Beirut in 1982, Darwish reflected on the relation between the fighter and the poet:

> The fighters are the genuine founders of a writing that for a long, long time will have to search for a linguistic equivalent to their heroism and their amazing lives. How can the new writing crystallize and take form in a battle that has such a rhythm of rockets? And how can traditional verse define the poetry now fermenting in the belly of the volcano? (*Memory* 62)

The fighter in Darwish's poetry is portrayed as a hero who through his self-sacrifice qualifies as a sacred, superhuman figure, the true lover of the homeland,[13] indeed her bridegroom, who through his violent death consummates a mythical marriage with her. The motif has been expressed by Darwish frequently from the early poem "Wa 'āda fī kafan" [He returned wrapped in a shroud] (from *Awrāq al-zaytūn*, in *Dīwān* vol. 1, 18–23) onward (see also Neuwirth, "Das Lied"). The notion of the mythic marriage of the martyr soon developed to become a hallmark of the Palestinian resistance.[14] One of the most overtly mythopoetic poems is "A'rās" (1977) ("Weddings," from *A'rās*, trans. Johnson-Davies in Darwish, *Music* 67):

> From the war comes a lover to the wedding-day
> Wearing his first suit
> And enters
> The dance floor as a horse
> Of ardor and carnation,
> And on the string of women's joyful trilling he meets
> Fatima
> And to them sing
> All the trees of places of exile
> And soft kerchiefs of mourning. (lines 1–9)
> [...]
> And on the roof of women's joyful trilling come planes,
> Planes,
> Planes,
> Snatching the lover from the butterfly's embrace
> And the kerchiefs of mourning,
> And the girls sing:

You have married
You have married all the girls
O Muhammad!
You have spent the first night
High on the roof-tiles of Haifa
O Muhammad!
O prince of lovers! (lines 13–25)

The idea of the mythic wedding of the dying fighter would be unthinkable in isolation from the ghazal tradition. In mythic love poetry the lover has to experience, indeed to welcome, the death of his ego in order to attain the desired union with the Beloved. In the Palestinian context, the concept of the "martyr of love" is embedded in a ritual reflecting the most important social rite in the rural milieu. The *shahīd* becomes a bridegroom, who like the real bridegroom through his marriage ensures the perpetuation of his community—not through procreation, but through the restoration of collective memory. The poem "A'rās" refers to the traditional marriage rites that culminate in a praise of the bridegroom, elevating him to rank of a ruler: *Yā amīr al-'āshiqīn* [O prince of lovers] (Combs-Schilling, *Sacred*). Messianic qualities had been ascribed to the *shahīd* in Palestinian literature earlier (see Embalo et al. 3–60) but the step remained an individual literary device that did not translate into ideology. Darwish incorporates the martyr into a drama that turns loss into redemption. Unlike the traditional Islamic imagination of the martyr, the postcolonial vision is not concerned with a reward in the beyond, his deed being an end in itself. He sacrifices himself, dedicating himself to the Beloved as a *fidā'*, a token of faithfulness. His achievement is primarily symbolic. It is the revival of memory, the crossing of the boundaries of gratuitous dreaming and fantasizing towards action. It is part of an Exodus into the disputed Promised Land.

In view of the closeness of the martyr poetry to social ritual it becomes plausible that this further act of canon-generating found a lively response in Palestinian society. Translating Darwish's poetical speech into a new rite, the freedom fighter [*fidā'ī*]—mythicized as a Dying God, as a figure dying a sacrificial death to redeem, or verbally "to marry" Palestine—was perceived as re-embodied in every fighter who died in action. Burials during the first intifada became similar in performance to wedding ceremonies. That the ensuing condolence ceremony was staged by women rather than by the male members of the household involved a striking subversion of the customary social order: the patriarchal order—already compromised by the powerlessness of Palestinian men due to the ongoing crisis—was temporarily made irrelevant. The *'urs al-shahīd,* the "wedding of the martyr," has been, at least since the first intifada, a powerful rite of commemoration.[15]

IV Re-entering the Lost Garden

Home in Exile: Mahmoud Darwish and Paul Celan

How do the mythical configurations—the homeland viewed as bride and the martyr viewed as redeemer—fare after the poet's disillusionment with the political developments that took place since 1982, after his definitely entering exile as a "land made of words" as Darwish himself labeled it in his poem "Nusāfiru kal-nās" [We travel like all people] from 1986? What remains of the counter-texts—written to challenge the other's canon—once the other no longer confronts the self but has become part of the self? Darwish, who can be considered as what Foucault termed a "founder of discursivity"—that is, one who plays a major role in producing a discourse—has in his more recent dīwāns not only reflected history, but also the history of the discourse that he himself initiated. Reconsidering his early love poetry on Palestine he has identified his role in *'Āshiq min Filasṭīn* [A lover from Palestine] as a poetic role that he had played in a kind of youthful ecstasy. In his dīwān *Sarīr al-gharība* [*The Stranger's Bed*], we find a poem entitled "Qanā' li-Majnūn Layla" ["A Mask of Majnūn Layla"] (121–123):

> I found a mask, and it pleased me
> To be my other. I was not
> Thirty yet and I thought, the limits
> Of being are the words. I was
> Sick for Layla like any young man, in whose blood
> Salt had spread. When she was not
> Present physically her spiritual image

Appeared in everything. She brings me close to
The circuit of the stars. She would separate me from
    my life
On earth. She is not death nor
Is she Layla. "I am you,
There is no escape from the blue naught for the last
Embrace." The river cured me when I threw myself
    into it to commit suicide... (lines 1–14)

The poet's estrangement from real life, his *Weltverlust*, could have lured him into self-annihilation as it lured Paul Celan, the great Jewish poet of exile, who in 1970 committed suicide in the Seine River. Darwish, however, is returned to life:

Then a man passing by brought me back.
So I asked him: Why do you give me back the air
And extend my death? He said
That you will know me better... who are you?
I said: I am Qays Layla, who are you?
He said: I am her husband.
So we went together through the streets of Granada
Recalling our days on the Gulf without pain,
recalling our days on the Gulf far away.
I am Qays Layla,
A stranger to my name and a stranger to my time.
(lines 15–25)

He is now prepared to step into the role of yet another exile: Louis Aragon's aged poet Mejdnoun, the hero of a Marxist-Surrealist adaptation of the Majnūn story, who wanders the embattled streets of Granada—the poetical locus of Arab exile—at the end of the fifteenth century before its fall, singing his mystic adoration for his future "Elsa" (Aragon's counterpart to Darwish's Layla), who does not yet exist but can come into being only when freedom and justice allow love to flourish (see Aragon, *Le fou*). Time, and with it political borderlines, are equally suspended in the poem. The speaker's former rival, his "other," has become his alter ego and together with him he recalls multiple exiles: not only the prototype of the Palestinian exile, the Arab exile from al-Andalus in 1492—which was also a fateful Jewish exile—but Badr Shakir al-Sayyab's exile from Iraq as well, which he had cried out standing on the shores of the Gulf and evoking his homeland.

While remaining Qays Layla, the speaker in our poem no longer walks in the footsteps of the ancient Arab Majnūn alone, but equally in those of modern poets of exile, Western and Eastern alike: Celan, Aragon, and Sayyab. As the allusions to these poets betray, his exile is no longer related to territorial exclusion, but is an existential estrangement, to the extent that the figure of the poet in the conventional sense is put into question. The concluding verses of the poem are unique in expressing a total renunciation of the modern self-perception as a subject and in dismissing any essentialist and monolithic understanding of identity, instead conveying a self-consciousness that no longer aspires to poethood but only to poetry (see Milich 116–127):

> I am a being that has never been. I am an idea for a poem
> That is without land nor body,
> Without son or father.
> I am Qays Layla, I,
> I am nothing. (lines 45–50)

The poet's exiles have come full circle: Darwish in the beginning of his poetical career had given the Palestinians a Genesis story, denarrating their exile. He later—when he celebrated the *fidā'ī* and the *shahīd*—created a Palestinian Exodus drama, dramatizing their "return" from exile (see Neuwirth, "From Sacrilege"). He has since the 1980s turned to exploring existential exile, the "other," or *al-gharīb*, having become part of his self. In his dīwān *Sarīr al-gharība* ("The stranger's bed"—the title is a pun on *ghurba*, "exile") numerous and heterogeneous experiences of exile merge. Similar to the Islamic mystic who considers the entire existence on earth to be an "exile of the soul" [*ghurba*] and similar to the religious Jew who views "the entire world to be in exile" [*galut*], the Palestinian Mahmoud Darwish perceives his world as an exile-home, "a land of words," *baladun min kalām*[16]—"ein aufgeschriebenes Vaterland" in the wording of the German exiled poet Heinrich Heine—which for an Arab without place must be located in poetry.

The Song of Songs versus Ghazal Poetry, or Shulamit versus Layla

The poetic re-creation of the figure of Palestine that the poet has achieved is not necessarily undone when he transforms his persona and ceases to claim the role of her sole partner, nor does he explicitly attempt to de-narrate this figure. Yet, his "ex-centric" self-location is, one would assume, indicative of a new mental condition attained in wider circles within the Palestinian intelligentsia.

With the retreat of Layla, the mythic Beloved, the memory of the first real Beloved re-emerges. Mahmoud Darwish had named the young Jewish woman whom he had been in love with as a young man when still residing in Haifa "Rita," or at other times "Shulamit" (see "Kitāb fī ḍaw' al-bunduqiyya" [Writing in the light of a gun] in *Ḥabībatī*), or the "strange woman." She is the heroine of a number of early poems that celebrate love but at the same time convey the relation between the couple as a love "impossible to live," a love located in sites impossible to inhabit such as an infernal place called Athina or a place simply called Sodom, both pseudonyms of Israel (see Klemm, "Poems"). She appears again in his war memoir *Dhākira lil-nisyān*, where in the apocalyptic situation of the bombardment of Beirut the poet in his daydreams has telephone conversations with her (5; *Memory* 3).

The most elaborate narrative of the love relation with Rita is, however, told in the dīwān *Aḥada 'ashara kawkaban 'alā ākhiri al-mashhadi al-Andalusī* [Eleven stars at the end of the Andalusian scene] from 1992, where a long poem entitled "Shitā' Rītā al-ṭawīl" [Rita's long winter] is dedicated to her (75–88). Here the scenario is markedly different from that of the early Rita poems. The piece is no less than a kind of translation of the biblical Song of Songs[17] into the reality of a Palestinian–Israeli loving couple—again threatened, not by the ancient city guards, but by a powerful modern ideology adverse to their love. The tension is not between female desire and patriarchal constraints, but between mutual love and political constraints. It is a poem full of motion and vitality, rich in striking bodily metaphors taken from the realm of fauna and flora. Darwish's poem starts with a nocturnal encounter, reflecting the likewise nocturnal scene of the beginning of the Song of Songs, and like the literary model more than once presenting an allusion to sexual arousal: in the Arabic poem, both lovers have already reunited in the "room," where a window, not the door, is opened—to invite the moon in, to let imagined palm trees rise up in the room. The room becomes spacious, a vast field, through Rita's presence (line 107). Rita's breasts are birds (line 15, cf. Song 4:5); she is a gazelle (line 56). Indeed, what has been said about the Song of Songs, that "the intricate metaphorical play whereby each one of the Beloved's body parts is likened to another object may in fact create an impression that the lover is attempting to fill in the gaps in his knowledge of her body, using as many vehicles as he can to grasp the tenor" (Pardes 138), could be applied to "Shitā' Rītā," lines 13–28, as well. The lover in being part of the local nature is closely related to his Beloved: he feels the needles of the cypress tree under his skin (line 76); both feel as if there were bees in their veins (line 27); she diffuses the smell of jasmine (line 72); when he found himself caught up in the hedge she freed him and cured him, washed him with her tears and spread anemones over him so that he could pass between the swords of her brothers (lines 80–83); she outwitted the watchmen of the city (line 105). As in the Song of Songs, on the threshold of fulfillment the Beloved vanishes and the lover is denied the possibility of consummating his desire. The tension between desire and fulfillment continues throughout the poem. In structural terms, as well, both texts are similar. In both the Song of Songs and "Shitā' Rītā," the lovers more than once reverse roles; in several scenes the young woman declares her love to him, curses or outwits her kinsmen for his sake, amorous dialogues being frequent. But in Darwish's poem, unlike in the Song of Songs, the male watchmen do not harass her but target him, blocking him from his familiar space (line 120) and in the end banning him from his happiness. But as the lover's self-assertions demonstrate, the modern poet is aware of his readers, reminding them that he is rewriting canonical texts, Hebrew as well as Arabic: he has "a part in the Book of Genesis, ... a part in the Book of Job, ... a part in the anemones of the *wādīs* in the poems of the ancient lovers, a part in the wisdom of the lovers demanding to love the face of the Beloved when killed by her" (lines 111–115). The last section is a kind of epilogue disclosing the end of the relationship—her pistol has been laid on the manuscript of his poem (lines 147–150)—and his being forced into exile.

Seven years later, "Rita" appears again, in a highly complex memory shaped in the poem "Ghayma min Sadūm" [A cloud from Sodom] from the dīwān *Sarīr al-gharība* (38–40). The title of the poem alludes to an early Rita poem ("Imrā'a jamīla min Sadūm" [A beautiful woman from Sodom] in *Al-'Aṣāfīr*), but it is first of all a quotation from Paul Celan, as discussed below:

> After your night, night of the last winter,
> the sea road was empty of its night guards,
> no shadow follows me after your night dried up
> in my song's sun. Who will say to me
> now: Let go of yesterday and dream with all
> of your subconscious?
> My freedom sits beside me, with me, and on
> my knees like a house cat. It stares at me and at
> what you might have left of yesterday for me: your lilac
> shawl, videotapes of dancing among wolves, and a
> jasmine necklace around the algae of the heart...
>
> What will my freedom do, after your night,
> night of the last winter?
> "A cloud went from Sodom to Babylon,"
> hundreds of years ago, but its poet Paul
> Celan committed suicide, today, in Paris's river.
> You won't take me to the river again. No guard
> will ask me: What's your name today? We won't curse
> war. We won't curse peace. We won't climb
> the garden fence searching the night for the two willows
> and two windows, and you won't ask me: When
> will peace open our citadel doors to the doves?
>
> After your night, night of the last winter,
> the soldiers pitched their camp in a faraway place
> and a white moon alighted on my balcony
> and I sat with my freedom silently staring into our night:
> Who am I? Who am I after your night
> night of the last winter?
> (trans. Fady Joudah, *Butterfly's Burden* 29)

The poem presents a new reflection of the story of Rita as told in "Shitā' Rītā al-ṭawīl" whose "plot" is now projected into the present ("videotapes"). The watchmen are no longer threatening, the soldiers have moved away, but hopes and expectations have vanished as well. The scenario of the Darwishian Song of Songs, "Shitā' Rītā"—recalled in this poem through the reminiscences of the wall of the garden, the willows, the interaction with the watchmen—has been relinquished. But the difference between both visions reaches deeper; as Stephan Milich has shown (Milich 108) the new poem relocates the Rita story, drawing the conclusion that the end of the relationship between the lovers can no longer simply be balanced by the poet's retreat to his subconscious and thus to poetical creativity. With the poet's entrance into definite exile and the disappearance of the "strange part" of his identity that was represented by the "strange Beloved," only the lonely "I" of freedom and silence remains. The poet himself now has to pose the question that until then he had been asked by the watchmen and soldiers:

> Who am I, after your night,
> The last winter night?

The spontaneous and self-affirmating assertion of Palestinian identity that was so often voiced in Darwish's previous poems has been replaced by a question; his identity has been made problematic by the loss of his lover.

The reminiscence of the infernality of the location, of Sodom—which was prefigured in the early Rita poem "Imrā'a jamīla min Sadūm" [A beautiful woman from Sodom]—brings the poet back to his impending exile: The poet will leave Sodom, the contemporary Israel, for Babylon, the land of exile par excellence. But Sodom is now associated with the experience of another poet of exile, Paul Celan, whose verse "Von Aug' zu Aug' zieht die Wolke/ wie Sodom nach Babel" (from "Marianne" in *Mohn und Gedächtnis*; see Milich 108) is rephrased by Darwish. The biblical locations of Celan's poem are reinterpreted; the words of the other are claimed as words of the self.

In Darwish's late revision of the stages of his poetical creativity as presented in this poem he overleaps, historically viewed, the long phase of his mythopoetic creation during his

Beirut activities when he was "temporarily exiled" still hoping for a return. He pre-dates his later attained consciousness of exile as a definite condition by projecting it onto a story that occurred in 1970, synchronizing his existence in a "land made of words" with that of Celan, who died in 1970. Stephan Milich has drawn attention to the fact that Darwish claims for himself the same stance toward poetry as Celan, who understood poetry as "a point of orientation and who strove to create an exile in language."[18]

Farewell to the Mythic Alter Ego, the Hero of the Palestinian Exodus

It proved no less problematic to rethink and ultimately revoke the second act of his invention of sacred history. Darwish had already in the 1980s tried to distance himself from the figure of the martyr,[19] exchanging the role of spokesman for the martyrs with the more modest role of their guardian, defending them against their relentless exploitation in political propaganda. Speaking to the martyred heroes perceived in the poem as having fallen asleep, and thus absent from the political scene, he had praised their integrity, their aloofness from the realm of propaganda. His "addresses to the sleeping martyrs" had been, however, of little avail to the consciousness of the Palestinian public; since Darwish had conceptually linked text and land, fighter and poet, the readers had cherished the figure of the martyr as closely related to that of the poet, a linkage that served as an anchor of hope in a situation of continuing siege and an ever-increasing desire for redemption.

The poetic creation of the martyr had been a powerful act. The martyr was closely related to traditional Islamic redeemer figures bearing strong mythic characteristics; his *hieros gamos*, his sacred marriage with the mythic earth of Palestine, the *'urs al-shahīd*, had bestowed on him semi-divine dimensions. The Palestinian martyr can be considered an Arab embodiment of the "dying gods" that K. J. Phillips has claimed are ubiquitous in Western literature of the twentieth century. Gods, once established through poetic words, do not die, but have—in order to disappear—to be "killed" by those whose words created them. About thirty years after the creation of the martyr, in 2002, Darwish turns the hierarchy of ranks upside down by exposing himself to the devastating critique of his poetic creature. He allows the martyr to correct his perception of martyrdom and to tell him that his entire martyr poetry was superfluous, nothing but idle noise. The martyr thus steps out of the creation of the poet, rejecting any part in his poetic imagination. To quote from the final section of Darwish's dīwān *Ḥālat ḥiṣār* [*State of Siege*] (98; trans. Elbendary 2002):

> The martyr besieges me when I live a new day.
> He asks me: "Where have you been?
> Return the words you gave me as presents
> To the dictionaries,
> Relieve the sleepers from the buzzing echo."

Step by step, the figure of the martyr as a poetic creation is deconstructed. Thus, the inverted social order—where not men but women determine the social life, staging a wedding instead of a funeral—needs to be revised:

> The martyr warns me: Do not believe their ululations
> Believe my father when he looks at my picture, crying
> Why did you change turn, my son, walking on ahead
> of me
> I was to be first.

Martyrdom is no longer a social rite with redemptive power, but an exclusively individual act motivated by personal pride and defiance of despair:

> To resist means: to be confident of the health,
> Of the heart and of the testicles, to be confident of
> your incurable malady,
> The malady of hope.

Martyrdom is viewed as an absolutely private endeavor; it resembles another intimate human experience of transgressing the borders between the self and the other: the transition from real time and real space into imagined sacred time and space familiar from the Islamic ritual prayer. This particular intertextuality is suggested by the concluding verse of the section on the martyr, which echoes the concluding phrase of Islamic ritual prayer, *al-salāmu 'alaykum* [Peace be upon you]. But whereas in prayer those words—uttered in the end of the ceremony and addressed to the real or imagined co-performers of prayer—mark the re-entrance of the praying person from imagined sacred time and space into reality, the martyr bids farewell for good: he addresses the "nothing" that has become of him; he bids farewell to his shadow [*shabaḥ*]:

> And in what remains of the dawn—I walk outside myself.
> And in what remains of the night—I hear the echoes
> of footsteps within me.
> Peace be upon him who shares my alertness at the
> ecstasy of the light,
> The light of butterflies
> In the night of this tunnel.
> Peace be upon my shadow.

By presenting a wholesale deconstruction of the poetical image of the martyr, Darwish ends his long personal history as a mythopoetic poet and thus concludes his role as a liminal figure, though he does not cease to reflect collective political issues in his poetry. But he certainly converts—or, more precisely, concludes—his long impending conversion from a sort of "magician poet" submersing vicariously for his community in mythic time and space, to a more personal artistic role that comes close to that of a modern, ideologically independent freelance writer. After creating a Genesis story and an Exodus drama for his homeland Palestine, Darwish has rewritten the Song of Songs, thus creating a scenario where the self and the other no longer exclude each other but, on the contrary, seek each other in unfulfilled longing. The supposedly apolitical Song of Songs provides a common biblical ground for both Palestinians and Jews. Exile becomes a space for desire that for the Palestinian Mahmoud Darwish, who perceives the world as an exile-home "made of words," can be best located in poetry. "In the end, we will ask"—he says in the poem "Fī al-masā' al-akhīr 'alā hadhihī al-arḍ" [On the last evening on this earth] (in *Aḥada*, *Dīwān* vol. 2, 471–557):

> Was Andalusia
> Here or there? On this earth… or in poetry?

8
Exile and the City: The Arab City in the Writing of Mahmoud Darwish

Hala Khamis Nassar

I walked like a foreign tourist
with a camera and a small guide book
It had poems describing this place
poems by many a foreign poet
—"Not as a Foreign Tourist Would," translated by Sinan Antoon

A POET IN (AND OF) EXILE, MAHMOUD DARWISH HAS LIVED MOST OF HIS life in both Arab and Western metropolises; it is hardly surprising, then, that a plethora of city references appears throughout his poetry and prose. In 1970, Darwish left Israel to study in Moscow. There he decided not to come back to Israel and instead left for Cairo. Since then, he has lived in Beirut, Tunisia, Paris, Jordan, and finally, in 1996, he was allowed to return to the West Bank and live in Ramallah. Darwish is not alone among Arab poets in espousing an "ambivalent attitude" toward the Arab cities.[1] Since at least the 1950s, most Arab poets have lived in cities for the opportunities they offer, while regarding the city with what Yair Huri has called "a unique ambivalence." Many of these poets, explains Huri, especially those who migrated from rural areas to the city, find the Arab metropolis an alienating space; at the same time, they appreciate the city for "the immeasurable possibilities and the immense cultural space the big city offers its inhabitants, especially its poets and artists" (Huri 185). But although Huri acknowledges that poets such as al-Bayyati, al-Sayyab, Abd al-Sabur, Hawi, and Adonis share with Darwish a rural background, he ignores the differing political, social, and cultural scenes from which these poets emerged, which must also be taken into consideration when thinking about the origins and forms of their ambivalence.

Translations in this chapter are by Hala Khamis Nassar unless otherwise noted.
For Tarik M. Ramahi

Mahmoud Darwish's ambivalence toward the Arab city is unique, I will argue, in that it emerges not simply from a rural/urban tension, but from the fact that he has been actively immersed in Palestinian politics, has been disappointed in Arab regimes, and most importantly has been living almost continuously in a self-imposed exile. I will also argue that Darwish's representations of various Arab and non-Arab cities collectively work to build a poetic home in exile for Darwish himself and for his Palestinian readers.

The polarization between the city and the countryside, as M.M. Badawi has pointed out, "is by no means a universal literary phenomenon. It is certainly a feature of European literature from the Greeks right down to modern times" (*Modern* 26). This dichotomy is perhaps best articulated by Raymond Williams:

> 'Country' and 'City' are very powerful words, and this is not surprising when we remember how much they seem to stand in for the experience of human communities... On the country has gathered the idea of a natural way of life: peace, innocence, and simple virtue. On the city has gathered the idea of an achieved center: of learning, communication, light. Powerful hostile associations have also developed: on the city as a place of noise, worldliness and ambition: on the country as a place of backwardness, ignorance, limitation. A contrast between country and city, as fundamental ways of life, reaches back to classical times. (qtd. in Badawi, *Modern* 26)

In the case of Arabic literature, Badawi argues that "a third factor comes into play, which in classical Arabic Literature of the Middle Ages is of much greater significance than the country, namely the desert" (27). Thus, the polarization between the city and countryside found in Western literature becomes in classical Arabic literature an opposition of the desert to the city. Huri claims that one of the main themes of classical Arabic poetry is "the distinct dichotomy between city and country life, or to be more specific, between the urban-sedentary and Bedouin-nomadic way of life" ("Seeking" 186). The struggle between the sedentary and the nomadic ways of life ended in favor of the city, to the extent that to the classical poets, writes Huri, "the Arab city—with its monuments, green spaces, and springs and rivers—became the embodiment of Paradise on earth."

The city as a positive, welcoming place continues to be a recurrent theme in classical Arabic poetry from the Middle Ages to the nineteenth and up to the start of the twentieth century, which marked the beginning of the Arab literary renaissance (187).

The development of modern Arabic literature, which began over a century ago, "was closely and inextricably connected with the growth of the modern Egyptian city, Cairo in particular" (Badawi, *Modern* 29). Literature and the modern city were the product of the same political, social, and intellectual forces, part of a wider process of revival and cultural assimilation known in Arabic as *al-Nahḍa*, which began in the nineteenth century. Badawi explains the relationship thus:

> they were both manifestations of the movement of westernization which was begun on a very limited scale, confined mainly to technology, by Muhammad Ali, but which, in the course of time, gathered momentum and widened its scope, especially in the age of Khedive Ismail, during whose reign many major changes, even topographical changes, in Cairo took place. (*Modern* 29)

The historical development of the Arabic novel and drama, and their dependence on the development of the modern Arab city, follows a familiar process. In the late nineteenth century, modern Arabic literature as a genre was fostered and shaped by a variety of factors, notably the spread of printing presses turning out translations of Western fiction, the rise of journalism, the growth of the educated urban middle class as a reading public, and the spread of Western political ideologies, particularly nationalism (Badawi, *Modern*).

The city became a frequent theme in modern Arabic poetry, with its treatment depending heavily on the attitude of each poet. One of the modern trends of contemporary Arabic poetry identified by Salma Khadra Jayyusi is the "frequent use of the theme of the *City*, [as] the center of exploitation and misery, of social injustice and political intrigue" (*Modern Arabic Poetry* 32). Jayyusi attributes this trend to al-Sayyab's poem "Jaykūr and the City," in which the lost village symbolizes a place of innocence, in direct opposition to the city as a place where corruption, cruelty, alienation, and isolation prevail (on al-Sayyab, see DeYoung, *Placing*). In discussing modern Arab poets and their political activism, sacrifice, and vision, Bassam Frangieh posits that the Arab city is used to represent a particularly pessimistic view of the Arab situation at large, since the city is "full of confusion and contradictions, corrupt leaders and thieves, gallows and prisoners and incinerators."[2] Jayyusi writes that the depiction of the city in Arabic literature is as a "cactus land, a mill, a wilderness, a bottomless sewer where alienation of the poet is complete" (*Anthology* 46). The Arab city is also a symbol for

> corruption, injustice and political conspiracies, and is employed as a symbol of evil, oppression and alienation. It is also a symbol for cruelty, inhumanity, and loss of innocence. As a result, poets are rejecting the ills of contemporary Arab society when they reject the modern city. (Frangieh, "Modern" 237)

It is not surprising that for al-Sayyab, al-Bayyati, and other poets, the Arab city generates negative images, since it has been, as Jayyusi reminds us, "the center of coercive government establishment, with its brutal police force and its hordes of informers, and was the home of thousands of social outcasts living in sordid conditions that drove them to the limits of their endurance" (*Modern Arabic Poetry* 156).

Although many poets would follow this critical trend, other themes would also surface: the city as a place of not only oppression but liberation, a place offering possibilities despite poverty, a space that could be both suffocating and liberating, a center for exploitation but also for modernization, a place lacking in spirituality but nonetheless overflowing with creativity, and much more.

However, the depiction of the city by Palestinian poets differs from that of other Arab poets, in that Palestinian cities are above all emblematic of the lost homeland yearned for by uprooted Palestinians. This longing for a place, writes Jayyusi, "is eternal in [Palestinian] poetry, unquenchable, unlimited and it can never be diminished.... The land, its flora and fauna, its villages and cities, are all integral parts of their lost and ever-sought-after dream" (*Modern Arabic Poetry* 35). Jayyusi notes that the central symbol for "Palestine lost and Palestine regained, of innocence lost and innocence regained" is the city of Jaffa and its orange grove.[3] Other Palestinian cities, including Jerusalem, Jericho, Acre, Haifa, and others, are recurrent symbols in poetry. Crucially, Jayyusi points out that in Palestinian literature the Palestinian city is never "delineated as a menace," and cannot "instill any hatred or rancor" (35). Moreover, the Palestinian city is often characterized as itself a victim, and a place of "resistance after death" (*Anthology* 47). This positive representation of the Palestinian city is rarely encountered in poetry describing other Arab cities.

It is worth noting that the dichotomy between the urban and the rural is not present in Darwish's poetry, since Palestine is predominantly represented as a rural landscape and a peasant country, as Johnson-Davies has pointed out (in Darwish, *Music* x). In Darwish's earlier poetic production, Palestinian cities are hardly mentioned; if harbor cities such as Acre, Jaffa, or Haifa are referred to, they are always associated with images of the sea and represent the embarkation point on the road to exile (Mansson, *Passage* 166). Therefore, the traditional polarization between the city and the country is not emphasized in Darwish's poetry, and instead the opposition is structured as, in Mansson's words, "exile versus home," with "'Home' cities belong[ing] to the same sphere as the rural country" (166).[4]

In addition, in his earlier works, Darwish generally addresses Palestinian cities as spaces empty of their inhabitants. This can be seen, for example, in the poem "Da'wa lil-tadhkar" ["A Call to Remembrance"] from *'Āshiq min Filasṭīn*, where he tackles the theme of the city for the first time (in *Dīwān* vol. 1, 135):

> The migrating sad birds
> Didn't forget anything except your face
> How did it get lost—
> You were my key to the heart of the city?
> (trans. Mansson, *Passage* 167)

Unlike the arguments of both Jayyusi and Barbara Parmenter—that Palestinian writers give Palestinian cities names and identities—Darwish's city here is nameless. His city is lost, notes Mansson, due to the departure of its inhabitants; the key to the city is also the face of the beloved. The only remaining link between the poet and the lover/the cities is memory, which is in danger due to forced emigration.[5]

Like the "migrating sad birds," Darwish had to leave Haifa and live in exile. As a wanderer, Darwish followed "the path of the Palestinians in their diaspora, wherever the winds of politics drive them" (Jayyusi, *Modern Arabic Poetry* 35–36). Therefore, my concern here will not be primarily with Darwish's representations of Palestinian cities, but rather with his depictions of the "other" Arab cities he inhabited while living in exile. It is worth mentioning that Darwish's Arab city cannot be easily categorized in his poetry. His attitude depends on location, fluctuates over time, and thematic shifts occur in his lyrics according to the winds of Palestinian politics.

On the question of exile in general, Edward Said warns us against imagining exile to be a purely "literary" concept, for this robs it of its historicity:

> [O]n the twentieth-century scale, exile is neither aesthetically nor humanistically comprehensible: at most the literature about exile objectifies an anguish and a predicament most people rarely experience first hand, but to think of the exile informing this literature as beneficially humanistic is to banalize its mutilations, the losses it inflicts on those who suffer them, the muteness with which it responds to any attempt to understand it as "good for us." Is it not true that the views of exile in literature and, moreover, in religion obscure what is truly horrendous: that exile is irremediably secular and unbearably historical, that it is produced by human beings for other human beings; and that, like death but without death's ultimate mercy, it has torn millions of people from the nourishment of tradition, family, and geography?

Edward Said, who befriended many poets in exile, writes that to "see a poet in exile—as opposed to reading the poetry of exile—is to see exile's antinomies embodied and endured with a unique intensity" (*Reflections* 174). Said lauds Darwish's poetry of exile and Palestinian national identity as "an epic effort to transform the lyrics of loss into the indefinitely postponed drama of return" (179).

Many Palestinian writers and intellectuals had to live in other Arab cities after 1948, specifically Beirut, Cairo, Damascus, and Amman, and in various metropolises in Europe and the Americas. Jayyusi and Parmenter both conclude that Palestinian writers in the diaspora do not offer any positive representations of Cairo, Baghdad, or Damascus (although they allow that Beirut, Sidon, and Tyre are mentioned affectionately). The city of exile in Palestinian literature, writes Parmenter, "is unrelenting in its ugliness. It is associated with crowds, strangers, vermin, corrupt bureaucrats, and hucksters" (*Giving* 60). In the same vein, according to Jayyusi, Palestinian diaspora literature, especially after the 1967 war, does not reflect a positive evaluation of the Arab city. Instead, as Jayyusi suggests, there is "a general identification with others, not simply with nationalities, and it is clear that Palestinian writers will identify with revolutionaries, the poor, the exile, and as in Jabra's work, the intellectuals" (*Anthology* 45–47). In addition, when Palestinian writers in exile refer to their Palestinian cities, the yearned for cities of home serve as a fixed mark against the rootless and often hostile life in exile (47).

One of the earliest poems in which Darwish articulates this feeling of exile is the poem "Risāla min al-manfā" ["Letter from Exile"] in the 1964 dīwān *Awrāq al-zaytūn* [Olive leaves]. In it, we encounter an adolescent young man who has left his village in search of work, and is working in a restaurant in a city. In a hostile and alienating environment, he lacks all but the most basic means of existence, is without friends or family, and has nothing to console him except writing.[6]

> Where shall I begin? Where end?
> The cycle of time is limitless
> And all I have in my exile
> Is a haversack containing a stale loaf, my yearning,
> And a notebook which somehow lightens my burdens
> [...]
> Night, Mother, is a hungry killer wolf
> Pursuing the wanderer wherever he goes
> And opens horizons to ghosts,
> And the forest of willows still embraces the winds
> (trans. Johnson-Davies; for entire poem, see Darwish, *Music* 6–8)

Like any impoverished worker, the young man's experience is one of torment, loneliness, hunger, and cold, with the night pictured as a wild animal chasing his prey. But note, moreover, the aching feeling of alienation, the lack of any sense of belonging, and the inability to return to the familiar place.[7] Darwish writes:

> To whom have I written these pages?
> What mail is there to take them?
> Blocked is the way by land and sea and air.
> [...]
> Perhaps like me you have no address.
> What's the worth of a man
> Without a homeland,
> Without a flag,
> Without an address?
> What is the worth of such a man?
> (trans. Johnson-Davies, *Music* 6–8)

The young man's exile in the city is not only expressed in physical uprooting and separation from the homeland, but also the anguish of losing his national identity, his sense of worth, and the inability to reconnect via familiar symbols of home: the address and the flag. Also, in exile the young man questions his own personal worth and equates it with the status of the lost homeland—just as Darwish at the age of six had to experience the loss of Palestine and had to reestablish a national connection with the homeland, unfortunately while in exile.

The first Arab city in which Darwish set foot after leaving the homeland to study in Moscow was Cairo, and he was immediately overwhelmed by the fact that everyone around him was speaking Arabic (Bitton and Sanbar, *Et la terre*). His initial enthusiasm for Cairo, as the first Arab city he lived in, changed over the course of time due to Egypt's position regarding the PLO and the signing of the Camp David agreement in 1978 (cf. Darwish, *Fī waṣfi ḥālatinā* 23). In a quick scan of Darwish's prose collections, one notices how at the beginning Egypt was put on a pedestal and regarded as a symbol of the greater Arab homeland and the center of support for the battle to liberate Palestine. Darwish eventually loses faith not only in Cairo, but also in the rest of the Arab regimes, as their support for Palestine became increasingly lip service only. After the signing of the Camp David agreement, Darwish felt disappointed and wrote in despair that "the Arabs should forget Arab nationalism, and the Palestinians should be aware that they are without a future" (27).

Darwish's next stop after Cairo was Beirut, where he moved in 1972. In the Arab world, Beirut has always been regarded as the center for the intelligentsia, and Beirut has a special significance for Darwish; he remained there for a decade, until the PLO was driven out of Lebanon in 1982. In both *Memory for Forgetfulness*, a quasi-autobiographical prose account of one day in Beirut, and in the poem "Beirut," Darwish recollects his ambivalence about the city. Darwish wrote the poem and the prose piece in Paris shortly after the 1982 Israeli invasion of Lebanon.[8] In "Beirut," Darwish sees the city as a mistress with a history made of "gold and fatigue":

> An apple for the sea, marble narcissus flower
> Stone butterfly, Beirut
> Shape of the soul in the mirror
> Description of the first woman, smell of early mist
> Beirut is built of gold and fatigue
> Of Andalusia and Damascus
> Silver, seafoam, bequests of earth in the plumage of doves
> Death of a cornstalk
> Vagrancy of a fugitive star between my love and me
> Beirut –I did not hear my blood before I uttered
> The name of the mistress
> Who sleeps across my blood, who sleeps....
> (trans. Lena Jayyusi and Christopher Middleton, in
> Jayyusi, *Modern Arabic Poetry* 204)

It is noteworthy that Beirut is described in terms of female attributes. Beirut is an "apple for the sea" and the first woman (perhaps an allusion to Eve, the mother of all and the original temptress in the biblical tradition), and is imagined as the poet's own mistress whom he reluctantly had to leave behind. Such gendered descriptions of the Arab city are yet another recurrent theme in Darwish's poetics that have not yet been adequately addressed.

In the same poem, Beirut is presented as the place where Palestinian refugees pitched their first tents after the 1948 war. It is where the second exodus took place, during which the Palestinians were held captive and under siege by the IDF in 1982, with nothing to mark their identity except posters of martyrs hung under the cover of the night:

> Captives we are in this flabby age
> Invaders have delivered us up to our kin
> [...]
> We found nothing to indicate our identity
> Except our blood that climbs the walls and in secret
> We sing:
> Beirut our tent
> Beirut our star
> [...]
> A grey horizon scattered in the distance
> Circle path of mother-of-pearl, not roads
> And from Hell to the Atlantic
> From the gulf to Hell right left and center
> I saw nothing but a scaffold
> With one single rope for two million necks
> [...]
> Is Beirut a mirror we can break
> To enter into the fragments
> Or are we mirrors for the drizzle to shatter? (206)

Moreover, Darwish points in the same poem to Beirut's ugly face, where human life is traded as a commodity in the context of a corrupt, boisterous, and booming economy, and where governments representing every religious or political party rule the city's streets. He says:

> Exporting martyrs in order to import whisky
> And the latest thing in sex and torture
> [...]
> Beirut, markets hung over the sea
> An economy that destroys production
> To build hotels and restaurants
> A government in a street or an apartment

And although Beirut has been left in ruins after the Israeli invasion, it remains for Darwish a symbol of his first kiss and of his childhood.

A moon shattered over the bench of darkness
Beirut is a lily of rubble
A first kiss
[...]
A rose that can be heard, Beirut
A voice that separates the victim from the sword
A little boy, who flung away the regulation and
commands
And the mirrors—
Then fell asleep (206)

In spite of the rubble, Beirut the mistress remains beautiful and delicate, like a lily or a rose that not only has a scent, but also a voice on behalf of the victims—which is to say the Palestinians—who were unjustly slaughtered. Despite Darwish's ambivalent feelings about Beirut, within the poem the city also represents a moment of self-reflection. Through the use of imagery like the moon and the mirror, the poet is using the battle of Beirut to condemn the injustices against the city's inhabitants and its Palestinian refugees.

In Darwish's more recent works, one cannot fail to notice yet another shift in his portrayal of the Arab city. Generally speaking, Darwish ceases to directly address the contemporary Arab city, and opts instead to invoke historical cities in Arab countries and Muslim Spain. The invocation of historical spaces is often accompanied by a string of references to both historical and modern poets. Amina Elbendary, in her review of *Lā ta'tadhir 'ammā fa'alta* [*Don't Apologize for What You Did*] (2004), says that Darwish "has always shown a willingness to situate himself within the pantheon of world poets, both contemporary and historical." In this collection alone, he names both historical and modern poets: Yanis Ritsos, Pablo Neruda, Federico Garcia Lorca, Abu al-Tayyib al-Mutanabbi, Amal Dunqul, and Badr Shakir al-Sayyab, and says:

And I, even if I be the last
Have found enough words...
(from "And I, Even if I be the Last" in *Lā ta'tadhir* 21)

In invoking historical and contemporary cities and poets, Darwish in *Don't Apologize for What You Did* addresses current political issues in the Arab city, as well as marking his return to the practice of poetry as poetry.[9] During the 2003 American invasion of Iraq, Darwish uttered a cry to remind the rest of the Arab world about what Baghdad stands for and why the oldest city should be defended. The US-led occupation of Iraq has been compared to the Israeli occupation of Palestinian lands, so Darwish's "invocation" of the Iraqi poet Badr Shakir al-Sayyab in this context is very à propos (Elbendary, "Like Him"). In remembering a fellow poet in exile (al-Sayyab was exiled from Iraq to Kuwait in 1953), Darwish writes in *Lā ta'tadhir 'ammā fa'alta* [*Don't Apologize for What You Did*]:

> I remember al-Sayyab… Poetry is born in Iraq:
> Be Iraqi to become a poet my friend!
> I remember al-Sayyab: he did not find life as he
> Imagined between the Tigris and the Euphrates: he
> didn't think,
> Like Gilgamesh, of the leaves of immortality,
> And he didn't think of resurrection afterwards…
> […]
> I remember al-Sayyab, when I am struck with fever
> And hallucinate: my brothers were preparing supper
> For Hulagu's army: no servants but they… my
> brothers!
> I remember al-Sayyab: we did not dream of the
> Food that bees do not deserve.
> […]
> I remember al-Sayyab. Poetry is experience and exile:
> Twins. And we haven't dreamt of a life more than
> Life, and to die our own way.
> 'Iraq;
> 'Iraq;
> 'No place but Iraq.'
> (trans. Elbendary "Like Him")

By summoning al-Sayyab, one of the most prominent modern Arab poets, and by remembering him in combination with references to the Sumerians, the ancient Greeks, and the first destruction of Baghdad by Hulagu's army, Darwish emphasizes both the historical and contemporary value of Baghdad. The poem is also a way for Darwish implicitly to condemn the Arab puppet regimes and their dependency on the US—"my brothers were servants"—in participating in yet another destruction of Iraq. However, in exile, both al-Sayyab and Darwish only "dreamt" of poetry and the dignity of life and death in their "own way," not dictated by new colonial forces. Although Darwish remembers al-Sayyab's poetry in terms of "experience" and "exile," and although al-Sayyab's early poetic representations of Baghdad were not especially positive, the poem maintains that Baghdad, the Arab city, must be remembered and defended for both its historical and poetical value (for more on al-Sayyab's Iraq, see DeYoung, *Placing*).

In the same collection, *Lā ta'tadhir 'ammā fa'alta* [*Don't Apologize for What You Did*], Darwish also pays tribute, in the guise of a poet/tourist, to cities, spaces, and sites that are of both personal and historical importance in the Palestinian struggle, such as Jerusalem, al-Sham/Damascus, Beirut, Egypt, and Tunisia. In the poem "Lā kamā yaf'al al-sā'iḥ al-ajnabī" ["Not as a Foreign Tourist Would"], Darwish writes:

> I walked like a foreign tourist
> with a camera and a small guide book
> It had poems describing this place
> poems by many a foreign poet
> I felt that I was the speaker in them
> were it not for the differences in rhymes
> I would have said:
> I *am* my other
> (trans. Sinan Antoon)

In exile, the poet is "like a foreign tourist" becoming his own double—both writer and reader searching unfamiliar streets and among unfamiliar faces (the double being a recurrent motif in Darwish's poetry).[10] In "Fī al-Quds" ["In Jerusalem"], the poet walks in different epochs, as a tourist, in the streets of the Old City where the "prophets share the history of the sacred.../ they ascend to the heavens and return less crestfallen and sad,/ for love and peace are sacred and coming to the city" (*Lā ta'tadhir* 47). The poet in Jerusalem is not just a tourist, but identifies himself with the prophets who ascended to Heaven: as he "walks in his sleep," the poet does not "see anyone behind" him or "in front of" him as he becomes "someone else in the manifestation." The whole poem seems to emphasize the holiness of the city from which prophets ascend to Heaven, but a strong change of tone occurs at the end of the poem, when Darwish asks "Who am I?" and the dream is abruptly interrupted by an Israeli female soldier who asks "Is it you again? Didn't I kill you?" The poet's reply:

> I said: you killed me and... like you, I forgot to die
> (48)

The lines underscore the way that Palestinian politics continue to occupy Darwish's poetry, despite his relentless efforts to get away from the heavy burden of being identified as a "poet of resistance" by emphasizing the fact that the essence of his poetry is simply poetry.

Another significant shift in Darwish's portrayal of the Arab city occurs with his depiction of Cairo in *Do Not Apologize for What You Did*. In the poem "Fī Miṣr" ["In Egypt"] the poet is in historic Cairo, and is not preoccupied with the search for his double: rather, he feels at home, paradoxically because he is both utterly unique and belongs to an ancient lineage. In Egypt, the poet says, "nothing is like me," for he is "the son of the Nile—this name is enough for me." Again, he finds himself in the company of prophets, this time with Moses of Egypt, "I was there. There the human being used to write the wisdom of death/life" (*Lā ta'tadhir* 119–120).

When Darwish continues to walk in another Arab city, he becomes more engrossed not only in the search for his double and/or his shadow, but also the search for himself, which he finds in al-Shām. Darwish says, "I know who I am among the crowd [...] I am I am in al-Shām, not my resembler and not my ghost" (from "Fī al-Shām" ["In Damascus"], *Lā ta'tadhir* 118–119). Unfortunately, this unrelenting search for the self is not just an embodiment of the harsh reality of exile, but leads to direct confrontations with it. In the opening lines of "Shukran li-Tūnis" ["A Thank You for Tunisia"], the poet/the self while reading poetry in Tunisia "cried among its women in the local theater." Darwish here alludes to a specific incident: Tunisia is the Arab city in which Palestinians sought sanctuary after leaving Beirut in 1982. During a poetry reading in 1994, Darwish bids farewell to Tunisia, the Arab city, and asks, "Have we left something behind? Yes, a longing heart and the best part of us. We left behind martyrs we commend to your care" (Bitton and Sanbar, *Et la terre*). Moreover, for a period of time the poet "pitches a new tent" in Tunisia, but he is restless because in his "language," there is a "mysterious" urge to "travel" and it cannot be controlled even by Carthage or "the winds of the southern Berbers." Therefore, the poetic self is compelled again to say thank you and bid farewell to Tunisia/the lover/the language. In other words, exile ends up being the perpetual state of living. In "A Thank You for Tunisia," Darwish writes:

> My language takes me and flies me to our eternal
>   unknown
> [...]
> My home here is not my home,
> and my exile is not like an exile.
> (*Lā ta'tadhir* 113)

While Darwish has been preoccupied with finding temporary substitutes for "home"—or even a permanent residence in exile—he has managed to build a sort of "home" or *bayt* in his poetic language.[11] It is a useful coincidence, for Darwish purposes that *bayt* means in Arabic both "home" and "line of poetry."

Furthermore, Darwish's life in exile has ultimately become a consciously chosen lifestyle. Even now that he has finally been allowed to live in the occupied territories, he still feels as if he is living in exile. Asked about his decision to live between Ramallah and Amman and not in his original home, the Galilee, Darwish replied:

> Galilee is my home. My personality was formed there. My personal nation is there, I have feelings for the place, for its hills and rocks and plants and sunsets.[12]

However, when it comes to language, he does not live in exile, for he always builds a home with his poetic language, on the page and in memory. Darwish says:

> Palestine is the group homeland, but my personal homeland is where I can *interpret* and *understand* [my emphasis] every flower; it is the place where I grew up. And that is Galilee, not Ramallah. Yet it is not possible for me to live in Galilee, and I am resigned to never making it my home again. (Shehadeh, "Mahmoud" 59)

Today, Darwish continues to portray the cities of his exile in complex and contradictory ways, as is apparent in his latest collection *Ka-zahr al-lawz aw ab'ad* [Like almond flowers or further] (2005). The dīwān consists of thirty-four poems divided into two main sections: "Personal Pronouns: You, He, I, and She" and "Exile no. 1, 2, 3, and 4," the last comprising a poem Darwish wrote in homage to Edward Said following Said's death in September 2003. The first section ("You") contains a poem entitled "Now in Exile" that sets the tone for the whole collection: "Now, in exile... yes at home." In that one line Darwish points to the paradox that although he now has the option of living in Ramallah, a symbol of a national home since the Palestinian National Authority is situated there, nonetheless, he feels even there as if he is living in exile.

In "Exile no. 1: Tuesday and the Weather is Clear" ["Manfā 1: Nahār al-Thulāthā' wa-al-jaww ṣāfin"], the poet walks aimlessly around an unnamed city, once again looking for his double:

> I walk lightly lightly. I look around me
> So that I might see a resemblance between my
> descriptions
> And the willow of this horizon I observe nothing
> That identifies me (106)

In the same poem, the poet not only is unable to identify himself, but also his cities go unnamed and his countries are unidentified. The poet says: "you walk as if you are someone else" (107), and "forget the old road to our house" (111), "I walk in a street that leads to nowhere" (114). To the poet, because he has for so long been living in exile, it becomes apparent that it is not important which city he ends up in. All cities look alike, in that walking in their streets leads you nowhere, and the danger of forgetting the road to your old home is always imminent. In Darwish's earlier poetry, forgetting the road to your old home is considered a sin; here, on the other hand, forgetting is a direct result of the inability to return home: "I do not look behind me, for I cannot/ Go back to anything, and I cannot disguise" (110).

It is noteworthy that in this collection Darwish not only "walks" through Arab cities but also revisits important personal spaces and junctures in the West, such as London, Paris, and New York. These Western cities become increasingly important in this collection, as they mark yet another shift in Darwish's depiction of his city of his exile. Some of these cities serve as sanctuary, poetic inspiration, and even the site of a celebration of exile.

Perhaps this new perspective is a function of age: in the course of the collection, the walking pace in these nameless cities and countries changes, from that of a young poet who treads lightly and quickly to a weary one whose steps are becoming heavy with age:

> … and I walk heavily heavily, as if I have a rendezvous
> with one of the losses. I walk and in me a poet
> gets ready for his eternal rest in a London night (121)

Here, the city of exile, where the poet's double/self longs to find eternal rest, is named all of a sudden: London. It is intriguing that the city of fog and the original imperial metropole would be the poet's place for eternal rest, rather than any of the previously mentioned Arab cities. Yet, the road to eternal rest and the end of exile is still not within reach. In the same poem and still on the road to exile, this time to a Western city [i.e., to London], the poet passes by al-Shām and asks, "how can I carry the burden of the *qaṣīda* from you and me?"(122) Continuing his journey in the same poem, the exiled poet searches no longer for himself or his double as he walks, but for his own language. In Paris at night he feels alienated; he and the French do not speak each other's languages. He says:

> Inside me there is a balcony no
> one passes to greet me.
> Outside me there is a world
> that does not return the greeting.
> My Language!
> Can I be what you are? Or you—my language—is
> what I am? (123)

Perhaps paradoxically, Darwish says that he loved Paris precisely because he does not speak French, a fact that kept him on the margins of French society.[13] He fondly recalls the French metropolis and claims that there he wrote the best of his writings. Being anonymous in the Parisian metropolis gave him a greater freedom to be what he wanted to be and act the way he wanted, free to write and to transform his poetic language (Bitton and Sanbar, *Et la terre*).

In "Exile no. 2: Thick Fog on the Bridge" ["Manfā 2: Ḍabāb kathīf 'alā al-jisr"], the poet is no longer in search of his double or his language. In what appears to be another reference to London, the poet seems to have found a friend to accompany him in exile. He is now in search of a different kind of place, not a place for eternal rest but rather:

> My friend told me, and the fog is thick
> On the bridge:
> Is a thing known from its opposite? (129)
> [...]
> I do not want a place to be buried in
> I want a place to live in and to curse if I want. (130)

In exile, both the poet and his imaginary friend or double are strangers, never in a state of belonging to a place. He says:

> On the bridge, in another country, he told me
> [...]
> the son of the country walks to a clear destination
> in a straight path. And the stranger circles around
> himself confused (135)

Again, we are no longer on a journey in search of the poetic persona, the double or the shadow; rather what we encounter, again, is a questioning of the nature of exile itself:

> I am two in one
> or
> am I one separated into two
> Oh bridge oh bridge
> which of the two exiles am I? (136)

The bridge here symbolizes the connection between home and exile, between exile and language, and between the self and its other, and between the two opponents striving for peace and reconciliation. It is an interim space, neither one place nor the other. The bridge also represents the actual Allenby Bridge, which the Palestinians walked across after the June 1967 war into Jordan. In "Exile no. 2: Thick Fog on the Bridge," Darwish evokes the image of this exodus across the bridge as an ongoing, uncomfortable, untenable state of being:

> [...] we walked on the bridge twenty years
> we walked on the bridge twenty meters
> coming and going,
> and I said: nothing remains but little
> He said nothing remains but little (136–137)
> [...]
> We stayed on the bridge twenty years
> we ate canned food for twenty years (146–147)

After the exodus across the bridge (an allusion to the 1967 war), the friend/double becomes weary with age and unable to continue crossing over or living on the bridge, leaving the original exiled speaker alone:

> If this road is long
> then I have work to do on the legends
> I was alone on the bridge, in that
> day, after Christ secluded himself on a
> mountain in the outskirts of Jericho... and before
> resurrection.
> I walk and I cannot enter and I cannot go out. I circle
> like the sunflower.
> At night I am awakened by the voice of the night
> guard
> as she sings to her friend
> Do not promise me anything
> and do not give me
> a rose from Jericho[14]

Caught on the bridge, the poet still has "more work to do" with rewriting the mythical and religious master narratives. Like Christ isolated in Jericho, he does not feel any particular affection for the historic city. He neither wants its promises, nor the gifts it offers; all he wants is to cross the bridge (alluding to the exodus of Palestinians to Jordan and other neighboring Arab countries) all the way to his old home. Once that home is liberated, he will no longer need to rework its historical or mythical narratives.

In "Exile no. 3" ["Manfā 3"] the poet takes us, yet again, to his obsession with the relentless search for the double and the shadow in the city. However, this search is different from previous searches in that it actively engages in a form of a dialogue with the shadow or the double for the sake of mutual recognition and reconciliation. In the opening lines of "Exile no. 3," the poet avoids reminding his shadow of what he used to have:

> I am he, walks in front of me and I follow him,
> I do not say to him: here, here
> Was something simple for us:
> Green stone. Trees. A street.
> [...]
> He walks in front of me
> I walk on his shadow, following... (153)

Although the poet keeps following his shadow, at one point he questions the connection: "Didn't we part? I said, he said: yes" (153). Also, the poet demands that the shadow reveal his intended destination:

> I said: where are you taking me?
> He said: toward the beginning, to where you were
>   born here, you and your name/ (154)

As the journey with the shadow to the poet's past begins, so do the reminiscences about past experiences. In "Exile no. 3," for example, there are many references to the poet's personal exodus in 1984 from his old village. While evacuating the village and walking northward to "other countries"—i.e., Lebanon—the poet says that if it was not for the moonlight "The walkers on the night [would not be able] to read their names suddenly ((refugees))/ guests on the wind" (156). In addition, none of the walkers mentioned the fact of exile:

> no one told me this place is called countries,
> beyond countries are borders, and beyond
> borders there is a place called exile and dispersion
> for us. Back then I was not in need of identity. (157)

Ultimately, the road to exile becomes permanent and reaches a full circle, as one cycle on the bridge of (no) return ends and another starts:

> I walk slowly with myself and my shadow follows me
>   and I follow him,
> Nothing brings me back
> Nothing brings it back (160)

In their journey of exile, both the poet and his shadow see how the poet's country's landscape has been changed and reshaped, with nothing remaining to mark his past inhabitance of the place except "signs telling us: you were not here" (158). Throughout the poem, one cannot fail to notice how the poet and his shadow engage in a dialogue in which each asserts his narrative over the landscape: "These are our remnants" (157). In spite of the erasure of these remnants by archeological digs, excavations, and the official renaming of places, the poet can still mark the place of his old school, now in ruins, and point out to his shadow where the family's cemetery used to be. In his exile, the poet attempts to reanimate the landscape with accounts of many living creatures and plants—deer, turtles, ants, birds, horses, and stalks of grain—but cannot place himself in the landscape: "a poem-song, a happy ending poem-song/ has no poet/" (162). He and his shadow have no real home to return to, but will remain in continuous exile, moving from one city to another:

> We asked him: where did you come from?
> He said: from nowhere, for every place
> away from God or his land is an exile. (167)

When the shadow or the other asks who "we" are, "We told him: we are the grandsons of the place's soul. We were born here" (167). Even while contesting the narrative and asserting ownership over the landscape, the poet reaches out for his other/the shadow and asks him more than once in the course of the poem to reconcile, since both of them are still in exile:

> I said: shall we make peace so that we can share this
> absence.
> For we are here alone in the *qaṣīda*? (171)

It seems, however, that reconciliation cannot take place, at least not at this moment. For the poet asks his shadow:

> I said: is this the end of your exile?
> He said: and this is the beginning of yours
> I said: what is the difference?
> He said: the subtlety of rhetoric (173)

Although it seems in the course of "Exile no. 3" that the poet's search for his double is finally at an end—with the two engaging in an active dialogue about their perspectives on the same landscape, where memories and ruins are key remnants that allow the poet to validate his past presence—reconciliation does not take place. It is as if the contested landscape cannot be home to both at once, but must always be the point of departure for yet another exile. Yet even in exile, again, Darwish manages to build a momentary refuge: this time his city of exile is his own *qaṣīda*, in the form of this powerful late collection.

The collection *Ka-zahr al-lawz aw ab'ad* [Like almond flowers or further] ends with "Exile no. 4: Counterpoint" ["Manfā 4: Ṭibāq"], which pays tribute to the late Edward Said. In "Counterpoint," Darwish recollects his encounters with Edward Said over the span of thirty years. The central theme of the poem is familiar, as the poet describes Said finding a home, an identity, and a meaning, even while living in perpetual exile. Describing their first meeting, the poem begins with a gloomy depiction of New York City:

> New York/ November/ Fifth Avenue
>
> The sun a plate of shredded metal/
> I asked myself, estranged in the shadow: Is it Babel or

Sodom? There, on the doorstep of an electric abyss,
high as the sky, I met Edward,
thirty years ago,
time was less wild then…
We both said:
If the past is only an experience,
make of the future a meaning and a vision.
Let us go,
Let us go into tomorrow trusting the candor of
imagination and the miracle of the grass.[15]

As the poem progresses, on the one hand, Darwish recaptures incidents that provide insight into Said's personal life and academic career. On the other hand, we get a glimpse of an engaging dialogue between Darwish and Said about past experiences, the lost homeland, the impossibility of visiting the remnants of home, and the life of the exile.

He said: I am from there.
I am from here and not there, and not here
I have two names that meet and depart
I have two languages, forgot in which I used to dream.
(182)

Darwish here reminds us that Said uses the English language for writing and the other—Arabic—for conversation and for the sense of connection to his birthplace, Jerusalem. But what is interesting in the above lines is that in spite of the fact that both the poet and the intellectual are living in exile, Darwish depicts Said as a person who has come to terms with exile. Darwish describes Said's notion of exile within the context of Orientalism, but also demonstrates that although exile is a painful experience, it can be rewarding and enriching, creating multiple identities that challenge dualistic notions of home and away:

No east is east exactly
and no west is west exactly
For identity is open from multiplicity
Not a fortress or trenches/ (185)

It seems entirely fitting that Darwish ends his collection *Ka-zahr al-lawz aw ab'ad* [Like almond flowers or further] with an elegy to Said. The last encounter between the poet and the intellectual was in 2002. Darwish writes that, back then, Said was not only battling against cancer but also against a "Sodom war," this time against the people of "Babel,"—i.e. the American invasion of Iraq. Said, in spite of feeling—as the title of his memoir puts it—"out of place," scattered, displaced, inhabiting multiple identities, made out of his future a "meaning" and a "vision" that will inspire generations. Likewise, Darwish's own past and present experiences of exile in all of the many cities where he has resided, his years spent searching for home and poetic inspiration, his lifetime of exercising his poetic imagination—all of this leads him to declare that the time has come, provisionally, to say to Edward Said and to all those in exile, whether in Arab, Western, or unnamed cities: "farewell, farewell to the poetry of pain!" (197)

9
Returning to the Wind: On Darwish's *La Ta'tadhir 'Amma Fa'alta*

Sinan Antoon

for Samera Esmeir

The P(r)oem

Proems do not always succeed in illuminating the texts before which they stand. Even when they do, their flicker is intermittent or does not survive the expanse and the distant borders of the text. There are those rare instances, however, when a proem encapsulates and performs the text's gestures and stands like a well of fire or a seductive sun guiding its readings. Such is the case in Mahmoud Darwish's collection *Lā ta'tadhir 'ammā fa'alta* [*Do Not Apologize for What You Have Done*], where the following excerpts introduce the main text (11; brackets in original, parentheses and translations added):

tawārud khawāṭir aw tawārud maṣā'ir
(A coincidence of thoughts, or of destinies)

lā 'anti 'anti
wa-lā 'd-diyāru diyāru
(You are not you
And the abodes are not the abodes)

[Abu Tammam]

wa-l'āna lā 'anā 'anā
wa-lā 'l-baytu baytī
(And now, I am no longer I,
the house no longer my house)

[Lorca]

Translations in this chapter are by Sinan Antoon unless otherwise noted.

Like a miniature of the entire work, the two excerpts bespeak the central themes and the dialectical relationship between them: "self" and "home" as effaced or irrevocably lost sites, the road(s) to them and the (im)possibility of an actual return to those spaces.

Let us return to the intriguing genealogy of the proem.[1] The first part, a famous line by the 'Abbasid poet Abu Tammam (805–845) "summarizes an entire poetic tradition" (Vazquez 127) crystallized in the elegiac stance of pre-modern Arab poets before the (real or imagined) *aṭlāl* [ruins] of *diyār* [abodes, deserted habitations, and encampments] (see Stetkevych, "Towards"). So central a topos was this that its reproduction and repudiation or variation defined and created various genres and trajectories in the history of pre-modern Arabic poetry.[2] Much can be said about the topos, but suffice it to say here that it engenders a space and mood of unparalleled melancholy in its invocation of all that is lost (see Stetkevych, *Zephyrs* 16–26). There is an added crystallization in Abu Tammam's line in that the self, too, becomes a ruined site in and of itself. Miguel Angel Vazquez has retraced the line's journey westward to al-Andalus where Ibn Khafaja (1038–1138) later used it in his lament for Valencia after it was conquered by El Çid (Vazquez 127–129). Ibn Khafaja's poetry was translated into Spanish, and Lorca (1898–1936) must have read it and appropriated the line in his "Somnambular Ballad."[3] While the first person feminine [*'anti*] in Abu Tammam's line is the self, in Ibn Khafaja it becomes the city (feminine in Arabic). In Lorca's poem there is a return to the "I" and the abodes [*diyār*] become the less abstract and more immediate "house."

So much so for the journey of a topos. The topos of the journey, as previously mentioned, is also at the heart of the poems. Journey(ing) always entails an arrival somewhere and a return of sorts, or a desire for a return, unless it is a perpetual journey. Return, both to the self in its various manifestations and temporal stages, as well as to various abodes/homes, is another thread linking these poems. What is particularly fascinating about this work is that Darwish, who is one of a few poets still able to successfully inhabit the Arabic tradition, yet who always manages to take it to new horizons, manipulates the classical Arabic topos of *raḥīl* [journey][4] throughout the collection in a novel way. The topos almost serves as the infrastructure of the entire collection. It does so, however, not in the traditional linear way, but rather in a circular manner as an eternal journey or series of journeys with no teleology or closure, but aborted and postponed ends, as this reading will show.[5] With this point in mind, the book's architecture is not dissimilar to that of a long Arabic ode [*qaṣīda*] with the proem serving as the opening *aṭlāl* section, but the entire text consisting of a maze of overlapping and intersecting journeys [*raḥīl*s]. This essay is an attempt to retrace and accompany the journey and its related tropes in the collection as a whole.

The Rhythm

The first section of the collection is entitled "Fī shahwati 'l-'iqa'," which can be translated as "In the lust for the rhythm," and includes 47 short poems. The first is entitled "Yakhtārunī 'l-'īqā'u" [The rhythm chooses me] (*Lā ta'tadhir* 15–16; italics added).

> The rhythm chooses me
> and cries through me
> I am the violin's echo—not its player
> I am, in the presence of memory,
> the echo of objects
> They utter me
> so I speak
> Whenever I listen to the stone,
> I hear a white dove cooing
> It gasps through me:
> Brother! I am your little sister
> so I shed the tears of speech in her name
> Whenever I see the trunk of the China tree
> on the way to the clouds
> I hear a mother's heart
> beating through me:
> I am a divorced woman.
> And I curse, in her name, the clay of darkness
> Whenever I see a mirror on a moon
> I see love as a devil
> eyeing me:
> *I am still here,*
> *but you will not be the same*

You will not return
And I will not return
The rhythm finishes its cycle
and cries through me

The poetic persona is in the confines of the rhythm here. The latter can be read as a certain division of, and relationship to, time (tempo). An intimate bond with objects (and hence space) is discernible as well. The persona is *not* the violin's player, but its echo—an extension of its sound. Regardless of the identity of the player, an echo will continue to bespeak the sound. The relationship constructed here is not of two separate entities, but a more intimate and inextricable one. It is important to note also that in the sentence "'anā raj'u 'l-kamanī" [I am the violin's echo], "raj'" [echo] is etymologically related to the same root [r-j-'] for [rujū'], meaning "return." This invisible bond with objects and space is re-established in the poem (and elsewhere in the collection): the stone bespeaks a dove who is a sister to the poet, the tree envelops the heart of a woman who speaks to the poet. The metaphors invoked to represent bonds to space and objects always humanize the latter. Moreover, the poetic persona speaks in the *name* of these *living* objects. The third exchange between the poetic persona and his own reflection (the mirror on a moon) is a disruption of previous (harmonious) relationships as he is told by love, which metamorphoses into a devil: *You will not be the same/ You will not return!* There is an important play on the word "ta'ud" here. In the first instance, the verb is transitive and can be read as "you will not be the same," but in the next two lines, when intransitive, it means "return": *you will not return/ And I will not return*. These last two lines convey a negativity that contrasts with the beginning of the poem. In the line before last, "'akmala/yukmilu" could mean both "to continue" and "to finish." If the rhythm is to come to an end and finish its cycle, then the sound and its echo will no longer be. This disruption in the rhythm of things in the shape of an impossible or an always aborted return will haunt many of the poems (especially toward their ends).

The rhythm of life coming to an end is at the heart of the second poem, "Lī ḥikmatu 'l-maḥkūmi bil-i'dām" [I have the wisdom of a man sentenced to death] (17–18). But this impending death is represented in positive terms:

> I slept bloodied and crowned with my tomorrow
> I dreamt that the earth's heart is bigger
> than its map
> and clearer than its mirrors and my noose

At dawn, the poetic persona is awakened and told by the night guard that his death is postponed and that he must "live another death":

> so amend your last will
> the execution has been postponed
> Until when? I asked
> Wait so you can live another death!

Even the end of the rhythm is not a proper end, but rather a postponement of the end. The end is unknown and time is out of sync. Living and dying overlap and are intertwined.

Poem 3, "Sāyajī'u yawmun ākhar" [Another day will come] (19–20), is a caesura in time in the larger sequence of the poems in section I. It is a dreamy caesura away from the present, but also from the past and its burdens. It is as if after the stay of execution, "time is on vacation," as one of its lines announces.

> no one feels a desire to commit suicide
> or to depart
> outside of the past, everything is natural and real

Death is at bay for now. When not finding a little nest to sleep in the lovers' bed, the doves sleep "in an abandoned tank." But this respite from death and the past is, once again, to be disturbed if not disrupted, with the sense of anxiousness and "lateness." In poem 4 (21–22), the anxiety over the poetic persona's legacy and the complex relationship with the poetic past is manifested. The poet reflects upon himself as a literary trace. The title itself takes us back to the first hemstitch from a famous line by Abū 'l-'Alā' al-Ma'arrī (973–1058) (with a slight change):

wa 'anā wa'in kuntu 'l-'akhīra [Although the last,
I…] (Darwish)

wa 'innī wa'in kuntu 'l-'akhīra zamānuhu
la'ātin bimā lam tastati'hu 'l-'awā'ilu
[Although the last, I will bring forth what my
predecessors could not] (al-Ma'arri)

The poet has arrived late, but is determined to anchor himself within the tradition and carry his burdens and carry on. He repeats this mantra to himself (note the repetition of "And I") as if to ward off the anxiety that he is unable to perform and carry out the impossible task of saying the unsaid/unsayable ("qawlu mā lā yuqāl" is one of the most famous definitions of poetry in Arabic). The anxiety of influence and legacy is clearly visible here[6]:

Although the last
I have found enough words
Every poem is a drawing
[…]
And I, the road will carry me
And I will carry it upon my shoulders
until the object regains its image
as it is
and, later, its original name
[…]
Every poem is a dream:
I dreamed that I had a dream
It will carry me and I will carry it (dream is the road,
poetry is the road)
until I write the last line
on the grave's marble:
I slept to fly

Poetic space is the space of the unconscious and the poet is set on it until the end (death). But death is merely "sleep" that will allow him to fly. There is an unconscious desire to escape teleology and seek alternative routes. Ends either are, or are made to be, elusive and non-ends. Dodging teleological ends and history requires an appeal to the mythological. To highlight this fusion and overlap of the miraculous/mythical with the real, which is important for the economy of the text, the last section in this poem reads:

> And I will carry Jesus' winter shoes
> So he may, like all people, walk from the mountaintop
> to the lake

The dream/unconscious is the space where one could fly, but where? Like Muhammad in his nocturnal journey to Jerusalem and ascent to heaven [al-Isra' walmi'raj], the poet, too, returns to Jerusalem in his sleep. There is an interesting point to be noted here about the overlap of the mythical and the real/mundane. To walk to the lake and perform his miraculous walk on water, Jesus needs winter shoes. The phrase "Like all people" is significant in this respect. I shall return to this point later in the section on Darwish himself becoming a mythical figure. Before his own mythical/imaginary journey to Jerusalem, the poetic persona makes a stop at his mother's house for more reflections.

A Guest to Oneself and One's Others

The eternal question posed in the proems about the irrevocable change to the self is redirected to the poet himself, but is now posed by his own representation (photograph) as a young man in "Fī baytī'ummī" [At my mother's house] (23–24; italics added). This reversal transforms the poet himself into a site of memory and splits him temporally. Interestingly though, he returns here as a guest to his own past/self and to a house not his anymore: "Are you, O my guest, *I*? Are you, O *my guest*, as *we* were?" (italics added) The question is repeated thrice before the answer:

> I said: I am you
> But I jumped over the wall to see
> What would happen if the unknown saw me
> respectfully plucking a violet
> from its hanging gardens?
> Perhaps it would have greeted me and said:
> Return safely!
> I jumped over this wall to see
> What cannot be seen
> and to measure the depth of the abyss

What is this abyss? Is it the abyss separating the past from the present? Or is it perhaps the abyss opened, and also bridged, by absence and representation, and hence poetry? These need not be mutually exclusive, of course. Elsewhere the poetic persona asks the figure of another poet, the Egyptian Amal Dunqul (1940–1983): "Can poetry save us from what time has done to us?" (145–146) Perhaps the leap over the wall signifies the poet's life trajectory, but also the decision to go into exile. This has obvious implications in the Palestinian context.[7] Is it also about the poet himself becoming a mythical figure of sorts? The unknown would have told the poet: return safely! In another poem in this collection, the figure of Yannis Ritsos (1909–1990), the famous Greek poet, tells our own poet: "Your Odysseus will return safely! He will return." The "you" has a plural referent [*Ūdīsukum*] and thus invokes the Palestinian collectivity (156).

In this first section in particular, but throughout the collection, the self is scattered and a dialogue among its various fragments manifests in the recurring use of pronouns (I, you, he, we) to refer to the self. The poetic persona no longer speaks to himself, but to his others. But what of the apology in the title of both the collection and the poem in section I? Is it the poetic persona's departure and choosing an exilic state of being that consciously or unconsciously calls for an apology? Poetry need not give us answers, of course, but sometimes it does:

> Do not apologize for what you have done!
> I say to myself
> I tell my personal other
> […]
> I whispered to my other:
> Is he the one who was you… I?
> He ignored me
> […]
> Then they turned to my mother to swear that I am the
>   one
> So she prepared to sing as she does:
> I am the mother who gave birth to him
> But the winds raised him
> I said to my other:
> Never apologize except to your mother! (26)

The series of concentric returns and attempted returns is occasionally punctuated with a meditation on the very nature of ends and returns. There is always a caesura, a recurring desire to bridge this abyss with death and love, or both. This is how "Fī mithli hādhā al-yawm" [On a day like this] (27–28) reads. In this poem, Darwish manipulates another classical topos in Arabic poetry, that of apostrophizing the poet's two imaginary companions. While in the classical tradition they represent two real or imagined companions, or, in other interpretations, the poet's sword and his horse, in the Darwishian variation they are the beginning and the end. This accentuates the solitude and alienation of the traveler whose life is measured in journeys and whose only companions are mere abstractions. Note the sense of unbelonging in the lines about being neither a citizen, nor a refugee:

> I will meet my end and my beginning
> And say: Woe unto you two!
> Take me!
> [...]
> I say: I am neither a citizen
> nor a refugee
> I want only one thing
> one thing:
> a simple quiet death
> On a day like this
> in the hidden ends of lilies
> a death that might compensate
> a little or a lot
> for a life I counted
> in minutes
> or journeys
> I want a death in the garden
> no more and no less...

Poem 9, "In 'udta waḥdaka" [If you were to return alone] (31–32), performs another attempt at a return and here it becomes clearer, perhaps, that "exile" or the path to exile could be what the poet is at pains not to apologize for. Abu Tammam's line from the proem is reproduced again here:

If you were to return alone, tell yourself:
Exile changed his features
Wasn't Abu Tammam startled before you
when he met himself:
"You are not you
And the abodes are not the abodes"
As for you,
The mirror has let you down
You… not you, say:
Where have I left my face?

Even if the abodes are unchanged and still the same upon this return, the self is not (not you/ missing two moons), let alone that it's a split self:

Have you found yourself now?
Tell yourself: I returned alone
Missing two moons
But the abodes are the abodes (32–33)

But are the abodes the abodes? The answer will come later.[8] Poems 10 to 16 read like various phases in the nocturnal journey and the mythical ascent to Jerusalem. There are constant references to "the horse," "our country," and to "Canaan" and its people, to whom poem 16 is dedicated:

Right here I saddled a horse to fly to my stars (33)
[…]
I broke the myth and was broken
I circled around the well until I flew from myself to
 what is not of it (34)
[…]
I become distant from my epoch
When I approach the place's topography (38)
[…]
Our country
so close to God's speech
has a ceiling of clouds
so distant from the name's attributes
Our country
has the map of absence (39)

[…]
The lemon seed glistens
like a lamp in the migrant's night
Geography shines
in holy scriptures
The hills become an ascent higher and higher (41)

Yet there is still anxiety about the journey itself:

If I were a bird, I would've burned my wings
The exile tells himself
Imagination opened to its sources
And became the place
The only real (42)
[…]
Nothing but light
I only stopped my horse
to pluck a red rose
from the orchard of a Canaanite woman (43)
[…]
I went on looking for my place
higher and farther
higher and farther
than my time (44)

In poem 17, "Fī 'l-Quds" ["In Jerusalem"] (47–48), the poet embarks on his own nocturnal journey to Jerusalem. It is worth noting that the notion of house is already present in the semantic history of "Jerusalem" [al-Quds]. Pre-modern sources used to refer to it as *bayt al-maqdis* [the abode of the holy]:

In Jerusalem

In Jerusalem—I mean inside the old wall—
I walk from one epoch to another
without a memory to correct me
There, prophets share the history of the sacred
They ascend to the heavens
and return less crestfallen and less sad
Love and peace are sacred
and coming to the city

I was walking over a slope and thinking:
How can narrators disagree
on the light's speech in a stone?
Do wars break out because of a stone's dim light?
I walk in my sleep
I gaze in my sleep
I see no one behind or before me
All this light is for me!
I walk, run, fly and become someone else in the
    manifestation
The words bloom like grass from Isaiah's prophetic mouth:
"You will not be safe unless you believe"
I walk as if I am someone else
My wound is a white Evangelical flower
My hands like two doves on the cross
flying and carrying the earth
I don't walk. I fly and become someone else
There is no place and no time
Who am I?
I am not I in the presence of the ascent
But I think: Only the Prophet Muhammad spoke
classical Arabic!
"What else?"
What else, a female soldier shouts suddenly:
It is you again?
Didn't I kill you?
I said: You killed me and... like you,
I forgot to die

Once again, the poetic subject "I" is holistic and unfractured at the outset of the poem, but soon afterward, it speaks its otherness and becomes "someone else" (repeated thrice) and then a total negation, "not I." Moreover, the biblical-Qur'anic serenity that characterizes the conciliatory mood of the poem and the liberation from time, space, and gravity aided by mythology and the unconscious are disrupted by the shout of the female soldier. Even in the dream and the realm of the unconscious, the real, or the threat of its existence, intrudes and aborts the return. There is an analytical reflection about this nocturnal journey in the next poem "Bighiyābihā kawwantu ṣūratahā" [In its absence I formed its image] (49–50), which is interspersed with anxiety about belonging:

Absence is the guide
Is the guide
[...]
So who am I after the visit?
A bird or a mere passerby
amidst the symbols and sellers of memory?
[...]
There is enough of the unconscious
to liberate objects from their history
and enough history
to liberate the unconscious from its ascent
[...]
Then I wake up
There is no city in the city
no "here" except "there"
and no there except here

The return was a dream; an attempt at using the unconscious for a momentary liberation from history. Perhaps prolonging the road and making the journey eternal is an antidote to the trauma of encountering the fateful end and the reality of what has become of one's obliterated homeland. Hence the desire expressed incessantly here for a never-ending road:

If I were someone else on the road
I would never look back:
O stranger!
Postpone our tomorrow
so the road may extend
and space may expand
and we may be saved from our tale:
You are so you... and I am so other
Here, before you!
If I were someone else
I would have belonged to the road
For I will not return
and neither will you (111)
[...]
If I were someone else on the road
I would have said to the guitar:
Let's rehearse on an additional string
For the house is farther

and the road to it is more beautiful
This is what my new song will say:
The longer the road
the newer the meaning
I have become two on this road:
I and someone else! (112)

In the remaining poems in section I, the poet revisits other important spaces and junctures that are of personal, but also historical, significance in the Palestinian saga, such as Beirut, Tunis, Damascus, and Egypt. These returns, too, are punctuated with reflective caesuras about death and love. Sections II and III are more pertinent to the thrust of this essay and the themes discussed above.

A Road Blocking the Road

"Tariqu 's-sāḥil" [The coastal road] occupies section II in the book. It consists of 26 statements; the first half of each starts with the signifier "ṭarīq" [road/path], whereas the second is a bracketed elaboration, or at times an anticlimax or negation, of the notion expressed in the first half. Considered within the larger narrative of the collection, it follows section I with its series of attempted returns through various roads and precedes one pivotal poem about a return to Galilee. It almost functions like a series of variations on the topos of the road itself. This is especially valid because many of the poems previously discussed are each encapsulated in a single line here (the road to oneself, the road to the sky's balconies, the road of contemplating love, etc.). There is, however, another function: to perform a multiplication and intensification of roads and journeys, as if to postpone their ends and prolong and question them at the same time. So many roads, but no arrival! There is the non-linear and circular road and the notion of the traveler being consumed by the journey:

The road of the traveler from… and to himself
[my body is a feather and the distance is a bird]

Anxiety about the teleology of the road:

The right road… the wrong road
[perhaps I erred, but it is an experience]…

A road leading to the thing or its opposite
[due to the extensive similarity between metonymy
and metaphor]

The road of peace crowned with Jerusalem
[after the end of wars with Crusader masks]
[…]
the road of spice, salt and wheat
[and war too]
[…]
the road of horses overpowered by distance
[and airplanes]

The road of old registered letters
[All letters are deposited in Caesar's caskets]

A road that is long or short
[according to Abu al-Tayyib al-Mutanabbi's mood][9]

And mythology being worn out by history:

The road of goddesses whose backs are bent
[like the banners of a retreating army]

A long road without prophets
[For they preferred difficult roads]

A road leading to the house's ruins
[under a settlement's garden]

The final section, the only one that consists of more than two sentences, collapses the notion of "road" so that the road becomes a block unto itself, an un-road:

A road blocking my road
And my ghost screams:
If
you want

to reach
your
unfettered self
do not
take
obvious roads! (125–129; brackets in original)

The poet heeds the advice of his ghost and never takes the obvious roads. The next poem in the collection, "Lā kamā yaf'alu al-sā'ihu 'l-'ajnabī" ["Not as a Foreign Tourist Would"] (131–138), traces one of those difficult roads of (no) return.

Not as a Foreign Tourist Would

I walked over what remains of the heart
Northward:
Three abandoned churches
oak trees on both sides
villages like dots on effaced letters
and a girl on the grass
reading something like poetry:
If I were older
the wolf would have surrendered to me!

I wasn't sentimental, or a Don Juan
so I didn't sit down on the grass
but, secretly, I said:
If I were twenty years younger
I would have shared some water and sandwiches with her
and taught her how to touch the rainbow

I walked like a foreign tourist
with a camera and a small guide book
It had poems describing this place
poems by many a foreign poet
I felt that I was the speaker in them
were it not for the differences in rhymes
I would have said:
I *am* my other
I was tracing the place's description:
more trees here

a moon missing there
and like the poems:
grass grows on a stone in pain
It is neither a dream
nor a symbol signifying a national bird
merely a cloud that bloomed
A step, two, three… I found that spring
was too short for apricot trees
As soon as I looked at the almond flowers
I was scattered between two dimples
I walked following the freckles
left by little birds in poems

Then I wondered:
how can a place become a reflection
of its image in myths?
or adjectives in speech?
Is the object's image
more powerful than the object itself?
Were it not for my imagination, my other would have said:
You are not here!

I wasn't realistic, but I don't believe the history
of the military man's *Iliad*
It is poetry: a myth that created a reality
and I wondered:
Had there been cameras and journalists
over the walls of the Asian Troy
would Homer have written anything other than the
    Odyssey?

I hold this sumptuous air
Galilee's air
with both hands
I chew on it as the mountain goats
chew on treetops

I walk and introduce myself to itself:
You, O self, are one of the place's adjectives

Three abandoned churches
broken minarets

oak trees on both sides
villages like dots on effaced letters
and a girl on the grass asking a phantom:
Why did you grow old and why didn't you wait for me
He says: I was not present
when the silk dress became too tight for two apples
Sing as you were just now:
If I were older
If I were older

As for me, I will enter the berry tree
where the silkworm will turn me into a thread
I will enter the needle of a woman
from the myths
and then fly like a shawl
with the wind

An intensely familiar space is being retraced, but the sense of effacement is immediate (remains/abandoned/effaced letters/broken minaret). The only human/living entity is the girl who is reading a myth. She appears to be at peace with her bucolic surroundings and unaware of the poet's presence. Is the poetic persona the terrifying wolf in question? Perhaps. He is not a Don Juan and would have joined her if he were younger, but the gap in time separates the two. They do not converse. The notion of the title is negated in the third section. The initial familiarity gives way to a foreignness. He *is* a tourist, or at least has to act like one, and is in need of instruments for recognition and identification (camera and guidebook). Although written by foreign poets, the poems describing the place sound familiar. The other's narrative has equal power. The poet admits that those poems could have been his. He is becoming the other or the other has taken or is able to appropriate his space and voice. But the next section will challenge this, as the poet ascertains that the land is identical to his own descriptions of it in his own poems (the reference to grass growing on stone is to a famous line by Darwish). The border between the real and its representation is blurred toward the end of this section (freckles left by birds from poems). The poet then ruminates about the power of representation and mythologizing and acknowledges that were it not for imagination his presence would have been negated by his other. The seventh part stanza recreates the real with powerful immediacy as if to reiterate the notion of non-foreignness contained in the title, but compromised early on in the poem. The self becomes one of the place's representations. The following section reintroduces assured familiarity with the remains of the place (and the heart). There is one addition that did not appear earlier, "broken minarets." The girl reappears and asks a phantom why he grew up and did not wait for her. Is the phantom the poet? He/it (the phantom) urges her to keep on singing as she would "If I were older." For he has come here for something else. The last section is perhaps one of the most important for our purposes. The poet/ic persona is about to become one with the place, but, once again, while the return is not disrupted, it is transformed into the realm of the eternal and mythological. Phantom or not, the poet/ic persona returns to a real space, but ends up in the realm of mythology, which is nothing but an eternal journey. His only companion is the wind:

> As for me, I will enter the berry tree
> where the silkworm will turn me into a thread
> I will enter the needle of a woman
> from myths
> and fly like a scarf
> with the wind

Poets/Houses

The remaining three poems in this collection all revolve around visits and salutes to poets' houses. These are poets who have had a personal friendship with Darwish and, like him, have acquired a mythical status in their own cultural context and are also exiled in their mythical space and eternal journeying. "Baytun mina 'l-shi'r/Baytu 'l-Janūbī" [A house of poetry/The Southerner's house][10] (139–148) is an imaginary visit to the Egyptian poet Amal Dunqul, whose work was highly politicized and who died prematurely. "Kaḥādithatin ghāmiḍa" [Like an obscure event] (149–156) is a visit to the Greek poet Yannis Ritsos and the last, "Laysa lil-Kurdī 'illā al-rīḥ" [The Kurd has nothing except the wind] is dedicated to the Syrian-Kurdish poet and novelist Salim Barakat.[11]

Like Darwish's poetic persona, Dunqul too is a scattered self and is on his own non-ending journey:

> He has no "there"
> nor "here"
> […]
> I am the voice of my communal self
> I he you and we I (142–143)

The title of the poem is deceptive, for Dunqul is not at home either. The house spoken of here is "baytun min al-shiʻr" (literally "a verse")[12]:

> He sleeps on dawn's stairs:
> this is the house, a house of poetry
> the Southerner's house (143)

Just as Darwish's poetic persona in the last poem entered a myth, Dunqul, who is a stranger in the real, demands to be taken to the metaphorical realm. The realm of poetry will be his final resting place:

> At the end of the night he said:
> Take me to the house!
> the house of the last metaphor
> for I am a stranger here, O stranger (146)

Darwish asks Yannis Ritsos for advice and seeks reassurances about poetry:

> I said: what is poetry
> What is it in the end?
> He said: it is that vague event
> that inexplicable yearning my friend
> as it makes the object a phantom
> and the phantom an object
> but it might explain our need to share public beauty (151)

The poetic persona (or Darwish) expresses some doubts about the resilience of myth and how it too can be subject to the vagaries of time:

Electra, the maiden, consoles
Electra, the old woman, and asks her:
Am I really you?

But Ritsos reassures Darwish:

Your Odysseus will return safely
he will return

Like Darwish, Ritsos is not at home anywhere. He enters his own myth and continues a journey that has no endpoint:

I remembered Yannis Ritsos at his house
He was entering one of his myths then
and saying to one of the goddesses:
If there must be a journey
then let it be an eternal one! (156)

In the last poem, the figure of the Kurd,[13] too, is at pains to postpone his tomorrow, as if to escape the intolerable teleology of history, at least to its victims:

When I visit him, the Kurd remembers his tomorrow
and pushes it away with his broom:
Away now!

He, too, is another perpetual traveler in language:

I travel in my metaphors...
my identity is my language. I... and I.
I am my language
I am exiled in my language (159)

Severed from their homeland and threatened with erasure, poets harbor that desire—and only great poets succeed in this—to recreate those homelands in language. They bridge the gaps created by time and space with poetry and mythology. There is always, however, the danger of being imprisoned in those very same representations and becoming mythical figures themselves. This is certainly true of Darwish. His disenchantment with his own mythical figure has become a prominent theme in his late poetry and this collection is no exception. In poem 28 "Ammā anā fa-aqūlu l'ismī" [As for me, I say to my name] (75–77):

> As for me, I say to my name:
> Leave me and go away!
> [...]
> I carried you when we were able
> to cross the river as one "You are me"
> [...]
> Where am I and where is my little story and tiny
>   pains?
> [...]
> A reader looks at my name
> and gives his opinion:
> I love his barefoot Jesus,
> but not his subjective poetry describing the fog
> [...]
> I say to my name: Give me all the freedom I lost!

Even in his monumental *Jidārīya* [*Mural*], conceived while he was battling death after a heart attack, one of Darwish's refrains and the last line in the book is "my name is not mine."

Even the name, the site of identity, and the self both become ruined and effaced or unattainable sites to which no return is possible. Perhaps this explains the prominence of the wind in these poems. Once again, the wind, which was to accompany Darwish's other poetic persona on his eternal journey in his eternal return to the Galilee, is the Kurd's home:

> The Kurd has nothing but the wind
> It inhabits him and he inhabits it
> They are addicted to each other
> The wind is the Kurd's plea to the Kurd in his exile (164)
> [...]
> with language you triumphed over identity
> I said to the Kurd
> with language you triumphed over absence
> He said: I will not go to the desert
> neither will I, I said

Then I looked to the wind
—Good evening
—Good evening! (165)

Note how the poet/ic persona looks to the wind before bidding farewell. As if it will usher a continuation of the eternal journey in exile. There is no sense of home or actual belonging except in language and metaphor. The self has already been scattered in various pronouns and spaces. The wind, here, makes a perfect companion. Not only because "the winds have no suitcases" as Darwish says in this last poem, but also because it will perpetuate this scattered state. More importantly, the wind has no telos and no clear itinerary. It does not promise a point of arrival or a return. Thus it makes the best companion for the exile, especially the eternally exiled. A beautiful poem in section I, "Lā a'rifu 'smakī" [I don't know your name] (103–104), illustrates this point and ties the theme of the wind to the desire of unbelonging and being unfettered by the shackles of identity. A stranger and the wind ask each other about their names, but they have none and refuse to take any:

[...]
—Name me so I can be whatever you name me!
—I cannot, because *I am a wind*
and you are a stranger like me
and names have a land
—Then I am "no one"
—Choose the name closest to forgetfulness!
[...]
—I am a woman traveling on the wind
and you are a traveler like me
names have a family and a clear house
—Then I am "nothing"
[...]
Nothing said: Life, with you, is beautiful.

One hardly needs to point to the immense symbolic capital encapsulated in the idea of and desire for "return" and for a "homeland" in the Palestinian context, let alone their actual material importance in the lives of millions of Palestinians. Palestine is the *ṭalal* [ruined site], par excellence, both real and imagined, in the collective unconscious of Palestinians and Arabs (perhaps only second to al-Andalus for the latter).[14] Its effacement continues to this moment. No poet has stood before it, recreated it, and safeguarded its memory like Darwish. He mythologized it and, in the process and because of it, became a mythical figure himself. He, too, is the only cultural figure who possesses the symbolic capital and cultural power capable of demythologizing it and celebrating a state of eternal exile, rather than return.

10
Language Places

Jeffrey Sacks

... [T]he words that repeat in us so that we'll follow them are the disaster.
—Mahmoud Darwish, *Hiya ughniya, Hiya ughniya*

UNDER SIEGE IN RAMALLAH IN JANUARY 2002, MAHMOUD DARWISH composed a poem entitled *Ḥālat ḥiṣār* [*State of Siege*]. This poem bespeaks a scene of address the thinking of which, today, bears a singular urgency; it is a scene which involves both the devastating modes of address of military targeting systems and the generosity and fragility of the dimensions of address in which the word of the poet partakes. This, as the devastation inflicted by the United States against Iraqis and by Israel against the Palestinians continues to work at registers which remain barely readable from America, having tuned itself out of the frequencies at which certain kinds of information could have infiltrated its closely policed borders. The scene of address which this poem bespeaks bears an essential relation to the ethical—to the act of bearing witness to colonizing violence and to the relation to haunting modes of alterity which always already touch upon the poetic word. Yet if Darwish's text bears a rapport with the ethical, it is not one which calls upon us to rush or to hastily speed-read, and thereby to transform his work into one slogan, program, project, future—perhaps most decisively, one decision—among others. It is a rapport which recalls the impossibility—the undecidability—which decision entails: decision may only take place there where decision is impossible. The time of the poem involves this aporia, and Darwish's work therefore takes time; it requires that one "linger at the words of an ode" (*Limādhā* 104). To refuse this lingering and to act according to the formulaic certitude of a decision which will have been secured in advance would be to partake in covering over the violence to which *State of*

Translations in this chapter are by Jeffrey Sacks unless otherwise noted.

Siege bears witness. Darwish's work insists that one not lose hold of such violence or the wounding and the pain which it will have inscribed upon the bodies of human beings. For this work recalls us to the lingering of disaster there where it will be said to have passed—there where it will be said to have sealed itself into a securely delineated period or epoch and receded into the past, finally, and once and for all. "Peace," Darwish writes in *State of Siege*, "is a god who leans the notes of a*l muwashaḥ*, on the heart of a bleeding guitar" (96). The leaning notes of the poem recall us to the fragile urgency of the demand imparted by the poetic word. The ethical dimension of this demand bears a relation to responsibility—and this is what the word of the poet calls us to read. It is a responsibility which remains essentially excessive: it is one which could never have been chosen in advance, could never have been recognized and reassuringly grasped, and could never merely have been carried out, and left, with a good conscience, behind.[2]

> What must be thought, therefore, is this exercise of force in language itself, in the most intimate of its essence, as in the movement by which it would absolutely disarm itself from itself.
>
> —Jacques Derrida, *Force of Law*

> My language is shrapnel.
>
> —Mahmoud Darwish, *Ahada 'ashara kawkaban*

Khudh al-qaṣīda 'annī. In a letter dated July 22, 1986 Mahmoud Darwish, writing to the poet Samih al-Qasim, offers a command to another: take the poem from me. Addressing another, the poet speaks, offers a call, and makes a demand. This command gestures toward something that precedes it: a speaker, an interlocutor, an alterity—another who came before. Gesturing toward another, the giving of the command divides the context within which language is said to find its parameters. For the one who speaks is preceded by something or someone else, if only something or someone to whom a word or an utterance may have been directed and from whom one may have sought a response. If this passage marks a certain thought of the poet as the one who speaks, it is only in order to disorganize the speaker. It is only in order to mark an experience, if it is an experience, in which the speaker divides and separates from himself. The force of this separation—which is also a separation that binds—is what goes in Darwish's work under the name language. "Take the poem from me. I can't bear, now, the betrayal of beauty. I can't bear the force of language which crams us into a passageway, and opens for it, not for us, the heroism of the horizon" (*Al-Rasā'il* 64). Language, the stuff of poetry, is never in Darwish's work something which could simply have been taken for granted—an inert tool with which one might work, an object which a scholar might study, a transparent bearer of information which would refer itself to something that will otherwise have remained obscure. "Deeply, deeply/ the imperfect verb continues/ the work of its hands/ beyond intention…" (*Ḥālat* 49). Partaking in a relation to something which one's intention will never have been able to manage, language is one name among others for a relation to an anteriority with which we are always already involved: one is always already touched upon by language—and this is one of the dimensions of the scene of address which Darwish's poetry calls us to read.

Language, rather than confirming the subject as an agent of referential determination, undoes and unsettles the subject who speaks. As Darwish writes in the same letter, "I can't bear the force of language which only alters the relation of the speaker to himself, who, when he goes out into the street, finds neither himself nor his language" (64). Going out into the street involves the subject's having lost himself; one does not lose one's self on the street, but one discovers there that "I" involves a relation to something which has always already been lost. Bearing an essential relation to loss, language acts: it crams, opens, and alters. It sends the poet onto the street and this sending partakes in the force of language to which Darwish calls our attention. For if "I can't bear the force of language," then "language" gestures toward a movement or a displacement which marks "I" in advance. But if language does bear—and bring to bear—a certain force, it is a not a force which marshals itself against a target, striking with the violence of the state and its apparatus: the police, the army—an American, Israeli,

Palestinian, or other security force. Aligning itself with another set of concerns, yet remaining implicated in these, language, in Darwish's work, is a force that cuts, displaces, disfigures, and divides. It is a force which attests to the fact that, as Darwish wrote in the preface to the second edition of a collection of essays first published in 1973, "language doesn't settle down" (*Yawmīyāt* 5).

Not settling down, language, in Darwish's work, unsettles. This, even as literary critical work on Darwish's poetry continues to diminish this dimension of his writing. It is a mode of literary critical work which involves Shakir al-Nabulsi's reading of Darwish's poetry as meeting, abstraction, and comprehension (*Majnūn* 52, 53, 81) and Sa'id Jabr Muhammad Abu Khadra's recent work which defines language as "units connected and bound in a single order" (*Taṭawwur* 12), and which, observing "the development of linguistic meaning in Mahmoud Darwish's poetic works," "confirm[s], objectively, the definition of the extent of this development, its nature, and its manifestations" (7). What is involved is a mode of reading and study which is also marked in Salah Fadl's circumscribing of Darwish's poetic text within the notions of expression and experience—"He is a poet of great expressive transformations. Perhaps what secured for him the preservation of 'the rule of artistic identity' is the signified in his poetry, the total experience that it expresses" (*Asālīb* 141)—and I'tidal 'Uthman's careful reading in which she nevertheless orients her work around an unquestioned metaphor and its cognates. Writing of her "fundamental understanding of the ideology of Mahmoud Darwish's poetic discourse," she explains that, "The ideology of discourse is a point of view, by way of which the writer expresses the reflection of reality in himself and his position in this reality. It is the meaning or the signified that the discourse carries" (*Idā'āt al-naṣṣ* 101). Despite the fact that an explicitly formulated set of reflections on language occurs in Darwish's poetic writings, these reflections remain to be read, and remain to be brought to bear upon the reading of Darwish's work. For they are not a set of reflections which come later—they are not an adjunct to a poetic text which will already have taken shape prior to their articulation—but they form an essential part of what it means for this poetry to be what it is; one will never have begun to read Darwish without them.

> The thing of language is that if it is there to be given, it is to be given away.
>
> —Avital Ronell, *The Telephone Book*

> Poetry is, finally, language.
>
> —Adonis, *Zaman al-shi'r*

Khudh al-qaṣīda 'annī. The force of this commanding gesture draws our attention to something in language that refuses to gather and to hold together. It draws our attention to the fact that if poetry will have been received it will have been as a gift, and that it therefore will have opened a relation between the poet and another that immediately comes undone—under the test and the burden of language. Opening this relation, the poet withdraws. "I withdrew, in order to bring all of the gifts of language/ to you," Darwish writes (*Hiya* 97). Yet if language opens a relation, it is one that could never have been measured, grasped, or consolingly ordered and set to work. It is a relation which remains bare, fragile, and exposed: at the margins of a certain impossibility. The command that Darwish offers, and the relation to which this command bears witness, then, calls upon us—it commands us—to attend to "the scant possibility of poetry" (Lacoue-Labarthe 22). Since the 1970s, reflections on Arabic poetry have taken an explicit interest in this scant possibility, orienting a set of reflections on language as a question that bears on the reading of poetic texts. As Yumna al-'Eid explains in the opening chapter of *Fī al-qawl al-shi'rī* [On poetic discourse], "We are no longer able, today, to consider the question of poetry in isolation from the question of language" (9). Al-'Eid's work offers a reading of poetry and its criticism which insists on the importance of language. "Insofar as poetry is a different vision of our one world, and insofar as criticism is a reading that attempts to produce knowledge of the text, the object of reading, I think that to speak about poetry is, in one of its aspects, to speak about language" (9). Linked to a certain difference—"a different vision of our one world"—poetry, within the terms of this emphasis on language for which al-'Eid calls, appears if only to withdraw. "The study of poetry becomes a study of the meaning of discourse and of its poetic distinctiveness, that is to say, it becomes a study of this linguistic text that in its dissimilarity from the reality of its world, or its withdrawal from it, creates, poetically, its discourse, its particular instance of speech" (22). Drawing our attention to an alterity that occurs in language, to a difference of language with respect to itself and its world—"a different vision of our one world," "its poetic distinctiveness," "this linguistic text in its dissimilarity from the reality of its world"—the reflections that al-'Eid offers open a space within which one might begin to speak of the force of language that Darwish gives us to read.

Yet if al-'Eid's work begins to open such a space, offering venues of reading that ought to be further pursued, it also closes this space down. For this work etches in a set of boundaries which circumscribe al-'Eid's object—"the text, the object of reading [*mawdū' al-qirā'a*]"—and which draw language into the order, *niẓām*, set by a pair of symmetrically related categories which she calls poetic trends. Posing a general frame that would guide the reading of modern Arabic poetry, al-'Eid identifies two, and each bears a relation to a fragmentation and shattering of language. The trends divide according to the measure of the desire of each to build from the fragmented and shattered place of language. "They attempted to fragment language [*sa'ū ilā tafkīk al-lugha*] or to shatter its structure [*taksīr bunyatiha*], for some in order to build a new expressive structure, or, for others, in order to leave speech as it was in its chaos and its absence of order" (22), she writes. But if al-'Eid's introductory essay describes a division between trends, this division is immediately recuperated and each of the two trends is connected by a third—a bridge—which insures the relations among them: "it is as if it stands as a bridge between the two trends that we have defined" (35). The triple structure which al-'Eid describes mirrors the reflection on language which she offers: language is always a matter of the active voice. The fragmentation and shattering of which she speaks involve language's having been acted upon. They involve the interruption of the continuity and interconnectedness which language is said to provide and to assure. "The fragmentation of language [*tafkīk al-lugha*] means the breaking of the structure of its symbolic system [*kasr bunyat niẓāmiha al-tarmīzī*], by means of which continuity and interconnectedness [*tawāṣul*] takes place" (22). The building up from fragments which al-'Eid's first trend seems to exemplify—and the second trend is merely the inverse of the first, affirming the categories which govern the analyses presented of each—continues and exemplifies this work of the active voice. It "fragments ossified language and shatters its symbolic, and, of course, poetic, system, but it builds another system [*niẓāman ākhar*], a substitute poetic world, a world that belongs to the time of the present" (28). Belonging to the present, the poet builds or does not build an order—it hardly matters which. Just as the triple structure which she describes mirrors her reflection on language, so too does her reflection on language find its double in the relations among poetic trends which she describes. The reflection upon the relations among language and poetry offered in the passages under consideration bespeaks a desire to seal the fragmented and shattered place of poetry; and if al-'Eid is able to write of a division between trends, and if she is able to write of an emphasis which ought to be placed upon language in the reading of poetry, it is only in order to reclaim a certain bringing together—a certain correspondence, *murāsala*—that would seal the divisions which have opened in criticism. "Speech is a relation. It is the activity of a binding cohesion [*tarābuṭ*]" (49). But the sealing of division and the affirmation of *tawāṣul* and *tarābuṭ*—connection, interconnectedness, binding—ends relation: the moment at which two are connected without division is the moment at which relation may no longer take place.

If al-'Eid's formulation is careful enough to mark the word relation in the singular, and to leave it indefinite, thus emphasizing a singularity that remains crucial—"Speech is *a* relation. It is the activity of *a* binding cohesion"—the gathering force that buttresses her language undercuts this noteworthy attention to the punch that would have been delivered by the definite article. The description which she offers of the second trend further calls attention to this undercutting gesture. "Here we are in front of a poetic text that does not construct, or that does not want to construct, its unified world, but rather tries, repeatedly, to shatter the regularity [*intiẓām*] of its context, to disorder or scatter the content, and cause it to lose its harmony.... The poets of this second trend construct poetry that does not speak [*shi'ran lā taqul*], poetry that fragments discourse, and in so doing kills it, substituting the logic of context and regularity and the unity of the world of discourse by the logic of the dispersion and fragmentation of this world" (40–41). "In this structure, the structure of fragmentation, poetic expression loses its ability [*qudratahu*] to speak," al-'Eid continues (43). Drifting from the question of language with which the essay seemed to open, al-'Eid's piece concerns itself here with a seeming loss of an ability to speak. This loss is linked to death. "The poets of this second trend construct poetry that does not speak, poetry that fragments discourse, and in so doing kills it." Yet the loss that is marked is immediately recovered. Linking poetry to an ability, if only one which has been lost, the impossible relation which occurs or fails to occur in language is set aside. A bridge is built and under the heading of *tarābuṭ* and *tawāṣul* one's losses are added up and the cutting of a wound that remains open is sutured. And an act of violence or a wounding—a death that al-'Eid seems to be at pains to avoid, if only by way of speaking of it—is mourned even as this mourning is refused: the return to the death of which she must speak haunts her discourse on poetry and bespeaks the refusal to mourn. And something appears as having been lost, as having been mourned, and, finally—or in the beginning?—left behind.

> The first thing that is required in explaining this matter is to know the border between what is lawful in poetry, and what is not poetry.
>
> —Qudama bin Ja'far, *Kitāb naqd al-shi'r*
>
> Writing about writing would be poetry itself.
>
> —Emmanuel Lévinas, *Otherwise than Being*

Khudh al-qaṣīda 'annī. Commanding the other to take the poem, Mahmoud Darwish's words recall us to the force that invests language—dislodging the relation which is said to hold between language and itself. The work of Yumna al-'Eid urges us to read this dislodging force, bringing a question of language to the scene of literary critical writing on poetry even as it closes this question down, folding it into the communicative privilege that her work calls us to read. For in her work the unsettling force of language is offered as a site at which poetry gives itself to be read even as this offering is withdrawn and a thinking of relation as *tawāṣul* and *tarābuṭ*—as continuity, interconnectedness, binding cohesion—is affirmed. This double gesture is one in which the literary critical text withdraws and differs from itself, dividing across the cut of an open wound, and it offers itself as a place to begin an extremely restricted reading of a passage taken from the literary critical corpus of the poet and critic Adonis. Adonis's literary critical writings, both before and after *Al-Thābit wa al-mutaḥawwil* [The stable and the changing], first published in Beirut in three volumes between 1972 and 1974 and later expanded to include four volumes, have been one of the decisive interventions in modern Arabic letters since World War II; this, even as they participate in the field of Arabic literary studies which was instituted in the early decades of the twentieth century and which drew much of its rhetorical force from the discourse of the *Nahḍa* [Renaissance] of the late nineteenth and early twentieth centuries.

In a passage offered in the opening pages of his introduction to the first volume of the three-volume anthology of poetry which he compiled and which was published first in Beirut between 1964 and 1968 and later in Damascus in 1996, Adonis writes of the place of poetry. "Poetry takes it value, finally, from its inside, from the richness of experience and expression, and not from the outside, from what it reflects or expresses" (*Dīwān* vol. 1, 13). Relating poetry to a distinction which is said to hold between inside and outside, Adonis further explains that "It is not possible to evaluate poetry according to a criterion that would consider it as a social or historical document, or as treating particular topics and not others. It is a voice that is self-sufficient, self-standing," and which finds its most proper place at an interior (*Dīwān* vol. 1, 13–14). But that poetry had to be delimited into an interior means that there is something excessive about poetry: it means that poetry involves a situation at which language may not be said to reside solely at an *inside*. The self-sufficient and self-standing quality of the voice of poetry requires that it be separated from what it is not—even as this separation seems to have been secured in advance by poetry's being what it is: self-sufficient and self-standing. The gesture which insists upon the self-sufficient and self-standing quality of the voice of poetry undermines and ruins this quality at the moment that it seems to insist on it. Already separated out from an outside, the quality of poetry which Adonis underscores is further emphasized with the particle *innahū*: *innahū ṣawtun kāfin bi-nafsihi, qā'imun bi-dhātihi*. This particle bears a force which marks a break with the previous sentence and in the force of this break an emphasis is inscribed. Yet the sentence also calls into question what it seems to be insisting on precisely because it insists on it. And the insistence doubles. Insofar as *innahū* opens a break, the sentence which says that poetry is a self-sufficient and self-standing voice performs the self-sufficient and self-standing gesture of which it writes by breaking itself off from what came before it. And this break is therefore also a link and a binding. The sentence which affirms self-sufficiency marks a certain relation—it marks a debt—to what has come before. If the relation marked by *innahū* may be considered, as Adonis writes elsewhere, "a connection of another kind" (*Muqaddima* 19), and if one may suggest that it is a connection which takes place across "a distance that remains distant" (*Zaman* 197), then the passage we are reading here both says and does not say that poetry involves a self-sufficient and self-standing voice. As Adonis further explains, "Voices have, usually, in places like this, their echoes" (*Fātiḥa* 105).

The relation which occurs in the reading that we are offering of Adonis's reflection upon poetry and its place gestures toward a consideration of relation that functions throughout Adonis's literary critical corpus. It is a relation wherein, "Perhaps, in order to draw near, you have to become distant" (*Fātiḥa* 97), and it directs us toward that letter which, in the title of what many consider to be his major literary critical work, operates across the two poles of a relation: the letter *waw* which falls between *al-thābit* and *al-mutaḥawwil*. This letter works in Adonis's text, in a certain sense, as a mark of separation. The title of *Al-Thābit wa al-mutaḥawwil* seems to want to tell us that *al-thābit* is not *al-mutaḥawwil*. Yet if it separates the one from the other, it does so only in order to draw them together. Adonis writes of his project in that text as an attempt to "study Arabic culture from the point of view of the stable and the changing and the relation between them" (*Al-Thābit* vol. 1, 47). He elaborates:

> Since I began to be interested in the study of the Arabic heritage, I was concerned in particular with the question of conformity and creativity, or the ancient and the modern, which is what I call the stable and the changing. At the beginning of the 1960s, when I began to attempt to present classical Arabic poetry to the modern Arab reader, I lived this question in theory and in practice. I was obliged to read this poetry one poem at a time, one verse at a time, and I left this reading with the *Dīwān of Arabic Poetry*, published in three volumes, in Beirut, between the winter of 1964 and the fall of 1968, which included, it seemed to me, the most beautiful and rich of what has been written by Arab poets from the *jāhilī* period through the first world war. But I left as well with a point of view which I presented in the three introductions with which I introduced the three volumes, the conclusion of which was that conformity guided Arab taste and governed the Arab view of poetry. (47)

Adonis further explains that

> "This reality revealed to me a principle in which I saw what could possibly be a starting point... in the study of Arabic poetry, and Arabic culture in its entirety. This principle is represented in that the origin of Arabic culture is not one but many, and that it contains the seeds of a dialectic, between acceptance and refusal, between the current and the possible, or, we would say, between the stable and the changing" (49).

The *and* which binds and separates *al-thābit* and *al-mutaḥawwil*—acceptance and refusal, the current and the possible, the stable and the changing—the one to and from the other, works in a way that participates in and complicates the definition of relation offered by al-Farabi in *Kitāb al-ḥurūf* [The book of letters], where relation is defined as "that by way of which each of the two related things is spoken according to the measure of the other" (*Kitāb* 85). For the measure which relates each of the two related things—even if the "two things that are related are connected each one to the other in a single, shared, meaning" (85)—is one that it remains impossible to take. It is one that, like poetry, "you are unable to grasp" for it "slips from between your arms like a wave"

(*Zaman* 159). Saying that "stability" is *and* is not "change," the literary critical text refuses what may be called a kind of auto-institutionalization. What is marked in this gesture of refusal is a tension that bears the "weight of history" (*Zaman* 161) and that recalls the violence that any instituted order, and any instituted decision, would have required—and would have sought to silence. "Each of us," Adonis writes, "sits on piles of ash" (*Muqaddima* 86). Saying two things at once, Adonis's writing is marked by a dislocation that highlights the linguistic or rhetorical dimension of the literary critical text. If Adonis's literary critical corpus draws upon a rhetoric of the total, of a unity that will have been the same as itself—from "Arabic culture considered as a totality" to "the condition of the human being considered as a totality" (*Al-Thābit* vol. 4, 267)—it is a rhetoric of totality or unity which partakes in this doubling; it bears witness to "the unity of the arabesque" (*Zaman* 132).

The double gesture that takes place in Adonis's reflections on poetry and on his work in *Al-Thābit wa al-mutaḥawwil*—a double gesture that is marked in the binding and separating force of the *waw*—begins to teach us about language and the place of language in Adonis's literary critical writing. It also helps us to situate a question about language, about relation, and about mourning which occurs in reflections on Arabic poetry. Yet if language bespeaks a relation to place, it speaks of a birth and of a scene at which something new appears: "the small room in which the alphabet was born" (*Fātiḥa* 45). Negotiating the space of this room, articulating the distances that open there, and naming, therefore, the dimension of language, remains both impossible and necessary. The distances traced and re-traced in this space evoke a dimension that, like language, "grows distant from us, to the extent that we try to approach it" (*Zaman* 187). It bespeaks "a world that slips away from our border" (*Muqaddima* 106). This dimension, this relation, recalls the possibility of which the poet dreams; it is, Adonis writes, "nothing other than another impossibility" (*Muqaddima* 86). This impossible possibility—which is given to be read in the *innahū* that binds as much as it separates, and the letter *waw* that links as much as it draws apart—marks a relation to an alterity. It bears witness to a debt to another and to a desire to mourn in which the literary critical text partakes and which it also disavows. And this impossible possibility marks criticism as much as it does poetry. If, as Adonis writes, "in every great Arabic poem there is a second poem: language" (*Dīwān* vol. 1, 11–12), then the double reading for which the literary critical texts calls signals the falling away of criticism from itself and its withdrawal from its place; it signals the force of language operating in—locating even as it dislocates—the literary critical text. In this unsettling call, the borders which have been erected and which continue to separate the literary critical from the poetic text, in Arabic literary studies and elsewhere, become, themselves, unsettled; and criticism appears as poetry.

> The *Here pointed out*, to which I hold fast, is... a *this* Here which, in fact, is *not* this Here, but a Before and Behind, an Above and Below, a Right and a Left. The Above is itself similarly this manifold otherness of above, below, etc. The Here, which was supposed to have been pointed out, vanishes in other Heres, but these likewise vanish. What is pointed out, held fast, and abides, is a *negative* This, which *is* negative only when the Heres are taken as they should be, but, in being so taken, they supersede themselves [*sich aufheben*]; what abides is a simple complex of many Heres.
>
> —G.W.F. Hegel, *Phenomenology of Spirit*

> Here, there—a clear furrow to the desert.
>
> —Mahmoud Darwish, *Arā mā urīd*

Khudh al-qaṣīda 'annī. Speaking to the other and demanding that he take the poem, Darwish offers poetry—and language—as bound to another. Never something that would have been born according to one theory or another of poetic inspiration or license, privileging the solitary intensity of a poetic subject, poetry bears witness to a relation to an alterity. Holding on to the question of language which Darwish has asked us to read, and having traced the modes in which this question is both given and withdrawn in the literary critical writings of Yumna al-'Eid and Adonis, I turn my attention here, and for the remainder of this essay, to a single poem—*State of Siege*. *State of Siege* betokens, strikingly and painfully, a specificity of place. It bears witness to the colonizing violence of the state and it also gives one to read the intimate inscription of a wounding upon the body of the poetic text; and it therefore partakes in what occurs, as Jacques Derrida has explained in his 1984 lecture on Paul Celan, there "where a singular incision marks language" (*Schibboleth* 88). *State of Siege* refuses to organize itself around a cut which would divide out the collective violence imparted by a colonizing force—the State of Israel—from the modes in which one is touched upon by personal loss and pain. The short passages which punctuate the poem bear witness to this refusal; they bear witness to a refusal to decide on a set of distinctions which remain barely tenable—between the public and private, between the collective and the intimate, between what is said to find its most proper place outside of the poem and what is said to take place at its interior. Bearing witness to this refusal, the punctuated, fractured, and fragmentary dimensions of *State of Siege* mime a wound: it is not a wound which comes from the outside, but which, while still something other than the poem, gives it to be what it is. And *State of Siege* sketches something that could have been neither articulated nor presented according to the classical values of presentation, emphasizing the unity of an object as it appears before a subject who will have mastered and comprehended it. The stitching together and coming apart of the fragments which constitute the poem remain, therefore, offered, given: they bear witness to an originary exposure. And *State of Siege* marks, in the words of Jean-Luc Nancy, "the tracing of the borders upon which or along which singular beings are exposed" (*Inoperative* 33; *Communauté* 83). Without anything to prop it up, without any security net—or security force—to protect it, the poem offers itself, a fragile exposition which divides across the cuts that separate and bind its fragments, the one to the other. Yet despite or because of this fragility, Darwish does speak and write—if only according to the valances and protocols linked to language and to poetry that are both lyrically and painstakingly set out in his work.

The place of the poetic text, the place of poetry, is what Darwish calls here, *hunā*. It is a place—if it is a place—that essentially withdraws: like the poet, like poetry, and like language. No mode of presentation or representation will have been able to account for it. Addressing this withdrawal and its relation to poetry, and the relation of each to the place names which mark Darwish's poetic corpus—Beirut, al-Andalus, Cordova, Granada, Damascus, Egypt, Samarkand, Baghdad, and more—I offer a reading of a single word: here. The word here—*hunā*—opens *State of Siege*. It is the first word of the poem and it offers itself without cover or alibis. In a certain and restricted sense it is merely there, and the word *here* marks a fragile exposure. Under occupation and under siege, *here* bears a relation to the political which may not be thought according to the structures of the state, of civil society, or of the city. Like the small stones which one may no longer use to add things up, these categories are also besieged. "Unintentionally the small stones become a language or an echo" (*Sarīr* 97). Leaving nothing untouched—least of all poetry—the siege compels a consideration of what it may mean to speak of one's being *here*. Like the city of Beirut, "a gazelle slaughtered by a sparrow's wing" (*Ḥiṣār li-madā'iḥ* 137), the modes in which *here* may be considered communicates with the scene of address of which I spoke in the opening sentences of this essay. *Here* has been thought perhaps most famously in the section on deictics in G.W.F Hegel's *Phenomenology of Spirit*. In Hegel's explication of deictics *here* is thought under the authority of the labor of the negative. Under this authority *here* is gathered into an abiding complex according to a gesture in which "the Heres are taken as they should be, but, in being so taken… supersede themselves [*sich aufheben*]." In the gesture of the Hegelian *Aufhebung*, alterity will have been taken in, consumed, raised up, conserved, and, finally, translated into a sameness—marking a mode of thinking relation in which the other is thought according to the measure of the self. The other, then, as Hegel explains in a later section of the *Phenomenology*, is rendered "as what is *null* and superseded [*als das Nichtige, Aufgehobene*; translator's emphasis]."[7] In the thinking of relation which takes place in this text, the other is drawn into a determination structured by and offered as the negative—*als das Nichtige*—and is therefore drawn into an economy of the same; this, even as this economy will have to have continued drawing the other in, raising up and conserving the other, once and again. As Werner Hamacher explains, "What is supposed to be closed, once and for all, can never cease to close" (*Pleroma* 1). The speculative economy is parasitical upon that which it seeks to sublate, upon the difference that it seeks to transform into a moment immanent to itself. "Only if an undialectical remnant persists can dialectic enter upon its course and combine what is true with what is untrue as a moment of the true itself" (8). This economy is able to persist because "something of what has been sublated, and which the course of dialectic seeks to erase until only a trace is left, must still remain" (8). Within this economy relation takes place as a linking bereft of separation, as a proximity bereft of distance. And despite or because of its sucking action—its constant drawing in, raising up, and conserving—the violence of this economy leaves something behind: shrapnel, unreadable words, the wreckage of language, the screams of victims of torture, the wounded and brutalized bodies of others.

Yet Darwish's poetic corpus opens with a command: *khudh al-qaṣīda 'annī*. Recalling and repeating an earlier command, one that was offered in the poem "Identity Card"—"*Sajjil, anā 'Arabī* [Record it, I am an Arab]"—his text opens with a gesture toward the other. If *here* maintains a certain sense of specificity and if it betokens a singularity of place—the scene or the site of *State of Siege*, the Israeli siege of the occupied city of Ramallah during the winter of 2002—then it also, like the poem, withdraws. And it remains something other than itself.

> The siege is waiting
> Waiting on a ladder, leaning over in the middle of a
> storm (*Ḥālat* 32)
>
> The pine trees, behind the soldiers, are minarets
> which prevent the sky from falling. Behind the iron
> fence soldiers urinate—under the protection of a
> bulldozer—
> while the autumn afternoon finishes its golden stroll
> across a wide street, like
> a church after Sunday prayer... (26)
>
> There is no Homeric echo for anything here
> For the myths knock upon our doors when we need them

> There is no Homeric myth for anything...
> Here a general searches for a sleeping state
> beneath the ruins of the coming Troy (16)

Here is a name for that place wherein there is neither Homeric echo nor myth. But the non-mythical dimension of the Homeric must double: it echoes and it appears as two. The division of the Homeric partakes in a relation to the undecidable division which cuts across Darwish's text; it bespeaks the site of exposure which *State of Siege* is and the exposed site to which this poem bears witness. *Here*—under siege—one appears as a cipher, as a being which comes into view at the end of the scope of a bulldozer: under siege one appears essentially as a target. There where the soldier is free to urinate "under the protection of a bulldozer" while "I" remained trained upon—never out of its sight. It is a site which marks the withdrawal of whatever ground will have been left in the wake of 1948, 1956, 1967, 1970, 1982, 1993, 1996—these dates which mark a history encrypted into Darwish's language; and it is a site which bespeaks a future which has already taken place: Israel's 34-day assault upon Lebanon during the summer of 2006. It is a history and a future-history of which Darwish's poetry speaks, all the while maintaining an austere discretion with respect to each. It is a discretion which recalls us to the inscription of irreparable loss upon the body of the poetic text. *Here* is the site of such inscriptions. It is also another word for this discretion.

> Here, after the poems of Job, we don't wait for
> anyone... (11)
>
> Here there is no I
> Here Adam remembers his clay (11)
>
> Here the days gather within us, red
> black. Were it not for the sins the Holy
> Book would have been smaller. Were it not for the
> mirage the steps
> of the prophets upon the sand would have been
> stronger, and
> the path to God shorter
> Let eternity complete its timeless acts...

As for me, I'll whisper to the shadow: Were
the history of this place less crowded
we would praise the topography of
the white poplar trees... more! (37)

Here, at the slopes of the hills, before the sunset
and the opening of time
near shadow-cut gardens
we do what prisoners do
and what those searching for work do:
we cultivate hope. (9)

Here, at the rising smoke, at the steps of the house
there is no time for time
We do what those ascending to God do
We forget the pain (15)

The discretion which marks Darwish's writing involves a relation to pain. It is a pain which one forgets under siege and which is also inscribed into Darwish's poetic text: there will not have been any poetry without it. To speak of this pain is also a part of what it means to speak of poetry and to speak of what may take place or fail to take place *here*. It is a mode of speech which involves a relation to bodies—to what is always *this* body, such as it is: *here*. Bodies, as Jean-Luc Nancy further explains in a text titled *Corpus*, involve "neither substance, nor phenomena, nor flesh, nor signification. But being-exposed" (29). Being-exposed involves one's being-there, deposed—*here*—before the bodies of others which always already press upon language and upon the poem. "Why is this body such as it is, and not another? Because it is another—and because alterity consists in being-*such*, in the without-end of being such and such and such of *this* body, exposed at its limits" (29). And this is what may allow one, according to a discrete yet firm displacement of the Hegelian deictics, to speak of a sense of *here* which withdraws from sense. "Bodies are the places of existence. And there is no existence without place, without *there*, without a 'here' or 'here is' for the *this*" (16). *Here* is also there where I am touched upon at my innermost interiority by the bodies of others. And bodies—like the poem—withdraw. "The place of the body is neither full nor empty, it is neither outside nor inside. No more than it consists in parts or functions, no more than it is a totality or that it ends" (16). Essentially withdrawing, the poetic text always already involves a relation to a body—and this is one of the lessons which Darwish's writing imparts. "The body is always departing, within the immanence of a movement, a fall, a gap, a dislocation" (31). This dislocation involves a relation to place, and it explains why the poem is never, simply, here. "There is nothing here to discover, nothing to communicate—but a body, and bodies, and bodies" (51). They are bodies for which no one—no literary critical idiom, no academic or scholarly metalanguage, no delicately or densely worded journalistic prose—may speak. "It is a matter, precisely, of that in language which no longer involves a message, but its excription" (99). The excription of language involves the modes in which language is inscribed by bodies, beyond calculation. "Bodies—murdered, torn, burned, dragged, deported, massacred, tortured, skinned, flesh tossed in mass graves, the relentlessness of wounds" (68). The place of poetry—"here"—is also poetry's displacement by bodies.

This displacement is inscribed into the fragmented pieces which bind and cut to form *State of Siege*. The seam along which this cut tears both binds *and* separates the poem to and from the siege to which it bears witness. And the poetic word reaches across an immeasurable distance.

> The soldiers measure the distance between being
> and nothingness
> with the scope of a bulldozer
>
> We measure the distance between our bodies
> and the bomb… with a sixth sense (17)

The poetic word does the impossible: it measures the immeasurable. "It is his right to measure the distance by the opening of a flute" (*Al-Rasā'il* 36; letter dated May 19, 1986). Measuring out an immeasurable distance—the distance which opens between the poem and the siege—the poem bears witness to a siege which will never solely have been exterior to it; the poetic text is touched upon in advance by the siege of which it speaks. It is a mode of touching which precedes the poem and which also precedes any mode of intention or bearing which will be said to have remained antecedent to its composition. Reaching across this distance one is left in the impossible place or non-place that remains—*hunā*, here. Without resolving inside into outside, without bringing the *exterior* of the siege into the *interior* of the poetic word, Darwish's language nevertheless remains touched by the siege. And the siege will always already have been touched upon by language and by the words of the poet; disarming the siege, the poetic text places in jeopardy the present and future present for which the siege seeks to bulldoze a place. Writing of an event which could never have allowed for a subject simply to be there—to be *here*—and to write from some point *outside* of the siege, Darwish's text bears witness to a singular instance of the giving of poetry: the fragile and exposed writing that is the poetic word.

Poetry—like *here*—in Darwish, withdraws. "The poem," Darwish explains, "draws away from me" (*Limādhā* 101). For if the first word of *State of Siege* is *hunā*, and if this word names a place toward which the poem will be said to refer, *here* is also preceded by a marker which in naming the place of the poem also displaces it. It is a marker which both affirms and undercuts the oppositions between inside and outside and between before and after—oppositions which continue to bear upon reflections on ethics and politics just as they do upon reflections on poetry and literature. Yet if these oppositions are in some sense required—How may one have spoken of the siege without them?—they also come apart in the face of the siege. On the page which follows the title page of poem, Darwish, placing his words between brackets, writes:

> [This text was written in January of 2002, in Ramallah ...]

Antecedent to the first word of the poem and thus marking the opening of the poem as preceded by something else—and therefore as not opening the poem—this remark between brackets orients our reading of *State of Siege*. That "[This text was written in January of 2002, in Ramallah ...]" means that the poem—"this text"—is not the siege. It means that the poem is different from and other than the siege, and that it writes of it. But the brackets also shield the poem. They hold it, embrace it, and with the cutting precision of a knife, slice "This text was written in January 2002, in Ramallah ..." out of the poem. And the poem is, therefore, already, from the beginning, under siege. It is touched by the siege to which it addresses itself and which is said to linger on the hither side of its borders. These brackets reappear throughout *State of Siege* and they commemorate this cut and the wounding to which Darwish's language bears witness.

> [To a critic:] Don't interpret my words
> with a cup of tea or the bird's snares!
> My words besiege me in my sleep
> The words that I didn't say
> They write me and leave me searching
> for the remains of my sleep... (*Ḥālat* 25)
>
> [To a killer:] Were you to reflect on the face of your victim
> and think, you would remember your mother in the gas
> chamber. You would be freed of the gun's wisdom
> and change your mind: Identity isn't restored like this!
> (29)
>
> [To a poet:] Whenever absence withdrew from you
> you became entangled in God's isolation
> So be the "subject" of your lost object
> and the "object" of your subject
> Be present in absence (56)
>
> When the helicopters disappear, the doves will fly
> white, white. They'll bathe the face of the sky
> with a free wing. They'll return its brilliance and own
> the sky and play. Higher and higher the doves
> fly. White, white. If only this sky
> were real [A man passing between two bombs said to
> me]. (23)

Under siege—the poem is besieged by the siege. It is touched by this onslaught that will never solely have come to it from an outside. Which will never solely have been an external and empirical fact that will have imposed itself on the poet and the poem.

> [To poetry:] Put your siege under siege.
>
> [To prose:] Lead your proofs from
> the scholars' dictionary to a reality which
> they destroyed. And explain your dust.
>
> [To poetry and prose:] Fly, together
> Like the wings of a sparrow bearing the blessed
> spring! (57)

But the wings of the sparrow gather together only to come apart. "We only meet parting at the crossroads of speech," Darwish writes elsewhere (*Limādhā* 80). It is a wounded meeting—or a farewell.

> Me or him
> This is how a war starts. But it
> ends with a wounded meeting:
> Me and him
>
> I am her until the end
> This is how love starts. But
> when it ends
> it ends with a wounded farewell:
> Me and her (*Ḥālat* 57)

The dimensions of this farewell mark the dimensions sketched by the word *here* and by the relations among poetry, language, and the siege. For just as the siege may be said to precede the poem that writes of it, so too the poem will have always already come before the siege. There is neither before nor outside with respect to the siege. And there is neither before nor outside with respect to poetry or with respect to language. In *State of Siege* the word here is given to be thought under the burden or pressure of this fact.

This fact marks the poem—and poetry—as under siege. Rather than an event external to the siege which would report on or about it, the poem, what Darwish calls "my words," *is* the siege: "My words besiege me." Complicating the difference that language makes between the poem and the siege, poetry besieges the poet. The tension which occurs in the scene in which the text places itself under siege is tightened. "[To poetry:] Put your siege under siege." The poet addresses poetry. The poet is, therefore, outside of poetry. He addresses the poetic word from a place exterior to the poem. But this opposition immediately comes undone. If the poet speaks to poetry, and if the poet says "Put your siege under siege," then poetry is already under siege; it is already being addressed—"*your* siege [my emphasis—J.S.]"—and it is already receiving an order or a command from another—if only from the poet. The scene evoked here communicates with the situation at which the poet offers a command to another: take the poem from me. And it is a situation which marks the relations among language and poetry throughout Darwish's poetic corpus. For "your siege [*ḥiṣāruka*]" is, on the one hand, the siege of the poem. It is the siege that the poem carries out and of which the poem is the subject. It is the siege that occurs when Darwish writes "My words besiege me in my sleep." On the other hand "your siege" is the siege of the poem as the siege to which the poem is subjected. It is a siege that comes at the poem; it bombards, invades, and wounds the poem. To write "[To poetry:] Put your siege under siege" means that poetry is *both* the *subject of* and *subjected to* the siege. It means that poetry, in Darwish's text, occurs, if barely, without recourse to anything—without recourse to a referent outside of the siege that will have secured and grounded it, without recourse to a unity or gathering of the poem that will have secured its relation to itself, and without recourse to the poet as the one who will have been its source and point of origin. Linked to what Elias Khoury has called a mode of writing, "which does not retrieve anything, or stand on stable points of reference" (*Zaman al-iḥtilāl* 57), poetry, in Darwish's work, is offered as a state of siege.

> And how could one, here, speak of arrival or departure?
>
> —Edmond Jabès, *The Book of Questions*

He said to her: What flowers do you like?
She said: I like carnations… black
He said: Where are you taking us—me
and the black carnation?
She said: To the light's center, within me

> And she said: And farther... farther... farther.
>
> —Mahmoud Darwish, *Ḥālat ḥiṣār*

Khudh al-qaṣīda 'annī. If the commanding gesture of these words marks poetry as bound to another, it also marks "me" as that from which poetry is taken. Poetry, then, recedes and withdraws, moving away—toward another. The withdrawal of the poem bespeaks its unreadability; it bespeaks the modes in which the poem is touched upon in advance by a wounding that also withdraws. The withdrawal of the poem mimes and repeats this wounding and it teaches us to read it—even as the word of the poet remains unreadable. What is given in Darwish's text is something which remains refractory to reading; it is something which may be neither appropriated nor spoken for—and of which the poetic text speaks. One dimension of the withdrawal of the poem under siege is the withdrawal of the "I" which speaks. For rather than being offered in the nominative case "I" appears—if it appears—in the accusative. The appearance of "I" in the accusative does not mean that "I" forms a stable and enduring identity upon which others may act, but that "I" has always already been touched upon by others. The dimensions of this prior relationality are essentially excessive and immoderate. They are abyssal—and there will have been no "I" without them.

> He said to her: Wait for me at the edge of the abyss
> She said: Come close.... come here. I am the abyss
> (41)

> The spirit must march
> walking upon its silk feet
> at my side. Hand in hand, the way two old
> friends divide an old roll of bread
> and an old glass of wine,
> to cross this path together
> Then their days pass in two different directions:
> I am metaphysics. As for her
> she chose to squat
> on a high stone (55)

The abyssal dimension of relation means that any mode of coming together also involves a parting. Walking hand in hand involves dividing a roll of bread and an old glass of wine, and crossing a path together involves passing one's days in two different directions. Just as the dimension of relation does not come to a being which will otherwise have been fully formed, so too the siege does not come to the poet later—according to some afterward. For the poet is besieged by "my words [*kalāmī*]." He is besieged by language. In a certain sense, if "I" is besieged it means that "I" has been struck by the siege. It means that "I" at a time prior to the siege remained outside of it and exterior with respect to it. It means that "I" will have remained untouched by the siege—from the very beginning. According to this reading the siege would have been an event that came to "I" and afflicted or wounded it. "I" would presuppose and refer itself back to a prior and unaffected state. But this reading is not sustained by the poetic text and this is why it urges us to consider the rapport between relation and accusation. "I" appears in the accusative. That "I" appears in the accusative means that "I"—at the place which Darwish has called *here*—is always already, from the beginning, in the accusative; it means that "I" is already accused, under accusation, and besieged. It means that there is no "I" outside of or without relation to the siege. And it also means that there is no poetry—neither poem nor poetic word—outside of or without relation to the siege and the disaster to which it bears witness.[8]

Rather than a site at which a subject will be said to have taken place, *here* bespeaks the subject's disarticulation; "I" is only what it is insofar as it bears a prior relation to something else and the site of this relation is *here*. This relation bears an ethical dimension and the text of Mahmoud Darwish gives one to read a scene at which one bears an originary obligation to another. It is a mode of obligation which precedes any relation which is said to obtain among the self and itself. Always already implicated with others—and with the bodies of others—Darwish's text scripts and de-scripts a scene of address. It is a scene which is given only in order to withdraw: one will never find one self there. And this is what is at stake when Darwish speaks of *here*. Bearing a relation to what Emmanuel Lévinas has called a *non-lieu*, it bespeaks an ethical relation which, today, urgently remains to be read—as so-called wars on terror and police interventions in the name of peace and democracy secure nothing but the security of the growing police and military apparatuses and their right to abuse the bodies of human beings, from Jenin to New York City and Guantánamo Bay and beyond. The literary critical work of the scholar runs the risk of partaking in the violence of the state, there where one responds to the cry of the other in advance—closing one's hand over the mouth of another with the speed-reading precision of a smart bomb. Yet the poem withdraws and the place of this withdrawal is *here*. It marks a wound, and one of its names is love.

> [To love:] Oh love, oh absent bird!
> Call us from eternal blue and the fever of absence
> Come to my kitchen so that we can prepare dinner
> together
> I'll cook, and you pour the wine
> and chose whichever songs you like, which remind us
> of the neutrality of the place and the chaos of our
> emotions: If
> it is said that you're one of the djinn… believe it!
> If it is said that you're a kind of influenza… believe it!
> Look at yourself and tear your veil. But you are, now,
> near me, intimate, gentle, peeling garlic. After dinner
> you'll choose an old, romantic film for me
> We'll watch it to see how the two heroes came to be
> there
> Here [*hunā*] two witnesses (62)

The scene of witnessing offered here mimes the dimensions of relation given in *State of Siege*. One calls upon the other in order that two may be proximate and intimate, but this proximate intimacy bears out two witnesses; the distance between them is like the distance between eternal blue and the fever of absence. Always already a witness, one does not linger exterior to that to which one bears witness. What is given is not the secure transmission of a communication but the unsettling dimension of language: that force which inhabits language and which offers love as a withdrawing greeting, as a coming together that parts; like language, it marks a wound.

> How will I bear my freedom? How will it bear me?
> Where
> will we live, after the marriage contract? What
> will I say to her in the morning: Did you sleep as you
> ought to,
> next to me? Did you dream of the sky's earth?
> Were you worried for yourself? Did you wake up after
> sleeping well?
> Will you drink tea or coffee with milk?
> Will you drink juice, or my kisses?
> [How will I free my freedom?] Oh stranger!
> I'm not your stranger. This is your bed. Be
> open, free, without end. Scatter my body
> one flower at a time, in your breath. My freedom!
> Accustom me
> to you. Take me to what lies behind concepts so that
> we'll become two in one!
> How will I bear her? How will she bear me? How will
> I become her master
> and her servant? How will I free my freedom
> without parting? (52)

Yet parting does not come to love from the outside. Parting is inscribed into the relation which Darwish calls love. It marks this relation from the beginning and this is what names "my freedom": "How will I free my freedom without parting?" It is a freedom given in the word of another to which one remains bound and which one is not free not to be subjected to. When Darwish writes of love and its relation to freedom it is also a way of writing of poetry, of language, of relation, and of "I." It is a way of writing of *here*.

> The martyr teaches me: There is no aesthetic exterior
> to my freedom. (79)

I am not free not to bear a relation to others, and this is what it means to speak of my freedom. There is no aesthetic—no poetry—exterior to it. Nor is there anything like "me" exterior to relation or to language. A text published in 1990 recalls the relations among language, relation, and "I." *Here* is the withdrawing place of this relation.

I am from here. I am here… I comb an olive tree this
fall.
I am from here. Here is I. My father cries out: I am
from here.
I am here. I am I. Here is here. I am I. I am here. Here
is
I. I am I. Here is I. I am here. I am here. I am I.
Our desire is an echo. Distance broke up. Rebirth was
reborn. An echo
that found an echo
The echo rang out… Forever here, forever here…
I
am
from
here
And
here
is
here
And
I
am
I
And
here
is
I
And
I
am
here. (*Arā mā urīd* 26)

In this passage "I" is distended. It bends and is stretched with the tension that gathers in language. This tension gathers like a taut string as the words of the poem no longer move horizontally but descend vertically the length of the page. Like the stroke of a pen they trace out *alif*—the first letter of the alphabet and the first letter of the word *anā*, I. But this *alif* is crushed by language; it is crushed by the words that have accumulated on top of it and the pressure which they exert.

> The siege transforms me from a singer into…
> a sixth string on a violin. (*Ḥālat* 82)

If Darwish writes that "I am from here" it is only to withdraw, translate, and repeat: "I am here." There is repetition insofar as the distance that is given with the word "from" is closed and "I" becomes "here." "I" and "here" undercut each other and "I" becomes another word for "here." "I am here" can thus be rewritten as "I am I." But the linking force of this copula also cuts. If "I am I" may seem to gesture toward a certain unity, it is a unity which comes apart with Darwish's short, choppy sentences. Language dislocates itself as much as "I" and "here" dislocate each other. In the accusative, "I" is addressed by the call of the other. And "here" merely names *here*, this place at which "we" occur and from which there is no exit or escape. It is the place at which "we" take place, bound to one another in a knot that binds and also marks a distance: the binding isolation between the one and the other.

> In what remains of dawn I walk outside of myself
> In what remains of night I hear the fall of footsteps
> within me (82)

That "we" communicates with isolation means that "we" does not gesture toward a consolidating or gathering event. It is a plural that leads to no joining—even as each moment of "we" remains enmeshed and entangled. If "we" occurs in Darwish it is not a "we" that would have consisted in the gathering together of a multiplicity. For if "we" marks anything it marks a wound. It is a wound that opens in language and that lies exposed—like Darwish's poetry, like language, and like those who continue to be subject to the violence of which Darwish has written—somewhere between domestication and obliteration, under siege.

> Let us then question the dictatorship of the text.
>
> —Mahmoud Darwish, *Dhākira lil-nisyān*

Khudh al-qaṣīda 'annī. Darwish's poetry offers a set of protocols for reading. It is a poetry which is generous and it teaches us how it may be read. One mode of this teaching comes in the form of a command: take the poem from me. That Darwish has commanded you to take the poem means that poetry may only be said to be what it is insofar as it always already bears a relation to you. The command to take the poem does not solely come from the poem's outside; it inheres within the poem and partakes in what it means for the poem to be itself. Unable to give place to this command—unable to find its place at the interior or exterior of the poem—the command to take the poem bears a relation to the discussion of decision which I offered at the opening of this essay. For one may not appropriate the poem according to a set of rules or formulae which will have secured decision in advance—relieving us of the trial and the test of decision; the moment at which one leaves this test behind, if one may leave it behind, is the moment at which one has ceased to read. And learning to read means learning to read poetry.

> This siege will continue until we teach our enemies
> examples of our *jāhilī* poetry. (*Ḥālat* 11)

But if *State of Siege* may partake in teaching one how to read, it only does so insofar as reading involves a situation where any rules which will have governed it in advance withdraw. The only mode in which one may be said to read is there where one no longer knows how to do so; there where reading remains—like decision—impossible. And the impossible is precisely what takes place in *State of Siege*. Doing the impossible—measuring the distance between the poem and the siege, "the distance between our bodies/ and the bomb"—the poetic word measures the immeasurable. It names the dimension of this measurement an opening.

> This earth, below or above
> holy or a prostitute
> We're not interested in parsing God's attributes
> For the opening,
> the opening of the heavens
> is geography! (76)

Yet it is an opening—like the word *here* with which *State of Siege* begins and does not begin—that is not one with itself; it repeats. Something like a stutter, a fragile and exposed poetic utterance, the text does not countenance beginning *here*—even as this is the only place where it may begin. Out of time and without shelter—for there is no off switch to the siege, even there where it is said to have ended—the poem begins at the only place where it can: the besieged and withdrawing site which Darwish calls *here*.

> Here, at the slopes of the rising smoke, at the steps of
> the house
> there is no time for time.
>
> Under siege, life is time.
> Between remembering its beginning
> and forgetting its end... (12)

Time, rather than marching forward, involves a certain lateness or belatedness. One will never have left *here* behind.

> Under siege, time becomes place
> It solidifies in its eternity
> Under siege place becomes time
> It is late for its appointment (74)

This untimeliness is linked to death and death comes as a surprise. It cannot be captured by the gathering gestures of understanding or cognition.

> Each death
> even if it is expected
> is a first death
> So how can I see
> a moon sleeping beneath each stone? (21)

Each death—each and every death—is inscribed upon the language of Darwish's poem. Not the abstract density of death but the singular intensity of *a* death; unreadable, death touches upon the poetic word. The poem is inscribed by those corpses which have been buried beneath the rubble of bulldozed houses and by the generosity of death which bespeaks the finitude of the subject. And death—each death—unsettles the rhythmic lyricism of the poem.

> This rhythm is not
> necessary. Neither in order to tune the voice
> nor to economize the pain
> It is an excess
> like a fly on the table (31)

The words which speak of rhythm are cut; the cut of the line slices the sentence in two: This rhythm is not/ necessary. It bespeaks a relation to the brutalized bodies of the dead and it recalls the cut of a wounding upon the body of the poem. It bespeaks "the memory of an incision at once unique and repeatable, cryptic and readable" (Derrida, *Schibboleth* 88). The line break of the poem interrupts the grammar of the sentence and the connective pull of the copula. It is an interruption which commemorates an irreparable loss and which also partakes in producing the poem. The unwritten force of the copula does the impossible; it gathers and divides the words of the poet even as these words speak of the unspeakable. And the place of the poem withdraws—it is neither inside nor outside, neither public nor private, neither collective nor personal; it will have been impossible to decide. It bespeaks a relation to an abyss.

> [To the reader:] Do not trust the poem,
> child of absence
> It is not intuition
> It is not thought,
> but it is a sense of the abyss (83)

And one is left, uncertain, without anything to grasp onto: out of time. "Time has broken and language has broken" (*Aḥada* 97). This broken time bespeaks a scene of waiting; one must wait—one must linger with the words of an ode—there where it has become impossible to do so; there where decision has become most pressing and most urgent.

> There's time for song:
> Waiting for you, I can't wait for you

> I can't read Dostoyevsky
> or listen to Um Kulthum or Maria Callas
> or others. Waiting for you the hands of
> my watch move to the left to a time
> without place
> Waiting for you I didn't wait for you. I waited for the
> end (*Ḥālat* 60)

One must wait where waiting is no longer possible just as one must decide there where the grounds of decision have been removed: Waiting for you, I can't wait for you; waiting for you I didn't wait for you. Not the stifled time of non-decision, but the unsettled and uncertain time of a decision which will never have left the hesitation—the waiting—of decision behind. The impossibility of decision mirrors the impossibility of placing the poetic text.

> Place is a scent
> When I remember the earth
> I smell the scent of blood
> and I long for my distant self (*Ḥālat* 75)
>
> Writing is a small cub that bites nothingness
> Writing is a bloodless wound (83)

State of Siege recalls us to a wound which it mimes and to which it bears witness. It bespeaks the technological-military address systems of the state and the devastating violence which they impart. But the siege, insofar as it partakes in a relation to language—insofar as it is always already touched upon by the poem—remains, itself, fragile; the poem which bears witness to the siege also unsettles and interrupts the siege and the politico-military regime which it seeks to secure. And the poem withdraws. This withdrawal marks a wounding—its place is *here*, and *here*, and *here*. Linked to what Darwish calls *life*, this wounding and its place linger, unreadable and unmournable—without reassurance and without end.

> Peace is the words of a traveler within himself
> to one traveling in the opposite direction…

Peace is the doves of two strangers, dividing the final
coo at the edge of the abyss

Peace is the longing of the two enemies, each on his
own
to yawn over the restless sidewalk

Peace is the wail of two lovers washing
in the moon's light (91–92)

Peace is one's acknowledgement, openly, of the truth:
what have you done with the ghost of the killed?

Peace is one's withdrawal to work in the field:
what shall we grow—in a little while? (95)

Peace is the eulogy of a young man, whose heart was
pierced—not
by a bullet, and not by a bomb, but by the birthmark
of a woman.

Peace is a song of life, here, alive
upon the string of a wheat stalk (97)

New York City
7 July 2005/1 April 2007

11
Alternative History, Expanding Identity: Myths Reconsidered in Mahmoud Darwish's Poetry[1]

Ipek Azime Celik

I used to fight in your twin trenches—
you'll never be absolved of my Asiatic blood,
you'll never be absolved of the obscure blood
coursing through the veins of your roses!
How cruel the Greeks were at that time!
How much that wild Odysseus loved to travel,
in search of his legend!
—Darwish, "O Helen, What a Rain," translated by Husain Haddawi in *The Adam of Two Edens*

THE SELECTION OF POEMS IN *THE ADAM OF TWO EDENS*, WRITTEN MAINLY during the first half of the 1990s in Paris, represents a new phase in Mahmoud Darwish's poetic expression. Darwish refers to this period as that of a transformation, during which his poetry engages critically with historiography and myth-making, with the ways history and mythology intertwine and become tools for power and domination. His poetry delves into the politics of narrating history and sustaining myths, in order to reveal the complexities and contingencies history writing and mythmaking bear for formulating Palestinian national identity. The poet shows that rigid mythologies, in the guise of past legacy and history, have maintained the present structures of apartheid in Palestine/Israel. Darwish makes his mark by re-delineating these mythologies to expose their multiple roots or "obscure blood."

Through an examination of the poems written during Darwish's Paris period, this essay will eventually explore the poet's identity politics, which imagine "nation" as plural and heterogeneous, in opposition to its classical sense. Darwish wishes Palestine not to limit itself to a nationalist space and dialogue bounded by uniformity; he reflects the plurality embedded in his perception of homeland and memory in his poetry. This essay will discuss the possibility of preserving the national ideal of Palestine while bypassing the national paradigm in Darwish's poetics, an ideal that echoes the political solution advocating Israeli and Palestinian coexistence in a binational state with equal rights and secular citizenship.

To analyze Darwish's project of bringing out the polyphonic possibilities of myth and history, this essay provides a reading of four poems taken from two different collections, both written and published during Darwish's so-called Paris period: "Ḥajarin kan'ānī fī al-baḥri al-mayyit" [On a Canaanite stone in the Dead Sea] and "Forassun lil-garīb" ["A Horse for a Stranger"] from *Aḥada 'ashara kawkaban* [*Eleven Planets*] (1992), and "Aṭwār Anāt" ["The Phases of Anat"] and "Al-Bi'r" ["The Well"] from *Limādhā tarakta al-ḥiṣāna waḥīdan?* [*Why Have You Left the Horse Alone?*] (1995). Darwish explains the transformation of his work in the poetry collections he composed in Paris as follows:

> Myth is not always the enemy of men… My last four books [*The Tragedy of Narcissus, The Comedy of Silver* (1989), *I See What I Want to See* (1990), *Eleven Planets*, and *Why Have You Left the Horse Alone?*] are part of an ambitious project I hope I'm able to complete. It's the project of a lyrical epic, of the liberation of poetic language toward epic horizons. History would serve as a scene through which peoples, civilizations and cultures could circulate freely. I am on a quest for my identity according to the laws of crossbreeding, of the shock and cohabitation of all identities. I want this hymn to take root in the open space of history. I don't know where this quest will lead me, but I know that its origin is the multiplicity of cultural origins. In such a project, poetry comes up against cultural racism and rejects any culture based on purity of blood. (*Boundary 2* 82–83)

The poet emphatically approaches the realm of history in order to open it up as a space for free circulation where various cultures can converse, but also to mark history's spots: "I had to defend the land of the past and the past of the land, the land of language and the language of the land. I feel that the past is subject to plunder… The past is more ambiguous than the future."[2] Before we contemplate further Darwish's account on his endeavor of raising history and myth as reconciliatory rather than hostile for his Palestinian and international audience, a brief overview of the context and conditions that carried him to this position within the trajectory of his poetics is necessary.

The critic Sinan Antoon describes Darwish's relationship with writing as "continuously tak[ing] his audience by surprise as he continues to rebel against his own style and reinvent his poetic discourse," while the poet's work "reads like a poetic panorama of Palestine and of the plight of Palestinians since 1948" ("Mahmud" 67). Darwish's early poetry is marked by a declarative and definitive voice that highlights pictorial landscapes, and formulates Palestinian identity primarily as it is attached to the land, a poetic zeal that has been epitomized by his famous poem "Identity Card" ["Biṭāqat hawīya"]. Published in 1964 in *Leaves of Olive* [*Awrāq al-zaytūn*], "Identity Card" confronts an Israeli officer with its renowned lines that became an emblem for the Palestinian resistance: "Write down,/ I am an Arab,/ Identity card number is 50,000" (Darwish, *Selected* 24).[3] Darwish's poetry in the 1960s and 1970s registers the displacement from homeland in language. The poems resist the seizure of the land of identity and the identity of land by stressing the existence and persistence in land.

In the documentary *Mahmoud Darwich: Et la terre, comme la langue* [Mahmoud Darwish: As the land is the language], co-directed by Israeli Simone Bitton and Palestinian Elias Sanbar, Darwish states: "My poems do not deliver mere images and metaphors but deliver landscapes, villages, and fields and deliver a place." His writing is a site of existential resistance, where the self and the space are intermingled: parts of home turn into metaphors for the body, and the body becomes a part of the flowering nature. Strong attachment to the land, laying roots deep and wide, becoming inseparable from the ground, eliminates spatial boundaries. Darwish says, "I find myself looking at an olive tree, and as I am looking at it, it transforms itself before my eyes into a symbol of the *ṣamidīn*, of our struggle, of our loss" (in Bowman 149). His poems eliminate the confinement beyond the barricades and curfews, the lyrics turning into material tools of struggle, as in "On Poetry," in which Darwish wishes, "If only these poems were/ a chisel in the hand of the proletariat/ a grenade in the palm of a struggler... a plow in the hands of a peasant,/ or a shirt, or a door, or a key" (*Selected* 35–36).

Up until the 1970s, Darwish wrote from within Palestine/Israel, where he lived under the legal status of "absent-present alien" (a term that can ironically reference both his aspiration to carve out a Palestinian topography and national identity against Israeli denial and the metaphorical homelessness and multifaceted identity prevalent in his later poetry) and was put in prison or under house arrest several times for his publications and readings of poetry. This period was followed by that of an exile in Beirut (1973–1982) during the civil war, where he edited *Palestinian Affairs*, published by the Center for Palestinian Studies, and joined the Palestine Liberation Organization. Later, in 1988 in Tunisia, he authored the Algiers declaration, the Palestinian Declaration of Independence, in which the PLO officially declared support for a two-state solution to the Israel–Palestine conflict. His direct involvement with the PLO came to an end when he finally resigned from the executive committee the day after the 1993 Oslo Accords, saying it was "an accord which did not provide the minimum level for the Palestinian to feel that he owns his identity, nor the geography of his identity" (in Antoon, "Mahmud" 76) and that the Palestinians "woke up to find they had no past" (in Jaggi, "The Profile"). He saw the accords as unworkable, likely to escalate the conflict rather than produce a viable solution for the Palestinians.[4]

Antoon suggests that Mahmoud Darwish's *Eleven Planets* "was poignantly prophetic of Oslo. In it, Darwish uses the Arabs' defeat and exodus from Spain in 1492 as a prism through which to accentuate the Palestinian predicament in 1992 and the fate they were about to face" ("Mahmud" 67). Although the Oslo Accords were crucial in shaping and sharpening Darwish's sensibility that Palestinians had no share in writing their own course of history, even before Oslo his poetry engaged in the Palestinian problematic of "[waking] up to find [they] had no past." In *Memory for Forgetfulness* (1986), which narrates one day in Beirut during the Israeli shelling in 1982, one can see the poet's ruminations on history and on the need to engender an original discourse to talk about what has generally been left out of history's bounds. This generically hybrid (combining poetry and prose, dreams, memoir, journalism, and poem) and fragmented work probes the possibility of narrating history especially on the eve of its making; it scrutinizes the poet's position as a bystander reporting the struggle.[5] In *The Tragedy of Narcissus* and *The Comedy of Silver*, his poetics began to challenge the linear and monologic narration of history, narratives that lay ground for genealogical reification, consecration, or legitimization of the victors' political claim.

> One cloudy day I pass by an old well
> Maybe it fills with heaven,
> maybe it flows past meaning…
> I drink a handful of its water
> and greet the dead around it…
> I hear ancestral desolation
> like an "abode of ruin"
> between the calling of my name's "mah"
> and the "mood" of its second syllable….
> I'm sure I'll return in a matter of hours alive
> from the well where I met neither Joseph
> nor his brothers' fears of ricocheting echoes…
> Like a woman, maybe it fills with heaven,
> maybe it flows past meaning and becoming,
> waiting for my birth
> from my first well!
> (*Adam of Two Edens* 57–60, trans. Ferial Ghazoul)

A reading of Darwish's poem "The Well," excerpted above, reveals the poet's approach to the past. For Darwish, the past is a cultural product comprising heterogeneous anarchical components, rather than an orderly, constructed, linear historical reality. The poet's "well" is a mirror that reflects a chaotic mixture of divisions, separations; it fragments the rigidity of "past meanings" into a fluidity of "becoming." The poet leans over the well, observes the flowing imagery and hears the echoes, "the voice loomed large, your voice—petrified image—a moment cracked open" (58). Images and voices of self and other mingle inside the well, which is saturated with "past meanings" flowing in, meeting, clashing, and getting lost into each other. The poet puts his own self through the fiery trial of the well, where the syllables of his name "mah" and "mood" are split apart by an "ancestral desolation like an 'abode of ruin'" (58). A history of ruins, an elusive mythic past cuts his name and self into two and abandons him at the edge of a well that becomes a mirror for self-reflection. Reflections and images of objects multiply: while the moon is idealized for its relationship to its reflection, or its other, as "hovering above [its] image but never sinking into it" (57), the poet's other-self turns into a traveler "on a caravan journey" who "couldn't complete anything but [his] ghost" (59). The impossibility of transgressing "self" other than by creating its ghost is resolved in the well, which "flows past meaning and becoming" (60), which includes the past not as a burden but as a source of renewal, a source of rebirth for the poet. This past enables a continuous "becoming" rather than a rigid "being."

This same well contains Joseph; the agrarian goddesses of Egypt, Syria, and Babylonia; and Gilgamesh. The well is saturated with these subjects and objects of epics, mythological characters who are created and recreated, used and abused, convoluted with meanings, figures whose different connotations through time have all eventually been rescinded. Mythical figures turn into evasive images that have abandoned the poet and the poem, a gesture that erases their "higher truths": the poet's void counters Gilgamesh's eternity, the agrarian goddesses become too busy with trivialities, and Joseph and his voice perish from the well. They are appropriated, taken away from "ordinary dailiness" to serve heightened meanings and thus get lost or abandon their creator. While Joseph is gone, however, his well stays; agrarian goddesses perish, but the cypress and the yellow inula plant are alive; Gilgamesh and the poet become voids, but the poem endures. Vigorous images of nature and poetry are sources of contradiction and life; they confront stagnant mythic images that revere the dead.

When the land became "Land," it "expelled [the poet] from itself," just like the myths that fracture and disappear as they are capitalized. Thus, the poet wishes to dissolve the possessive power implied in all past meanings, all mirages abstracted and detached from social meaning. The continuity of becoming enables the "birth from the first well," from a well without any institutionalized memory or perceptions. This is (as Darwish's description of his "liberation of poetic language toward epic horizons" connotes) "the open space of history" where alternative stories disable absolute truths, ongoing dichotomies flow in endless becoming. The well makes possible "cohabitation of all identities," "the theatre of interactions, both positive and negative," ("Poetry and Palestine" 83) as long as it debilitates the possessive legacies of certain mythologies and arrests the dual images of identities that refuse to sink into each other.

Making a Myth, Breaking a Myth

"The Well" alludes to the discursive oppression of Palestinian identity through the "scientific" or theological possession of the past: the realms of history, archeology, religion, and myth. The poem spells a break from the mechanisms that support monolithic structures for imagining history. It establishes a link between everyday reality, the past, and the mythic realm. "The Phases of Anat" goes one step further; it *employs* mythology as a narrative tool for deciphering everyday reality as well as for reading into the constructedness of this reality. The poet explores the interaction that emerges from the meeting of two seemingly separate realms (myth and reality), and explores what this meeting means in terms of the politics of narration and identity-making.

Darwish's employment of myth[6] and discussion of mythmaking reflect a historical understanding of the concept as a mode of perceiving the world and as a model that continues to generate a discourse. Rather than simply a traditional story dealing with ancestors, heroes, and customs that is transmitted to the present from some distant past, myth is for Darwish a narrative of knowledge continually produced for/by the present. In his alternative definition of myth, Darwish reevaluates tradition, history, and "civilization" to allow multiple (often contrasting) testimonies, documentation, and evidence. The poet "brush[es] history against the grain" (Benjamin, "Theses") by adding in the discarded pasts of "obscure blood," and by resisting the amnesias imposed by orderly myths/histories.

In "The Well," the reader can observe Darwish's poetry becoming more introspective and can see that the poet's vision of self-identity is a complicated dialectic construction inherently including its mirror image or Other. In "The Phases of Anat," the dual identity is more distinctly framed in allusions to ancient myths as the rhetorical instruments that accommodate such oppositional dualities in dialogue. Darwish's alternative employment of the mythopoesis subverts the convention of constructing homogeneous national identities with "finished, definitive and consecrated myths" (Darwish, "Poetry and Palestine" 82). Darwish's re-writing or reconsideration of certain mythologies such as Anat becomes a tool to draw landscapes of memory and cultural history with multiple roots, an endeavor that delineates a more inclusive Palestinian and Israeli identity.

> ... two women never to be reconciled
> one bringing water to fountains.
> the other driving fire to forests...
> Anat, I want you both together
> in love and in war
> and I find myself in Hell,
> for I love you.
> Anat kills herself within herself
> then recreates that distance inside herself
> so that before her image far away
> all creatures pass,
> over Mesopotamia and Syria...
> Come back, and bring
> the land of truth and connotation
> the first land of Canaan,
> land of your public breasts and thighs,
> so that miracles return to Jericho,
> return to the deserted temple door
> where there is neither life nor death,
> where there is only chaos in doomsdays arch,
> where no future arrives and no past returns..."
> (from "The Phases of Anat," trans. Husain Haddawi,
> in *Adam of Two Edens* 99–102)

"The Phases of Anat" mourns the loss and calls for the return of the moon goddess, the ancient goddess belonging to several cultures in Canaan, Syria, and Phoenicia (Astarte in Hebrew, Ishtar in Assyrian and Babylonian, Inanna in Sumerian), the goddess of fertility and war, life and death; a personality of contradictory roles: virgin, mother, whore, and warrior. The poem wishes her to come back to the city of Palestine to give birth to, revive the land and the people. After the death of Anat, goddess of multifarious genealogies, "all is lifeless... for life died out like the conversation of/ people on the way to Hell" (100). The poet grieves her absence in the present time of suspension in chaos, a time when Anat remains "in the underworld" to be discovered as a potential productive resource to illuminate the depths and complexities of self and identity, "like a mirror for the hopeless lovers/ as she wends her way to the deserts of the soul" (99). This poem is a "ladder to the moon" (99), an elegy for the goddess of multiple roots and kins. When asked which Anat he is looking for in this poem, Darwish replies:

> Je crois qu'Anath est... le produit de l'affrontement dialectique entre l'Anath qui vient de la Mésapotamie et de la Méditerranée, et celle, hellénique, qui part derrière les vaisseaux grecs. Anath dit également les étapes de ces bouleversements dans le temps et l'espace (1997: 82)/ I think that Anath is... the product of a dialectical confrontation between the Mesopotamian and Mediterranean (Hellenic) Anath, who follows suit with Greek vessels. Anath also tells the stages of these dislocations in time and space. [my translation]

As the poet explains, Anat is a mythical figure not only capable of crossbreeding and embracing multiple traditions and belief systems across time and space, but also embodying multiplicity in her dual self. She epitomizes inherent dialectics—containing birth and death, fertility and destruction, love and war: "two women never to be reconciled,/ one bringing water to fountains,/ the other driving fire to the forests" (99). Her Other is always already within herself, creating a distance inside herself, allowing the possibility of self-reflection in an inner mirror with the eyes of an Other. If her identity cannot expand to withhold the two poles in opposition, then "there is neither life nor death... there is only chaos under doomsday's arch... no future arrives and no past returns" (101). The present is suspended in the chaotic singularity when "the land of truth and connotation," associations, connections, relations are evaded with the erasure of Anat. Time leaves the space of decay, lacking the fertility of generously all-encompassing Anat's collectivity, her "public thighs and breasts." As the poet uncovers "the phases of Anat," the layers of her meanings and connotations, he seeks the reason for her human creator's dismissal of the multifarious goddess. He suggests the reason might be "unknowingly accepting the mirage" of other gods or goddesses "afloat in the dusty air" with their illusory mystical auras, rather than facing the challenge of the complexity of Anat's double-edged self. To love her is to "find [one]self in Hell," a love of inconsistencies, struggles, but to erase her is to contain the time, space, and identity in "two bottomless pits," "prancing forever" in irreconcilable divisions, unproductive and inconclusive chaos; without her inclusive and indefinite duality, geography and history are doomed to be "the wells [that] dried up."

Anat is a controversial figure; she is elusive. Darwish's choice of the goddess as the protagonist of his poem in search of both producing and destroying a myth is not a coincidence. The figure is ambiguous and open to a variety of interpretations; she does not restrain the reader to a certain tradition belonging to a specific community or a particular historical background. In "On a Canaanite Stone at the Dead Sea," the poet employs (or appropriates) "authoritative" biblical myths, a more controversial act compared to exploring pagan myths like that of Anat. This poem raises the following question more emphatically: why is Darwish drawing upon/rewriting/alluding to *myths* in order to resist/undermine authoritative cultural histories?

Darwish was not the first to set his eyes on the realm of myths for articulating a critique of those dominating "the past." Several postcolonial[7] authors and poets have previously reconsidered "official" triumphalist colonial histories as well as imperialist models of nationalism by questioning the construction of the past based on "pure" myths. African-American novelist Toni Morrison goes back to communal tales for "dusting off the myth, looking closely at it to see what it may conceal" (Morrison in Cowan, "Introduction" 9). Similarly, Caribbean author/poet Derek Walcott also refers to myths in his epic poetry, to reveal his mixed ancestry "descended in blood from men of Warwickshire and in ink from the bard of Avon" and from "slaves whose history and language have all but disappeared from the official record" (Farrell 274).

Walcott's strategic mythopoesis in *Omeros* is proclaimed to be "an antithesis of imperialist social discourse" that is "powered by sublimation of violence" (Callahan 122), or a "revisit [to] the infinitely diverse field of the past not to discover the origins but to contest the idea of a unified and inevitable continuity of the same, by uncovering and celebrating difference, then and now" (Burnett 68).[8] Morrison, on the other hand, emphasizes the narrator's role in redeeming marginalized cultures as well as performing as the mediator, a healer between the self and the community, the past and the present (Mobley, *Folk Roots*). In the novelist's words, "dusting off the myth" is an essential tactic of resistance against the narrative power of the colonizer; inserting alternative stories is a necessary part of the struggle against imperialist narratives.

Edward Said states that imperialism produces "pure (even purged) images of... a privileged, genealogically useful past, a past in which we exclude unwanted elements, vestiges, narratives" (*Culture* 15). For the postcolonial authors above, as for many others, "dusting off the myth" means to deconstruct/raise their controversial voices against the image in the colonial historiographies of a fixed, eternal, "clean" past. This past still perpetrates colonial identities and divisions—ethnic/religious/racial divides, the legacies of colonial "divide and rule" strategy—and therefore has to be rewritten by the colonized and oppressed. As in the works of Walcott and Morrison, Darwish's poems provide alternative Palestinian histories and mythologies, and suggest the multiplicity of meanings to "Palestinian" identity—becoming Anat, an Indian who lost his battle in "Speech of the Red Indian," a wandering Granadan in "Eleven Planets in the Last Andalusian Sky," Lot exiled from his city in "On a Canaanite Stone at the Dead Sea," or the daughter of a Yemenite Jew in "A Horse for the Stranger."

The discovery, institutionalization, and degradation of the "native Palestinian's" past (and thus present) have been—still are—established features of appropriation in Israel/Palestine, as in other colonial regimes. In Bitton and Sanbar's documentary, Darwish says, "I'm a poet whose text has been lost, a Trojan poet." As implied in these words, which compare Troy and Palestine as places that have been represented mainly through the victors' narratives, Palestine has a unique place within the corpus of cultural imperialism, given the extensive amount of literature written on this theologically and mythically convoluted territory.[9] The land is rediscovered repeatedly through a wide variety of discourses by Western travelers, archeologists, anthropologists, biblical historians, and Zionists. Eventually, Palestine has become a fictive place, between the historical and the mythical, detached from its present for the sake of its biblical past, subjected to the manipulation of myths around it. The relationship between Palestine and its mythical aura is made unique by the fact that here the absurdity of shaping reality according to an adopted myth seems to have been purposefully neglected.

The nineteenth-century European accounts of Palestine depict Palestinian natives, the colonized inhabitants of the land, as between being nonexistent and a part of the mute landscape[10]—as the later Israeli legal term "present absentees" ironically echoes. Palestine was pictured as a fictive landscape devoid of its inhabitants, who would taint the ancient image of purity; it was turned into a void to be filled by biblical myths. Later, Zionism, or the Israeli nationalist ideology, would similarly distort history and eliminate the existence of Palestinians, claim it as "a land without people for people without land."[11] Israeli myths of nationhood monopolized not only the right to own history and geography but "all roles available in the conflict, the roles of the criminal and the judge, of the murderer and the mourner, of the perpetrator and the victim. This leaves no role for the Palestinians, who are thus, by force, eliminated from the historical scene..." (Leeuwen 265). The ongoing Israeli use of the rhetoric of victimhood, to deny or distract from their own role in victimizing Palestinians, effectively covers up the Palestinian everyday reality and erases the possibility of a dialogue between the two parties. As Darwish implies in "As He Walks Away,"[12] the rhetoric of allowing victimhood to one side only ("Don't blame the victim!") cuts down the voice of the other side and brings any interaction to a deadlock.

Under these circumstances of ancient (biblical possession of the land) and modern (monopoly on victimhood after the Holocaust) mythifications, Palestinian identity has had to assert itself among the Zionist symbolism that legitimizes historical appropriation and hegemony of the land. Initially, some poets belonging to the Tammuzi movement in Arabic literature[13] revived ancient mythology in referring to the Palestinian situation. For instance, the idea of sacrificial death and rebirth in T.S. Eliot's use of fertility myth in *The Waste Land* offered the poets novel means to narrate the state of desolation after the 1948 catastrophe.[14] As Khalid A. Sulaiman explains in his book *Palestine and Modern Arab Poetry*, the prominent Palestinain mythic symbols were heroes of epic adventures such as Odysseus and Sindbad, or martyrs such as Christ or al-Huseyn, while the Israeli is represented as the Tartar or the seductive Delilah (Sulaiman 162, 163, 169). In these early poems of frustration, anger, alienation, and self-condemnation, the myths create Palestinian victims, heroes, or mourners. In pursuit of a language capable of narrating the Palestinian self, these poems defined "Palestinian" negatively, as the Israeli's Other. The figures of *fidā'īyūn*, martyr, or Beloved-woman-home provided a strong base that supported Palestinian consciousness and struggle against the occupation; however, in time they too became stereotypes incapable of productively articulating or addressing the complexities of the situation. The myths that created these national heroes become arid, unable to deconstruct the underlying problematic of monologic and homogeneous mythification that is the basis of British as well as Zionist colonial appropriation.

Myth as the Heterogeneous Past

In "On a Canaanite Stone at the Dead Sea," Darwish looks primarily into biblical mythologies. The poet's approach to the politics of myth-making—what it would mean to "forge" consecrated myths, reinterpret them, and challenge their conventional meanings—is more apparent here than in "The Phases of Anat." The moon goddess appears again, but this time to make the poet the sacrificial lover of the fertility myth: "Father, how many times must I die/ on the bed of the legendary woman Anat chose for me/ so fire can ignite the clouds?" (77). Then the poet personifies a descendant of Lot:

> ... This is my absence,
> a master who imposes his laws
> on the descendants of Lot
> and sees no scapegoat for Sodom but myself.
> This is my absence,
> a master who imposes his laws
> and mocks my visions.
> Of what use is mirror to a mirror?
> (*Adam of Two Edens* 78–79, trans. Mona Asali van Engen)

Darwish's Lot is taken out of the city by force, but still bears both the guilt of the city and of his absence when exile is imposed upon him. The myth of fertility and that of Sodom coincide as a Palestinian's story; Darwish positions "the master" and his own "absence" to mirror each other. Such a scene of facing mirrors hints at the dialogic relation he has with "the master." Mirror images are going deeper and deeper within, infinitely reflecting each other and themselves through the Other. As the poet also professes in "A Horse for the Stranger," "my dagger is on my image, my image is on my dagger" (109); the victim and the victimizer face each other in an interchanging role.

> A family bond exists between us, but you will not
> rise from history, nor erase
> foaming sea from your body
> And the sea, this very sea,
> smaller than its myth, smaller than your hands,
> is a crystalline isthmus,
> same from the beginning to end (78)

By contextualizing the interaction with the Other in the realm of myth, Darwish displays the indispensability of this realm as a part of the identity-making process. The poet is rewriting myths in order to break the identifying homogeny of the signifier and the signified, in order to attach multiple significations and identifications to the always already politicized myth (the myth of Lot, the myth of the Dead Sea). Darwish's lines suggest that tradition and identity enclosed in rigidly defined biblical myths inhibit dialogue between communities of the same heritage, those that have "a family bond between [them]." He wishes to erase the sacred grandeur of mythic symbols that distances them from their humanistic roots and natural correspondents. He wants to bring back the Dead Sea, which has not only been the "sea of Moses" but also the sea that contained "Canaanite stone"—the stone that represents an ancient unity, the root of connection between the self and the Other: the Palestinian and the Israeli.

As in "The Well," here again the poet's name and his inner self are dissected: "I looked for the root of my name/ but I'm split apart by a magic wand" (74). Alluding again to the biblical-mythical story of Moses, Darwish too finds salvation in the act of "splitting." The end result of this splitting is an expansion in perception as the poem continues: "Do my dreams reveal my visions or my victims?" (74)—as visions of self and the Other mingle, the poet also takes on the role of "the victim," eliminating the Israeli monopoly on suffering. With these augmented sources of identification, the poet then claims that "all the prophets are my kin" only to disenchant his audience from falling for a nostalgic multiculturalism—a brotherhood of religion despite centuries of conflict: "But heaven is still far from its earth/ and I am still far from my words" (74).

The duality of identity—which has to be unearthed beneath the dust and soil of the past, through re-writings of the past—accommodates the possibility of co-existence and dialogue. Nevertheless, attaining peace as a material reality is still distant, as the poet, too, is far from the language that will dissolve the monologic readings of the ancient and modern myths: "No wind lifts me above the past here,/ no wind rips a wave from the salt of this sea. There are no white flags for the dead to wave/ for surrender, no voices for the living to exchange/ declarations of peace" (74). The poem is a quest for the near impossible, for nature's wind, the human's white flag, or the voice of peace, which are buried under the fictive and non-fictive representations of the past.

In the next verse, the poet returns to the Dead Sea and meditates on its age-old existence, its connotations of concert and hostility, life and death. The sea "carries [the poet's] silver shadow at dawn/ shepherds [him] to [his] first words, laps [him] to the first woman's breast" (74). In a metaphorical journey similar to that toward "the first well" in "The Well," the poet dives into the mythical sea in order to approach the depths and history of the sea, of his own self and of the Other. Inside the sea, or inside the memory it contains, the poet finds out that "the sea lives dead in the pagan's dance/ circling his space/ and dies alive by the joining of poem and sword" (74). The Dead Sea "lives dead" for human memory when its relationship with those around it is merely spatial rather than textual. Once it becomes the mythic inspiration for a narrative of violence, the *mise en scène* where the poetic narration merges with the sword, the instrument of violence, then the natural sea "dies alive" beneath the textual sea. In both cases, the contradiction of being and non-being, living and death, cannot be resolved. The Dead Sea is neither simply an unmarked space nor a narrative tool for violence, but it always is a resource for artistic creativity.

On Poetry

Darwish's ruminations on his art take a different path between the time of "On Poetry" and that of "A Horse for a Stranger," but his poetics loses nothing from its extensive political situatedness and only becomes deeper. The three poems above expound on the identity of the poet, the narrator, while "A Horse for a Stranger" focuses more on the narration, on poetry, the mythologies and silences it creates and upholds.[15] "A Horse for a Stranger" is dedicated "to an Iraqi poet" and was written in the aftermath of the Gulf War. Poetry is denounced as its elevated speech gets nullified, shattered under the burden of history: "Poetry is a grave,/ a grave made of wind/ O stone of the soul, O our silence!" (109), but again the poem promises a ceasefire, a dialogue to let the foes "open two windows onto a street of shadows" (113). The poem moves between two opposite poles of meaning—the lightness, transience, and dynamic vigor of the wind, and the weight, memory, persistence, and stability of the grave. The poets of war and conflict zones, however, inevitably have to move from the first pole to the second: "this air which we used to carry on our shoulders/ like bunches of grapes from Mosul/ is now a cross" (110) destined to carry the cross of memories and sufferings.

Mythological characters, histories, and stories sustained by poetry are laid out in the poet's existential search for the present meaning of writing a poem. The poet relates his ideal poem as he converses with his dead colleague: "Didn't you tell me on the way to the wind/ we'd soon be filling our history with meaning? That the war would soon be over,/ that we'd soon build Sumer in song again,/ soon open the theater doors to everyone/ and to every kind of bird?/ That soon we'd return to where the wind first found us?" (106). Its author is searching for a poem that is not alienated from its original function: initiating a conversation with the past, a dialogue between the past and the present, cultivating communication beyond the confused meanings of words. The poet is, however, again "far from his words" as the poem becomes a burden, the cross on his shoulder at the point where "Time is shattered,/ language is shattered" (110). He aspires for a utopia where language and time are organic, so that words can be shaped free from their past and present connotations. Now, canonical voices, "tablets of law," "Shakespeare," "prophets and scientists," determine, narrate, and obliterate meanings of the past and thus the present. They phrase and rephrase space to bury it in time and language. In the face of these discursive burdens, the poet writes: "the last Arab writes:/ I am the Arab that never was/ the Arab that never was" (111), in his inexhaustible voice hoping to erase all past categorizations that refute the complexities of self, Other, and collective identity.

Darwish's ideal poem wipes out all the assumed pasts and their suffocating knowledge in favor of expanding the dialogue between peoples through time and space. His ideal poem resonates with the ideal poet, a poet in a state of permanent, metaphorical exile: "The relation between homeland and exile is much more complex than we imagine... exile is the laboratory of experience. It is also a poet's destiny in his ongoing dialogue with the Other, and between the inner and the outer" (in Mosbahi, "Interview" 6–7). Exile for Darwish is the ability to be without the ultimately limiting security provided by the formulaic definitions of self—as monologic opponent of the Other—and of home. Toward the end, "A Horse for a Stranger" suggests a standing point that has a panorama of all sides: "my outside is inside me" (114). This is a spot free of corpses and vengeance—a perspective shared by the author known for existential angst and insurrectional metamorphoses, Kafka:

> I'll beget you and you'll beget me
> and very slowly, very slowly
> I'll remove the fingers of my dead from your body,
> the buttons of their shirts and their birth certificates
> You'll take the letters of your dead to Jerusalem.
> We'll wipe the blood from our glasses, my friend
> and reread our Kafka
> and open two windows onto a street of shadows.
> (*Adam of Two Edens* 113; trans. Sinan Antoon)

Conclusion

Darwish's poems give insight to Said's conception of an extended identity that critically approaches the pure, homogeneous categories sustained by certain mythologies:

> No one today is purely *one* thing... Imperialism consolidated the mixture of cultures and identities on a global scale. But its worst and most paradoxical gift was to allow people to believe that they were only, mainly, exclusively, white, or Black, or Western, or Oriental... Survival is in fact about the connections between things; in Eliot's phrase, reality cannot be deprived of the 'other echoes [that] inhabit the garden.' (Said, *Culture* 336)

The new direction of Darwish's poetry aims to defy the Zionist/imperialist discourses of purity and claims of private property on the right to delineate memory. Like Walcott and Morrison, Darwish uses myths as narrative tools. He refers to the pagan/oral myth of Anat, the literary myth of Gilgamesh, and the biblical myth of Sodom, which have all emerged from the same geography. The poet delineates these myths' multiple geneses and interpretations in order to interpose a parallel discourse for the right to the homeland, past, and memory.

Darwish's depiction of an expanded Palestinian identity and memory—which includes the Israeli Other as well as similar communities of the dispossessed—transgresses the paradigmatic boundaries of homogeneity in nationalism. Reflection on the recent political agenda reveals the strategic positioning that Darwish's narratives take concerning the Palestinian national struggle. Underlining the multicultural, multiethnic, and multireligious history of Palestine, Said wrote, "I see no other way than to begin now to speak about sharing the land that has thrust us together, sharing it in a truly democratic way, with equal rights for each citizen… it means self-determination for both peoples" ("Real Peace" 6). As a viable alternative to the homogenization of culture in Israel that has radicalized Palestinian culture for years, Darwish, like Said, suggests a novel definition of communal identity, home, and belonging in bi- or multi-national lands. The poet's linguistic heterotopia describes a nation shaped by a reterritorialized exilic experience grounded in linguistic openness; a nation that, with its expanded definition of citizenship, is more benevolent to its hybrid components.

"Don't hanker for your grandfather's black cloak/ or your grandmother's bribes./ Take off like a colt into the world/ and be who you are/ wherever you are./ Shoulder the burden of your heart/ and then come back/ if your country is really/ big enough to be a country" ("Hooriyya's Teaching" in *Adam of Two Edens* 88–89). Darwish revives mythmaking and memory not simply to mourn for the dead and grieve over the present situation in Palestine. The poet redefines myth and memory as products of an "obscure blood" against all acclaimed purities and as tools for poetic agency. As the critic Mary Layoun claims more generally for the novels of the displaced, these are not simply nostalgic stories about the lost past: "They are acts of remembering against a master narrative of coercive unity, homogeneity, and absolute propriety of place" (62). By deconstructing the hegemonic homogeneities in canonical myths, the poet expands identity, homeland, and memory beyond nationalist constraints: "If [the personal aesthetic of the author] is open enough, it will set a horizon for the homeland; if it is too narrow, the homeland will feel constrained in it" ("Poetry and Palestine" 83).

12
The Art of Repetition: The Poetic Prose of Mahmoud Darwish and Mourid Barghouti

Stuart Reigeluth

Indeed, what would life be if there were no repetition?
—Søren Kierkegaard, *Repetition*

THE POETIC PROSE WORKS OF MAHMOUD DARWISH AND MOURID Barghouti shed light on the current predicament of Palestinian existence. The lives of both poets overlap at meaningful intervals and their poetic prose works complement each other by depicting contiguous eras of the contemporary history of the Middle East. As they walk through Beirut and Ramallah, both poets embody modern conceptions of the nineteenth-century *flâneur*. As they transcribe observations and contemplations, both use literary repetition. However, where Darwish transmits nostalgia, Barghouti conveys Nietzsche's *ressentiment*, a feeling of deep frustration due to the inability to change a situation. The evocation of pivotal eras and communal feelings elicit the particular Palestinian and the broader Arab collective memory. Beneath the umbrella of historical recurrence, Darwish uses literary recurrence and Barghouti employs the notion of the "swing of life." Both inquire into the nature of the repeated Israeli assaults on Palestinian identity and contribute to reasserting the Palestinian place in history. Pertaining to Palestinian resistance literature, their respective poetic prose works place the Palestinian life in the limelight. Confronted with the wreckage of war and military occupation, conversing with the dead while longing for repose, both poets provide a profound and mutual literary perspective of Palestinian existence.

Congruent Lives and Complementary Prose

Both leading Palestinian poets have suffered imprisonment, deportation, territorial exile, and existential estrangement from their land and people. Their most recent poetic prose works complement each other chronologically by depicting pivotal eras of contemporary Palestinian history. In *Dhākira lil-nisyān* [*Memory for Forgetfulness*] (1986), Mahmoud Darwish narrates a quasi-autobiographical account of one day in his life during the Israeli bombardment of Beirut in the summer of 1982, when the Palestinian era in Lebanon was coming violently to an end. Mourid Barghouti was in Beirut prior to the repeated Israeli invasions of Lebanon (1978 and 1982), when he worked for the Palestinian Radio Station in Beirut to cover the Syrian bombardment of Tal al-za'tar [the thyme hill] Palestinian refugee camp in 1976. In *Memory*, Darwish writes:

> The years piled up, one on top of the other. For ten years now I've been knocking on this door, avoiding the sea. I used to prefer the route, the path I walked thirty years ago and walked again to go back *there*. Did I forget to return, or did I forget to remember? (172; *Al-Zamān* 91)[1]

Just as the Lebanese poet Kahlil Gibran prophetically foresaw the demise of Beirut with his lines "pity the nation" (*Garden* 9–10), so Darwish involuntarily foreshadows the return voyage after 30 years of exile across the wooden bridge into Palestine as described by Mourid Barghouti. In his memoir *Ra'aytu Rāmallah* [*I Saw Ramallah*] (1997), Barghouti narrates a twelve-day visit to Ramallah and his home village of Deir Ghassanah in the occupied Palestinian territories when the implications of the Oslo Accords (1993) had become overtly perceptible. Congruently, Darwish has returned on numerous occasions prior to and after the implementation of the Oslo Accords. Both authors are therefore highly aware of the subject matter each is addressing. Using literature as a point of encounter, the symbolic meeting between the two poets occurred in Ramallah where they "talked about many things, among them the possibility of issuing *Al-Karmel* magazine once again from Ramallah" (*I Saw* 115; *Ra'aytu* 138). Similar to the nineteenth-century "novel of disillusionment" as examined by Georg Lukács (see *Theory of the Novel*), Barghouti and Darwish reveal poetic prose works of twentieth-century Arab embitterment.

The Modern *Flâneur*

The prose works of Darwish and Barghouti are journeys to cities of their respective pasts. Through the mental portals of recollection, both repeat a voyage to a time foregone in a place that is no longer the same. According to Kierkegaard, repetition is "a crucial expression for what 'recollection' was to the Greeks." Though both terms refer to the same movement of memory, he claims there is sadness to recollection not present in repetition (*Repetition* 131, 324). Unlike Kierkegaard, who undertook a journey to Berlin to see if repetition was possible, Darwish and Barghouti do not set out to prove a philosophical theory based on a psychological experiment. They are acutely aware that repetition within existence is not possible. They will not return from exile with a full sense of belonging.

In the streets of Beirut and Ramallah, Darwish and Barghouti observe the routine of everyday life and contemplate the current Palestinian predicament. Both perceive the devastation of war and suffocation of military occupation as detrimental to Palestinian identity, but they do not take up arms. Both meander through and record their impressions of a respective era of contemporary Palestinian history. As they walk and talk about their experiences, they become modern conceptions of the nineteenth-century *flâneur*.[2] And in the diurnal repetition of being, they perceive the endurance of existence.

In *Memory*, Darwish moves through the streets and debris of Beirut in search of a newspaper. He is defying death and proclaiming life: "I walk slowly. Slowly, I walk. I walk slowly… I walk down the street, exactly in the middle," not caring where he is going and ignoring the menacing "silver fish"—the Israeli fighter jets—in the sky. "And I walk on. I walk, to see myself walking, with firm steps, free even of myself, in the middle of the street, exactly in the middle" (41, 45, 51; *Al-Zamān* 22, 24, 28). These short excerpts are obviously very repetitive in style, but distinctively portray the repetitive behavior of a seemingly purposeless stroll. He meets friends at a hotel, another at a butcher's. He sees the destruction of his office at the Palestinian Research Center and witnesses an apocalyptic scene near a garden. He imagines a woman he loved and converses with the dead.

In *I Saw Ramallah*, Barghouti observes the stagnant life in the streets as he meanders through thirty years of occupation. He "walked in the streets of Ramallah," for he wants "to recapture the old images, the old rhythms." When meeting with friends in the evening, Barghouti goes "on the promised outing into the Ramallah night" and "on this outing, and the others before it, I saw most of my places" (*I Saw* 30, 116–117; *Ra'aytu* 62, 139–140). He meets with friends at a café in the evening and walks through the marketplace during the day. He too is accompanied by and converses with the dead. Both poets search, through contemplation, for meaning in the chaos of the city.

In *Das Passagen-Werk* [*The Arcades Project*] (1927–1940), Paris provides a means for Walter Benjamin to explain the metaphysical passageway of existence through time and space. The physical outings through the streets of Ramallah and the village square of Deir Ghassanah serve as a means for Barghouti to explain the predicament of Palestinian existence. The mind meandering between the broken buildings of Beirut portrays the sinuous passage of time through traumatic memories for Darwish. The city acts as a microcosm for the plurality of succession in the general recurrence of history, but also permits the *flâneur* to perceive the singularity of events in the repetitious cadence of daily realities:

> Just as on the street one hears the smallest part of a solitary flute-player's piece, and almost instantly the rattle of the carriages and the noise of the traffic make it necessary even for the market-woman to shout loudly so that the madame standing there can hear the price... and then for a brief instant it is quiet and again one hears the flute-player. (*Repetition* 303)

Here Kierkegaard concludes that repetition is continually interrupted by the noise of life. Barghouti echoes Kierkegaard in a similar passage, recollecting a walk through a market in Ramallah:

> Is it possible that I should go to the vegetable market in Ramallah, after an absence of thirty years to find it in the same decrepit state it was in thirty years ago, as though the stallholders had not changed... Is it possible that I should find the ground here exactly as it used to be, like the surface of a marsh... Is it possible that I

> should look at the façades of the buildings on the main street and find that they resemble the ground of the vegetable market? (*I Saw* 147; *Ra'aytu* 176)

This highly intertwined and circular passage about the market challenges Kierkegaard's conclusion and asserts that life is continually interrupted by the noise of repetition. Barghouti inquires about the possible recurrence of the past by using the literary style of repetitive questions.

Though Darwish prefers to make broad historical parallels, he also asks questions. When drawing a distant parallel between the horrors of Hiroshima and the bombardment of Beirut, the recent ruins of the city compel him to imagine the scene of a wasteland: "Sanayi' Gardens is like a sight from Judgment Day... pushing humanity into a bottomless pit... letting us imagine we are an exception to the only truth." Though he transmits an exaggerated reality, he is also compelled to ask: "what is the name of this thing?" (*Memory* 75; *Al-Zamān* 41)[3] W. B. Yeats writes:

> And send imagination forth
> Under the day's declining beam, and call
> Images and memories
> From ruin or from ancient trees,
> For I would ask a question of them all.
> (*Collected* 201)

Just as Darwish recollects images from ruins, Barghouti is enticed to remember by the "ancient" fig tree. Barghouti expects to see, upon returning to his family's house in Deir Ghassanah, the "huge fig tree with a massive trunk and spreading branches [that] dominated both house and courtyard. This tree fed our grandfathers and our fathers—there was not one person in the village who had not tasted its delicious fruit." But the old fig tree is no longer there. Barghouti realizes: "I saw the fig tree—solid in my memory—absent from its place" and asks: "Who cut down the fig tree?" (*I Saw* 55; *Ra'aytu* 66–67) The destroyed city of Beirut and the severed tree in Palestine are symbolic of the continual repression of Palestinian identity. Both poets have developed the propensity to ask questions, which is a characteristic trait of the modern *flâneur*.

However, Darwish's and Barghouti's "footsteps" lead them to different geographic locations.

Geographic Location and Time Lapse

In both narratives, the present city includes aspects of past cities. In *I Saw Ramallah*, the return voyage across the "Bridge of Return" reminds Barghouti of when he first went to study in Cairo during the tumultuous end of the Nasir era in Egypt (1952–1970). Similarly, in *Memory*, Darwish remembers Haifa when he is in Beirut. The view of the sea and its symbolism for the reality of exile propel him to imagine a possible return to the slopes of Mount Karmel overlooking Haifa. Also located in the Upper Galilee was his home village of al-Birwa, which was destroyed by Jewish militias in 1948. Darwish and his family fled north to Lebanon. This was a time of initial and forced exile for hundreds of thousands of Palestinians.

Though both cities elicit memories of past times in other cities, two important differences arise between these poetic prose works. The first is the geographical location. The stage for *Memory for Forgetfulness* is Beirut, which once served as the center for Palestinian armed resistance *outside* Palestine. In a revealing description of Beirut, Darwish claims: "everything that passed in the world also passed through here, sometimes reflecting what went on outside, sometimes setting a pattern for it" (53; *Al-Zamān* 28). *Memory* reflects what went on *outside* of Beirut (the external recurrent historical events) and refracts what went on *inside* Beirut (the terminal phase of the Palestinian era). Barghouti revisits Ramallah, which now serves as the political capital *inside* Palestine. Moreover, Darwish witnesses the recent destruction of Beirut, whereas Barghouti sees the effects of the prolonged Israeli occupation of Palestine. The different locations of the narratives thus provide insights into the repeated and multifarious Israeli assaults on Palestinian identity.

The second difference is the time lapse between the moment of writing and the event being related. Barghouti recorded his experiences in the occupied Palestinian territories immediately upon returning to Amman, "without order, without structure" (180; *Ra'aytu* 217). He later finished his memoir in Cairo. He allows very little time for memory to become enticed by imagination or to succumb to the whims of the mind. After the destruction of Beirut, after the "heroic" defeat of the PLO in Lebanon, after the Palestinian *fidā'īyūn* ("the ones who sacrifice themselves" or "the freedom fighters") and their leader Yasir Arafat were sent off to sea on a Greek ship bound for Tunisia, after the Palestinian intellectual resistance scattered around the Arab world and Europe, Darwish isolated himself in his Parisian apartment and composed *Memory for Forgetfulness*. Three years had elapsed since the Israeli bombardment of Beirut.

An immediate trend emerges from Darwish's prose works. In his previous quasi-autobiographical prose work, *Yawmīyāt al-ḥuzn al-'ādī* [Diary of ordinary sadness] (1973), he wrote about Haifa when he was in Beirut; when he was in Paris he wrote *Memory for Forgetfulness* about his experience in Beirut. Each new exile provides recollections of a past exile. And for the diaspora intellectual, every displacement is a new beginning: there is no end to exile.

During the composition of *Memory*, Darwish also mimicked reality by establishing a self-siege in his Parisian apartment for approximately three months. This is also the approximate duration of the Israeli siege of Beirut. With the passage of more time and the mnemonic assistance of mimicry, there is enough time for imagination to work its way into his narrative, ample time for Darwish to construct a work of literary art. Though their "footsteps" equally instigate memories, the different lapses of time allow for divergent mechanisms to be used.

Mechanisms of Memory

Though both narratives are voluntarily set within a determined time frame, the sequence of events is defined by different mechanisms of memory. Due to more conducive means of writing or compelled by the immediacy of what he witnessed, a short period of time elapses between the events experienced and the composition of *I Saw Ramallah*. "I chattered an entire lifetime to myself," Barghouti claims and uses *mémoire involontaire*, in which the chronological account of the twelve-day visit to the occupied Palestinian territories is marked by tangents into the past (182; *Ra'aytu* 219). The spontaneous transitions are natural and create an authentic flow to the narrative. Similarly, Darwish asserts: "Memory does not remember but receives the history raining down on it" (*Memory* 146; *Al-Zamān* 76). However, he uses *mémoire volontaire* to put order and structure to his one-day account of the Israeli bombardment of Beirut. He has more time to select and include specific intertextual passages from Arab historians, references to other poets, quotations from the Bible, and citations from the Qur'an. The use of intertextual passages in *Memory* permits him to "cut the thread connecting the beginning with the end," to carry on his search for something in the streets and "to reach an end that we forget" (75; 41). Darwish refines this mosaic style of texts, which he employed previously in *A Diary of Ordinary Sadness*, and reaches a very high level of fluidity between the texts. The transitions between the "mosaic of texts of diverse genres, bound together by their thematic content and the perspective of the author" (see Leeuwen 258), transforms the fragmented component of *Memory* into a smooth stream of consciousness. However, this is an artificial construction that only resembles the movement of selective memory.

Darwish selects fragments of his life and intersperses intertextual passages according to the image he wants to transmit. He also uses mnemonic devices to facilitate the recollection of the past. The most notable example is the smell of coffee, which acts like a Proustian madeleine and prompts the initial deluge of memories. According to Walter Benjamin, the olfactory trigger of memory is the most tenacious and instigates the opening of the "fan of memory":

> He who has once begun to open the fan of memory never comes to the end of its segments; no image satisfies him, for he has seen that it can be unfolded, and only in its folds does the truth reside...[4]

As the creases of the "fan of memory" unfold, the opening gaps between the older memories are filled by forgetfulness. Entrenched in a battle against forgetting, memory succumbs to the whims of imagination, which in turn satisfy the hope of recovering pieces of memory. Truth does not reside between the folds, but rather something resembling the truth. Similarly, Maurice Halbwachs asserts:

> We preserve memories of each epoch of our lives, and these are continually reproduced; through them, as by a continual relationship, a sense of our identity is perpetuated. But precisely because these memories are repetitions, because they are successfully engaged in very different systems of notions, at different periods of our lives, they have lost the form and the appearance they once had. (*Collective* 47)

The mnemonic trigger of the coffee's aroma and the reliving of a past reality via his self-siege in Paris are Darwish's devices to assist voluntary memory. Barghouti does not use either: he presents a "basket of memories" put on spontaneous display by involuntary memory, which is provoked by the wooden planks of the bridge, the languid flapping of Israeli flags, a Jewish propaganda poster, and an old fig tree. Whether instantaneously or deliberately, voluntary and involuntary memory brings the past into the present: the mechanisms resemble Vladimir Nabokov's butterflies: fluttering "messengers of memory" (Boym).

Though Darwish is more preoccupied with the conveyance of memory, neither Darwish nor Barghouti forget to remember. They are remembering to counter the presence of forgetfulness. The act of writing becomes an act of intellectual resistance against both the internal natural propensity to forget and the external Israeli forces in favor of Palestinian forgetfulness. Darwish writes:

> No one wants to forget. More accurately, no one wants to be forgotten... it has a long history, this double operation of searching for a place or a time on which to put a signature and untie the knot of the name facing the long caravan of oblivion. (*Memory* 15; *Al-Zamān* 10)

Darwish uses the cliché of "long caravans" to symbolize both the chain of historical events and the unrelenting procession of time. Writing becomes a means of transmitting historical experiences and collective emotions.

The pivotal eras of contemporary Palestinian history related by Darwish and Barghouti and the emotions aroused by their inquiries into the nature of the Israeli bombardment and the Zionist Jewish colonization of Palestine appeal to Arab collective memory. In his self-siege in Paris, Darwish appears to be, in the words of Fyodor Dostoyevsky:

> particularly oppressed by an old memory. It came back to me clearly a few days ago and, since then, it's been like an exasperating tune that I can't get out of my head. But I must get rid of it. (*Notes*)

In the Middle East, the traumatic memories of Beirut are not "old" and they do not come back suddenly. The repercussions of the 1982 Israeli siege continue to be felt today. The memories are still present and remain painfully "exasperating." The composition of *Memory for Forgetfulness* therefore becomes a personal, and by extension a communal, catharsis for the unpleasant past. Barghouti picks up the chronological thread and presents *I Saw Ramallah* as a testimony that Israeli aggression against Palestinian identity continues within what remains of Palestine. Whether against the internal propensity to repress traumatic experiences or the external forces of forgetfulness, both *Memory for Forgetfulness* and *I Saw Ramallah* are essential Palestinian manifestos of memory.

Individual Palestinian Dream and Collective Arab Memory

Both Palestinian poets employ different means to reinforce the particular Palestinian and broader Arab collective memory. Darwish transmits the Palestinian predicament in the diaspora through the individual dream. As a depiction of Palestinian identity, Barghouti relies on family ties within the occupied Palestinian territories for the maintenance of memory.

The narration of *Memory for Forgetfulness* starts before the break of dawn and ends after the fall of night. The same phrases, related to the notion of sleep and the dream-like state of being, are repeated at the beginning, middle, and end of the narrative:

> Out of one dream, another dream is born.
> *Are you well? I mean, are you alive?*
>
> ... a dream that came, born from another dream. *Are you still alive? When did it happen?*

I am awakened from one dream by another, itself the
interpretation of the dream?
That's what's happening now. Are you alive?
(*Memory* 3, 119, 182; *Al-Zamān* 4, 62, 96)

The repetitive phrases related to the inevitable cycle of night and day bring the narrative full circle by making it end where it began. The cyclical literary style echoes the verse of T. S. Eliot's "Little Gidding":

What we call the beginning is often the end
And to make an end is to make a beginning.
The end is where we start from. (*Four Quartets* 42)

Through the repetitive dream-related phrases, *Memory* also resembles *Finnegans Wake*. In his "nightbook," Joyce ties the entire state of unconsciousness together by having the last sentence lead into the first:

A way a lone a last a loved a long the

riverrun, past Eve and Adam's, from swerve of shore
to bend of bay, brings us by a commodius vicus of
recirculation back to ... (628, 3)

In order to "recirculate" the end into the beginning of *Memory*, Darwish uses repetitive phrases, as well as the sea image. At the beginning of *Memory*, the aroma of coffee instigates a flood of memories tightly intertwined by scenes of the sea. The evacuation of the PLO will occur by sea, but the era of the Palestinian presence in Beirut is already over. In reference to the biblical flood, *Memory* ends with the sea—symbolic of the reality of exile—inundating the city.

Just as Joyce's *Wake* is "a dream of the human family, with the 'history of the world' as its memory" (Heaney, introduction xi), so *Memory* can be seen as a dream-nightmare of the Arab family, with the history of the Middle East as its memory. In this sense, Darwish rearticulates a particular period in the history of the Middle East to reinforce Arab collective memory. It is important to note that though

Memory for Forgetfulness is shrouded in an outer dream shell, the internal narrative occurs within a nightmare. The recurrent dream of existence adds a surreal element to the narrative, while the nightmare depicts the reality of experience.

"Outside the dream, in reality the past does not recur," Maurice Halbwachs asserts, and claims that history is preserved in the collective memory of societies; more precisely, collective memory is preserved through the ties of generations and the bonds of family (39). Where Darwish fulfills the first part—the dream—of this theory, Barghouti exemplifies the second part—the familial relations—by physically revisiting his family in Ramallah and their home village of Deir Ghassanah.

The Israeli intention to evict Palestinians from historical time and geographic place has not been successful in breaking the relations between the Palestinian diaspora and the occupied Palestinian territories. Edward Said claims the two Palestinian communities

> are beginning to form a different kind of community, which is based not on everyday experience but on long-distance telephone calls and other activities that occur infrequently. (*Politics* 118)

Barghouti also relates the use of the telephone as a means of keeping Palestinian families and their communities together:

> The Palestinian has become a telephonic person, living by the sound of voices carried to him across huge distances...
>
> A ring of joy, a ring for sorrow, a ring for yearning.... the displaced person can never be protected from the terrorism of the telephone. (*I Saw* 126–127; *Ra'aytu* 151–152; 161)

The telephone ring causes apprehension because the call may announce a wedding or a funeral; it may be the birth of a new family member or it may be the death of a relative. Geographic displacement does not permit the Palestinian to know until the voice on the telephone enunciates the news:

> At one-thirty in the morning Mounif informed me from Qatar of the death of my father in Amman. I was in

> Budapest. At two-fifteen in the afternoon, seven years later, my brother ‘Ala informed me from Qatar of the death of Mounif in Paris. I was in Cairo. (127; 152)

The collective Palestinian experience is determined by different locations of exile. The random telephone calls announcing death or birth, sadness or happiness, leave the individual in limbo, suspended between life and belonging "here," and death and exile "there." Edward Said calls this type of life: "a marginal existence, with no center to it" (*Politics* 111). In this sense, the community of the Palestinian diaspora appears to have centers everywhere with no delineated or established periphery. In *I Saw Ramallah*, Palestinian life appears in suspension, as if in a dream; much like the coexistence of dream and nightmare as conveyed by Darwish in *Memory for Forgetfulness*.

Both prose works recollect contiguous eras of contemporary Palestinian history. According to the French historian Jacques Le Goff, when a historical time is particularly evocative of communal identity, then the pivotal turning point becomes a "fundamental axis of memory" (95). On the linear timeline of history, the "axis" of memory straddles a threshold between "then" and "now" and thus elicits the collective memory. For Israel, the conquest of Palestine is twofold: on the military level, the conquest is carried out through the occupation and colonization of the land; on the collective level, the conquest is carried out through the superimposition of history, the deletion of Palestinian and the substitution of Israeli memory. Darwish and Barghouti intellectually counter the Israeli political use of memory as "an instrument and an objective of power"; each "seeks to save the past in order to serve the present and the future" (98–99), and thus both pertain to Palestinian resistance literature. Palestine remains, however, a dream for the Palestinian diaspora and a nightmare for those besieged in the occupied Palestinian territories.

Palestinian Diaspora and Resistance Literature

Both Palestinian poets belong to the Palestinian diaspora. Writing from exile, they repeat their journeys to a specific era of contemporary Palestinian history. Salman Rushdie once asked Edward Said: "Doesn't this need to go back again and again over the same story become tiring?" Said answered: "It does, but you do it anyway… there seems to be nothing in the world which sustains the story; unless you go on telling it, it will just drop and disappear."[5] According to Edward Said, for "a Palestinian—it is as if the activity of repeating prevents us and others from skipping us or overlooking us entirely" (*Politics* 111). Moreover, he claims in other instances: "Memory is a powerful collective instrument for preserving identity… it is one of the main bulwarks against historical erasure. It is a means of resistance" (Said and Barsamian 182–183). As demonstrated by the prose works of Darwish and Barghouti, the repetition of memory reinforces Palestinian identity and acts as a means of literary resistance to the Israeli superimposition of history.

Representative of the popular discourse of the Palestinian resistance, Darwish "repeatedly states that the Israeli versions of history have been imposed by force, that the Israeli interpretations of justice have been imposed by force and that the Israeli meanings of words and concepts have been imposed by force" (Leeuwen 271). This is why the translator of *Memory*, Ibrahim Muhawi, claims that the wars on "borders" alluded to by Darwish "are not only those between Israel and the Arab countries, but also those of writing itself" (introduction to *Memory* xx). Barghouti experiences the reality of these "border wars" and how Israel attempts to "obliterate history and turn it into private or collective mythology."[6]

As he walks across the "Bridge of Return," Barghouti encounters a poster of the Masada "massacre" hanging from the gate of the Israeli *mahsoum* [military checkpoint]. According to Jewish history, the mountain fortress of Masada, which overlooks the Dead Sea, was besieged by the Roman legionaries of Emperor Titus in 73 CE. However, Masada was only taken after some 900 Jewish zealots finally resolved to commit mass suicide and thereby save themselves from surrender and slavery. Barghouti does not provide answers, but asks: "Is this their message to us… to remind us that they will stay here forever?" (*I Saw* 14; *Ra'aytu* 20)[7]

If so, then the extremist Palestinian answer to avoid surrender has also been suicide. The radical Palestinian resolve of suicide, when confronted with the option of Israeli military domination, demonstrates the general recurrence of historical behavior. Once a practice revered by zealous Jews when confronted with foreign occupation, the contemporary Palestinian use of suicide as a means of resistance is now highly condemned internationally and is effectively used by Israel as propaganda against the Palestinians. Both Darwish and Barghouti perceive the counterproductive nature of suicide terrorism and express existential ennui with the morbid practice of martyrdom based on aspirations to the afterlife, and agree that the repetition of death incites boredom: "Heroism invites boredom when the scene goes on too long and the initial excitement fades," Darwish states. However, he also concedes that boredom with the banal always leads to "something resembling wisdom" (*Memory* 98–101; *Al-Zamān* 52–53). And Barghouti responds: "Prolonged wars generate boredom" (*I Saw* 107; *Ra'aytu* 128).

During the Palestinian era in Beirut, the repetition of modern martyrdom acquired new proportions. In *I Saw Ramallah*, Barghouti remembers when he was in Beirut and Abu Tawfiq would drive around the neighborhood of Fakihani "repeating the unchanging phrase 'O our beautiful martyr!'" For Barghouti, the first scene is emotionally moving, but the repetition of self-sacrifice, "of falling martyrs, the repetition of funerals, the repetition of favorite sentences, 'O our beautiful martyr!' started to color the tragedy with a tint of routine familiarity." Accordingly, posters of martyrs' faces covered the city walls, "but as more and more martyrs fell, the posters crowded each other on the walls" and the new faces covered "parts of the older ones" (176–177; 212–213). Similarly, in *Memory*, Darwish sees the repetition of posters along the façades of buildings in Beirut. He sees the resolute faces of martyrs "freshly emerging from life and... death is a remake of itself. One martyr replacing the face of another, taking his place on the wall, until displaced by yet another, or by rain" (*Memory* 53; *Al-Zamān* 28). Death becomes banal when life loses its importance. Death is forgetfulness and life is remembrance, but both forsake the dead as repetition overwhelms memory.

Darwish and Barghouti become critical of both the external Israeli assaults on Palestinian memory and the internal practice of martyrdom that defines a facet of contemporary Palestinian identity. However, their paths of intellectual resistance remain divergent. Though both used literary resistance to counter Israeli occupation and colonization, at a young age, Darwish was propelled to the forefront of Palestinian resistance literature with his "Biṭāqat hawīya" ["Identity Card"] (1964). He subsequently wrote an introduction to Ghassan Kanafani's conclusive work *Al-Adab al-filasṭīnī al-muqāwim taḥt al-'iḥtilāl, 1948–1968* [The literature of Palestinian resistance under occupation] (1968), which often mentions the up-and-coming poet. A collection of Palestinian resistance poems entitled *The Palestinian Wedding* (after a verse from a poem by Darwish) was dedicated to Ghassan Kanafani after he was killed by an Israeli Mossad car bomb in Beirut on July 8, 1972 (Harlow, *Resistance* 11).

Darwish solidified his position as the "poet laureate of Palestine" and increasingly affiliated himself with the Palestinian leadership. He followed the PLO from Beirut to Tunis. Barghouti, who disapproved of the leadership's corruption, moved to Budapest. In Paris, at the end of *Memory*, the famous lines—"Sajjil!/ Anā 'Arabī" [Record!/ I am an Arab]—return, but this time, Darwish is disappointed: "I didn't realize it was necessary to say it here in Beirut" (*Memory* 174; *Al-Zamān* 92).[8] However, he does not criticize the PLO and maintains that there was no other political body representative of the Palestinian people. He later resigned as cultural attaché for the PLO Executive Committee in protest of the dire implications of the 1993 Oslo Accords. In *I Saw Ramallah*, Barghouti remains highly critical of the Palestinian "leadership" before and after the ominous Oslo Accords. Toward the end of *I Saw Ramallah*, Barghouti wonders if he was wrong to return. In the words of Abu Muhammad:

> On the contrary. Anyone who can come back and live here should come back immediately.... Build in your villages if you can. Build Palestinian settlements in Palestine. How can you ask if it was wrong? Come, my friend—come! (*I Saw* 142; *Ra'aytu* 169)

Darwish has higher personal ambitions. Just as he became the "poet laureate of Palestine" and the "poet of Canaan," after Beirut he wanted to become the modern "poet of Troy" (see Darwish, *La Palestine* 152). According to Edward Said:

> with literally hundreds of air sorties flown unchecked and the city cut off from electrical, water, food, and

> medical supplies, a UN Security Council resolution calling on Israel to let pass humanitarian supplies was vetoed by the U.S. on the grounds that it was 'unbalanced.' ("Reflections")

Beirut was bombarded beyond recognition into a state of non-existence. However, during the Israeli siege of Beirut, those demonstrating against the siege were not the Arabs, but the Israelis.[9] In *Memory*, Darwish claims, "I didn't rejoice over the demonstrations in Tel Aviv, which continues to rob us of all our roles" (109; 54–55). And commenting on the motivation behind the writing of *Memory*, he asserts:

> I feared that these manifestations, good or positive, would bring the cameras to Israeli territory and would leave us in the shadow... It was important to show the paradox... I wanted to say that the victim had nowhere to demonstrate, because others were demonstrating for them. (*La Palestine* 143)

The Arabs contented themselves with the images of the Israeli "Peace Now" demonstrations, as though the Israelis were representing them. Darwish's ambition is to depict how the world listens when Israelis speak up and turns a deaf ear to the voice of the Palestinians; his ambition is to present a counternarrative to the Israeli representation of reality. In becoming the modern "poet of Troy," he hoped to rectify the imbalance between the image of the victor and reality of the victim. Both Darwish and Barghouti present a literary perspective of Palestinian existence, but Barghouti's call for collective resistance is more direct than Darwish's fancy "footsteps" of literary repetition.

Literary Repetition: Nostalgia and *Ressentiment*

Both poets use repetition as a literary device in their prose works. When Darwish employs literary repetition, he transmits nostalgia. This is noticeable in his overall poetic work, excessively so in his later poetry and particularly in nostalgic parts of *Memory for Forgetfulness*. When Barghouti uses literary repetition, he conveys *ressentiment*. In both cases, the English translations made noticeable cuts to the literary repetition of their Arabic prose.[10]

Memory for Forgetfulness is tied together by the desire to sing the Song of Songs. When confronted with the immediacy of death, Barghouti also feels compelled to write a poem about life (see "War Butlers"). However, he is not motivated by the desire to recover an unrequited love, as symbolized by Darwish's hope to see the "Lily of the Valley" blossom at dawn. Darwish's reference to Solomon's Song of Songs fulfills a poetic purpose. The lily image recurs in the opening, middle, and closing scenes and provides an evident undertone of nostalgia to the flow of *Memory*.

With intense longing, Darwish now eulogizes his moments with a woman prior to Beirut, thereby critiquing the perpetual situation of present war. In the most intimate passage of *Memory*, Darwish is enraptured with a woman, who is essentially "a rose of Sharon, a lily of the valleys" (Song of Sol. 2:1). Throughout this passage, he obsessively repeats the sentence: "each will kill the other outside the window" (*Memory* 122–126; *Al-Zamān* 62–66). Muhawi claims this verse is "repeated like a leitmotif every time the poet recollects his passion for his Israeli lover" and that the line is repeated by Darwish in a previous poem called "A Beautiful Woman in Sodom" (1970) (*Memory* 122n). The image of the lily most probably represents the reincarnation of Rita, the Israeli lover of Darwish's youth: inside they are products of the same land and can consume their love, but outside they are political enemies. Darwish associated his notion of forgetfulness as leading to the annihilation of these historical confrontations, but forgetfulness is also death and "leads to another pathway: 'each will kill the other outside the window'" (*Memory* 173; *Al-Zamān* 91). The repetition of this line expresses his internal desire to forget the political differences, but also his awareness of the present inability to do so because of the recurrent external circumstances. The use of literary repetition reflects the seemingly insoluble Palestinian–Israeli conflict: the lover and the loved, like the executioner and the executed, and the colonizer and the colonized are wed until death do they part.

In the lyrical and circular passage that follows the "lily," Darwish sees a mare "born from the praise poetry of the Arabs" emerge from the far corner of the room and burst forth challenging language and the unknown. Darwish calls her "D" because she is,

> the dawning of madness, the dawning of hell, the
> dawning of paradise, and the dawning of all passions

> that can win a war by an act of love not realizable except
> in the fear of death. (127; 166)

As the rhythmical cadence of the passage progresses, the mare turns into a beautiful woman with high heels, then embodies the "pride of a gazelle" as the passage exalts the power of spontaneous sex, and turns suddenly into a testament about the devastating effects of war. The confluence of the woman's absence with the presence of the feeling causes Darwish to refer again to the emotional persistence of the "Lily of the Valley, born from the Song of Songs." The literary repetition of the phrase "and you will be born out of a dream that is born out of another dream" ties the narrative of *Memory* together, and the addition of "as the Lily of the Valley was born this dawn" recreates the prevalent feeling of nostalgia for a future pertaining to the past (131; 68).

In *Memory*, Darwish masters the art of repetition. The chain of images leads back to the first time he came to Beirut as a six-year-old. The streetcar passage "on two parallel lines made of iron" carries young Darwish around the circuit of the city and back to the same place where a cap was put on his head (86–87; 46–47).[11] The circular scene of the streetcar moving through the streets of Beirut epitomizes the cyclical motion of time in *Memory*, just as the narrative of *I Saw Ramallah* comes full circle when Barghouti prepares for his departure and journey back across the bridge. And just as there are no longer any streetcars in Beirut, so the wooden bridge Barghouti crossed has disappeared.

Barghouti claims that generally "nostalgia comes when one chooses to live away from their homeland" and that particularly for him, "nostalgia is replaced by this feeling that your will is broken… by the Occupation, by the Arab regimes, by the existing laws, by not having the passport, by being threatened to be arrested at the borders… This generates anger not nostalgia" (Reigeluth, interview). Darwish also wonders in the opening scenes of *Memory*: "Where's my will?" (10, 13; 8, 9) Barghouti resolves nonetheless to make the trip into the occupied Palestinian territories. Darwish resigns himself to the sobering fact that "he who lives, lives by chance," but eventually decides that: "I don't want to die under the rubble. I want to die in the open street" (27; 15–16).

The use of literary repetition is most prevalent in *I Saw Ramallah* when Barghouti asks questions about the nature of the Zionist Jewish colonization and the Israeli military occupation of Palestine. The removal of communal freedom and the breaking of personal will caused by the Israeli occupation create *ressentiment*, but the occupation cannot give parameters to questions. When arriving in Ramallah, Barghouti wonders:

> Is it not odd that when we arrive at a new place living its new moment we start to look for our old things in it? Is there something new for strangers? Or do they go around the world with baskets full of the stains of the past? (50–51; 62)

Barghouti is also repetitive when touched by doubt:

> How did I sing for my homeland when I did not know it? Should I be praised or blamed for my songs? Did I lie a little? A lot? Did I lie to myself? To others? What love is it that does not know the beloved? And why were we not able to hold on to the song? (61; 73)

He is particularly repetitive when preoccupied by the occupation:

> Generations… Generations… Generations… The Occupation has created generations without a place whose colors, smells, and sounds they can remember; a first place that belongs to them, that they can return to in their memories in their cobbled-together exiles. (62; 74)

And later concerning the symbolism of Jerusalem:

> They took the addresses… They took the city's throngs and its doors and its lanes, they took even the secret brothel… They took… They took the yawning of the pupils… They took the footsteps… They took… They took that shop I traveled to specially from Ramallah… for I was returning to Jerusalem. (144; 172–173)

The repetition of questions and the use of repetitive phrases is Barghouti's form of resistance to the Israeli military occupation and the Israeli monopoly on the image of victimhood, to the decadent Arab rulers and the corrupt Palestinian leadership, to "those who give answers"; in brief, to his world (Reigeluth, interview).

In contemporary history, no conflict has been more prolonged than the Arab–Israeli conflict. Furthermore, almost all the wars related to the ongoing conflict have been related to the question of Palestine. Indeed, the recurrence of history in the Palestinian–Israeli conflict—by way of a long list of wars and truces related to territorial borders, of sieges and the sacking of cities, of invasions and the subsequent occupation of land—reflects with the intensity of a prism the broader notion of historical recurrence in the Middle East.[12] A product of the seemingly endless conflict has been the use of literary recurrence by Darwish and the "swing of life" by Barghouti.

Literary Recurrence and the "Swing of Life"

Darwish also conveys nostalgia when he uses literary recurrence. He transmits the "sadness of recollection" when desiring to recover a poetic "love" or to recuperate a tangible "land" in what was Palestine. If nostalgia is about "the repetition of the unrepeatable, [the] materialization of the immaterial," as Svetlana Boym claims, then Darwish is clearly affected by this "fundamental ambivalence" (*Future* xvii). The most notable example of territorial nostalgia occurs at the end of *Memory*, concerning the impossibility of returning to Haifa by sea. Darwish borrows a wooden rowboat from a short story by Ghassan Kanafani called "Kafr al-manjam" ["The Mine Hamlet"]. Darwish sends a young Palestinian named Kamal out to sea from Lebanon, returning to Haifa on the same wave that had taken him into exile. In the distance, Kamal sees the "Dove's feathers" and remembers the streets and windows of Haifa. At the end of this passage, the switch to the future tense is reminiscent of the end of "Kafr al-manjam":

> I will walk down the street, climb the stairs, and open the door to my room. I will take off my shoes and go to bed fully dressed… just like every day. (Kanafani, "Kafr" 26)

In the passage from *Memory*, Kamal will ascend the "ancient stone steps"; he will find his house; finally, the door will open with his mother's keys and he will "*sleep for hours, hours, hours. He will sleep forever.*" In the rowboat, Kamal wakes and finds himself surrounded by the Israeli Coast Guard. They nail his hands, feet, and shoulders to the wood of the boat. He bleeds and looks at the "ring of the Dove" growing smaller in the distance (168–172; 88–91). The idea of the ring of the Dove as a description of Haifa—

while the narrative in *Memory* takes place during the bombardment of Beirut—is reminiscent of description of the downfall of Cordova in *Ṭawq al-ḥamāma* [*The Neck-Ring of the Dove*] by the Muslim literary figure Ibn Hazm.[13] And just as a necklace is comprised of attached links, history is a chain of recurrent events and memory is filled with a series of intertwined images.

A plethora of literary references are interspersed throughout Darwish's poetic work. In *Memory*, he refers to the famous poem "Waiting for the Barbarians" by the Greek poet Constantine Cavafy to describe how car bombs, modern Trojan horses, "perfected by the MOSSAD" paved the way for the Israeli invasion. Every car promised the possibility of death, so Darwish exclaims: "Let the barbarians come in, then!" (*Memory* 71; *Al-Zamān* 39; see also Cavafy, *Collected*)

For Darwish, the similarity of tragic historical events also serves to fulfill a poetic purpose. It is not coincidental that the events in *Memory* took place on the Day of all Days, "that apocalyptic day, 6 August 1982, Hiroshima Day" (Muhawi, introduction to *Memory* x). Darwish attempts to draw a parallel between the horrors of Hiroshima and the bombardment of Beirut. During the recollection of his actual visit to Hiroshima, he mentions a film based on the novel *Hiroshima mon amour* by Marguerite Duras, but he can only imagine what Hiroshima must have been before and asks: "Who will remind Hiroshima that Hiroshima was here?" and "Where is Hiroshima?" (*Memory* 84–86; *Al-Zamān* 44–45) *Memory* becomes an attempt to keep Beirut from suffering the same fate. With the innumerable sieges of cities throughout history, Darwish could have chosen from an abundance of other sieges, which may have provided closer historical comparisons.[14]

According to Barghouti, "Our catastrophes and our pains are repeated and proliferate day after day" (*I Saw* 171; *Ra'aytu* 205). This simple statement demonstrates Barghouti's awareness of the contemporary historical recurrence of events in Palestine. Darwish is also cognizant of the effects of the siege and describes them throughout *Memory* with a certain "restraint of rage."[15] However, he prefers to circumvent the simplistic historical comparisons to other sieges and intentionally chooses a more popular parallel by drawing a broad parallel between the Israeli invasion and the invasions of the *franj* [the "Franks" or "Crusaders"].[16]

The most important historical intertextual passage included in *Memory* is taken from a book by the Hanbali Sunni historian Ibn Kathir, entitled *Al-Bidāya wa al-nihāya* [The beginning and the end].[17] The title conveniently supports the cyclical notion of history in the Middle East as depicted through the use of literary repetition in *Memory*. The following passage comes at the end of the referential inclusion and may illustrate Darwish's political stance:

> That year, a truce was signed to stop the war, after thirty years and six months. The Franks would keep what lands they held on the coast, and the Muslims would keep the hill country; the districts in between were to be divided half and half... (*Memory* 115; *Al-Zamān* 60)[18]

Darwish includes this passage purposefully near the middle of *Memory*. Ibn Kathir intentionally repeats "that year" at the beginning of each paragraph of the passage as a way of reinforcing the memory of that time. However, the date of "that year" is never given in *Memory*, which also makes it conveniently applicable to the year Israel besieged Beirut.

Barghouti does not use literary recurrence directly. He perceives a confluence of the tragic and the comic in Palestinian existence. He employs his observations of the Israeli occupation and his experiences as a Palestinian to depict his notion of the "swing of life." This notion is probably influenced by Marx's famous remark that a historical event occurs "the first time as tragedy, the second time as farce."[19] Similar to Emile Habiby, who refers directly to Marx, Barghouti writes:

> Life does not allow us to consider repeated uprootings as tragic for there is an aspect to them that reminds us of farce, and it will not allow us to get used to them as repeated jokes because there is always a tragic side to them. (89; 106)

The incremental recurrence of detrimental historical events for the Palestinian on the tragicomic "swing of life" leads to absurdity in the French existentialist sense of the word, in which life is devoid of apparent meaning and seemingly futile:

> The person on a swing gets used to moving in two opposing directions; the swing of life carries its rider no further than its extremes, farce and tragedy. The world swings on, a light mist hiding the two horizons (89; 106).

The hidden horizon compels Barghouti and Darwish to express the existential immediacy of the Palestinian predicament. Where Barghouti feels *ressentiment*, Darwish transmits nostalgia. Where Darwish employs literary recurrence, Barghouti relies on the notion of the "swing of life." In both cases, they converse with the dead and long for sleep.

The Dead and Sleep

As both poets repeat their journeys of recollection, the act of writing alleviates a mutual feeling of existential estrangement from their people and of geographic displacement from Palestine. This type of repetition, Kierkegaard claims, "not only is for contemplation, but is a task for freedom, it signifies freedom itself" (*Repetition* 324). Barghouti is aware that "the newborn feeling of freedom is temporary" (*I Saw* 48; *Ra'aytu* 59). Darwish's defiance of the Israeli bombardment of Beirut and Barghouti's defiance of the Israeli military occupation of Palestine both enhance this ephemeral feeling. Both Darwish and Barghouti walk and talk, observe and contemplate: the presence of the dead speaks louder than the absence of the living.

In *I Saw Ramallah*, Barghouti is accompanied by the leading Palestinian resistance writer Ghassan Kanafani, the famous Palestinian political cartoonist Naji 'Ali, and his older brother, Mounif. All died violent deaths. In *Memory for Forgetfulness*, Darwish plays chess with the Lebanese poet Khalil Hawi, has a surreal conversation with another Palestinian writer, Izz al-Din al-Qalaq, and talks casually with another Palestinian poet, Mu'in Bsseisso. All died violent deaths. Fatigue inundates both poetic prose works. Darwish and Barghouti long for rest, but find no respite from the persistence of memory. Barghouti writes: "It is the field of memory that has been plowed and fertilized and watered in the darkness that is ours" (*I Saw* 180; *Ra'aytu* 217).

As modern conceptions of the *flâneur*, Darwish and Barghouti wander through Beirut and Ramallah. They offer no answers, only observations of the follies of war and military occupation. Darwish goes in and out of a state of reverie and Barghouti becomes affected by gradual fatigue and the silence of approaching sleep. During his last night in Ramallah, Barghouti is with family and guests, but prefers "listening." Later that night, he is lying on his pillow. The trip back across the bridge in the morning is irrevocable. "I try to sleep—I cannot sleep." The narrative returns to the beginning, where Barghouti is standing on the wooden bridge that no longer exists: "I contemplate the scene. I have nothing to do except contemplate" (162, 8; 194, 13).

At the end of *Memory* and *I Saw Ramallah*, both Palestinian poets are like the "Angelus Novus" by Paul Klee. As described by Walter Benjamin:

> he is about to move away from something he is fixedly contemplating. His eyes are staring, his mouth is open, his wings are spread. This is how one pictures the angel of history. His face is turned toward the past. Where we perceive a chain of events, he sees one single catastrophe which keeps piling wreckage upon wreckage and hurls it in front of his feet. (*Illuminations* 257)

Darwish contemplates the ruin of Beirut and sees the succession of wars over Palestine reflected in the historical recurrence of the Middle East. Barghouti contemplates the severed tree of Deir Ghassanah and sees the succession of repeated historical fallacies and political ploys used to expropriate the geography of Palestine.

Both Darwish and Barghouti want "to stay, to awaken the dead" with whom they converse, but they are moving away, to contemplate what they see, to recompose the wreckage through the freedom of literary expression; as Hannah Arendt asserts:

> in this angel... the *flâneur* experiences his final transfiguration. Just as the *flâneur*, through the *gestus* of purposeless strolling, turns his back to the crowd even as he is propelled and swept by it, so the 'angel of history,' who looks at nothing but the expanse of ruins of the past, is blown backwards into the future. (introduction to *Illuminations* 13)

Darwish calls out to his youth with his typical juxtaposition of terms: "Oh, for a living time rising from a dead time!" and confirms that in Beirut: "Here, I didn't die; I haven't died yet" (*Memory* 173–174, 178–179; *Al-Zamān* 91–92, 94–95). As the night fades into morning, Barghouti is already leaving; he hovers momentarily over a lifetime of exile, engages the freedom to remember again, and before the inevitable departure he asks a final question:

> *What deprives the spirit of its colors?*
> *What is it other than the bullets of the invaders that*
> *have hit the body?* (*I Saw* 182; *Ra'aytu* 220)

Darwish moves into that nebulous area between night and day, tries to free himself from memory, and repeats: "I'll try to sleep now... Sleep is peace. Sleep is a dream, born out of a dream." Dawn will break again, but when he wakes, the nightmare will continue. Once again the anonymous woman figure asks: "Are you alive?" Darwish responds: "In this middle region between life and death" and Barghouti adds: "in this pale wasteland."[20]

This is the mutual result of a suspended existence spent in exile. This is the product of being neither here nor there, of being a stranger, not by their own volition, but due to displacement and estrangement. In *Memory for Forgetfulness*, Mahmoud Darwish contemplates the bombardment of Beirut as a reflection of existence in the Palestinian diaspora. In *I Saw Ramallah*, Mourid Barghouti observes the results of the occupation of Ramallah and the village of Deir Ghassanah as a reflection of the dire condition of Palestine. Equally well, both could have asked: "Sleep, where in the waste is the wisdom?" (Joyce, *Finnegans Wake* 114)

13
Interview with Mahmoud Darwish: On the Possibility of Poetry at a Time of Siege

Interview by Najat Rahman

IN THE SPRING OF 1996, MAHMOUD DARWISH RETURNED TO RAMALLAH. I had the chance to meet him then for the first time. A span of nine years separates that meeting from this interview, which took place in the late morning on Monday, July 18, 2005, at the Sakakini Cultural Center in Ramallah.

In 1996, he seemed elated to have returned, hopeful for the future, elegant and generous. In this second interview, Darwish was still a familiar mixture of these impressions. He seemed, however, more preoccupied, perhaps ever conscious of how critical projects are undertaken to address his work. He wanted to discuss the contributors to this edition—sometimes openly expressing concern that a particular critic "only offers political readings" of his poetry or commending the skills of another. He seemed, in short, more conscious of his legacy. At one point during the interview, a woman entered his office and offered him a large framed placard of his poem, "Identity Card." She told him that it was "from the Americans," and he made a few remarks about how this poem still follows him around, and how surprised he was about the attention of the Americans.

During the first interview, we talked about his return to Palestine; about his poetry after the experience of Beirut in 1982 in relation to his earlier work of the 1960s and 1970s; about the meaning of "return"; about the difference between *qaṣīda*, song, and *nashīd*. The focus was primarily on his poetic period of the epic-song.

This second interview centers more on the period after *Why Have You Left the Horse Alone?* (1995), with particular emphasis on

State of Siege (2002). *Why Have You Left the Horse Alone?* is a powerful synthesis of his earlier poetic periods in its focus on the relation between history and myth, as well as in its interrogation of poetry and of the self. In Darwish's latest period, the metaphors and the realities of exile and journey are more about the relations between the self and the self, between the self and language, the poet and his poetry.

NR: In your work *Ḥālat ḥiṣār* [*State of Siege*], you explore the many states of siege, and you seem to imply that poetry is also a state of siege. For instance, you write:

> My speech besieges me in sleep,
> my speech that I have not said,
> it writes me then leaves me searching
> for the remnants of my sleep … [*Butterfly's Burden* 129].

How has poetry become a state of siege for you? And, has the state of siege ended?

MD: The siege has not ended. I don't know how to assess it. I tried to widen the notion of siege from its usual sense of military siege to an existential condition [*ma'nā wujūdī*], in incorporating the siege of the martyr, the siege of language. National themes, topics, questions have besieged the poet. This work was an attempt to end the siege from the collective. It was announcing a complaint and a daring acknowledgement. The poem *Ḥālat ḥiṣār* is similar to a journal that takes up the meaning of siege. There is a siege from the reader—a siege of image, in case he [the poet] will not arrive at a stereotypical state, as if the text is expected to adhere to previous expectations, as if there is a reading that precedes the poem. It is essentially a siege of reading. I try to surprise my readers, and they have come to expect that I will surprise them. With time, I have been able to build a relation of trust with my readers.

NR: Do you distinguish between reader and critic?

MD: There are two critics of my poetry: One reader consists of academics and students who produce schoolbooks and university theses at institutions not interested in modern poetry. I am often embarrassed and utterly depressed reading them. I used to ask myself: Is this my fault or the fault of the critic who has not carefully read my poems? I would mostly lay the blame with myself. I did not learn anything reading these studies. It was the kind of criticism that does not add anything. Outside of academic life, there are young writers and poets who are good readers of my work. Subhi Hadidi in particular has been the best who has written on the subject. The *Qāhira* special edition on my poetry [June 1995] is particularly impressive. There is a large gap between modern poetry and criticism. Perhaps this is due to the deplorable state of our universities here [in Palestine and in the Arab world]. The universities are more like high schools. It is true that poetry and literature always precede criticism, but the gap is especially remarkable here in the Arabic context. In the West, criticism mostly happens in a university context. Criticism in the Arab world remains mostly an attempt at deciphering or explanation of meaning—it does not seek the movement of meaning, even though one of the most remarkable developments in modern Arabic poetry is its move away from referential meaning to signification [*min al-ma'nā ilā al-dalāla*], directing its attention to the movement of meaning rather than meaning itself. Poetry produced after the 1960s is not even read. There is also a political, accusative reading of my poetry that reads more like a political prosecution, but I do not attach to it any importance or interest.

NR: You describe the role of poet under siege as almost extraneous, as you do in *Ḥālat ḥiṣār* when you declare

> The siege transforms me from a singer into …
> a sixth string in the violin [*Butterfly's Burden* 165]

This is strikingly different from the role of the poet during the siege of Beirut, where a poet as you indicated in various places was asked at every turn to respond poetically to the event, to contribute with poetry against a state of siege. What happened to the role of the poet?

MD: This is the most difficult question that is directed toward a poet. And what is often intended by this question is the interrogation of his social role, and not his aesthetic role. An Italian poet has asked, Is poetry necessary? I would ask: Is poetry possible? The poet has to cultivate the illusion that poetry is necessary and is able to transform, even if its role is receding in the world. It is not possible for poetry to affect change, but it is perhaps possible to change consciousness. Poetry might transform the reader's relation to his surroundings. The aesthetic experience is an individual experience and it develops into the possibility of saving the world from ugliness. Its possibility of humanizing is doubtful. Its role is to resist that which is an obstacle to the reader's humanity, to his being. Its role is to deepen the idea of beauty in human beings. The idea of beauty leads to the idea of peace: peace between the individual and himself, between the individual and his being, between the individual and nature. Now, that is where there seems to be a rupture between poetry and society. The reasons for which are (a) the poet wants his solitude, and (b) society is busy with consumerism and with speed, and this is manifested in the lowering of the standard of language, with the hegemony of the media and of the political discourse. There is an illusion that literary language is no longer necessary. The one who is responsible for this in the Arab world is the poet himself. Poets are engaged in formal experimentation and they have broken with rhythm as well as with modernity in its historical context and from within an Arabic heritage. Any modernity that does not emerge from a historical context will remain a false and fabricated modernity.

For the Beirut siege, I wrote *Madīḥ al-ẓill al-'ālī* [In praise of the rising shadow] and *Dhākira lil-nisyān* [*Memory for Forgetfulness*]. The first was much more popular with readers, but the anger overwhelmed its poetic quality. In my opinion, *Memory for Forgetfulness* is more poetic. Distance allows for better vision. Experience becomes more complete, riper. In the Ramallah text [*State of Siege*], the text seems quieter; it is disrobed from any ornamentation. It becomes almost neutral. There is a larger space for the other. In the search for the common, it is necessary to accept the other on the condition that the other accepts me as well. In looking at the faces of soldiers, one inevitably sees their humanity, a humanity that implements terrible and destructive politics. The search for normal life in this country has to include a solution for the other. This is the paradox, and unlike any other in history—the victim has to also find a solution for its oppressor.

I am influenced by the poetry of René Char, especially when he says that the poet has to transform enemies to adversaries. This is especially the role of the Palestinian poet now.

NR: You write you are

> … the last of the poets who
> are insomniac by what makes their enemies
>   insomniac:
> Perhaps the earth is too narrow
> for people,
> and for the gods [*Butterfly's Burden* 135]

How are you the "last poet"? Are you *also* the last poet in the sense of the pre-Islamic Arab poet who is inextricably connected to the collective when he speaks himself?

MD: I mean to say that the self and the enemy are entangled and embroiled, trapped in a land with too much history and too many prophets. Perhaps the time I write has the chance, the potential for peace. Self and other are always interlinked. I can also be myself's other.

NR: For many Palestinians in the diaspora, belonging has been fostered through poetry and other cultural forms rather than through physical attachment to land or to people. What will happen when the *nashīd* disappears? In your view, where is the *nashīd* today? You address the reader in *Ḥālat ḥiṣār* by saying

> Don't trust the poem,
> this daughter of absence
> […]
> she's chasm's sense [*Butterfly's Burden* 167]

As your poetry increasingly addresses such existential conditions as love and death, is there still a "fragile force" in poetry as you indicated in other places?

MD: The *nashīd* is linked with a certain period of transition, and it has a collective voice. This *nashīd* rises and falls and it has a relationship to the multiple journey, with general developments and questions. Myth is a collective story and a divine act [*fi'l ilāhī*], whereas history is a human act. As such there is no place for myth in modernity. As the collective is closer to achieving its project, as the *nashīd* becomes less serious, arrival is the last stanza. And when arrival has been achieved and identity with it, then beauty allows for an individual voice. So the repressed within the individual has an opening and a possibility for expression. The Palestinian question has not been resolved, but it has been transformed from its human dimension to its administrative dimension. We are not present and we are not absent. But we are linked to the idea of state. We are now in the middle of a workshop on the state [*warshat al-dawla*] on a theoretical level. The image of epic has ended and has been transformed to the image of the state. We cannot be preoccupied with national nostalgia. It has been stripped off. [*inqashata*—literally skimmed off.] I wrote *nashīd* more than once, and now, even in the national sense, it is better for Palestine to have a plurality of subjects and poetic topics.

NR: You often choose the long poem in your late stages—*Jidārīya* [*Mural*], *Ḥālat ḥiṣār*, *Madīḥ al-ẓill al-'ālī*, *Qaṣīdat Bayrūt*. Is there a relation between the long poem and writing in critical moments?

MD: I remember the poetry of epic: the use of the long poem has a relation to profound individual experiences or historical experiences where there is a need for archaeological work. The construction of the poem [*qaṣīda*] allows the poem to incorporate what it likes. The long poem, like the novel, can accommodate and incorporate human knowledge from culture, cinema, and reportage. It also allows for more poetic experimentation. I believe in meter—and this makes me conservative in comparison to other poets. Poetry for me is rhythm. Otherwise, it is not poetry. I am rich with rhythm. I can mix meters in one meter. The long poem has vitality. It is like a forest, whereas the shorter lyrics have to be as pure as crystal.

NR: In *Ḥālat ḥiṣār*, the poetic voice takes on the voice of Christ when it cries:

> My lord ... my lord! why have you forsaken me
> while I'm still a child ... and you haven't tested me
> yet? [*Butterfly's Burden* 141]

It is said that Christ's address in Aramaic to his father is quite intimate and familiar. [Thanks to Terry Cochran for this observation.] The poetic voice in your works is often that of the son. In the *Dīwān*, you say "every absence is my father" (102). How do you view the figure of the father? Is the questioning of the father, for instance, in *Why Have You Left the Horse Alone?*, a disappointment or simply an acknowledgement of the limits of the ability of that generation?

MD: The cry of Jesus is different from how I feel or how I use the father figure. The father figure is also present in *Arā mā urīd* [I see what I want]. In this, as in other places, there are no horizons further than a simple relation of the father and his son. Perhaps there are other dimensions, but they are not dominant, such as the dimension of heritage, of we the sons who inherit from other fathers. First, I myself have a lot of guilt toward my own father who was very shy and very attentive. He took care of the land before Israel was established. We were a landowning family. After Israel, he turned into a worker. His work and preoccupations gave the impression that he didn't pay attention to us. Second, after I left in 1970, I didn't see my father again. It was said that when he died he had a deep regret [*ḥasra*] that he wasn't able to see me. The dialogue with my father was clear and from one side, since he wasn't present. After I grew up, I don't remember him ever sitting with me alone. The relation with the mother is filled with symbols, because it could be associated with land, with continuity, with legitimacy. One does not doubt the mother as source. The land of Palestine is one, but the fathers have been many. So I did not use the father figure in the sense of the authoritarian father. My own father did not have a controlling, authoritarian presence. The conflict is with the mother. So I speak about my family, and not in a general sense. This interpretation [*bu'd*, literally what is far, the horizon] is not one that readily comes to mind [*wārid*].

NR: One notes a notable presence of the command verb in your poetry and wonders why. Does this indicate an opening toward a dialogue of sorts or a temporality that is more open-ended?

MD: Really? Where do you see this?

NR: Yes, for example in *Do Not Apologize for What You Have Done* and in poems such as "When He Walks Away."

MD: In the end, it is directed toward me. It's not a controlling tendency.

Warm thanks to Mahmoud Darwish for generously offering his time. Special thanks to Hala Khamis Nassar for helping to arrange the interview.

Contributors

Sinan Antoon is a poet, novelist, and translator. He studied English literature at Baghdad University before moving to the US after the 1991 Gulf war. He did his graduate studies at Georgetown and Harvard, where he earned a doctorate in Arabic literature in 2006. In 2002, he was awarded a Mellon Grant to support his research on the tenth-century poet Ibn al-Hajjaj. His poems and essays (in Arabic and English) have appeared in *As-Safīr*, *Al-Nahār*, *Al-Adāb*, and *Mashāref*, as well as the *Nation*, *Middle East Report*, *Al-Ahram Weekly*, *Banipal*, and the *Journal of Palestine Studies*. He has published a collection of poems *Mawshūr Muballal bil-Ḥurūb* [A Prism; Wet with Wars] (Cairo, 2003), which was published in English as *The Baghdad Blues* in April 2007 by Harbor Mountain Press, and a novel, *I'jaam*, which was published in March 2007 by City Lights Books. His poetry was anthologized in *Iraqi Poetry Today*. He has also contributed numerous translations of Arabic poetry into English. His co-translation of Darwish's poetry was a finalist for the PEN Prize in Translation in 2004.

Antoon returned to Iraq in 2003 as a member of InCounter Productions to co-direct/produce the documentary "About Baghdad," about the lives of Iraqis in a post-Saddam occupied Iraq. He is a senior editor with the *Arab Studies Journal*, a member of PEN America, a contributing editor to *Banipal*, and a member of the editorial committee of *Middle East Report*. Antoon is an assistant professor at New York University.

Rim Bejaoui is a doctoral student in comparative literature at the University of Montreal. Her research interests include: modern theater, particularly that of Kateb Yacine, contemporary Arabic and Francophone literature of the Maghreb and the Middle East, women's writing, and theories of postcolonialism.

Ipek Azime Celik is a Ph.D. candidate in the Department of Comparative Literature at New York University. She is writing her dissertation on the literary and filmic representations of Middle Eastern migrants and minorities in Europe.

Faysal Darraj (b. 1943) is a distinguished Palestinian critic. He studied at the University of Damascus and earned his Ph.D. in France. Darraj has had a long career writing for Palestinian cultural and political journals. He is widely published; his books include *Ḥiwār fī 'alāqāt al-thaqāfa wa-al-siyāsa* [Dialogue in cultural and political relations] (1984); *Naẓariyāt al-riwāya wa-al-riwāya al-'Arabīya* [Theory of the novel and the Arabic novel] (1999), awarded a prize for best book written in Arabic at the 2000 Cairo Book Exhibit; *Al-Riwāya wa-ta'wīl al-tārīkh: naẓarīyat al-riwāya wa-al-riwāya al-'Arabīy* [Interpretation of history in the Arabic novel] (2004); and *Al-ḥadātha al-mutaqhqira* [Retreating modernity] (2005). Darraj divides his time between Amman and Damascus.

Subhi Hadidi is a prominent Syrian critic, columnist, and translator. He has published extensively on contemporary Arabic literature, and translated into Arabic several works of poetry, fiction, and theory. His forthcoming book discusses the lyric-epic interactions in Mahmoud Darwish's later poetry. He lives and works in Paris.

Areeg Ibrahim was a Fulbright Scholar in 2006 at the Yale Center for International and Area Studies and a visiting assistant professor at the Department of Middle Eastern Languages and Civilizations at Yale University. She obtained her Ph.D. in 2003 from the University of Connecticut and teaches in the English Department at the Helwan University in Egypt. Her areas of research interest are comparative literature and modern drama. In addition to her published articles, she is also a published creative writer, with two short story collections and a novel in Arabic.

Sulaiman Jubran is a senior lecturer of modern Arabic literature in Tel-Aviv University. His publications include three books: *Structure and Language in the Poetry of 'Abd al-Wahab al-Bayyati* (Acre, 1989), *The Book of al-Fariyaq: Structure, Style and Satire* (Tel-Aviv University, 1991), and *Majma' al-Dād: A Study of Jawahiri's Biography and Poetry* (University of Haifa, 1994). He has also published articles in Arabic, English, and Hebrew dealing with modern Arabic poetry and prose.

Bassam K. Frangieh was born and raised in the Middle East and received a BA from Damascus University in 1976 and a Ph.D. from Georgetown University in 1987. He is a senior lecturer at Yale University. His research focuses primarily on modern Arabic literature and its relationship to Arab culture. He has published extensively on modern Arabic poetry and on the Arabic novel. In addition to writing numerous articles, he has authored several books, including *Anthology of Arabic Literature, Culture, and Thought from Pre-Islamic Times to the Present* (2004) and *Al-Ightirāb fī al-riwāya al-Filasṭīnīya* [Alienation in the Palestinian novel] (1989).

Hala Khamis Nassar is an assistant professor of modern Arabic culture and literature in the Department of Near Eastern Languages and Civilizations and in Women's, Gender, and Sexuality Studies at Yale University. She studied at Birzeit University in Palestine, as well as in Scotland (British council scholarship), the US, and Germany (DAAD scholarship), where she did her Ph.D. in theater studies at the Free University of Berlin. She came to the US as a Rockefeller Fellow at the University of California at Berkeley. She has taught many courses on contemporary Arab culture and literature at Bethlehem University in the West Bank, UC Berkeley, Columbia University, and Evergreen State College. She has published articles on Palestinian and Arab cultural productions and currently she is working on two manuscripts, one on Palestinian theater (forthcoming from Interlink) and another on the Palestinian culture of martyrdom.

Angelika Neuwirth is the chair of Arabic Studies at the Free University of Berlin, Germany. Previously she was a guest professor in Amman (1977–1983) and Cairo (1988–1989), and director of the Orient Institute of the German Oriental Society in Beirut and Istanbul (1994–1999). Her main research is on the Qur'an and Arabic literature.

Najat Rahman is assistant professor of comparative literature at the University of Montreal with a specialty in modern and contemporary Arabic literature and poetry. She is the author of

Literary Disinheritance: Home in Writing in the Works of Assia Djebar and Mahmoud Darwish (Lexington Books, forthcoming). Her present research, which explores constructions of gender and masculinity in relation to contemporary articulations of home, has appeared in Routledge, Zed, and Palgrave Macmillan. She has published translations of selected poetry of Mahmoud Darwish and Abd al-Wahhab al-Bayyati (*Flyway*, 2003; *Modern Poetry in Translation*, 2003). She has also written on the work of Rachid al-Daif, Amin Maalouf, and Leila Sebbar. She was a recipient of a Fulbright Scholar Grant to Beirut, Lebanon.

Stuart Reigeluth has a Masters degree from the Center for Arab and Middle Eastern Studies (CAMES) at the American University of Beirut (AUB). He covered the Israeli disengagement from the Gaza Strip in August 2005 and has contributed articles to the *Daily Star*, *Al-Ahram Weekly*, and and *Foreign Policy Edición Española*. He is a freelance writer and works for the Africa and Middle East Program at the Toledo International Center for Peace (CITpax) in Madrid, Spain.

Jeffrey Sacks is a writer, translator, and scholar living in New York City. He has translated Mahmoud Darwish's *Why Did You Leave the Horse Alone?* (New York: Archipelago, 2006) and is completing a book on the relations among literature and mourning in modern Arabic and Arab Jewish letters entitled *Opening Figures*. He teaches Arabic at Columbia University.

Reuven Snir is a professor of Arabic language and literature at the University of Haifa. He has published in English, Arabic, and Hebrew on various aspects of Arabic prose, poetry, and theater, as well as on the Arabic and Hebrew writings of Arab Jews. His last books are *Rak'atān fī al-'ishq: dirāsa fī shi'r 'Abd al-Wahhāb al-Bayyātī* [Two Rak'as in Love: A Study of 'Abd al-Wahab al-Bayyati's Poetry] (Beirut: Dar al-Sāqī, 2002); *'Arviyut, yahadut, tsiyonut: ma'avak zehuyot ba-yetsira shel yehude 'Iraq* [Arabness, Jewishness, Zionism: A Struggle of Identities in the Literature of Iraqi Jews] (Jerusalem: Ben-Zvi Institute, 2005); *Palestinian Theatre* (Wiesbaden: Reichert, 2005); and *Religion, Mysticism, and*

Modern Arabic Literature (Wiesbaden: Harrassovitz Verlag, 2006). Professor Snir is also a translator of Arabic poetry into Hebrew and Hebrew poetry into Arabic, and serves as the associate editor of *Al-Karmel: abḥāth fī al-lugha wa-l-adab* [Al-Karmel: studies in Arabic language and literature], published in Haifa.

Notes

INTRODUCTION

1 For an excellent development of the idea of the poet as an exile, see Maurice Blanchot, The Space of Literature, translated by Ann Smock (Lincoln: University of Nebraska Press, 1982).

2 Note that several exceptions to this statement have been published since we began this project: Randa Abou-baker, *The Conflict of Voices in the Poetry of Dennis Butrus and Mahmud Darwish: A Comparative Study* (Wiesbaden: Reichert, 2004), and Anette Mansson, *Passage to a New Wor(l)d: Exile and Restoration in Mahmud Darwish's Writing, 1960–1995* (Uppsala: Uppsala University, 2003).

CHAPTER 2: RAHMAN

I would like to thank Mary Layoun and Sam Slote for looking at earlier drafts of this paper, Jeffrey Michels for his invaluable help in translating "Crypts, Andalusia, Desert," as well as Pam Thompson and Hilary Plum for their careful readings.

1 Interview with Mahmoud Darwish on 10–11 April 1996 in Ramallah. This meeting corresponded with Darwish's first return to Palestine since the early 1970s. In this meeting, he also expressed that he only considers his writing after the Beirut 1982 period to be "poetry." Many thanks to Elias Mikhail and Nadia Rahman for arranging this interview.

2 In the Greek myths, Orpheus is a poet celebrated for his voice, the sung word. In the myth, Orpheus loses his wife Eurydice, who is stung by a snake as she is pursued by the desire of another, Aristaeus. Orpheus descends to the underworld to return her to life and is allowed to take Eurydice back by the infernal powers only if he does not turn back as he walks in front of her. Unable to abide by the prohibition, Orpheus loses Eurydice once again, this time definitively, for he turns back to look at her. Orpheus withdraws, a solitary and sad figure, and the women who feel scorned by the poet tear him to pieces. For a rendition of this myth, see for instance *Encyclopédie Universalis*. See also Maurice Blanchot, *Space* 171–173, for a detailed reading of this myth. For the added emphasis on Orpheus's floating head, which continues to sing after the dismemberment, see Adonis, *La Prière et l'épée*.

3 Asked by *Libération* why he writes, Darwish responds that in writing poetry he is really conducting a dialogue with himself, but admits that the "drive" for writing "is the desire to find a compensation for a loss that cannot be found outside of writing. When I lose love, the homeland, time, a beautiful scene, I recall it in writing" (*Libération* 13).

4 The siege of the city of Beirut has initiated an examination of the role of writing among writers and poets. In an interview, "A pressing longing for Beirut," Darwish points to the transition in his work: "What I wrote before Beirut was derivative. The experience demands a new kind of writing, because what

happened in Beirut is more than just the ordinary experience of people's history" (see Harlow, "Memory" 192).
5 In the April 1996 meeting with Darwish, he described the crypt as a suspended space: "a refuge, a closed and at the same time an open space, a place where strangers gather, meet, and talk." In configuring it as a place of possibility, it is not unlike Andalusia.

CHAPTER 3: DARRAJ

1 Translated by Areeg Ibrahim, from Darwish, "Ilā al-qāri'" [To the reader] in *Awrāq al-zaytūn* (*Dīwān* vol. 1, 7).
2 "To the Reader," trans. Nassar.
3 "'An al-shi'r," trans. Ibrahim.
4 From *A'rās*, in *Dīwān* vol. 1, 581–657. Translated by Nassar.
5 "Poem of the Land," translated in Jayyusi, *Anthology* 150–151.
6 "Poem of the Land," trans. Jayyusi, *Anthology* 148.
7 "Poem of the Land," trans. Nassar (*Dīwān* vol. 1, 623–630).
8 Jayyusi, *Anthology* 149, 151.
9 "Poem of the Land," trans. Nassar and Ibrahim (*Dīwān* vol. 1, 629).
10 *Ḥālat ḥiṣār* 41; trans. Elbendary 2002.
11 *Ḥālat ḥiṣār* 43; trans. Nassar.
12 *Ḥālat ḥiṣār* 56; trans. Elbendary 2002.
13 *Ḥālat ḥiṣār* 27; trans. Nassar.
14 *Ḥālat ḥiṣār* 27, trans. Ibrahim.

CHAPTER 5: HADIDI

1 A reference to Darwish's famous poem "Rītā wa al-bunduqīya" [Rita and the gun], from the collection *Ākhir al-layl* (1967) [The end of the night], in which the poet proclaims: "Between Rita and my eyes a gun."
2 From his collection *Awrāq al-zaytūn* (1964). This poem is better known under the first line, "Sajil anā 'Arabī," or "Record I am an Arab."
3 All translations from *Sarīr al-gharība* are by Fady Joudah, from Darwish, *Butterfly's Burden* (Port Townsend, Washington: Copper Canyon Press, 2007); page numbers given refer to this volume. *Trans.*
4 Arabic poetry relies on the Khalīl meters, codified in the eighth century by Khalil bin Ahmed, which determined the character of Arabic poetry through meter and rhyme until the last few decades. Rhythm has been traditionally created through the use of *'urūḍ* (prosodic or metrical divisions) or *taf'īla* (foot of a verse meter or measure). While some poets like Adonis see a certain rigidity in the conception of Arabic poetry along *'urūḍ*, Darwish finds a treasure: "No other language possesses sixteen different meters like Arabic. The Arabic meter is based on the number of musical units: one long syllable and one short" (Yeshurun 125) Joudah explains Darwish's use of *taf'īla* (the basic unit of prosody in Arabic) thus: "Darwish abides by the taf'eelah, but employs a 'circular' prosody, wherein the line does not consist of a discrete whole or fixed number of taf'eelahs. This is like saying that the line is often not made up of a whole number of metrical measures. Instead, the unity or wholeness (of prosody) is within the stanza or poem entire"

(*Butterfly's Burden*, xvi). *Trans.*
5 Please note that Darwish's *Sarīr al-gharība* and Joudah's translation in *The Butterfly's Burden* do not use section divisions. Effectively, they are Hadidi's sectioning of the poems. *Trans.*
6 Darwish uses the word "Sonata" to mean the sonnet, not the musical form of sonata. Arab poets have often employed "sonata" to mean sonnet. *Trans.*
7 A play on the word *nathr* as prose and dispersal. *Trans.*
8 Short vowel indicators are not part of the Arabic letter system; instead they are written as diacritic marks (*fatḥa* or vowel "a", *ḍamma* or vowel "u", *kasra* or vowel "i") over or below the consonant: with the *fatḥa*, *dhahab* becomes *dhahaba*; with *ḍamma*, *mushāt* becomes *mushātu*; with *kasra, ḥayāt* becomes *ḥayāti*. However, sometimes the voweling is implicit and the characters are not used as designators. In this case, the reader is called upon to determine the vowel sound; in the poem of Darwish for example, this opens possibilities for rhyming on the part of the reader. *Trans.*
8 *Rubā'iyāt* are quatrains (four-line stanzas) and *khumāsiyāt* quintains (five lines).

CHAPTER 6: SNIR

1 This saying is found in different forms in various medieval works, e.g. Ibn Qutayba, *'Uyūn al-akhbār* vol. 2, 185; al-Suyuti, *Al-Muzhir* vol. 2, 470. Cf. Lyall, *Translation* xv. For an examination of the above saying with regard to the change in perception of poetry and its function during the emergence of Arabic-Islamic society, see Ouyang, *Literary Criticism* 56–60.
2 Ibn Rashiq al-Qayrawani, *Al-'Umda* 65; al-Suyuti, *Al-Muzhir* vol. 2, 473. The translation is according to Lyall, *Translation* xvii, with minor modifications. See also Nicholson, *Literary History* 71.
3 Muhammad ibn Isma'il refers to the marginalization of Arabic poetry in relation to politics as being a metaphor for the rupture between poetry and culture in the contemporary Arab world ("Bayna al-siyāsa").
4 Cf. Adonis on the value of contemporary poetry: "Our success has been substantially and paradoxically due to our marginality" (Adonis, *Hā anta* 180). Muhammad 'Ali Farhat sees this development as corresponding to the disappearance of the "spirit of the countryside" [*al-rūḥ al-rifīya*] and the dominance of the town in the Arab world (Farhat 51). On the dichotomous roles played by town and country in modern Arabic poetry, see Moreh, "Town and Country."
5 *Al-Akhbār*, 11 August 1993, 11. Cf. the special volume of *Fuṣūl* 12.1 (Spring 1993) entitled *Zamān al-riwāya* [The time of the novel] as well as Jabra, *Ta'ammulāt* 11–26. See also Ihsan Abbas's words, "'aṣrunā huwa 'aṣr al-riwāya dūna adnā rayb," in *Ghurbat al-rā'ī* 230).
6 Preminger, *Princeton Encyclopedia* 582–583. Cf. Eliot, *Selected Essays* 248. On obscurity in modern Arabic literature and the reasons for it, see Adonis, *Muqaddima* 43–47, 124–125; Adonis, *Zamān al-shi'r* 158–159, 276–284; Adonis, *Al-Thābit* 290, 297; 'Abd al-Sabur, *Riḥla* 37–44; Isma'il, *Al-Shi'r al-'Arabī* 194; Lu'lu'a, *Al-Baḥth* 151–154.
7 Darwish was born in the village of Birwa, near Acre (Akka), which was

destroyed by Zionist forces in June 1948 after they had expelled all its inhabitants. Darwish's family fled to Beirut, but after a year managed to make it back across the border and find refuge in the village of Judayda. Darwish published his first poetry collection, *'Aṣāfīr bilā ajniḥā* [Birds without wings], when he was nineteen (1960). In 1961 he joined the Israeli Communist Party but in 1971 decided to leave Israel. Since then he has moved from one place to another (Cairo, Beirut, London, Paris, Tunis) and currently has homes in Ramallah and Amman. He edits the Palestinian cultural and literary journal *Al-Karmel*.

8 Darwish, *Ward aqall* 9. This translation is based on that of al-Udhari, *Maḥmūd Darwīsh* 23. For another English translation, see Darwish, *Unfortunately, It Was Paradise* 5. For a German translation of the collection *Ward aqall*, see Mahmud Darwisch, *Weniger Rosen*; for this poem in particular, see page 11.

9 On the motif of the road in *Ward aqall,* see also Mansson, *Passage* 155–157.

10 On al-Andalus in Arabic literature, see Uthman, *Idā'āt* 5–72; Noorani, "The Lost Garden of al-Andalus"; Reuven Snir, "'Al-Andalus Arising from Damascus.'"

11 For the argument that traces the beginnings of the Renaissance in Europe to al-Andalus, see Anwar G. Chejne, "The Role of al-Andalus in the Movement of Ideas between Islam and the West," in Semaan, *Islam* 110–133; Recapito, "Al-Andalus and the Origin of the Renaissance in Europe."

12 One of the first uses of al-Andalus as a mirror for Palestine appeared in 1910, when the Damascene *Al-Muqtabas*, edited by Muhammad Kurd 'Ali (1876–1953), wrote: "We fear that the new settler will expel the indigenous [population] and we will have to leave our country en masse. We shall then be looking back over our shoulder and mourn our land as did the Muslims of Andalusia" (*Al-Muqtabas*, 15 March 1910, as quoted in Yazbak, *Haifa* 221).

13 Darwish, *Aḥada 'ashara kawkaban* 29–31. The poem is structured like a classical *qaṣīda*, consisting of ten stanzas each in a kind of couplet: a pair of lines that are the same length and rhyme and form a complete thought. The first couplet imitates the *bukā' 'alā al-aṭlāl* [weeping over the ruins] of the beloved homeland and it is repeated in the fourth stanza and again in a different order in the lines in the tenth stanza. The meter of the poem is *mutadārak* (- U -) and the rhyme scheme is aa/bb/cc/aa/dd/ee/ff/ff/gg/aa. On the metrical system in Arabic poetry, see below.

14 On the story of Cain and Abel in ancient sources, see Busse, *Islam* 68–70. On this story as an archetypal conflict in classical and modern Arabic literature, see Sebastian Günther, "Hostile Brothers in Transformation: An Archetypal Conflict in Classical and Modern Arabic literature," in Angelika Neuwirth, et al., *Myths* 309–336.

15 Darwish, *Ward aqall* 77. For a German translation, see Darwisch, *Weniger Rosen* 79. On the story of Joseph (Yusuf) in the ancient sources, see Busse, *Islam* 88–92; Tottoli, *Biblical Prophets* 28–31. On this story as employed in modern Arabic literature, see Hartman, *Jesus, Joseph and Job*. For a study of the poem, see Husayn Hamza, "Anā Yūsufun Yā Abī."

16 The song was released on the album *Rakwat 'Arab* [Arabic coffeepot] (Nagam

Records, 1995). Khalifa divided the song into four stanzas with short musical intervals between them; the duration of the song is 6 minutes and 30 seconds and the division is as follows: Musical prologue (21 seconds); first stanza (1 minute and 8 seconds); musical interval (7 seconds); second stanza (1 minute and 9 seconds); musical interval (13 seconds); third stanza (2 minutes); musical interval (19 seconds); fourth stanza (1 minute and 32 seconds).

17 While some Muslim clerics maintain that all singing of the Qur'an is forbidden, others have had no qualms about making lyrical recordings of the Qur'an, and tapes of clerics singing Islam's holy book can be bought in many places. Also Qur'anic verses, whether in the original Arabic, or translated into Persian, have been routinely used in Iranian revolutionary songs since 1978. According to early Islamic tradition, listening to the recital of the Qur'an accompanied by music is considered a sin of disobedience against God (Kister, "Exert Yourselves" 61). On the issue of setting verses of the Qur'an to music, see Diya' al-Din Baybars, "Talhīn al-Qur'īn bayna Ahl al-Fann wa-Rijāl al-Dīn," *Al-Hilāl*, December 1970, 118–127.

18 Following the case, *Al-Jadid* (Los Angeles) published an issue dealing with the freedom of artists, intellectuals, and media in Lebanon (11 [September 1996]). Among the articles in this issue were Elie Chalala, "Arab Artists, Intellectuals, Condemn Charges Against Khalife as Attack on Liberty, Civil Freedom"; Marcel Khalifa, "We Turn the Page from City to City"; Paul Sha'ul, "Marcel Khalife and the Modern Inquisition"; Michelle A. Marzahn, "Lebanese Media Restrictions Stir Broad Opposition." On the case, see also *Al-Jadid* (Los Angeles) 28 (1999), 7–9, 16; 'Abd al-Rahman, "Al-Qur'ān."

19 Because of the meter, the poet used *imra'a* instead of *mra'a*.

20 For example, see C. D'Ohsson, *Histoire* vol. 1, 387 (quoted in Browne, *Literary History of Persia* vol. 2, 427); Nicholson, *Literary History* 129; I. Goldziher, *Short History* 141. Cf. Browne, *Literary History of Persia*, vol. 2, 463.

21 For example, see Ghanim, *Maḥasīn* 153; Hasan, *Tārīkh al-Islām* vol. 1V, 160; Majid, *Tārīkh al-ḥaḍāra* 291; al-Sayyad, *Mu'arrikh* 42; al-Alusi, *Baghdad* 136.

22 For example, see Zaydan, *Tārīkh* vol. 2I, 10; Husayn et al., *Al-Mujmal* 139–140; al-Iskandari and al-'Inani, *Al-Wasīṭ* 290; Nadim 'Adiyy, *Tārīkh* vol. 1, 360; al-Fakhuri, *Al-Jadīd* vol. 1V, 470; al-Ghazzawi, *Tārīkh al-adab* 300–301; al-Zayyat, *Tārīkh al-adab al-'Arabī* 400; al-Jundi, *Al-Ra'id* vol. 1, 544; al-Fiqqi, *Al-Adab* 8–9; Dayf, *'Aṣr al-duwal* 240–241.

23 For example, see al-Rusafi, *Dīwān* vol. 2, 192–202; 'Abd al-Mu'ti Hijazi, *Dīwān* 410, 430; al-Qasim, *Dīwān* 540; Darwish, *Al-Jiyad* 67–68; Habib, *Al-'Awda ilā al-āti* 35–41. Cf. Mahmoud Darwish, "Hudna ma'a al-Maghūl"; 'Izz al-Din, *Al-Riwāya fi al-'Irāq* 31–32.

24 Gibb, *Arabic Literature* 141. Cf. Lewis, *Islam* 179–198; Lewis, *The Middle East* 12; Wiet, *Introduction* 243; Smith, *Islam* 40.

25 Zurayk, *Meaning of the Disaster* 48. See also Gharayiba, *Al-'Arab* 185–186; Abu al-Khashab, *Tārīkh al-adab al-'Arabī* 141–154. Cf. Grunebaum, *Modern Islam* 255; Lewis, *Islam* 182.

26 On the linear and ironical modes of intertextuality, see Somekh, *Genre* 53, 61.

27 For example, see the figure of Hulagu in "al-Kutub" [The books] by Mishil

Haddad (1919–1997), first published in *Al-Sharq* (Shfram) (January–April 1985), 3. The poem was incorporated in Haddad's collection *Fī al-nāḥīya al-ukhra* 9.
28 Elias Sanbar, www.autodafe.org/correspondence/chroniques/elias2.htm, June 2002. It should be noted that only Cafavy's poem is called "Waiting for the Barbarians" and that neither this nor Darwish's poem illustrate Sanbar's point—it seems that Coetzee's novel is much more suitable as an illustration of the message he wished to convey.
29 See the interview with A. Shavit in www.haaretzdaily.com, 9 January 2004. In response to the interview, the Palestinian scholar Salim Tamari refers to the "barbarians" as including also the Mizrahi people inside Israel (www.haaretzdaily.com, 16 January 2004). On how the Israeli establishment created the "barbarians" in the image of the oriental Jews, see Nissim Rejwan, *Outsider* 111–136.
30 The daughter of Leda and Zeus, Helen was reputed to be the most beautiful woman in the world. When she reached marriageable age, she was wooed by the most illustrious men of Greece. She married Menelaus and lived happily with him for a number of years and bore him a daughter, Hermione. After a decade or so of married life, Helen was abducted by—or ran off with—Paris, the son of King Priam of Troy. As a result, the Greek leaders mobilized the greatest army of its time, placed it under the command of Agamemnon, and set off to wage what became known as the Trojan War. After the fall of Troy, Menelaus took Helen back to Lacedaemon, where they lived an apparently happy married life once more. At the end of their mortal existence, they were reunited in Elysium.
31 Cf. the poem "Maṭār Athīnā" [Athens Airport], where *zawāj sarī'* means, though ironically, sexual intercourse, but full of compassion toward two young refugees (*Ward* 23; Darwish, *Unfortunately* 12).
32 *Al-Karmel* 18 (1985), 4–9. The article was later incorporated into Darwish's *Fī waṣfi ḥālatinā* 169–175.
33 Darwish, *Dīwān Maḥmūd Darwīsh* 73–76. For other translations of the poem, see Darwish, *Music* 10–12; Asfour, *When the Words Burn* 199–200. For a French translation, see La'abi, *La poésie* 33–35. The influence of the poem has sometimes traversed the national field and spread into the religious sphere, as we find, for example, in "Sajjil! anā Islāmī" [Write it down! I am an Islamist] by the Moroccan poet Muhammad Bin'Amara, (b. 1945) in *Min al-shi'r al-Islāmī al-Ḥadīth* 311–318.
34 Already in 1969 Darwish had published an article entitled "Anqidhūnā min hādhā al-ḥubb al-qāṣī" [Save us from this cruel love!], in which he voiced strong dissatisfaction with the injustice Arab critics were doing to Palestinian literature by avoiding objective criticism in their readiness to accept unconditionally anything that was Palestinian—poetry of slogans included—as a positive contribution to the spirit of the nation. Asking the Arabs not to allow affection for the Palestinian cause to be a decisive criterion when assessing literary works, he points out that Palestinian poetry should not be looked upon as if it had suddenly come from nowhere—"it is only a stream originating from and pouring into the big river of Arabic literature."
35 The legendary dwelling place of the demons, according to Arab tradition,

which maintains, like the Greek theory of the muses, that poetry has its source in divine forces.

36 On the impossibility or difficulties of expressing the mystical experience through human language, see al-Ghazzali, *Al-Munqidh* 96; Scholem, *Major Trends* 4–5; Eliade, *Sacred* 10; Knox, *Enthusiasm* 249; Scharfstein, *Ineffability*. On the psychological aspects of ineffability, see Tart, *Altered* 16: "Most often, because of the uniqueness of the subjective experience associated with certain ASC [Altered States of Consciousness—R.S.] (e.g. transcendental, aesthetic, creative, psychotic, and mystical states), persons claim a certain ineptness or inability to communicate the nature or essence of the experience to someone who has not undergone a similar experience." See also ibid. 23, 40–42, 405–406.

37 First published in *Al-Karmel* 38 (1990), 33–43; incorporated in his collection *Arā mā urīd* 79–99. For an English translation, see Darwish, *Unfortunately* 31–51. For a Hebrew translation with clarifying notes, see Snir, "Mahmoud Darwish—Birds without Wings."

CHAPTER 7: NEUWIRTH

1 Agnes Imhof in *Relgiöser Wandel* shows how some *mukhadram* poets had to take their fates into their own hands and change sides when they were held responsible by the new community for the official stance held by their tribal groups.

2 In an interview, Darwish has affirmed the impact this international group of communist poets (Lorca and Neruda wrote in Spanish, Aragon in French, Hikmet in Turkish) has had on his early poetry (see *Palästina*, 33).

3 An early testimony of a comparable elevation of a young man to the rank of a cosmic figure is found in one of Darwish's earliest poems celebrating a resistance fighter: "Wa 'āda fī kafan" [He returned wrapped in a shroud] from *Awrāq al-zaytūn* [Olive leaves] (1964), in *Dīwān* vol. 1, 18–23. See Neuwirth, "Das Lied."

Likewise, the Palestinian novelist Jabra Ibrahim Jabra has repeatedly portrayed himself as a liminal figure; for his self-stylization as Tammuz in the first part of his autobiography, *Al-Bi'r al-ūlā* [The first well], see Neuwirth, "Jabra Ibrahim Jabra's Autobiography" 115–127. The second part of his autobiography, *Shari' al-amirāt* [Princesses Street], contains a particularly striking self-portrayal as Jesus (with whom he shared his place of birth, Bethlehem); see chapter "Sayyidat al-buḥayrāt" [Lady of the lakes] in Jabra, *Shari' al-amirāt* 53–66.

4 Mahmoud Darwish employs the genre of "Psalms" [*mazmūr*, pl. *mazāmīr*], otherwise unfamiliar in secular literature; he refers repeatedly to biblical stories, sometimes equally known from the Qur'an, such as that of Yusuf/Joseph.

5 Paul Celan, who was born in the Bokovina and survived the Nazi terror, is one of the outstanding modern poets in the German language. He emigrated to Paris in 1948, where in 1970 he committed suicide in the Seine.

6 Darwish, *Hiya ughniya, Hiya ughniya* (1984); *Ward aqall* (1986); *Arā mā urīd* (1990); *Aḥada 'ashara kawkaban* (1992); *Limādhā tarakta al-ḥiṣāna waḥīdan?* (1995).

7 Valk, "Der Dichter als Erlöser" 71–81; 71: "Da der Poesie eine weltverwandelnde

und zeitaufhebende Dimension zugeschrieben wird, rückt die Reflektion über ihr Wesen häufig in einen eschatologischen Horizont. Der Dichter trägt (im Werk des Novalis) die Züge des antiken Dichters Orpheus. Wie dieser tritt er als mächtiger Magier auf, der die Gesetze von Raum und Zeit außer Kraft setzt, entlegenste Wirklichkeitsbereiche mit einander verbindet und alle Geschöpfe in einen umfassenden Dialog eintreten läßt."

8 Ibid., 73: "Der Dichter nimmt eine besondere Vorrangstellung ein, da er einen geradezu mystischen Zugang zum Goldenen Zeitalter besitzt. Für ihn ist die Einheit der idealen Ursprungssphäre auch in den disparaten Erscheinungen der gegenwärtigen Welt erfahrbar."

9 Emile Habiby (d. 1996), a novelist and publicist. Habiby's chief work, the novel *Al-Waqā'i' al-gharība fī ikhtifā' Sa'id abī l-naḥs al-mutashā'il* (1974) [*The Secret Life of Saeed: The Pessoptimist*] discusses the collective memory of both the Jews and Arabs in Israel, paying particular attention to the issue of naming and inscribing places and landscapes; see Neuwirth, "Israelisch-Palästinensische Paradoxien." His criticism of the political myths cherished on both sides has been acknowledged by Silberstein in *Postzionism Debates: Knowledge and Power in Israeli Culture*, who draws a close connection between Habiby's thinking and that of the later Israeli New Historians.

10 Darwish, *'Āshiq min Filasṭīn* (1966), in *Dīwān* vol. 1, 77–83. For a detailed discussion of the intertextuality, see Neuwirth, "Mahmud Darwish's Re-staging" 153–171.

11 The poem is highly autobiographical, since it opens a poetical dialogue in response to a famous earlier poem by the Iraqi poet Badr Shakir al-Sayyab, modifying particular poetic views of the earlier poet; see Neuwirth, "Mahmud Darwish's Re-staging."

12 The pre-Islamic poet 'Antara, b. Shaddad, celebrated in a medieval romance, *Sirat 'Antara*, which was particularly well-known in pre-modern rural Palestine; see Embalo, et al. *Kulturelle*, subject index, s.v. Roman, 548.

13 See e.g., Darwish "'Ā'id ilā Yāfā" [Returning to Yafa] from *Uḥibbuki aw lā uḥibbuki* [I love you or I do not love you] (1972), in *Dīwān* vol. 1, 401–405.

14 See the novel by the Syrian author Adib Nadwi, *'Urs al-shahīd* [The wedding of the martyr].

15 These rites emerged in the 1970s. They are reflected in several prose works, such as Habiby's *Al-Mutashā'il* and Sahar Khalifeh's *Bāb al-sāḥa*. The implicit mythicization was questioned with the beginning of the second intifada; see section four of this essay. Yet the militant groups have maintained the concept of martyrdom as applying to those killed in the armed struggle.

16 From the poem "Nusāfiru kal-nās" in *Ward aqall*; translation in *Unfortunately, It Was Paradise* 11, slightly modified.

17 Darwish has asserted the deep impression that the Song of Songs has had on him; see *Palästina* 34.

18 "In dieser Sprache habe ich in jenen Jahren und in den Jahren nachher Gedichte zu schreiben versucht: um zu sprechen, um mich zu orientieren, um zu erkunden, wo ich mich befand und wohin es mit mir wollte, um mir Wirklichkeit zu entwerfen," from Celan's speech on the occasion of his receiving the Bremer

Literaturpreis 1958, quoted in Milich 92.

19 See the poems "'Indamā yadhhabu l-shuhadā' ilā al-nawm" [When the martyrs go to sleep] and "'Alā al-ssafḥial-a'lā min al-baḥr nāmū" [On the slope, higher than the sea, they slept], both from *Ward aqall*; English translations in *Unfortunately, It was Paradise* 16, 22.

CHAPTER 8: NASSAR

The author would like to recognize the insights of Jolisa Gracewood and Ellen Lust-Okar and thank them for their comments and feedback on the article.

1 I am borrowing the term "ambivalent attitude" from Yair Huri, which he introduces in his article "Seeking Glory in the Dunghills: Representations of the City in the Writings of Modern Arab Poets." *Archiv Orientální* 73 (2005): 185-202.

2 Bassam Frangieh contends that a negative image of the city is also seen as a characteristic of all modern Arabic art: "without exception, the Arab artist's position towards the city was one of hatred and rejection" ("Modern Arabic Poetry" 238).

3 *Modern Arabic Poetry* 35. Jayyusi says of Jaffa's orange groves: " I suspect [the frequency and power of the image] may be due, among other reasons, to the fact that the orange, one of Palestine's most inspiring flora symbols, is connected to Jaffa, where so many Arab orange groves flourished in Palestine prior to 1948."

4 Mansson's study of the Palestinian city in Darwish's poetry argues that the mythological cities of Jerusalem and Jericho "are not mentioned with any particular affection" (*Passage* 166). She also presents a detailed study of the mythological Babylon and Jerusalem from a variety of perspectives.

5 Jamal Ahmad al-Rifai has noted that the Jewish exile and the imprisonment in Babylon have become a metaphor for the Palestinian exile. He declares that "the poet Mahmoud Darwish designates the Palestinian exile in the 20th century with the expression Babylon to suggest that the trial of the Palestinian exile doesn't differ much from the Jewish trial of dispersion. In reading these verses we find the poet uses the word 'fetters' [*salāsil*] not to express a word rhyming with 'Babylon' [*Bābil*] but to suggest that staying in Babylon, synonym [for] exile, will make the fettered Palestinians [the equivalent of] prisoners of Chaldeans, uncapable [*sic*] of outlining their destiny and future" (qtd. in Mansson, *Passage* 169).

6 Mansson argues that in Darwish's early collections of poetry one finds a frequent use of words reflecting exile and dispersion (*Passage* 55–67).

7 Mansson finds interesting parallels between migrant/immigrant Jews and Palestinians (*Passage* 50).

8 A quick glimpse at Darwish's prose works reveals a trend of writing about previous experiences of exile: in his early quasi-autobiographical prose *Yawmīyāt al-ḥuzn al-'ādī* [Diary of ordinary sadness] (1973), Darwish wrote about Haifa, and when he lived in Paris after 1982 he wrote about Beirut in *Memory for Forgetfulness* (1986). For more information on Darwish's prose work, see Stuart Reigeluth's essay in this collection.

The poem "Beirut" was originally published in the collection *Ḥiṣār li madā'iḥ al-baḥr*, and can be found in *Dīwān* vol. 2, 194–223. The English translation of Darwish's poem, by Lena Jayyusi and Chirstopher Middleton, is taken from Jayyusi, *Modern Arabic Poetry* 204–207.

9 Elbendary argues that *Lā ta'tadhir 'ammā fa'alta* "is in many ways also a return for Darwish to poetry as poetry. Not that he has ever left poetry properly so-called, but he has so often been labeled a 'poet of resistance' that some have tended to lose sight of the fact that the essence of Darwish's poetry is always poetry, even when resistance is its subject-matter" ("Like Him").

10 Elbendary argues that a "characteristic motif in Darwish's work is that of doubles, negatives, reflections and shadows, the idea of an object being both itself and its opposite at the same time" ("Like Him").

11 To further investigate these ideas, please see the work of Najat Rahman.

12 Since Darwish left Israel in 1970, he was only allowed to come back to the West Bank in 1994 under the Oslo peace accords. If Darwish wants to visit his family in Galilee, he still needs to have a military permit from the Israeli authorities.

13 Darwish moved to Paris after the PLO was evacuated from Beirut in 1982, instead of joining his countrymen in Tunisia; he says that relocating to Paris was a pure coincidence and completely unplanned move (Bitton and Sanbar, *Et la terre*).

14 *Ka-zahr* 149, an allusion to the Oslo Accords, signed between the PLO and Israel in 1994. Specifically, at a ceremony in Cairo on May 4, 1994, Israel and the PLO signed the Gaza-Jericho Agreement, sometimes called the Cairo Agreement. Israel withdrew from all of Jericho and most of Gaza on May 18, 1994, and instead Palestinian police were deployed there. Darwish here refers to this agreement and says that it is full of empty "promises," and that if Gaza is still surrounded with Israeli settlements then "do not give me" the same empty promises of peace—the rose, also from Jericho.

15 Ibid. 179. The English translation is taken from *Al-Ahram Weekly* online 774, 22–28 Dec. 2005.

CHAPTER 9: ANTOON

1 Although an impressively voracious reader, Darwish seems to have been unaware of how the line traveled from Abu Tammam to Lorca and that this was no mere coincidence. This is evidenced by the question with which he prefaces the proem: "a coincidence of thoughts or of destinies." For more on the journey of the line, see Vazquez's "Poetic Pilgrimages." Lorca has appeared in Darwish's poetry before. See, for example, "Lī khalfa al-samā'i samā" [I have a sky beyond the sky], where he writes: "Some speech about love will descend in Lorca's poetry/ which will live in my bedroom and see the bedouin moon I have seen. . ." (see Darwish, *Aḥada* 11–12).

2 One example is that of Abu Nuwas (755–813) who adopted an anti-*aṭlāl* stance in favor of gaiety and bacchism and pioneered the *khamrīya* [winesong].

3 For the complete text of the poem in Spanish and English, see the appendix in Vazquez, "Poetic Possibilities" 134–135.

4 For more on *raḥīl*, see Stetkevych, *Zephyrs* 28.

5 In his late works Darwish has been more particular about the architecture of his collections in terms of a unifying theme and narrative that structures the individual poems. This present collection is no exception, exhibiting even more of this heightened sensitivity to internal divisions and thematic harmony. It is no coincidence that the table of contents, usually at the end of Darwish's collections, is placed at the beginning as if to serve as a map for the reading. The six sections are as follows: I. In the lust of the rhythm, II. The road to the coast, III. Not as a foreign tourist would, IV. A house of poetry/The southerner's house, V. Like an obscure event, VI. The Kurd has nothing but the wind. This trend can be seen as early as *Limādhā tarakta al-ḥiṣāna waḥīdan* [*Why Have You Left the Horse Alone?*] (1995).
6 Poem number 27 in this same section portrays this anxiety in a beautiful dialogue between the poet and his other. The latter addresses the poet, saying: "You will be forgotten, as if you never were... You will be forgotten, as if you never were a person, or a text." In the poet's answer, he acknowledges: "What I say has already been said/ A passing tomorrow precedes me/ I am the king of the echo/ My only throne is the margins.../ perhaps the ancients left something undescribed/ I will stir a memory and a sensation in it" (71–73).
7 Emile Habiby (1921–1996), the great Palestinian novelist, playwright, and politician, chose to have the following inscribed on his tombstone: "Emile Habiby: stayed in Haifa."
8 See the section on "Roads" below.
9 The famous pre-modern Arab poet (915–965 CE), who was a restless soul and was killed on his way back to Iraq.
10 There is a play on the word *bayt* here. In poetic terminology "bayt" signifies "verse."
11 Salim Barakat (1951–) is one of the most innovative poets and novelists writing in Arabic. His works chronicle the plight of the Kurds and the traumatic events that have structured their history. There is a personal relationship to Darwish here as well, as Barakat was the managing editor of the prestigious Palestinian journal *Al-Karmel*, whose editor was, and still is, Darwish.
12 In Simone Bitton's documentary about Darwish, he makes the point that the poetic line or verse [*bayt*] for him is a home. The terminology for prosody and the various parts of the verse in Arabic were modeled after the tent and its parts.
13 The plight of the Kurds in terms of genocide, displacement, and the cultural and linguistic erasure to which they were, and still are, subjected to by nation-states that deny their existence has many obvious parallels to that of the Palestinians. This, of course, is important to the mood of this poem.
14 See Anton Shammas's article "Autocartography: The Case of Palestine." I would like to thank Samera Esmeir for bringing it to my attention.

CHAPTER 10: SACKS

1 I wish to thank Avital Ronell, Ammiel Alcalay, Hamid Dabashi, Noha Radwan, and Muhsin al-Musawi for the generous comments which they have offered regarding earlier versions of parts of this essay. I wish to thank Najat Rahman for inviting me to contribute to this volume and for her insight, and Hilary Plum for her helpful editorial suggestions.

2 The discussion of decision which I offer here draws upon Jacques Derrida's extensive reflections upon the relations among decision and responsibility. One may consider in this regard Derrida's discussion of the Nietzschean *perhaps* in *Politics of Friendship*: "The crucial experience [*épreuve* —J.S.] of the *perhaps* imposed by the undecidable—that is to say, the condition of decision—is not a moment to be exceeded, forgotten, or suppressed. It continues to constitute the decision as such; it can never again be separated from it; it produces it *qua* decision *in and through* the undecidable; there is no other decision than this one: decision in the matter and form of the undecidable" (*Politics* 219/*Politiques* 247; emphasis in original). For a compelling discussion of the undecidable dimensions of the test—*épreuve*—which bears upon the relations among testing and the ethical valances of reading and decision one may consider Avital Ronell, *The Test Drive*.

3 Criticism of Darwish's work has, from the beginning, perhaps with Ghassan Kanafani's *Adab al-muqāwama fī Filasṭīn al-muḥtalla* [The literature of resistance in occupied Palestine] and Raja' al-Naqqash's *Maḥmūd Darwīsh: shā'ir al-arḍ al-muḥtalla* [Mahmoud Darwish: the poet of the occupied land] minimized the question of language that his work seems to require that one ask. I trace some of the lingering impact of this work, and its relation to language, here.

4 On the *Nahḍa*, see Albert Hourani's *Arabic Thought in the Liberal Age*.

5 I wish to distinguish the reading that I offer here from that presented by Muhammad 'Abid al-Jabiri in *Naqd al-'aql al-'Arabī* 114: "'The stable' for him [Adonis] is 'the ancient,' and 'the changing' is 'the new.' This correlation is imprecise, not to mention the insufficiently founded conclusions and interpretations that are derived from it." See also, in a slightly different idiom, Nasr Hamid Abu Zeid, "The Stable and the Changing in Adonis' View of the Heritage" 251: "In his view of the present, he [Adonis] has united the dominant culture with the inheritance. From this point, he considers creativity to be complete revolt against everything inherited." Abu Zeid formulates the point as follows, objecting that Adonis' "binary vision of the current cultural reality, his uniting, entirely, between the dominant culture and the past, his inability to realize the dialectical relation between the two cultures, and between the past and the present, makes him—at the practical level—flee from the past, in the way that he flees from the dominant culture" (232). Yet in offering this objection—one in which he argues that Adonis mis-articulates the relation with which he is working—Abu Zeid confirms the separation between "the stable" and "the changing" that he is at pains to demand that Adonis clarify. What remains noteworthy in Abu Zeid's essay, in the context that I underscore here, is the extent to which it insists on the word relation, *'alāqa*, and demands that it be offered as a "dialectical" one (228, 229, 232, 233, 237, 239, 244, 250). If what is marked in this reading of Adonis is a certain anxiety about relation, and a certain demand that Adonis mark his relations, and in particular his relation to the past, and the relation of his reading of the past to the present—Adonis' work is grounded in a "dissociation from any prior given" (244) and "despite its apparent dynamism," it "still works with the heritage as if it were an entity in the past" (232), we read—I wish to underline that the rhetorical scene that Abu Zeid sets up and from which

he offers his argument does precisely what it accuses *Al-Thābit wa al-mutaḥawwil* of having done. The reading that is offered of Adonis, therefore, sets a protocol for the reading of "The Stable and the Changing in Adonis' View of the Heritage." Indeed, the essay opens offering a scene of difficulty and the swirling and uncontrollable approach of danger: "The study of the heritage is a task surrounded by many difficulties, the most dangerous of which is a lack of consciousness that our position in the present towards our reality determines our vision of this heritage, and colors our judgment of it" (227). The scope of the danger is intensified, insofar as it occurs in the wake of an act of violence. "Since Taha Husayn threw the bomb *On Jahili Poetry* into the horizon of our cultural life, the consciousness of the Arab intellectual has not stopped reflecting on the identity of the heritage and his relation to it" (227). Returning to "the present"—a moment that is offered in Abu Zeid's essay as that which will have come after Taha Husayn and his book *On Jahili Poetry*—Abu Zeid writes of "intellectuals" who work with "the traditional delusion that divides the present position of the intellectual from his vision of the heritage" (227) and who set to work "as if the past were something neutral, independent of our present consciousness of our current position" (227–228), and he then proceeds to take evasive action in order to get the danger and delusion about which he is anxious under control. Two gestures take place. First, he divides "existence" into "ontological" and "epistemological" sectors, shoring up a separation between "the past" and "the present" that he derides others for seeming to maintain. "The past has its independent existence, without doubt, in the sense that it has an historical existence in the past (existence in the ontological sense), yet in the epistemological sense, the past is something continual, that forms the present, just as our present consciousness repeats its re-formation" (228). Instituting a separation barrier, "the researcher" then gains "consciousness" of "the dialectical nature of his relation with the heritage" and is able to "do away with the delusion of an objective view" (228). "This consciousness makes it possible for the researcher to get control over his position" (228). With everything under control, the past—danger and delusion—is left behind. And the essay begins again, disavowing its relation to what has come before and placing it in the past—just as he wanted those whom he is attacking not to have done. "Setting out from the consciousness of this dialectical relation between the past and the present, between the researcher and his object" (228), Abu Zeid turns to read Adonis. Having secured "the dialectical relation between the past and the present" he sets out in his work having disavowed his relation to the past—to a violence, to a wounding, and to Taha Husayn—to which this work remains bound.

6 The relations among the refusal to mourn and Arabic literary studies remain to be examined in detail. For work that suggestively begins to explore these relations, see the important intervention of Sayyed al-Bahrawi, *Al-Baḥth 'an al-manhaj*: "Behind the studies that constitute this book," al-Bahrawi explains, "are practical and scientific motives that gather around the passing of a century since the birth of Taha Husayn and his generation of 'enlighteners'"(7). Al-Bahrawi's work here, he further comments, does not intend to "level an accusation at anyone," but rather, was carried out "in order to know our wounds, and, perhaps,

in order to be able to scrape off their scabs, so that the putrid blood, the continued existence of which threatens us with death, will flow from them"(13). For a politico-historical account of the literary and poetic climate of the late nineteenth and early twentieth centuries that underlines a context of loss, and therefore of mourning, to which this climate is related, see the opening pages of Elias Khoury, *Dirāsāt*:

> On a literary and poetic level, everything, since the coming of the imperialist West as a conqueror, was shaken.... At the level of culture and thought the response led to frameworks that resembled madness. The tragic attempt to repel what al-Afghani's thought expressed was a mixture of speechlessness and an attempt to build in a context of collapse. At the literary level, this was the first time that a model came, like a stroke of lightning, from the outside. Arabic literature had not been exposed, in its history, to a shock as violent as this. It is not possible to compare this new condition to the period of the growth of Persian and Indian translations, or to the shattering of poetic meter and the appearance of the modern with Abu Tammam and Abu Nuwwas. What took place, on the literary level, was that the classical model lost, in a single moment, all of its exemplarity and all of its magic. For with the accumulation of translations, the new city, and the national miscarriage, the literary movement faced itself, for the first time, bare before the new model and its challenges (11–12).

7 Since the object is the True and universal, the self-identical, while consciousness is alterable and unessential, it can happen that consciousness apprehends the object incorrectly and deceives itself. The percipient is aware of the possibility of deception; for in the universality which is the principle, *otherness* itself is immediately present for him, though present as what is *null* and superseded [*aber als das Nichtige, Aufgehobene*]. His criterion of truth is therefore self-identity, and his behavior consists in apprehending the object as self-identical. Since at the same time diversity is explicitly there for him, it is a connection of the diverse moments of his apprehension to one another; but if a dissimilarity makes itself felt in this course of this comparison, then this is not an untruth in the object—for this is the self-identical—but an untruth in perceiving it (Hegel *Phenomenology* 70; translator's emphasis/*Phänomenologie* 82–83).

8 The reflections offered by Emmanuel Lévinas on the relations among the responsibility and the accusative inform the argument which I present here. "The subjectivity of the subject, as being subject to everything, is a pre-originary susceptibility, before all freedom and outside of every present. It is accused in uneasiness or the unconditionality of the accusative, in the 'here I am' which is obedience to the glory of the Infinite that orders me to the other" (*Otherwise* 146; *Autrement* 228). One may further consider the following passage in which Levinas considers the relations among responsibility and the one who calls out: "Here I am."

> Responsibility for the other, going against intentionality and the will, which intentionality does not succeed in dissimulating, signifies not the disclosure of a given and its reception, but the exposure of me to the

> other, prior to every decision. There is a claim laid on the same by the other in the core of myself, the extreme tension of the command exercised by the other in me and over me, a traumatic hold of the other on the same, which does not give the same time to await the other.... There is an assignation to an identity for the response of responsibility, where one cannot have oneself replaced without fault. To this command continually put forth only a 'here I am' can answer, where the pronoun 'I' is in the accusative, declined before any declension.... (*Otherwise* 141–142; *Autrement* 221–222).

CHAPTER 11: CELIK

1 I have to acknowledge that due to my limited knowledge of Arabic, my criticism of Mahmoud Darwish's oeuvre mainly depends on reading his works through translation, from Arabic to English or to French. So unfortunately this essay lacks a sense of what it is like to read the poems discussed in their original language. I would like to thank Vangelis Calotychos, Elias Khoury, Angelika Neuwirth, and Najat Rahman for their invaluable assistance with the problems that appeared due to my linguistic limitations, and for their precious comments at various stages of this essay.

2 The whole quote is: "In *Eleven Planets* I put our case in the context of history. You might be surprised to know that I consider *Why Have You Left the Horse Alone?* to be one of the most sublime kinds of aesthetic resistance. In this collection I had to defend a forgotten history; or to put it more clearly, I had to defend the land of the past and the past of the land, the land of language and the language of the land… I feel that the past is subject to plunder, and have always said that it should be the arbiter of the conflict. The past is more ambiguous than the future" (Darwish in Mosbahi, "Interview" 8).

3 Of "Identity Card," Edward Said claimed, "If there is anything written by a Palestinian that can be called a national poem, it would have to be Mahmoud Darwish's short work *Biṭāqat hawīya*" (*Question* 155).

4 Sinan Antoon's article "Mahmud Darwish's Allegorical Critique of Oslo" examines the poet's reaction to the Oslo accords in detail through a reading of Darwish's poem "A Non-Linguistic Dispute with Imru'al-Qays" which Antoon himself translated into English in *The Adam of Two Edens*.

5 "It is galling that we should be ready during these air raids to steal time for all this chatter, defending the role of a poet… at a moment in which everything has stopped talking, a moment of shared creativity when the people's epic is shaping its own history. Beirut itself is the writing, rousing and creative. Its true poets and singers are its people and fighters… They are the genuine founders of a writing that for a long, long time will have to search for a linguistic equivalent to their heroism and their amazing lives" (*Memory* 64).

6 Some clarification of the broad and ambiguous term "myth" has to be made for a further understanding of what is meant by Darwish's allusion to or re-writing of myth or certain mythological characters and concepts. Literary scholar Gregory Lucente explains the term as follows: "Traditionally, 'myth' has been the term par excellence for falsehood, whether intentional or innocent, strategically invoked or

blindly accepted, but, at the same time, the word has retained a connotation of higher truth. In this sense, it has been used to combine the functions of *gnoscere* and the privileged vision of *narrare*" (*Narrative* 26). This definition suggests the elevating and legitimating power politics of myth entrenched in knowledge and narration. Myth's liminal standing between fact and fiction creates the illusion that it is detached from social history. "The creation of myth in support of political and social ideology is a recurrent phenomenon and is one reason why subsequent interpretations of mythic discourse always carry the potential both for demystification of prior norms and legitimation of current, authentically 'knowledgeable' ideologies" (27–28).

7 The term "postcolonial author" is used here to refer to those who pose a theoretical critique of and resistance against imperialist and neo-imperialist narrative strategies of domination and appropriation rather than any temporal connotation that might mean they (and we) are past colonialism.

8 During a conversation with Najat Rahman, she mentioned that in a private interview with Darwish, the poet related that his admiration for Walcott's *Omeros* was so intense that he was not able to write for a year after reading the work. Also in *La Palestine comme métaphore* he admits, "Walcott et Heaney sont les deux derniers poètes que j'ai lus de façon approfondie, et je ne cache pas mon parti pris pour Walcott" (69)/ "Walcott and Heaney are the two last poets that I read in depth, and I don't hide my preference for Walcott" [my translation].

9 Israeli historian Yehoshua Ben-Arieh estimates that about 5,000 books and articles were written between 1800 and 1878 about the area (Parmenter, *Giving* 8).

10 A missionary's comment on the land written in mid-nineteenth century explains his frustration with the incongruity of what he was experiencing and Josephus' exuberant description of Galilee: "The soil may be as good as ever, the climate the same, but where are the walnuts, the figs, the olives, the grapes and other fruits?... Alas! all gone... and there are no inhabitants... to cultivate this 'ambition of Nature'" (Parmenter, *Giving* 11).

11 A canonical Israeli text, A.B. Yehoshua's short story *Facing the Forests* is a striking example of this "absentification" with its mute Arab peasant character.

12 In 1950 Yemenite Jews settled in what used to be al-Birwa, Darwish's village, and started the Kibbutz Moshaff. I am indebted to Elias Khoury for informing me on this point, because it is crucially connected to the identity of the two characters that the poet is speaking to/about in the poem. "As He Walks Away" raises the possibility of conversation or interaction with the guest/stranger/other/neighbor who is currently living in the poet's home, al-Birwa. This is a Yemenite Jew who has "a daughter with thick eyebrows, brown eyes and long hair/ braided over her shoulders/ like a night of songs" (*Adam of Two Edens* 51). The poet sends greetings to the house, the landscape—which includes the fig tree (a Palestinian symbol) as well as the pine tree (an Israeli symbol)—and the Yemenite Jew's daughter who "has an absent friend/ who wishes to visit her, to enter her mirror/ and see his secret" (53).

13 In the early 1950s, poets such as Badr Shakir al-Sayyab, Ali Ahmad Said, Tawfiq Sayigh, Buland al-Haydari, and Jabra I. Jabra turned to mythological and religious resources (such as Greek, Babylonian, Phoenician, Egyptian, Christian,

and Islamic). Although the Tammuzi movement initiated by these poets started out primarily as an attempt to thematically and formally emancipate Arabic poetry from the confines of traditional conventions, and the Tammuzi poets' use of mythic imagery was considered to be dense and remote from everyday language, they did not neglect the political realm. However, in a comparison of Darwish's use of myth to that of the Tammuzi poets', Munir Akash concludes that the latter "erect a wall between themselves and their readers by forcing them to refer to a dictionary of world mythology to make heads or tails of them. Darwish, on the other hand, instead of employing myth as a merely presumptuous intellectual texture, uses the dimension of myth as field to indicate life's unlimited possibilities" (Akash, "Introduction" 33).

14 Angelika Neuwirth explores how Badr Shakir al-Sayyab, in a manner reminiscent of Eliot, addresses the fertility myth to personify Iraq in "Hymn of the Rain" ["Unshudat al-matar"]. She accepts the poem's influence on Darwish's personification of Palestine in "A Lover from Palestine" [*'Āshiq min Filasṭīn*], but concludes that the latter managed to extend the use of myth from inactive suffering to a struggle for freedom.

15 Darwish alludes to his own previous works, especially on the meta level, in order to reconsider his definition of poetry. This gives his poems the sense of being a draft of a draft, never perfect but in continual evolution. Darwish refers to his famous poem "Identity Card" in *Memory for Forgetfulness* with an implication of his desire to change this poem's reception as an identity card for his poetry: 'Put this in your record'—I recognize this voice, whose age was twenty-five. Oh, what a living time! Oh, what a dead time! 'Put this in your record: I'm Arab!' I said that to a government employee whose son might now be piloting one of these jets. I said it in Hebrew to provoke him. But when I put it in a poem, the Arab public in Nazareth was electrified by a secret current that released the genie from the bottle. I didn't understand the secret of this discovery, as if with the gunpowder of identity I had stripped the minefield of its thunderbolt. This outcry then became my poetic identity, which has not been satisfied with pointing to my father but chases me even now" (174).

CHAPTER 12: REIGELUTH

1 All quotations for Darwish's prose are taken from *Memory for Forgetfulness: August, Beirut, 1982*, trans. Ibrahim Muhawi; the corresponding page numbers in parentheses are taken from the original Arabic text, which appeared in *Al-Karmel* 21/22 (1986) under the title *Al-Zamān: Bayrūt, al-makān: Āb* [The time: Beirut, The place: August].

2 The term *flâneur* was first used by the French poet Stéphane Mallarmé. Based on Walter Benjamin's analysis of the nineteenth-century *flâneur* in Paris, the term is used here to denote the idle movement through the streets of a city. Similar to those of the Parisian idlers, the Palestinian "footsteps" instigate memories, as perceived by Benjamin in *Das Passagen-Werk* and in *Beroliniana* 242–248. However, contrary to the Parisian idlers, the modern Palestinian *flâneurs* barely recognize their respective cities: Beirut is so severely damaged by war and Ramallah is distorted through the passage of time.

3 *The Waste Land* by T. S. Eliot had a significant influence on Arab poetry. Many studies have been written on this subject; see, for example, Daghir, *Al-Shi'rīya al-'Arabīya* 136.
4 Benjamin, "A Berlin Chronicle" 6: Throughout this autobiographical essay, Benjamin refers to the domineering presence of his nursemaid in his childhood, the souvenirs associated with the different streets of Berlin, the narration and literary style of memories bumping into each other and flowing together somewhere, where it does not matter. Everything "smells" of Proust: Benjamin's intellectual affinity to Proust exemplifies the influence of ideas and the mimicry or imitation of literary style.
5 Edward Said, *The Politics of Dispossession* 118. The title of Said's account of Lebanon *After the Last Sky; Palestinian Lives* (New York: Pantheon, 1986; reprinted Columbia University Press, 1998) is borrowed from a poem by Darwish called "Taḍīqu bi-nā al-Arḍ" [The earth is closing on us].
6 Boym, *Future* xv. For the recent political controversy in Israel over whether or not to include Darwish's poetry in education, see Darwish, *Palestine, mon pays* and Darwish, *La Palestine comme métaphore*.
7 Jewish interest in the Masada story was reignited only with the rise of Zionism in the early twentieth century. The "massacre" was most effectively popularized by the publication in Palestine of a heroic poem called "Masada" by a Ukrainian Jewish immigrant Yitzhak Lamdan in 1927. Famous lines read: "O God, save Masada…" and "Masada shall not fall again." Masada became a key symbol of Jewish resistance and resilience of immense popular appeal: "It was transformed into a state-sponsored cult of the heroic resistance fighters. The enthusiastic reception led in its turn to moving these two-thousand-year-old events into the very core of Jewish Israel's national and social consciousness."(Halbwachs 33) The distorted document was reinforced when music was adapted to the "Masada" poem, requiring a full orchestra. The 40-day Nazi siege of the Warsaw ghetto in 1942 was compared to Masada. The poster of Masada is no longer present at the King Hussein-Allenby Bridge border crossing. The Masada archaeological excavation (1963–1965) was carried out and recorded by Yigael Yadin in *Masada: Herod's Fortress and the Zealots Last Stand* (1966). The massive archaeological site of Masada now benefits from popular tourism in Israel.
8 The Palestinians had problems with the Israelis, but also with right-wing factions of the Christian Maronites, notably the militant Phalangists, who committed the massacres of Sabra and Shatila (September 15–17, 1982) under the supervision of the Israeli Army, then commanded by Ariel Sharon.
9 The Beirutis brought televisions into the streets to watch the Algerian national soccer team make a run at the World Cup championship in Spain in 1982. Neighboring Arab countries were equally ineffective in providing support to the Palestinians and Lebanese during the Israeli siege.
10 Comparing the prose works with their respective English translations is a long but worthwhile task. The translator of *Memory for Forgetfulness*, Ibrahim Muhawi, and the translator of *I Saw Ramallah*, Ahdaf Soueif, both made cuts to the original texts when the writing became overly repetitious. To enumerate all the small phrases that were excluded by the translators would be an excessive

exercise. Suffice it to say that the translators had noticed the literary repetitions and chose to eliminate them on more than one occasion.

11 Muhawi prefers the term "streetcar," but the term used by Darwish is "tram," which demonstrates the linguistic transmission of foreign terms as a result of French colonialism in Lebanon.

12 During the establishment of Israel (1947–1949), hundreds of thousands of Palestinians either fled from fear or were expelled by force from British Mandate Palestine. This year became known as *al-Nakba* [the disaster] to the Arabs. The Israeli invasion of the Sinai Peninsula ensued in 1956, followed by the preemptive Israeli attack of June 1967. The defeat of the Arab armies was so complete that it became known as the second *Nakba* or the *Naksa*, which literally implies a tragic relapse or degeneration. More Palestinians were evicted and Palestine further dwindled with "the repeated geographic scattering after the war." (*I Saw* 47; *Ra'aytu* 57). The Palestinian resistance decided to rely solely upon their *samūd* [steadfastness]. Subsequently, the Palestinian *fidā'īyūn* were routed from the Jordan Valley during Black September in 1970. They found refuge in Lebanon and established a "state within a state." The first Israeli invasion of Lebanon came in 1978; the second Israeli invasion and the siege of Beirut in the summer 1982. The PLO went to Tunisia. The first Palestinian intifada (popular uprising) erupted in the occupied Palestinian territories in 1987. The late Palestinian President Yasir Arafat returned to Gaza in July 1994. The second intifada, instigated in September 2000, was largely quelled by the *Tsahal,* or Israeli Defense Forces (IDF), and "periodically the demolition of houses on the West Bank and in Gaza is repeated" (*I Saw* 133; *Ra'aytu* 59).

13 Ibn Hazm (994–1064) was a Muslim theologian and served as vizier on repeated occasions to the Umayyad Caliphate of Muslim Spain. As a result of his political activities, he suffered imprisonment, banishment, and exile from Cordova. He dedicated the last thirty years of his life to literary activities and composed his famous *Ṭawq al-ḥamāma* [*The Neck-Ring of the Dove*, trans. A. J. Arberry (London: Luzac, 1953)], which contains highly lyrical prose and poetic passages about the art and practice of Arab love. Originally written during and revised after the fall of the Cordova Caliphate, the parallel with Darwish's account of the fall of Beirut and his descriptions of love in war is noteworthy.

14 When trying to eliminate an enemy cloistered within the precincts of a city, the siege has been a commonly used war tactic and recurs through history. Nonetheless, Edward Said refers to the overshadowing of larger events as also foreshadowing smaller events, which he calls the "adumbration" of history. Accordingly, the atrocious repercussions of an atomic bomb would permit lesser forms of destruction to be disregarded. *Memory* can therefore be perceived as an intellectual effort to avoid neglecting the devastating effects of other bombs.

15 In Muhawi's introduction to *Memory*, he claims that "we can comprehend that the purpose of the complexity [of the pattern of writing] is to reach for the sublime by expressing rage through restraint" (xxx). Concerning the ambitions of the US in the Middle East and Zionist Israeli aspirations in Palestine, this "restraint of rage" is further elucidated by the Palestinian scholar Rashid Khalidi in *Resurrecting Empire: Western Footprints and America's Perilous Path in the Middle East*.

16 This historical parallel is often made among Arabs in the Middle East and highlights the popular role Darwish plays as the leading national poet of Palestine.
17 Ibn Kathir (1301–1372) was a Syrian teacher and scholar of Islamic theology and history. He wrote a highly respected *Tafsīr* (commentary and explanation) of the Qur'an. His fourteen-volume historical compilation, *Al-Bidāya wa al-nihāya* [The beginning and the end], contains the stories of the Prophets and other nations, the *Sīrat* [Biography] of the Prophet Muhammad, plus an additional volume called *Al-Fitān*, which deals specifically with the "Final Hour."
18 Curiously, the sixth edition of *Dhākira lil-nisyān* (Beirut: Dar al-'Awda, 1994) omits this entire passage. This erroneous edition also excludes the final apocalyptic scene of the sea "walking in the streets." The omission of this reference is important not only because the Apocalypse is prevalent in the Bible and the Qur'an, but also because Ibn Kathir wrote a text entitled "Apocalypse" (see note 17).
19 Marx, *Eighteenth Brumaire* Ch.1. This famous phrase recurs in the tragicomic novel *Al-Mutashā'il* by Emile Habiby: "You used to assure us, honored sir, that history, when repeating itself, does not reproduce itself precisely. If the first occurrence were tragedy, the second would be a farce" (Habiby, *The Secret Life of Saeed* 44.) Habiby also borrows the scene of the sea from Ghassan Kanafani's famous short story "Kafr al-manjam" ["The Mine Hamlet"].
20 *Memory* 181; *Al-Zamān* 95. *I Saw Ramallah* 12. See also note 3. This mutual "pale wasteland" in the "middle region between life and death" is reminiscent of Dante's *Divine Comedy*; however, here there is no hint of reaching Paradise.

Works Cited

All references to Darwish's Dīwān *in the edition are to the two volumes cited below. Other collections by Darwish have appeared as* Dīwāns *in different years. Some of Darwish's works have appeared in different translations. We have tried to make note of the different versions to honor the difficulty and fluidity of poetic translation.*

By Mahmoud Darwish

———. *'Ābirūn fī kalāmin 'ābir* [We pass through passing words]. 2nd ed. Beirut: Dār al-'Awda, 1994.

———. *The Adam of Two Edens: Selected Poems by Mahmoud Darwish*. Ed. Munir Akash and Daniel Moore. Syracuse: Syracuse University Press, 2000.

———. *Aḥada 'ashara kawkaban 'alā ākhiri al-mashhadi al-Andalusī* [Eleven stars (or planets) over the last (at the end of the) Andalusian scene]. Beirut: Dār al-Jadīd, 1992.

———. *Ākhir al-layl* [The end of night]. Acre: Maṭba'at al-Jalīl, 1967.

———. "Anqidhūnā min hādhā al-ḥubb al-qāsī" [Save us from this cruel love]. *Al-Jadīd* June 1969: 2–4.

———. *Arā mā urīd*. Casablanca: Dār Tubqāl, 1990. Translated in part as *I See What I Want to See* in *Unfortunately, It Was Paradise*.

———. *A'rās* [Weddings]. Acre: Maktabat al-aswār lil-ṭibā'a wa al-nashr, 1977.

———. *'Aṣāfīr bilā ajniḥa* [Birds without wings]. Beirut: Dār al-'Awda, 1960.

———. *Al-'Asafīr tamūtu fī l-Jalīl* [The birds die in Galilee]. Beirut: Dār al-Adāb, 1970.

———. *'Āshiq min Filasṭīn* [A lover from Palestine]. Beirut: Manshūrāt Dār al-Adāb, 1966.

———. *Awrāq al-zaytūn* [Olive leaves]. Haifa: Maṭba' at al-Ittiḥād al-Ta'āwnīya, 1964.

———. "Bayt, thawm, baṣal, mā'iz wa mafātīh" [House, garlic, onions, goats, and keys]. *Al-Karmel* 33 (1989).

———. *The Butterfly's Burden*. Translated by Fady Joudah. Port Townsend, WA: Copper Canyon Press, 2007.

———. *Dhākira lil-nisyān: al-makān āb 1982, al-Zamān Bayrūt*. Beirut: al-Mu'assassa al-'Arabīya lil-Nashr, 1987. Translated as *Memory for Forgetfulness: August, Beirut, 1982* by Ibrahim Muhawi. Berkeley: University of California Press, 1995.

———. *Dīwān* [Collected works]. 2 vols. Beirut: Dār al-'Awda, 1987–1994.

———. "Fī intiẓār al-Barābira" [Waiting for the barbarians]. *Al-Karmel* (Nicosia) 18 (1985): 4–9.

———. *Fī waṣfi ḥālatina* [A depiction of our state]. *Al-Karmel* 3 (1981). Reprinted, Beirut: Dār al-Kalima, 1987.

———. *Ḥabībatī tanhaḍu min nawmihā* [My beloved awakes from sleep]. Beirut: Dār al-Jadīd, 1969.

———. *Ḥālat ḥiṣār* [*State of Siege*]. Beirut: Riad al-Rayyis, 2002. Translation of extracts by Amina Elbendary in *Al-Ahram Weekly* online 581 (11 April 2002). Also translated in *The Butterfly's Burden*.

———. *Ḥiṣār li-madā'iḥ al-baḥr* [Siege for the praises of the sea]. Beirut: Dār al-'Awda, 1984.

———. *Hiya ughniya, Hiya ughniya* [It is a song, it is a song]. Beirut: Dār al-Kalima, 1986.

———. "Hudna ma'a al-Maghūl. Amāma Ghābat al-Sindiyān" [Truce with the Mongols. In front of the oak tree]. *Filasṭīn al-thawra* 24 February 1991: 30–31.

———. *Jidārīya* [Mural]. Beirut: Riad al-Rayyis Books, 2000. Translated in *Unfortunately, It Was Paradise*.

———. *Ka-zahr al-lawz aw ab'ad* [Like almond flowers or further]. Beirut: Dār al-Rayyis, 2005.

———. *Lā ta'tadhir 'ammā fa'alta*. Beirut: Riad al-Rayyis Books, 2004. Translated in *The Butterfly's Burden* as *Don't Apologize for What You've Done*.

———. *Limādhā tarakta al-ḥiṣāna waḥīdan?* Beirut: Riad al-Rayyis Books, 1995. Translated in part as *Why Have You Left the Horse Alone?* in *Unfortunately, It was Paradise*. Translated as *Why Did You Leave the Horse Alone?* by Jeffrey Sacks. New York: Archipelago Books, 2006.

———. *Madīḥ al-ẓill al-'ālī*. [In praise of the rising shadow]. 1983 (audio recording); printed in *Kul al-'Arab* (Lebanon), 16 March 1983.

———. *Muḥāwala raqam sab'a* [Attempt number seven], 1973. Beirut: Dār al-'Awda, 1973.

———. "Mu'īn Bssīsso lā yajliss 'alā maq'ad al-ghiyāb" [Mu'in Bsseisso does not occupy a seat of absence]. *Al-Karmel* 11 (1984).

———. *The Music of Human Flesh: Poems of the Palestinian Struggle*. Translated by Denys Johnson-Davies. Washington, DC: Three Continents Press, 1980.

———. "Not Like a Foreign Tourist Would." Trans. Sinan Antoon. *Banipal* 23 (Summer 2005).

———. *Palästina als Metapher: Gespräche über Literatur und Politik* [Palestine as metaphor: conversations about literature and politics]. Trans. Michael Schiffman. Heidelberg: Palmyra, 1998.

———. *La Palestine comme métaphore: entretiens* [Palestine as metaphor: interviews]. Trans. Elias Sanbar and Simone Bitton. Paris: Actes Sud, 1997.

———. *Palestine, mon pays: L'affaire du poème* [Palestine, my country: the affair of the poem]. Ed. Jérôme Lindon. Paris: Les Éditions de Minuit, 1988.

———. "Poetry and Palestine." *Boundary 2* 26 (1999): 81–83.

———. *Psalms*. Translated by Ben Bennani. Washington, DC: Three Continents Press, 1994.

———. *Qaṣīdat Bayrūt* [Beirut poem]. *Al-Karmel* (Nicosia) 1 (1981): 220–221.

———. *The Raven's Ink: A Chapbook*. Translated and edited by Munir Akash,

Carolyn Forché, Amira al-Zein, and Sinan Antoon. The Lannan Foundation, 2001.
———. *Sand and Other Poems*. Translated by Rana Kabbani. London: Routledge and Kegan Paul PLC, 1986.
———. *Sarīr al-gharība*. Beirut: Riad al-Rayyis, 1999. Translated in part as *A Bed for the Stranger* in *Unfortunately, It Was Paradise*. Translated as *The Stranger's Bed* in *The Butterfly's Burden*.
———. *Selected Poems*. Translated by Ian Wedde and Fawwaz Tuqan. Manchester: Carcanet Press, 1973.
———. *Shay' 'an al-waṭan* [Something on the homeland]. Beirut: Dār al-'Awda, 1971.
———. "Thalāthat shahādāt shafawīya" [Three oral testimonies]. *Al-Karmel* 7 (1983).
———. *Tilka ṣūratuhā wa hādhā intiḥār al-'āshiq* [That is her image and this is the lover's suicide]. Beirut: Markaz al-Abḥāth, Munaẓẓamat al-Taḥrīr al-Filasṭīnīya, 1975.
———. *Uḥibbuki aw lā uḥibbuki* [I love you or I do not love you]. Beirut: Dār al-Adāb, 1972.
———. *Unfortunately, It was Paradise: Selected Poems*. Translated and edited by Munir Akash and Carolyn Forché, with Sinan Antoon and Amira al-Zein. Berkeley: University of California Press, 2003.
———. *Ward aqall*. Acre: Dār al-Aswar, 1986. Translated in part as *Fewer Roses* in *Unfortunately, It Was Paradise*. Also *Weniger Rosen*. Trans. Khalid al-Maaly und Heribert Becker. Berlin: das Arabische Buch, 1996. Also translated by 'Abd al-Rahim al-Shaykh, unpublished ms.
———. *Why Did You Leave the Horse Alone?* Translated by Jeffrey Sacks. New York: Archipelago, 2006.
———. *Yawmīyāt al-ḥuzn al-'ādī* [Diary of ordinary sadness]. Beirut: al-Mu'assassa al-'Arabīya lil-Nashr, 1973.
———. *Al-Zamān: Bayrūt, al-makān: Āb* [The time: Beirut. The place: August]. *Al-Karmel* 21/22 (1986). Later republished as *Dhākira lil-nisyān*.
——— and Samih al-Qasim. *Al-Rasā'il* [The letters]. Beirut: Dār al-'Awda, 1990.

By Others

Abbas, Ihsan. *Ghurbat al-rā'ī*. Beirut: Dār al-Shurūq, 1996.
———. *Ittijāhāt al-shi'r al-'Arabī al-mu'āṣir* [Directions of contemporary Arabic poetry]. Kuwait: Al-Majlis al-Waṭanī lil-Thaqāfa wa al-Funūn wa al-Adab, 1978.
Abdel-Malek, Kamal and Wael Hallaq, eds. *Tradition, Modernity, and Postmodernity in Arabic Literature*. Leiden: Brill, 2000.
Abu Deeb, Kamal. "Conflicts, Oppositions, Negations." *Kalimāt* (Bahrain) 10/11 (1995): 27–35.
———. "Conflicts, Oppositions and Negations: Modern Arabic Poetry and the Fragmentation of Self and of Text." Unpublished ms. University of Sana'a, 1989–1990.

Abu Khadra, Sa'id Jabr Muhammad. *Tatawwur al-dalālāt al-lughawīya fī shi'r Maḥmūd Darwīsh* [The development of linguistic meaning in the poetry of Mahmoud Darwish]. Beirut: Al-Mu'assasa al-'Arabīya lil-Nashr, 2001.
Abu al-Khashab, Ibrahim 'Ali. *Tārīkh al-adab al-'Arabī fī al-'aṣr al-'abbasī al-thānī* [History of Arabic literature during the second Abbasid period]. Cairo: Dār al-Fikr al-'Arabī, n.d.
Abu Zeid, Nasr Hamid. "The Stable and the Changing in Adonis' View of the Heritage." In *Ishkālīyāt al-qirā'a, aliyāt al-ta'wīl* [Problematics of reading, instruments of interpretation]. Ed. Nasr Hamid Zeid. Casablanca: Al-Markaz al-Thaqāfī al-'Arabī, 1994.
'Adiyy, Nadim. *Tārīkh al-adab al-'Arabī* [History of Arabic literature]. Vol. 1. Aleppo: Maktabat Rab'i, 1954.
Adonis. *Fātiḥa li-nihāyāt al-qarn* [Opening of the ends of the century]. Beirut: Dār al-Nahār, 1998.
———. *Hā anta, ayyuhā al-waqt* [There you are, O time]. Beirut: Dār al-Adāb, 1993.
———. *Hadhā huwa ismī* [This is my name]. Beirut: Dār al-Adāb, 1969.
———. *Al-Kitāb: ams al-makān al-ān* [The book: the place's yesterday is now]. Beirut: Dār al-Sāqī, 1995.
———. *La Prière et l'épée: essais sur la culture arabe*. Choice of texts by Anne Wade Minkowski. Trans. Leila Khatib and Anne Wade Minkowski. Ed. Jean-Yves Masson. Paris: Mercure de France, 1993.
———. *Muqaddima lil-shi'r al-'Arabī* [Introduction to Arabic poetry]. Beirut: Dār al-'Awda, 1971.
———. *Al-Shi'rīya al-'Arabīya* [Arabic poetics]. 2nd ed. Beirut: Dār al-Adāb, 1989.
———. *Al-Thābit wa al-mutaḥawwil—ṣadamāt al-ḥadātha* [The stable and the changing—the challenges of modernity]. 3 vols. Beirut: Dār al-'Awda, 1972–1974; vol. 4, Beirut: Dār al-'Awda, 1986, reprinted in 1994. Page citations to vol. 4 are to the reprinted edition.
———. *Zaman al-shi'r* [The time of poetry]. Beirut: Dār al-'Awda, 1972.
———, ed. *Dīwān al-shi'r al-'Arabī* [Collection of Arabic poetry]. Damascus: Dār al-Madā, 1996; 1964.
Adorno, Theodor W. *Prisms*. Trans. Samuel and Shierry Weber. Cambridge, MA: MIT Press, 1967.
Akash, Munir. "Introduction." *The Adam of Two Edens: Selected Poems by Mahmoud Darwish*. Eds. Munir Akash and Daniel Moore. Syracuse: Syracuse University Press, 2000.
———, trans. and ed. *See under* Darwish, *The Raven's Ink*.
———, trans. and ed. *See under* Darwish, *Unfortunately, It was Paradise: Selected Poems*.
Alloush, Naji. Introduction to *The Collected Works of Badr Shakir al-Sayyab*. Beirut: Dār al-'Awda, 1986.
al-Alusi, Jamal al-Din. *Baghdād fī al-shi'r al-'Arabī* [Baghdad in Arabic poetry]. Baghdad: Al-Mujama' al-'Ilmī al-'Irāqī, 1987.
Antoon, Sinan. "Mahmud Darwish's Allegorical Critique of Oslo." *Journal of*

Palestine Studies, 31 (2002), 66–77.
———, trans. *See under* Darwish, "Not Like a Foreign Tourist Would."
———, trans. *See under* Darwish, *The Raven's Ink*.
Aragon, Louis. *Le fou d'Elsa*. Paris: Gallimard, 1964.
Arazi, Albert. "Une Epitre d'Ibrahim b. Hilal al-Sabi sur les genres litteraires." *Studies in Islamic History and Civilization in Honour of Professor David Ayalon*. Ed. M. Sharon. Jerusalem: Cana & Leiden: Brill, 1986.
Asfour, John Mikhail, ed. *When the Words Burn: An Anthology of Modern Arabic Poetry 1945–1987*. Dunvegan, Ontario: Cormorant Books, 1988.
'Awad, Rita, intro. *See under* Hawi, *The Collected Works*.
al-A'zami, Ahmad 'Izzat. *Al-Qaḍīya al-'Arabīya: asbābuhā, muqaddimātuhā, taṭawwūruhā wa-natā'ijuhā* [The Arab leadership: reasons, beginnings, development and consequences]. Vol. 4. Baghdad: Maṭba'at al-Sha'b, 1932. Translated in G. Haim, *Arab Nationalism: An Anthology*. Berkeley: University of California Press, 1962.
Badawi, M. M. *Modern Arabic Literature and the West*. Oxford: Oxford University Press, 1985.
———. *A Short History of Modern Arabic Literature*. New York: Oxford University Press, 1993.
al-Bahrawi, Sayyid. *Al-Bahth 'an al-manhaj fī al-naqd al-'Arabī al-hadīth* [The search for method in modern Arabic criticism]. Cairo: Dār al-Sharqīyāt, 1993.
al-Baqi, 'Abd and Muhammad Fu'ad, eds. *Al-Mua'jam al-mufahras li-alfāẓ al-Qur'ān al-karīm* [The collected anthology for the expressions of the Holy Qur'ān]. Beirut: Dār Ihyā' al-Turāth al-'Arabī, 1945.
Barakat, Halim. *The Arab World: Society, Culture and State*. Berkeley: University of California Press, 1993.
Barghouti, Mourid. *Rā'aytu Ramallah*. 1997. 2nd edition: Dār Baidā' al-Maghreb: Al-Markaz al-Thaqāfī al-'Arabī, 2003. Page citations are to the second edition. Translated by Ahdaf Soueif. *I Saw Ramallah*. New York: Anchor Books, 2003.
———. "War Butlers and their Language." *Autodafe* 3 (spring 2003). <www.autodafe.org/autodafe/autodafe_03/art_07.htm>
Baybars, Diya' al-Din. "Talhīn al-Qur'ān bayna ahl al-fann wa-rijāl al-dīn" [The musical composition of the Qur'an between the aesthetes and the theologians]. *Al-Hilāl* Dec. 1970: 118–127.
al-Bayyati, Abd al-Wahab. *Al-Mawt fī al-ḥayā* [Death in life]. Beirut: Dār al-Adāb, 1968.
———. *Al-kitāba 'alā al-ṭīn* [Writing on Clay]. 1970. 3rd ed., Cairo: Dār al-Shuruq, 1985. Page citations are to the later edition.
Benjamin, Walter. "A Berlin Chronicle." In *Reflections*. Trans. Edmund Jephcott. New York: Schocken Books, 1978.
———. *Beroliniana*. München and Berlin: Koehler and Amelang, 2001.
———. *Illuminations: Essays and Reflections*. Ed. and introduction by Hannah Arendt. Trans. Harry Zohn. New York: Schocken, 1969.
———. *Das Passagen-Werk*. Ed. Rolf Tiedemann. Frankfurt: Suhrkamp

Verlag, 1982. Translated as *The Arcades-Project*. Trans. Howard Eiland and Kevin McLaughlin. Cambridge: Harvard University Press, 2002.
———."Theses on the Philosophy of History." In *Illuminations: Essays and Reflections*.
Bennani, Ben, trans. *See under* Darwish, *Psalms*.
Beydoun, Abbas. "The Palestinian Tragedy Will Find Its Most Sublime Expression." Interview with Mahmoud Darwish. *Masharif* (Haifa) 3 (1995).
———. "Qui impose son récit hérite la terre du récit" [Whoever imposes his narrative inherits the land of narrative]. In Darwish, *La Palestine comme métaphore*.
Bin'Amara, Muhammad. *Min al-shi'r al-Islāmī al-Hadīth: mukhtārāt min shu'arā' al-rābiṭa* [From modern Islamic poetry: selections from al-Rabita poets]. Ammān: Dār al-Bashīr, 1989.
bin Ja'afar, Abi al-Faraj Qudama. *Kitāb naqd al-shi'r* [The criticism of poetry]. Ed. Muhammad 'Abd al-Mun'im Khaffaja. Beirut: Dār al-Kutub al-'Ilmīya, n.d.
Bitton, Simone and Elias Sanbar, dirs. *Mahmoud Darwich: Et la terre, comme la langue* [As the land is the language]. Co-produced by France 3 and Point du Jour. Paris: Sindbad, 1997 (video).
———, trans. *See under* Darwish, *La Palestine comme métaphore: entretiens*.
Blanchot, Maurice. *The Space of Literature*. Trans. Ann Smock. Lincoln: University of Nebraska Press, 1982.
Boullata, Issa. *Badr Shākir al-Sayyāb: ḥayāhtuh wa shi'ruh* [Badr Shakir al-Sayyab: his life and poetry]. Beirut: Dār al-Nahār, 1971.
Bowman, Glenn. "'Country of Words': Conceiving the Palestinian Nation from the Position of Exile." *The Making of Political Identities*. Ed. Ernesto Laclau. London: Verso, 1994.
Boym, Svetlana. *The Future of Nostalgia*. New York: Basic Books, 2001.
Browne, Edward G. *A Literary History of Persia*. Vol. 2. Cambridge: Cambridge University Press, 1951.
Burnett, Paula. *Derek Walcott: Politics and Poetics*. Gainesville: University Press of Florida, 2000.
Busse, Herbert. *Islam, Judaism, and Christianity: Theological and Historical Affiliations*. Trans. Allison Brown. Princeton: Markus Wiener Publishers, 1998.
al-Bustani, al-Mu'allem. *Muḥīt ul-muḥīt* [The ocean of the ocean]. Beirut: Librairie du Liban, 1993.
Callahan, Lance. *In the Shadows of Divine Perfection: Derek Walcott's* Omeros. New York: Routledge, 2003.
Cavafy, Constantine P. *Collected Poems*. Trans. Edmund Keeley and Philip Serrard. London: Chatto & Windus, 1998.
———. *The Complete Poems of Cavafy*. 4th ed. Trans. Rae Dalven. New York: Harcourt, 1961.
Celan, Paul. *Mohn and Gedächtnis: Gedichte*. Stuttgart: Deutsche Verlagsanstalt, 1950.

Coetzee, J. M. *Waiting for the Barbarians*. Hardmondsworth: Penguin Books, 1983.
Combs-Schilling, M.E. *Sacred Performance: Islam, Sexuality, and Sacrifice*. New York: Columbia University Press, 1989.
Cowan, Louise. "Introduction." *The Epic Cosmos*. Ed. Larry Allums. Dallas: Dallas Institute of Humanities and Culture, 1992.
Daghir, Sharbil. *Al-Shi'rīya al-'Arabīya* [Arabic poetics]. Casablanca: Dār Tubqāl, 1988.
Dakrub, Muhammad. "My Life, My Cause, and My Poetry." Interview with Mahmoud Darwish. *Al-Ṭarīq* 10–11 (1968).
Dalman, Gustav. *Palästinischer Dīwān: Als Beitrag zur Volkskunde Palästinas gesammelt, mit Übersetzung und Melodien herausgegeben* [Palestinian dīwān: A contribution to the Palestinian popular culture, collected and edited with translation and melodies]. Leipzig: J.C. Hinrichs, 1901.
Darwish, Zaki. *Al-Jiyād* [Stallions]. Acre: al-Aswār, 1989.
Dayf, Shawqi. *'Aṣr al-duwal wa al-imārāt* [Age of states and emirates]. Cairo: Dār al-Ma'ārif, 1983.
Derrida, Jacques. "Force of Law: The 'Mystical Foundation of Authority.'" Trans. Mary Quaintance. *Acts of Religion*. Ed. Gil Anidjar. New York and London: Routledge, 2002; *Force de loi: Le "Fondement mystique de l'autorité*." Paris: Galilée, 1994.
———. *The Politics of Friendship*. Trans. George Collins. London: Verso, 1997; *Politiques de l'amitié*. Paris: Galilée, 1994.
———. *Schibboleth: pour Paul Celan*. Paris: Galilée, 1986.
DeYoung, Terri. *Placing the Poet: Badr Shakir al-Sayyab and Postcolonial Iraq*. Albany: State University of New York Press, 1998.
——— and Issa Boullata, eds. *Tradition and Modernity in Arabic Literature*. Fayetteville: University of Arkansas, 1997.
D'Ohsson, C. *Histoire des Mongols depuis Tchinguiz-Khan jusqu'a Timour Bey ou Tamerlan* [History of the Mongols from Ghanghis Khan to Tamerlane]. 2nd ed. Vol. 1. The Hague and Amsterdam, 1834–1835.
Dostoyevsky, Fyodor. *Notes from the Underground*. Trans. Andrew R. MacAndrew. New York: Signet Classics, 1961.
al-'Eid, Yumna. *Fī al-qawl al-shi'rī* [On poetic discourse]. Casablanca: Dār Tubqāl, 1987.
Elbendary, Amina. "Like Him, Like Me: *Lā ta'tadhir 'ammā fa'alta* [Don't apologize for what you did]." *Al-Ahrām Weekly* online 678, 19–24 February 2004.
Eliade, Mircea. *The Sacred and the Profane*. New York: Harcourt Brace Jovanovich, 1959.
Eliot, T.S. *Four Quartets*. London: Faber & Faber, 2001.
———. *Selected Essays*. New York: Harcourt, 1950.
Embalo, Birgit, Angelika Neuwirth, and Frederike Pannewick. *Kulturelle Selbstbehauptung der Palästinenser: Bio-bibliographischer Survey der modernen palästinensischen Dichtung*. [Palestinian cultural self-assertion: a bio-bibliographic survey of modern Palestinian poetry]. Beirut and Würzburg: Ergon-Verlag, 2001.

Fadl, Salah. *Asālīb shi'rīya al-mu'āṣira* [Styles of contemporary poetry]. Beirut: Dār al-Adāb, 1995.

al-Fakhuri, Hanna. *Al-Jadīd fī al-adab al-'Arabī* [New trends in modern Arabic poetry]. Vol. 4. Beirut: Maktabat al-Madrasa wa-Dār al-Kitāb al-Lubnānī lil-Ṭibā'a, 1954.

al-Farabi. *Kitāb al-ḥurūf* [The book of letters]. Ed. Muhsin Mahdi. Beirut: Dār al-Mashriq, 1990.

Farhat, Muhammad 'Ali. "Al-Shi'r rīf wa al-riwāya madīna" [Poetry is the countryside; the novel is the city]. *Al-Wasaṭ* 2 March 1992.

Farrell, Joseph. "Walcott's *Omeros*: The Classical Epic in a Postmodern World." *Epic Traditions in the Contemporary World: The Poetics of Community*. Eds. Jane Tylus, Margaret Beissinger, and Susanne Wofford. Berkeley: University of California Press, 1999.

al-Fiqqi, Muhammad Kamil. *Al-Adab fī al-'aṣr al-Mamlūkī* [Literature under the Mamluks]. Cairo: Al-Hay'a al-'Āmma lil-Kitāb, 1976.

Fish, Stanley E. "Literature in the Reader: Affective Stylistics." *Reader-Response Criticism: From Formalism to Post-Structuralism*. Ed. Jane P. Tompkins. Baltimore: Johns Hopkins University Press, 1980.

Forché, Carolyn, trans. *See under* Darwish, *The Raven's Ink*.

———, trans. and ed. *See under* Darwish, *Unfortunately, It was Paradise*.

Frangieh, Bassam. "Modern Arabic Poetry: Vision and Reality." *Tradition, Modernity and Postmodernity in Arabic Literature*. Eds. Kamal Abdel-Malek and Wael Hallaq. Leiden: Brill, 2000.

Garcia Marquez, Gabriel. *Chronicle of a Death Foretold*. Trans. Gregory Rabassa. New York: Alfred A. Knopf, 1983.

Ghanim, Muhammad. *Maḥāsin al-sulūk fī tārīkh al-khulāfā' wa al-mulūk* [Good manners in the history of the caliphs and the kings]. Cairo: Maṭba'at al-'Ulūm, 1938.

Gharayiba, 'Abd al-Karim. *Al-'Arab wa al-Atrāk* [The Arabs and the Ottomans]. Damascus: Damascus University, 1961.

al-Ghazzali, Abu Hamid. *Al-Munqidh min al-dalāl wa al-mūṣil ilā dhi al-'izza wa al-jalāl* [To be saved from signification and linked to the Exalted One]. Eds. Jamil Saliba and Kamil 'Ayyad. Damascus: Maṭba'at al-Jāmi'a al-Sūrīya, 1956.

al-Ghazzawi, 'Abbas. *Tārīkh al-adab al-'Arabī fī al-'Irāq* [History of Arabic literature in Iraq]. Baghdad: Al-Majma' al-'Ilmī al-'Irāqī, 1960.

Gibb, H.A.R. *Arabic Literature*. Oxford: Oxford University Press, 1962.

Gibran, Kahlil. *The Garden of the Prophet*. London: Heineman, 1934.

Goldziher, I. *A Short History of Classical Arabic Literature*. Hildesheim: Georg Olms, 1966.

Grunebaum, G.E. von. *Modern Islam: The Search for Cultural Identity* (Berkeley & Los Angeles: University of California Press, 1962.

Habib, Shafiq. *Al-'Awda ilā al-ātī* [Return to the future]. Nazareth: Maṭba'at al-Hakīm, 1990.

Habiby, Emile. *Al-Waqā'i' al-gharība fī ikhtifā' Sa'īd abī l-naḥs al-mutashā'il*. Haifa: Dār ibn Khaldūn, 1974. Translated by Salma Khadra Jayyusi and

Trevor LeGassick, *The Secret Life of Saeed: The Pessoptimist*. Northampton: Interlink Books, 2001.

Haddad, Mishil. *Fī al-nāhīya al-ukhrā* [In the other end]. Shfaram: Dār al-Mashriq, 1985.

Haddad, Qasim. *'Uzlat al-malikāt* [The solitude of queens]. Cairo: Al-Ghad Publishing House, 1985.

———, and Amin Salih. *Al-Jawāshīn*. Casablanca: Dār Tubqāl, 1989.

Hadidi, Subhi and Basheer al-Baker. "Nulle demeure pour la poésie hors un canon poétique" [No place for poetry outside a poetic canon]. In Darwish, *La Palestine comme métaphore*.

Haim, G. *Arab Nationalism: An Anthology*. Berkeley: University of California Press, 1962.

Halbwachs, Maurice. *On Collective Memory*. Ed. Lewis A. Coser. Chicago: University of Chicago Press, 1992.

Hamacher, Werner. *Pleroma: Reading in Hegel*. Trans. Nicholas Walker and Simon Jarvis. Stanford: Stanford University Press, 1999.

Hamoudeh, Hussein. "*Missār al-nā'ī... madār al-ghiyāb: 'An shahādāt Maḥmūd Darwīsh fī dīwānuh al-akhīr:* Limādhā tarakta al-ḥiṣāna waḥīdan" [The path of remoteness and the circle of absence: The testimony of Darwish in *Why Did You Leave the Horse Alone?*] *Al-Qāhira* 45 (1995).

Hamza, Husayn. "Anā Yūsufun Yā Abī—Maḥmūd Darwīsh bayna marji'īyāt al-Naṣṣ wa al-ta'wīl" [I am Joseph my father—Mahmoud Darwish between context and interpretation]. *Al-Sharq* Mar. 2004: 52–56.

Harlow, Barbara. "Memory and Historical Record: Literature and Literary Criticism of Beirut, 1982." In Lennard J. Davis and M. Bella Mirabella, eds. *Left Politics and the Literary Profession*. New York: Columbia University Press, 1990.

———. "Palestine or Andalusia: The Literary Response to the Israeli Invasion of Lebanon." *Race and Class* 26: 33–43.

———. *Resistance Literature*. New York: Metheun, 1987.

Hareven, Alouph, ed. *Ehad mi-Kol Shishsha Yisraelim* [One out of every six Israelis]. Jerusalem: Van Leer, 1981.

Hartman, Michelle. *Jesus, Joseph and Job: Reading Rescriptings of Religious Figures in Lebanese Women's Fiction*. Wiesbaden: Reichert Verlag, 2002.

Hasan, Ibrahim Hasan. *Tārīkh al-Islām* [History of Islam]. Vol. 4. Cairo: Maktabat al-Nahḍa, 1967.

Hawi, Khalil. *The Collected Works of Khalil Hawi*. Introduction by Rita 'Awad. Beirut: Dār al-'Awda, 1993.

Herzl, Theodor. *The Jewish State: An Attempt at a Modern Solution of the Jewish Question*. Trans. S. D'Avigdor. London: Central Office of the Zionist Organization, 1936.

Hegel, G.W.F. *Phenomenology of Spirit*. Trans. A.V. Miller. Oxford: Oxford University Press, 1977; *Phänomenologie des Geistes*. Hamburg: Felix Meiner Verlag, 1988.

Heidegger, Martin. *Poetry, Language, Thought*. Trans. and introd. by Albert Hofstadter. New York: Harper & Row, 1971.

Hourani, Albert. *Arabic Thought in the Liberal Age: 1798–1939*. 1962. Cambridge: Cambridge University Press, 1983.

———. *History of the Arab Peoples*. New York: Oxford University Press, 1990.

Huri, Yair. "Seeking Glory in the Dunghills: Representations of the City in the Writings of Modern Arab Poets." *Archiv Orientální* 73 (2005): 185–202.

Husayn, Taha, ed. *Al-Majmū'a al-kāmila: Abū al-'Alā' al-Ma'arrī* [The complete works: Abu al-'Ala' al-Ma'arri]. Vol. 10. Beirut: Dār al-Kitāb al-Lubnānī, 1974.

———, et al. *Al-Mujmal fī tārīkh al-adab al-'Arabī* [Arabic literary history]. Cairo: Maktabat al-Adāb, 1948.

———. *On Jahili Poetry*. s.l.: s.n., 1926.

Ibn Hazm. *The Neck-Ring of the Dove*. Trans. A.J. Arberry. London: Luzac, 1953.

Ibn Kathir. *Al-Bidāya wa al-nihāya* [The beginning and the end]. Ed. Hamed Ahmed al-Taher. Cairo: Dār al-Fajr lil-Turāth, 2003.

Ibn Qutayba, 'Abd Allah ibn Muslim. *'Uyūn al-akhbār* [The eyes of news]. Vol. 2. Cairo: Maṭba'at Dār al-Kutub al-Miṣrīya, 1928.

Imhof, Agnes. *Religiöser Wandel und die Genese des Islam: Das Menschenbild altarabischer Panegyriker im 7. Jahrhundert*. [Religious change and the beginning of Islam: the image of man in old Arabic panegyrics of the seventh century] Würzburg: Ergon-Verlag, 2004.

al-Iskandari, Ahmad, and Mustafa al-'Inani. *Al-Wasīṭ fī al-adab al-'Arabī wa tārīkhihi* [The medial in Arabic literature and its history]. Cairo: Maṭba'at al-Thaqāfa, 1931.

Isma'il, 'Izz al-Din. *Al-Shi'r al-'Arabī al-mu'āsir: qaḍāyāhu wa-ẓawāhiruhu al-fannīya wa al-ma'nawīya* [Modern Arabic poetry: issues of aesthetics and signification]. Cairo: Dār al-Fikr al-'Arabī, 1978.

Isma'il, Muhammad ibn. "Bayna al-siyāsa wa-l-thaqāfa 'inda al-'Arab 'abra al-tārīkh" [Between politics and culture among the Arabs through history]. *Fikr wa-fann* 72 (2000): 44–48.

'Izz al-Din, Yusuf. *Al-Riwāya fī al-'Irāq* [The novel in Iraq]. Cairo: Ma'had al-Buḥūth wa al-Dirāsāt al-'Arabīya, 1973.

Jabès, Edmond. *The Book of Questions*. 2 vols. Trans. Rosemarie Waldrop. Hanover and London: Wesleyan University Press, 1972, 1983; *Le livre de questions*. 2 vols. Paris: Gallimard, 1963, 1973.

al-Jabiri, Muhammad 'Abid. *Naqd al-'aql al-'Arabī: takwīn al-'aql al-'Arabī* [Critique of Arab thought: The formation of Arab thought]. Beirut: Markaz Dirāsāt al-Wiḥda al-'Arabīya, 1994.

Jabra, Jabra Ibrahim. *Al-Bi'r al-ūlā: Fuṣūl min sīra dhātīya* [The first well: a Bethlehem boyhood]. London: Riad al-Rayyis, 1987. Translated as *The First Well: A Bethlehem Boyhood* by Issa Boullata. Fayetteville: University of Arkansas Press, 1995.

———. *Shāri' al-amirāt*: *Fuṣūl min sīra dhātīya*. London and Beirut: Al-Mu'assasa al-'Arabīya lil-Nashr, 1994. Translated as *Princesses Street: Baghdad Memories* by Issa Boullata. Fayetteville: University of Arkansas Press, 2005.

———. *Ta'ammulāt fī bunyān m'amari* [The visual diary of an Arab architect]. London: Riad al-Rayyis, 1989.

Jaggi, Maya. "The Profile, Mahmoud Darwish: The Poet of the Arab World," *Guardian Unlimited* 8 June 2002. 23 August 2005 <www.guardian.co.uk/Archive/Article/0,4273,4428829,00.html>

Jayyusi, Salma Khadra, ed. *Anthology of Modern Palestinian Literature*. New York: Columbia University Press, 1992.

———. Introduction to *A Mountainous Journey, an Autobiography of Fadwa Tuqan*. Minneapolis: Graywolf Press, 1990.

———. *Modern Arabic Poetry: An Anthology*. New York: Columbia University Press, 1987.

———. *Trends and Movements in Modern Arabic Poetry*. 2 vols. Leiden: E. J. Brill, 1977.

Johnson-Davies, Denys. *See under* Darwish, *The Music of Human Flesh*.

Joudah, Fady, trans. *See under* Darwish, *The Butterfly's Burden*.

Joyce, James. *Finnegans Wake*. 1939. Introduction by Seamus Heaney. London: Penguin Books, 1992.

al-Ju'aydi', Muhammad 'Abd Allah. "Ḥuḍūr al-Andalus fī al-adab al-Filasṭīnī al-ḥadīth" [Al-Andalus in modern Arabic literature]. *'Alam al-Fikr* 28.4 (2000).

al-Jundi, In'am. *Al-Rā'id fī al-adab al-'Arabī* [The pioneer in Arabic literature]. Vol. 1. Beirut: Dār al-Rā'id al-'Arabī, 1979.

Kabbani, Rana, trans. *See under* Darwish, *Sand and Other Poems*.

Kanafani. Ghassan. *Adab al-muqāwama fī Filasṭīn al-muḥtalla 1948–1966* [The literature of resistance in occupied Palestine]. Beirut: Dār al-Adāb, 1966.

———. *Al-Adab al-filastīnī al-muqāwim taht al-ihtihāl, 1948–1968* [Palestinian literature of resistance under occupation]. 1968. Beirut: Institute for Palestine Studies, 1986.

———. "Kafr al-manjam." Translated as "The Mine Hamlet" by Malak Hasem. In *Flights of Fantasy: Arabic Short Stories*. Ed. Ceza Kassem and Malak Hashem. Cairo: Elias Modern Publishing House, 1985.

Khalidi, Rashid. *Resurrecting Empire: Western Footprints and America's Perilous Path in the Middle East*. Boston: Beacon Press, 2004.

Khalifeh, Sahar. *Bāb al-sāḥa* [The gate quarter]. Beirut: Dār al-Adāb, 1990.

Khouri, Mounah. *Poetry and the Making of Modern Egypt*. Leiden: E. J. Brill, 1971.

———. *Studies in Contemporary Arabic Poetry and Criticism*. New York: Jahan Book Co., 1987.

Khoury, Elias. *Al-Dhākira al-mafqūda* [Lost memory]. Beirut: Mu'assassat al-Abhāth al-'Arabīya, 1982.

———. *Dirīsāt fī naqd al-shi'r* [Studies in the criticism of poetry]. Beirut: Mu'assasat al-Abḥāth al-'Arabīya, 1979.

———. "Mahmoud Darwich: Rita et la poetique du couple" [Mahmoud Darwish: Rita and the poetic of the couple]. *Revue d'Etudes Palestiniennes* 21 (2001): 58–69.

———. Zamān al-ihtilāl [Time of the occupation]. Beirut: Mu'assasat al-Abhāth al-'Arabīya, 1985.

Khoury, Philip. "Syrian Political Culture in the Light of the Notables Paradigm: 1800 to the Present." Yale University, New Haven, 22 April 1997.

Kierkegaard, Søren. *Fear and Trembling: Repetition*. Trans. and ed. Howard V. Hong and Edna H. Hong. Princeton: Princeton University Press, 1983.

Kister, M.J. "'Exert Yourselves, O Ban, Arfida!': Some Notes on Entertainment in the Islamic Tradition." *Jerusalem Studies in Arabic and Islam* 23 (1999).

Klemm, Verena. *Literarisches Engagement im arabischen Nahen Osten: Konzepte und Debatten* [The commitment of literati in the Arab Near East: concepts and debate]. Würzburg: Ergon-Verlag, 1998.

Klemm, Verena. "Poems of a Love Impossible to Live: Mahmud Darwish and Rita." *Ghazal as World Literature I: Transformations of a Literary Genre*. Eds. Angelika Neuwirth and Thomas Bauer. Beirut/Würzburg: Ergon-Verlag, 2005.

Knox, R.A. *Enthusiasm*. Oxford: Clarendon Press, 1951.

La'abi, Abdellatif. *La poésie palestinienne de combat* [Palestinian poetry of struggle]. Honfleur: Pierre Jean Oswald, 1970.

Lacoue-Labarthe, Philippe. *Poetry as Experience*. Trans. Andrea Tarnowski. Stanford: Stanford University Press, 1999.

Layoun, Mary N. *Wedded to the Land?: Gender, Boundaries, and Nationalism in Crisis*. Durham: Duke University Press, 2001.

Le Goff, Jacques. *History and Memory*. Trans. Steven Rendall and Elizabeth Claman. New York: Columbia University Press, 1983.

Leeuwen, Richard van. "The Poet and His Mission: Text and Space in the Prose Works of Mahmud Darwish." *Conscious Voices: Concepts of Writing in the Middle East*. Eds. Stephan Guth, Priska Furrer, and Johann Christoph Bürgel. Beirut and Stuttgart: Steiner, 1999.

Lévinas, Emmanuel. *Otherwise than Being, or, Beyond Essence*. Trans. Alphonso Lingis. Pittsburgh: Duquesne University Press, 1981; *Autrement qu'être ou au-dela de l'essence*. The Hague: Martinus Nijhoff, 1978.

Lewis, Bernard. *Islam in History: Ideas, Men and Events in the Middle East*. London: Alcove Press, 1973.

———. *The Middle East and the West*. London: Weidenfeld and Nicolson, 1968.

"Libération: 'Why Do You Write?'" 1991. In *Aswār* 11.

Lindon, Jérôme. *See under* Darwish *Palestine, mon pays*.

Lucente, Gregory L. *The Narrative of Realism and Myth: Verga, Lawrence, Faulkner, Pavese*. Baltimore: Johns Hopkins University Press, 1981.

Lukács, Georg. *The Theory of the Novel*. Trans. Anna Bostock. Cambridge: MIT Press, 1971.

Lu'lu'a, 'Abd al-Wahid. *Al-Baḥth 'an ma'nā* [The search for meaning]. Baghdad: Dār al-Ḥurrīya, 1973.

Lyall, Charles James, ed. *Translation of Ancient Arabian Poetry*. London: Williams & Norgate, 1930.

al-Ma'arri, Abu al-'Ala'. *Ta'rīf al-qudamā' bi-Abū al-'Alā'* [Introducing the ancients through Abu al-'Ala']. Ed. Taha Husayn. Cairo: Dār al-Kutub al-Miṣrīya, 1944.
Mahmoud Darwich: Et la terre, comme la langue (video), *see under* Bitton, Simone.
Majid, 'Abd al-Mun'im. *Tārīkh al-ḥaḍāra al-Islāmīya fī al-'uṣūr al-wusṭa* [The history of Islamic civilization during the medieval period]. Cairo: Maktabat al-Anglo al-Miṣrīya, 1972.
Mansson, Anette. *Passage to a New Wor(l)d: Exile and Restoration in Mahmoud Darwish's Writings, 1960–1995*. Uppsala: Uppsala University, 2003.
Marx, Karl. *Eighteenth Brumaire of Louis Napoleon*. 1852.
Masalha, Salman. "'Anāwīn lil-nafs" [The soul has addresses]. *Al-Ittiḥād* 24 July 1987.
Milich, Stephan. *'Fremd meinem Namen und fremd meiner Zeit': Identität, Fremdheit und Exil in der Dichtung von Mahmud Darwisch*. [Strange is my name and strange is my time: identity, alienation, and exile in Mahmoud Darwish's poetry] Berlin: Schiler, 2004.
Mobley, Marilyn S. *Folk Roots and Mythic Wings in Sarah Orne Jewett and Toni Morrison: The Cultural Function of Narrative*. Baton Rouge: Louisiana State University Press, 1991.
Moore, Daniel, ed. *See under* Darwish, *The Adam of Two Edens*.
Moreh, Shmuel. "Town and Country in Modern Arabic Poetry." *Asian and African Studies* 28 (July 1984): 161–185.
Mosbahi, Hassouna. "Interview with Mahmoud Darwish: There Is No Meaning to My Life Outside Poetry." *Banipal* spring 1999: 5–12.
Muhawi, Ibrahim. *See under* Darwish, *Dhākira lil-nisyān*.
al-Mu'ti Hijazi, Ahmad 'Abd. *Dīwān*. Beirut: Dār al-'Awda, 1982.
al-Nabulsi, Shakir. *Majnūn al-turāb: dirāsa fī shi'r wa fikr Maḥmūd Darwīsh* [Mad for land: a study in the poetry and thought of Mahmoud Darwish]. Beirut: Al-Mu'assasa al-'Arabīya lil-Dirāsa wa al-Nashr, 1987.
Nadwi, Adib. *'Urs al-shahīd* [The wedding of the martyr]. Damascus, 1969.
Nancy, Jean-Luc. *Corpus*. Paris: Métailié, 2000.
———. *The Inoperative Community*. Ed. Peter Connor. Minnesota: University of Minnesota Press, 1991; *La Communauté désoeuvrée*. Paris: Christian Bourgeois, 1986.
al-Naqqash. Raja'. *Maḥmūd Darwīsh: shā'ir al-arḍ al-muḥtalla* [Mahmoud Darwish: the poet of the occupied land]. Beirut: Mu'assasat al-Abḥāth al-'Arabīya, 1972.
———. *Udabā' mu'āsirūn* [Contemporary writers]. Cairo: Dār al-Hilāl, 1968.
al-Nasir, Jamal 'Abd. *Falsafat al-thawra* [Philosophy of the revolution]. Cairo: Dār al-Ma'ārif, n.d.
Neuwirth, Angelika. "Das Lied des 'Sängers ohne Hoffnung': Zur Ghazalrezeption in der palästinensischen Widerstandsdichtung" [The singer's song without hope: the reception of the ghazal in Palestinian

poetry of resistance]. *Ghazal as World Literature II: From a Literary Genre to a Great Tradition. The Ottoman Gazel in Context*. Eds. Angelika Neuwirth, Judith Pfeiffer, Michael Hess, Börte Sagaster. Beirut and Würzburg: Ergon-Verlag, 2006.

———. "From Sacrilege to Sacrifice: Observations on Violent Death in Classical and Modern Arabic Poetry." *Martyrdom in Literature: Visions of Death and Meaningful Suffering in Europe and the Middle East from Antiquity to Modernity*. Ed. Friederike Pannewick. Wiesbaden: Reichert, 2004.

———. "Israelisch-Palästinensische Paradoxien: Emil Habibis Roman *Der Peptimist* als Versuch einer Entmythisierung von Geschichte" [Israeli–Palestinian paradox: Emil Habibi's novel *The Pessoptimist* as an attempt to demythologize history]. *Quaderni di Studi Arabi* XII (1994): 95–128.

———. "Jabra Ibrahim Jabra's Autobiography, *Al-Bi'r al-ulā'*, and his Concept of a Celebration of Life." *Writing the Self: Autobiographical Writing in Modern Arabic Literature*. Eds. Robin Ostle, Ed de Moor, Stefan Wild. London: Saqi Books, 1998.

———. "Mahmud Darwish's Re-staging of the Mystic Lover's Relation Towards a Superhuman Beloved." *Conscious Voices: Concepts of Writing in the Middle East*. Eds. Stephan Guth, Priska Furrer, Johann C. Bürgel. Beirut and Stuttgart: Steiner, 1999.

———, B. Embalo, S. Günther, and M. Farrar, eds. *Myths, Historical Archetypes and Symbolic Figures in Arabic Literature*. Beirut: Orient-Institut der DMG, 1999.

Nicholson, Reynold A. *A Literary History of the Arabs*. 1907. Cambridge: Cambridge University Press, 1969.

Nietzsche, Friedrich. *On the Advantage and Disadvantage of History for Life*. Indianapolis: Hackett Publishing Co., Inc., 1980.

Noorani, Yaseen. "The Lost Garden of al-Andalus: Islamic Spain and the Poetic Inversion of Colonialism." *International Journal of Middle East Studies* 31 (1999): 237–254.

Nye, Naomi Shihab. "Meeting Edward Said at the Alamo." *Texas Observer*, 16 January 2004.

Obenzinger, Hilton. *American Palestine: Melville, Twain, and the Holy Land Mania*. Princeton: Princeton University Press, 1999.

Oppenheimer, Paul. *The Birth of the Modern Mind: Self, Consciousness, and the Invention of the Sonnet*. New York: Oxford University Press, 1989.

Ouyang, Wen-chin. *Literary Criticism in Medieval Arabic-Islamic Culture: The Making of a Tradition*. Edinburgh: Edinburgh University Press, 1997.

Pardes, Ilana. *Countertraditions in the Bible: A Feminist Approach*. Cambridge, MA: Harvard University Press, 1998.

Parmenter, Barbara M. *Giving Voice to Stones: Place and Identity in Palestinian Literature*. Austin: University of Texas Press, 1994.

Peteet, Julie. "Male Gender and Rituals of Resistance in the Palestinian Intifada: A Cultural Politics of Violence." *Imagined Masculinities: Male Identity and Culture in the Modern Middle East*. Eds. Mai Ghoussoub and

Emma Sinclair-Webb. London: Saqi Books, 2000.
Phillips, Kathy J. *Dying Gods in Twentieth-Century Fiction*. Lewisburg, PA: Bucknell University Press, 1990.
Post, G., ed. *Fihris al-Kitāb al-muqaddas* [The index of the Holy Book]. Beirut: Maktabat al-Mash'al, 1981.
Preminger, Alex. *Princeton Encyclopedia of Poetics and Poetry*. Princeton: Princeton University Press, 1974.
Qabbani, Nizar. *Hal tasma'īn ṣahīl aḥzānī* [Do you hear the sound of my sorrows]. Beirut: Manshūrāt Nizār Qabbānī, 1991.
———. "Imbarāṭūrīyāt al-kalām al-'Arabī" [The empire of Arabic words]. *Al-Mustaqbal* 29 May 1983: 6–7.
al-Qasim, Samih. *Dīwān* [Collected works]. Beirut: Dār al-'Awda, 1987.
——— et al. *Maḥmūd Darwīsh: Al-Mukhtalif al-ḥaqīqī dirāsāt wa shihādāt* [Mahmoud Darwish: the real difference: studies and testimonies]. Amman: Dār al-Shurūq, 1999.
——— and Mahmoud Darwish. *See under* Darwish, *Al-Rasā'il*.
al-Qayrawani, Ibn Rashiq. *Al-'umda* [The mayor]. Ed. Muhammad Muhyi al-Din 'Abd al-Hamid. Cairo: Al-Maktaba al-Tijarīya al-Kubrā, 1963.
Racy, A.J. *Making Music in the Arab World: The Culture and Artistry of Tarab*. Cambridge: Cambridge University Press, 2003.
Rahman, Najat. Interview with Mahmoud Darwish. Ramallah, Palestine. 10–11 April 1996.
al-Rahman, Wa'il 'Abd. "Al-Qur'ān bayna shi'r Maḥmūd Darwīsh wa-Alḥān Marsīl Khalīfa" [The Qur'an between the poetry of Mahmoud Darwish and the musical compositions of Marcel Khalifa]. *Star* 7 November 1996: 4–5.
al-Ra'i, Ali. *Al-Riwāya al-'Arabīya fī al-waṭan al-'Arabī* [The Arabic novel in the Arab world]. Beirut: Dār al-Mustaqbal al-'Arabī, 1991.
Recapito, Joseph. "Al-Andalus and the Origin of the Renaissance in Europe." *Indiana Journal of Hispanic Literatures* 8 (Spring 1998): 55–74.
Rejwan, Nissim. *Outsider in the Promised Land: An Iraqi Jew in Israel*. Austin: University of Texas Press, 2006.
Reigeluth, Stuart. Interview with Mourid Barghouti. Amman, Jordan. 13 August 2004.
"Al-Riwāya mir'āt al-sha'b" [The novel is the mirror of the people]. *Al-Ṭalī'a*, August 1971.
Ronell, Avital. *The Telephone Book: Technology, Schizophrenia, Electric Speech*. Lincoln: University of Nebraska Press, 1989.
———. *The Test Drive*. Urbana: University of Illinois Press, 2004.
al-Rusafi, Ma'ruf. *Dīwān* [Collected works].Vol. 2. Beirut: Dār al-'Awda, 1986.
al-Sabur, Salah 'Abd. *Riḥla 'alā al-waraq* [A voyage on paper]. Cairo: Maktabat al-Anglo al-Miṣrīya, 1971.
Sacks, Jeffrey, trans. *See under* Darwish, *Limādhā tarakta al-ḥiṣāna waḥīdan?*
Said, Edward. "Barbarians at the Gates." *Al-Ahram Weekly* 11–17 March 1999.
———. *Culture and Imperialism*. New York: Vintage, 1993.
———. *Orientalism*. New York: Random House, 1978.
———. *The Politics of Dispossession: The Struggle for Palestinian Self-*

Determination, 1969–1994. New York: Pantheon Books, 1994.
———. "Real Peace Can Come Only with a Binational Israeli-Palestinian State." *Arab American News* 5 February 1999: A6.
———. *Reflections on Exile and Other Essays*. Cambridge: Harvard University Press, 2002.
———. "Reflections on Twenty Years of Palestinian History." *Journal of Palestine Studies* 20:4 (summer 1991): 5–22.
———. *The Question of Palestine*. New York: Vintage, 1992.
——— and David Barsamian, *Culture and Resistance: Conversations with Edward W. Said*. London: Pluto Press, 2003.
Sanbar, Elias. *See under* Bitton, Simone.
al-Sayyab, Badr Shakir. *Dīwān Badr Shakir al-Sayyab*. [*The Collected Works of Badr Shakir al-Sayyab*]. Beirut: Dār al-'Awda, 1986.
al-Sayyad, Fu'ad 'Abd al-Muti. *Mu'arrikh al-Maghūl al-kabīr Rashīd al-Dīn* [Rashid al-Din, the historian of the grand Moghul]. Cairo: Dār al-Kātib al-'Arabī, 1968.
Scharfstein, Ben-Ami. *Ineffability: The Failure of Words in Philosophy and Religion*. Albany: State University of New York Press, 1993.
Schiffman, Michael, trans. *See under* Darwish, *Palästina als Metapher*.
Scholem, Gershom G. *Major Trends in Jewish Mysticism*. New York: Schocken, 1954.
Semaan, Khalil I., ed. *Islam and the Medieval West: Aspects of Intercultural Relations*. Albany, NY: State University of New York Press, 1980.
Shammas, Anton. "Autocartography: The Case of Palestine." *The Geography of Identity*. Ed. Patricia Yaeger. Ann Arbor: University of Michigan Press, 1996.
Sharabi, Hisham. *Neopatriarchy: A Theory of Distorted Change in Arab Society*. Oxford: Oxford University Press, 1988.
Shehadeh, Raja. "Mahmoud Darwish." *Bomb* 81 (Fall 2002): 54–59.
Shklovskij, Viktor. *Theorie der Prosa* [Theory of prose]. Frankfurt am Main: Fischer, 1966.
Shurayh, Mahmoud. *Khalīl Ḥawī wa Antūn Sa'āda* [Khalil Hawi and Antoun Sa'ada]. Sweden: Dār Nelson, 1995.
Silberstein, Laurence J. *Postzionism Debates: Knowledge and Power in Israeli Culture*. London: Routledge, 1999.
Sivan, Emmanuel. *Mitosim Politiyim Arviyim* [Arab political myths]. Tel Aviv: Am Oved, 1988.
Smith, W.C. *Islam in Modern History*. New York: Mentor, 1963.
Somekh, Sasson. *Genre and Language in Modern Arabic Literature*. Wiesbaden: Otto Harrassowitz, 1991.
Snir, Reuven. "'Al-Andalus Arising from Damascus': Al-Andalus in Modern Arabic Poetry." *Hispanic Issues* 21 (2000): 263–293.
———. "Mahmoud Darwish—Birds without Wings." [Hebrew] *Helicon: Anthological Journal of Contemporary Poetry* 18 (1996): 47–61.
———. *Rak'atān fī al-'ishq: dirāsa fī shi'r 'Abd al-Wahhāb al-Bayyātī* [A study of the poetry of 'Abd al-Wahhab al-Bayyati]. Beirut: Dār al-Sāqī, 2002.

Stetkevych, Jaroslav. "Towards an Arabic Elegiac Lexicon: The Seven Words of the Nasīb." In *Reorientations/Arabic and Persian Poetry*. Ed. Suzanne Pinckney Stetkevych. Bloomington: Indiana University Press, 1994.

———. *The Zephyrs of Najd: The Poetics of Nostalgia in the Classical Arabic Nasīb*. Chicago: University of Chicago Press, 1993.

Subhi, Muhyi al-Din. *Al-rū'ya fī shi'r al-Bayyati*. [*Vision in Al-Bayyati's Poetry*]. Baghdad: Dār al-Shu'ūn al-Thaqāfīya al-'Amma, 1987.

Sulaiman, Khalid A. *Palestine and Modern Arab Poetry*. London: Zed Books, 1984.

al-Suyuti. *Al-Muzhir fī 'ulūm al-lugha wa-anwā'ihā* [The luminous work concerning the sciences of language and its types]. Vol 2. Cairo: Dār Iḥyā' al-Kutub al-'Arabīya, n.d.

Swift, Todd, ed. *100 Poets Against the War*. Cambridge: Salt Publishing, 2003.

Tart, C.T., ed. *Altered States of Consciousness*. New York: John Wiley, 1969.

Thomson, William. *The Land and the Book: Or, Biblical Illustrations Drawn from the Manners and Customs, the Scenes and the Scenery of the Holy Land*. 2 vols. New York: Harper and Brothers, 1858.

Tottoli, Roberto. *Biblical Prophets in the Qur'an and Muslim Literature*. Richmond: Curzon, 2002.

Tuqan, Fawwaz, trans. *See under* Darwish, *Selected Poems*.

al-Udhari, Abdullah, ed. and trans. *Maḥmūd Darwīsh, Samīh al-Qāsim, Adonīs*. London: Al Sāqī Books, 1984.

'Uthman, I'tidal. *Idā'āt al-naṣṣ: qira'āt fī al-shi'r al-'Arabī al-ḥadīth* [Illuminating the text: readings of modern Arabic poetry]. Beirut: Dār al-Ḥadātha, 1988; 2nd ed. Cairo: Al-Hay'a al-Miṣrīya al-'Ama lil-Kitāb, 1998.

Valk, Thorsten. "Der Dichter als Erlöser: Poetischer Messianismus in einem späten Gedicht des Novalis." *Poetologische Lyrik von Klopstock bis Grünbein*. Ed. Olaf Hildebrand. Köln/Weimar/Wien: Böhlau, 2003.

Vazquez, Miguel Angel. "Poetic Pilgrimages: From Baghdad to Andalucia, Abu Tammam's *Lā anta anta wa lā al-diyāru diyāru*." *Journal of Arabic Literature* 34.1–2: 127–137.

Wadi, Taha. *Al-Qiṣṣa dīwān al-'Arab: qaḍāya wa-namādhij*. [Fiction is the new annals of the Arabs: issues and examples]. Cairo: Al-Sharika al-Miṣrīya al-'Ālamīya lil-Nahsr, 2001.

Wedde, Ian, trans. *See under* Darwish, *Selected Poems*.

Wehr, Hans. *A Dictionary of Modern Written Arabic*. Beirut: Librairie du Liban, 1974.

Weir, Shelagh. *Palestinian Costume*. London: British Museum Press, 1989.

Wensinck, A. J. and J. P. Mensing, eds. *Concordance et indices de la tradition muselmane* [Concordance and indexes of the Muslim tradition]. Leiden: Brill, 1936–1969.

Wiet, Gaston. *Introduction à la littérature arabe* [Introduction to Arabic literature]. Paris: Maisonneuve et Larose, 1966.

Yadin, Yigael. *Masada: Herod's Fortress and the Zealots' Last Stand*. 1966. New York: Welcome Rain, 1998.

Yazbak, Mahmoud. *Haifa in the Late Ottoman Period, 1864–1914: A Muslim Town in Transition*. Leiden: Brill, 1998.

Yeats, W. B. *Collected Works*. London: Vintage, 1992.

Yeshurun, Helit. "Je ne reviens pas, je viens." In Darwish, *La Palestine comme métaphore*.

Zaydan, Gurji. *Tārīkh adāb al-lugha al-'Arabīya* [Literary history of the Arabic language]. Vol. 3. Cairo: Maṭba'at al-Fajjala, 1913.

al-Zayyat, Ahmad Hasan. *Tārīkh al-adab al-'Arabī* [The history of Arabic literature]. Cairo: Maktabat Nahḍat Miṣr, 1960.

al-Zein, Amira, trans. See under Darwish, *The Raven's Ink*.

Ziyad, Tawfiq. "Maḥmūd Darwīsh: *'Āshiq min Filasṭīn*" [Mahmoud Darwish: *Lover from Palestine*]. *Al-Jadīd* 3 (1966).

Zurayk, Constantine K. *Ma'nā al-Nakba*. [The meaning of the disaster]. Beirut: Khayāṭ, 1956.

———. *Ma'nā al-Nakba mujaddadan* [The meaning of the disaster anew]. Beirut: Dār al-'ilm lil-malāyīn, 1967.

Acknowledgments

We wish to sincerely offer our heartfelt thanks to Hilary Plum and Pamela Thompson for their tremendous work in editing this volume and to our contributors for their important scholarship. Special thanks to Rim Bejaoui for her careful work on the index.

A

Index